T0397673

Hero Projects

Hero Projects

*The Russian Empire and Big Technology
from Lenin to Putin*

PAUL R. JOSEPHSON

OXFORD
UNIVERSITY PRESS

Oxford University Press is a department of the University of Oxford. It furthers the University's objective of excellence in research, scholarship, and education by publishing worldwide. Oxford is a registered trade mark of Oxford University Press in the UK and certain other countries.

Published in the United States of America by Oxford University Press
198 Madison Avenue, New York, NY 10016, United States of America.

CIP data is on file at the Library of Congress

ISBN 978–0–19–769839–6

DOI: 10.1093/oso/9780197698396.001.0001

Printed by Integrated Books International, United States of America

Contents

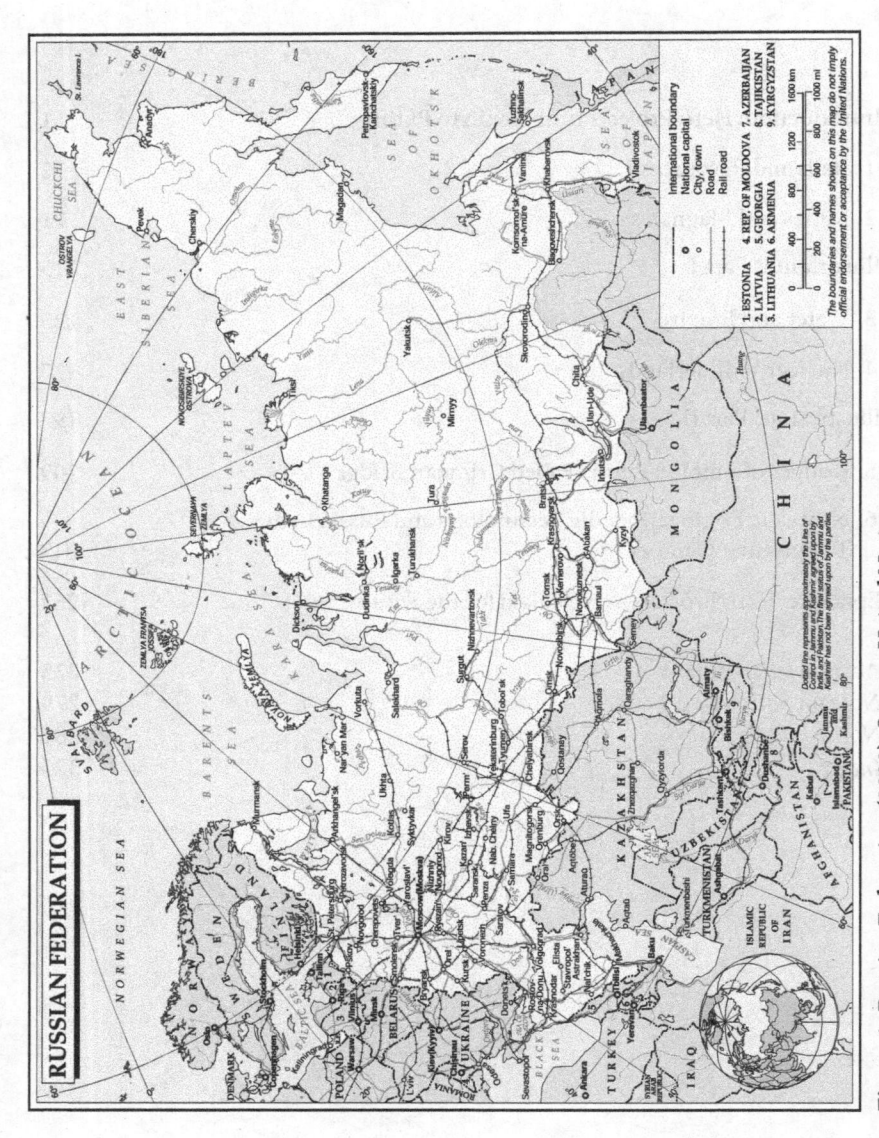

Figure 1 Russian Federation (2020). Source: United Nations.

Introduction

Hero Projects from Lenin to Putin

Russia's imperial technologies—big state-funded projects—have captured our imagination: the Tsar's Trans-Siberian Railroad from Moscow to Vladivostok on the Pacific Coast built in the 1890s; Lenin's visionary state electrification plan of the 1920s; Stalin's magnificent yet murderous Magnitorogorsk steel combine, mines, railroads, and scores of other gulag projects; powerful icebreakers, first diesel, later nuclear, to keep the Great Northern Sea (Arctic) Route open in the dead of the polar night; stepped hydropower stations on major rivers that provided electricity for local industry including aluminum smelters and plutonium factories; and massive transfer and transport canals, dating to the 1920s and brought to completion in the 1950s, 1960s, and 1970s, that have created agricultural oases in the steppe, in Central Asia, and elsewhere. These and other large-scale technologies have been the centerpiece of Russian economic development projects. In many cases completed, in others persistently proposed and reaching only the blueprint stage, in others finished at great delay, human and environmental cost, and budgetary overruns, these projects served simultaneously to bring masses of workers together at distant sites across the empire, meld them together into industrial armies, extract the nation's great mineral, fossil fuel, and natural resources, and fill perceived empty spaces of the Arctic, Far North, and Far East with mines, smelters, railroads, and other hero projects—and with Slavic peoples. This book is about these projects and their continuities of design, construction, technological verve, and symbolism over the past century of Russian history.

Hero projects remain a major tool of economic growth and military power in Russia. They moved ahead because of the unbridled interests of state officials, the hubris of engineers, and the coalescence of the masses under a national ideology of glorious achievement and military necessity. Russia's citizens have had great pride in these modern technological wonders, as

Hero Projects. Paul R. Josephson, Oxford University Press. © Oxford University Press 2024.
DOI: 10.1093/oso/9780197698396.003.0001

well they might: gleaming new railway "magistrals," enormous mines that brought copper, platinum, and diamonds to the surface, and first-in-the-world nuclear power plants. But they must also pay for them indirectly with stagnant salaries, poorly stocked stores, and miserly pensions, not to mention the public health costs of water and pollution and ruined landscapes and waterways.

Dating to the reign of Peter the Great (1682–1725), Russian leaders have believed that the nation's future depends on production, extraction, and trade of natural and mineral resources: furs, forest, and fish; and later, oil and gas, nickel, copper and platinum, electricity, and water.[1] When the Bolsheviks seized power in the 1920s, Soviet commissariats (later "ministries") were directed to ratchet up production of these and other strategic natural resources, minerals, and fossil fuels. In their activities and programs, the ministries and state corporations of today's Russian Federation continue to rely on megaprojects to master fossil fuels, iron and steel, copper and nickel, and other commodities. Because Russia's great power, its leaders never doubted, depended on its resources, they intended to mine them, tap them, drill for them, process them, fire up boilers and turn turbines with them, and sell them abroad. This view of resources—seeing natural systems and resources as goods to be processed, apprehending nature with an industrial ethos, and treating it as a commodity machine for the benefit of the state—has been a major feature of political rule from Tsarist times to the present. And the embrace of "hero projects," "projects of the century," and megaprojects, as successive regimes have called them, indicates their importance to leaders and citizens alike. Even as their nomenclature changed, the hero projects remained. And if the tools and devices were modernized and became more powerful and efficient, the purposes of enhancing state power and military might have remained across three regimes: Tsarist, Soviet, and post-Soviet Russia.

Some of the projects—icebreakers and nuclear power—are high tech. Others—in hydroelectricity, rails, and bridges—are modernized versions of projects from earlier eras. And virtually all of them—coal and other mines, oil and gas pipelines—represent the prevailing activities of the Russian state as an excavator, bulldozer, track layer, concrete pourer, tunnel borer, oil derrick, a producer of electricity, a locomotive to transport coal. Hero technologies beyond these narrower technical purposes are the tools of opening the interior of the vast Russian land mass, a way to bring workers together for common purposes, and a brute force means of transforming local people and indigenes perceived as being backward or hostile to the state into reliable citizens, or at least employees of state enterprises.

Many Soviet-era and Soviet-inspired projects have been reborn in the twenty-first century through massive infusions of state funding and are run through state-owned and managed technologies. All of them reflect the desire to enhance state power, placate citizens in a time of economic or military challenges, demonstrate to the world the nation's technological verve, and draw Russia's great natural and mineral wealth into the Kremlin's hands, while also ostensibly benefiting the citizen. Across all regimes, Russian leaders have pursued hero projects for their military and economic significance, for their importance to generating international recognition of the prowess of a technologically advanced nation, for their facility in conquering nature and shaping citizens' expectations and beliefs, and for their symbolic importance at home and abroad.

Large-scale engineering projects are paradigmatic for development across the globe. In states like Russia with closed political structures and limited access to protest avenues, they move ahead seemingly with a power of their own. Indeed, it is hard to see differences between projects to control and harvest natural and mineral resources in Russia today and those of the Soviet period, in particular concerning their great environmental and social costs, the political culture of authoritarianism that undergirds them, and the military adventurism that hero projects serve. Granted, large projects have spread throughout the globe in pursuit of transport, agricultural, industrial, and other ends. These "brute force" technologies, as I call them, exist in Brazil, the United States, China, and elsewhere. These projects also require brute force *politics* to succeed: government, engineering, and financial authorities use a variety of means to force projects ahead, often pushing local residents out of the way to enable the projects to plow to the horizon.[2] Historical experience indicates they are nearly irreversible, go forward on low budget estimates to get started and result in massive cost overruns, have very low elasticity of substitution of inputs, especially in nations like Russia with heavy reliance on tight capital, and no matter the long-term plans the projects generally encounter significant unexpected obstacles en route to completion. Take, for example, water-related projects and the people ousted from their homes to be completed. Agricultural engineering in the Central Valley of California, irrigation projects of the Transvaal, dozens of massive hydroelectric power stations damming Amazon basin rivers to produce electricity for Rio de Janeiro and São Paulo, Jawaharlal Nehru's promotion of dams as "temples of modern

India" coming to brute force fruition in the Sardar Sarovar project in the Narmada district, Chinese interbasin water transfer projects and its Three Gorges Dam on the Yangtse that required the removal of nearly two million residents—all of these waterworks supported state plans to pursue rapid economic growth. They were profoundly important for their symbolism of modernity and hubris, even if they have provoked concerns about their budgets, their environmental impacts, and their unintended social costs. Those costs include millions of "oustees" forced into unfamiliar lands and homes, and with their cultures and traditions destroyed.

This book examines the challenges and successes in building large-scale technologies, in particular infrastructures, in Russia over the last one hundred years or so, from the time of the Russian Revolution to the present, although it will refer to a number of projects with Tsarist roots. It considers the motivations of the past and present leaderships to pursue these expensive, long-term projects. It places them within a framework of political history, institutional history, and history of technology. I examine railroads, coal mines, bridges, waterworks, and nuclear power plants as both hero projects and as systems of economic development, resource management, and political control to understand their broader political, economic, and cultural meanings. My focus is how people have engaged natural and mineral resources across a vast Eurasian landscape through a variety of infrastructures and systems in the effort to change production and consumption patterns, and to direct and control the activities of people in that landscape as part of an imperial effort. Unfortunately, all hero projects have acquired renewed significance under Vladimir Putin in his war on Ukraine and his determination to recreate a Russian empire through them. In the end, I examine how a leading military and political power of the modern era—Russia—determined to overlay its great landscape and people with hero projects: technological infrastructures of transport, energy, and water resources to build and maintain an empire.

Big Technology in the Russian Empire

It will help to understand the argument of this book to recall that, inheriting the great land mass of the Tsarist empire and its desire to control the territory to the Pacific Ocean and to the mountains of South Central Asia and all of its inhabitants, the USSR was also a great empire. The Red Army was constituted not only to win the Civil War (1918–1920) against the White Army and other monarchist forces, but to regain control over Tsarist holdings to incorporate them into an invincible proletarian power. And the Russian Federation also seeks to enhance its imperial legacy, both through economic partnerships and treaties with the former republics of the USSR, and through adventurous and dangerous efforts to reincorporate territory from other nations: Georgia in 2008 (war over South Ossetia and Abkhazia), Ukraine in 2014 (the annexation of Crimea and the Donbas), Moldova (an ongoing conflict), and continuing its war on Ukraine (2022–present). In each empire—Tsarist, Soviet, and Russian—hero projects played a significant role in conquest, control, and resource extraction.

Thus, this book contributes to a special understanding of empire, that concerning the relationship between technology and empire. Many of the studies in this area focus on science and medicine, and less so on technology, and if they consider technology centrally, then they tend to focus on the military enterprise. To be sure, science and technology have long served conquest and colonialism—by indicating to Europeans that their "mastery" and understandings of nature confirmed their belief in the superiority of the civilization that they brought to others when they sought to civilize and control that colonial world.[3]

Already in the Tsarist period, the state employed the scientific enterprise to enhance its control over the growing empire. The imperial science of the Tsarist government—as represented in the activities of its various independent societies of geographers, foresters, and others, and in its Academy of Sciences—provided crucial information through state-sponsored and private endeavors to survey the landscape, prospect for mineral resources, and tabulate and evaluate the peoples within the nation's borders. Explorers and military engineers, university and academy specialists, and gentlemen scholars saw in one way or another a wild frontier, porous borders, and vast national wealth, at the same time characterizing the people and their practices in provincial Russia and its distant lands as backward. One nobleman, a chemist by profession, Nikolai Engelgardt, lamented outmoded agricultural practices in the late nineteenth century, and he urged the training of peasants to ensure more modern, rigorous, and scientific approaches to improve the farming situation in the empire.[4]

Specialists and engineers of all profiles contributed to an effort to place the bureaucratic and military imprint of the Russian government on the expanding empire, at the same time harnessing its resource potential to technological advance. A number of important state-sponsored expeditions, military outposts, and other endeavors sought to bring stability and control to the periphery of the empire through the settlement of Slavic soldiers and farmers. One such effort at the beginning of the nineteenth century unfolded under a favorite of Tsar Aleksandr I, General Aleksei Arakcheev, who also served minister of war. Arakcheev's military-agricultural colonies were intended to ensure the presence of standing armies in border regions by allowing soldiers to farm and have a family, and indeed regimented life to require women to bear a child annually, as a way to increase Russian family presence.[5] Several other early projects for building transfer canals to bring Siberian water to the Caspian Sea were pursued by military men and entrepreneurs to assist Russian peasants in bringing sedentary agricultural to the region while facilitating the control the Muslim herders and other indigenes.[6]

And yet Tsarist support for and interest in the exploratory, surveying, public health and other aspects of nineteenth-century science was episodic and insufficient to enable significant growth of the research enterprise. Only in times of crisis did the government move firmly to support specialists: after the debacle of the Crimean War in the 1850s that showed Russia's technological, military, and social backwardness; in the aftermath of the 1891 famine that revealed, among other things, outmoded agricultural practices; and in the support of a special Academy of Sciences commission late in World War I to secure domestic resources needed to wage battle, including chemicals for explosives, after European sources were shut off from Germany. But strive they did, the explorers and chroniclers, amateurs and professionals, scientists and naturalists, and engineers, to explore the nation from its European borders to the Pacific Ocean, and from the Arctic regions to Central Asia's deserts. Social critics joined in with their observations about the empire's great natural and mineral wealth to communicate their worries about the threats to Russia's forests or waterways of unbridled development and the plight of Russia's poverty-stricken peasant, about plunder of Russia's forests, and so on.[7]

Tsarist specialists after the revolution became "bourgeois specialists" under the Soviets. It would be years before there existed a large cohort of engineers and scientists trained fully in the Soviet system, and the relationship between scientists, engineers, and the Soviet state remained tense.[8] In any event, many of these specialists welcomed the increased support for their work after the Bolsheviks seized power. The Bolsheviks embraced science and technology as a panacea for construction of the modern resource empire.

They endorsed projects with proclamations, supported the creation of new institutions, and increased funding for the specialists' research programs, especially after the end of the Civil War in the 1920s. And if scientists rejected revolutionary Bolshevism as anathema to their beliefs, which tended to be moderate or conservative, or saw the Bolsheviks as temporary interlopers to political power, the specialists joined the endeavors to build new factories and foundries, to improve transport systems, to modernize and expand electrical energy production, and to establish new institutions and create professional societies to lobby the government—all in support of harnessing the scientific and engineering enterprise to the strengthening of the Soviet empire. Many of the engineers were pleased to learn that their projects to rework and improve upon nature that had languished during the Tsarist period—canals, dams, generating stations, transport systems—had a sympathetic, indeed a supportive Communist Party and government whose officials sought rapid economic development through the most modern technology.

Several of the efforts to catalog and engage Russia's rich natural resources indicate an important tension between what is often called universal science and local knowledge. Universal scientific knowledge is seen as objective and rigorous, set forth as the only accurate way to understand nature, and considered the best foundation for developing mineral, natural, and other resources rapidly and effectively. The knowledge of local people in a community about climate, resources, and seasons that has developed over time and is communicated through shared experience and handed down by tradition was perceived as less rigorous. For empires—for the Tsar in St. Petersburg, the Bolsheviks in the Kremlin, the oligarchs in Moscow—the distant regions invited conquest and assimilation to enhance state power, with local knowledge and local people evidently an obstacle to progress, even of questionable loyalty to the government, and plainly quaint and backward. Roads and rails, bridges and canals, mines and foundries, and other technological means would enable exploitation of resources and settlement of sparsely populated regions. They could be built properly only on the basis of surveys, studies, and maps produced by scientific and military expeditions.

Ultimately, the science and technology of empire building had little patience for the ways of life of local people that to officials and engineers prohibited full exploitation of strategic resources. Of course, local understandings of climate, flora, and fauna are crucial complements to the balanced use of resources to benefit all citizens, not only privileged urban residents. One attempt to celebrate the importance of "local knowledge," the accumulated wisdom of the larger environment created through the experiences of local people—trappers, peasants, indigenes, and others—comes from the fictional *Dersu Uzala* (1923), written by the explorer of the Ussuri region of the Far East, Vladimir Arsen'ev (1872–1930). *Dersu Uzala* is a loving paean to the spirits of the forest and the glories of nature before conquest by Tsarist soldiers, and to the friendship between a Tsarist captain in 1908, tasked with charting Ussuri resources with a detachment of simple conscripts and his notebooks, surveying instruments, cameras, and the like, and Dersu, a Goldis (Nanai) hunter who truly comprehends the rhythms of nature in a way that, the captain realizes, he will never master with his imperial engineering. In all events, local understandings of nature and resources, and local practices and traditions, were subjugated to big engineering projects, from Lenin and Stalin to Putin.

The Soviets had less patience than the Tsarist government with inefficient and incidental accumulation of data that they believed characterized the efforts of so-called bourgeois specialists during the autocracy. They claimed that socialism was unquestionably scientific, and they would bring modern science and technology to bear on creating the socialist economy. They supported expeditions through professional societies, ministries (commissariats), and military detachments. From the 1930s, authorities used the gulag camps to accelerate the efforts of compilation, construction, control, and subjugation of resources with the camp prisoners being moved to thinly settled regions. Gulag bosses often employed incarcerated geologists, geographers, botanists, and other specialists in the effort to provide a scientific foundation to slave labor infrastructure projects from mines to roads to runways to forestry combines, and later to the space and nuclear programs.[9] The gulag bosses aimed at speed of study, as well as the construction of infrastructure forced rapidly forward through the wilderness to facilitate industrial and agriculture works in the Far North, Arctic, and Far East. They insisted upon applications that immediately served the worker state through increased production, greater security, and resource assimilation. Many of the contemporary hero projects discussed in this book not surprisingly have gulag roots.

Geopolitical reasons were also a crucial impetus to hero projects. Beyond economic reasons for employing hero projects throughout the empire, the Bolsheviks worried about dangerous "capitalist encirclement." Indeed, the revolutionary nation was surrounded by capitalist powers, had just engaged in the Great War, and faced allied intervention; American and British troops set up shop in Arkhangelsk region on the White Sea and in Siberia in an effort to keep the Russian state in the war against Kaiser Wilhelm's armies. During World War II, German armies again pushed far inland, to the Leningrad outskirts that survived a 900-day blockade of starvation and mass death, to the suburbs of Moscow, to the oil wells of the Caspian Sea, and to the Volga River. In response, the Soviets evacuated what they could just ahead of the Blitzkrieg to the Ural mountains to produce war equipment. After the war and into the 1980s, Soviet officials accelerated programs to access Siberian resources and build production facilities from the ground up and turned to Arctic regions and the Far East as well. Hence exploration, prospecting, construction of infrastructure, and industrial development in the interior ensured access to strategic minerals, fuels ,and building supplies in the event of an invasion, far from the borders and the front.

In all cases, the pursuit of hero projects was closely connected with military needs and goals. Military bases and their harbors and airfields clearly have a strategic role. But hero projects are also closely connected with military policies and doctrines in the effort to make the nation safe from attack, facilitate resource exploitation, and enable the transport of people, products, and things by river, road, railroad, and airplane. This dual purpose of the projects is evident in the twenty-first century in the efforts of the Putin administration to develop the extensive fossil fuel resources of Arctic regions at the same time as extending the Russian military presence in the name of protecting the interests of the nation to unquestioned Arctic ownership. Nuclear icebreakers, Yamal pipelines, a new Arctic magistral (freight railroad)—all of these technologies reflect the geopolitical goals of the Russian empire.

A number of analysts of "empire" suggest that the term is not fully appropriate for such states as the Tsarist empire and the Soviet Union precisely because they consider empires to be those nation states with colonies across the water.[10] But the control and management of distant reaches of nation within its own borders—internal colonization—was another major stimulus behind the adoption of hero projects to wed science, technology, settlement and resource development within national borders.[11] This book argues that technologies of construction, mining, forestry, communications, transport and so on served as instruments of control over what imperial leaders saw as peripheral lands, perhaps even devoid of people. Kremlin leaders have long believed that empty spaces required settlement by deserving Slavic peoples—as Arakcheev's military-agricultural colonies were intended.

As in the case of other empires whose leaders justified expansion, conquest and control through "manifest destiny," that is, a civilizing mission over corrupt, inferior, and uncivilized people, so many officials and citizens of the Russian empire believed that the Slavic peoples would bring their higher standard of living, superior education, and unquestioned higher quality of life to the "little peoples"—the minority nationalities. Already from the 1920s, the Soviets embarked on an effort to incorporate minority nationalities much more fully into the socialist enterprise as capable citizens. By the Stalinist period this effort transformed into a violent, impatient, and coercive effort. Soviet linguists set out to build alphabets to ensure literacy, educate, and make the "little peoples" accessible to cultural assimilation. For example, they opened schools, mobile hospitals, veterinary clinics, and "workers' clubs" for reindeer herders to force a sedentary life on them and enable better control of their movements and economic activities.[12] Ultimately, technologies of modernization—factories, roads, railroads, bridges, pipelines, mines and smelters, forestry operations, power stations and pipelines, and electrical power grids—enabled control over local people, while transferring the fruits and bounties of lands of the periphery—lumber, furs, reindeer meat, coal, copper and nickel, and so on—to the center.[13]

The Great Russian Landmass

The great landmass of the Russian empire presented party officials, economic planners, geographers, geologists, botanists, foresters, and a variety of other visionary nature transformationists with a rich variety of landscapes and resources. Generally, the Soviet/Russian empire consists of five different zones: the tundra zone; the taiga, or forest, zone; the steppe, or plains, zone; the arid zone; and mountains. This description of the empire from north to south, and from west to east, will help the reader to understand both the reasons for the centuries-long effort to pursue hero projects and the great human, financial, engineering, and other challenges to the effort.

In the Arctic northwest on the Kola Peninsula that juts out into the Barents Sea Soviet geologists discovered in the 1920s and 1930s significant mineral resources just underneath the rock surface—iron, nickel, bauxite, apatite, and many others—in a land largely inhabited by reindeer herders. The Soviets established a series of metallurgical towns including Nickel, Monchegorsk,

Kirov and Kandalaksha to develop this ore.[14] Tundra, an Arctic desert of scraggly vegetation of dwarf shrubs, grasses, lichens, mosses, and some flowering plants that appear over a four- or five-week frenzy of birth and death, stretches from the Finnish border to the Bering Strait and encompasses about 10 percent of Russian lands. Prospectors and other researchers charted great mineral and carbon wealth—coal, oil and gas, rare metals—in the tundra. During the Soviet period they built gulag operations to extract them in frigid, permafrost conditions. Some of these operations still exist, for example, in the decrepit Arctic cities of Vorkuta and Norilsk. The tundra now houses massive Siberian oil and gas industries as well.[15]

Also, in the northwest is the Republic of Karelia, situated between the White and Baltic Seas, including lands stolen from Finland in the Winter War of 1939–1940, that recall Maine or Minnesota with multitudinous lakes—some 60,000 of them—and swampland. Pine forests followed by spruce and birch fill the area; it has logically become a site of major lumber, paper, and pulp mills. Karelia is the western reach of extensive forested lands, the taiga. South of the tundra, also stretching across the country from west to east and as far south as Lake Baikal, this taiga, a boreal or mixed forest with spruce, fir, cedar, birch and hemlock, and larch, is 57 percent of world's conifer forest and 23 percent of all the world's woodlands, larger than Amazonia and about the size of United States. It is a region of very hot summer temperatures and, in spots, the coldest winter temperatures in the world. A third of Russia's population lives in the taiga zone. It is rich with bear, moose, reindeer, sable, weasels, otter, beaver, lynx, wolves, swans, eagles, and other animals, although these animals have declined under the strain of poaching. The forested regions of European Russia have longer summers and more rain than the eastern forests, and here much of the forest has been pushed back and plowed up for agriculture. Under Soviet rule, powerful paper, pulp, and lumber industries, especially in zones of the Russian Federation, opened new operations, frequently assisted by gulag camps.

South of the taiga is the steppe, a broad band of treeless, grassy plains that extend from Hungary across Ukraine, southern Russia, and Kazakhstan before ending in Manchuria; some Russian steppe is located mainly between Ukraine and Kazakhstan southward toward the Black and Caspian seas. The steppe has been an area of intensive and extensive activity in the Russian empire, important for agriculture, if often at risk because of insufficient precipitation and at times droughts. It drew waves of Slavic settlers drawn to its rich soil (*chernozem*, black earth), who displaced nomadic herders and pastoralists.[16] The steppe has also been the focus of afforestation and irrigation efforts, the latter especially after the formation of a variety of Soviet organizations and ministries determined to provide planned regularity—and certainty—to the agricultural production of the area, notably in Stalin's Plan to Transform Nature.[17]

Large areas of Russia are covered by bog and swamps. It may be that Russia contains more wetlands than any other country. There are between one and two million lakes and ponds, and forests are often a mix of pine groves, bogs, and swamps—and often the subject of reclamation efforts. When not bubbling forth with black flies and mosquitoes in the spring and summer, these regions are snow and ice covered, many for more than half the year. They come to a new life with the spring melts, flooding the land. In Siberia the generally northward flow of rivers means that source areas thaw before areas downstream that flood with water, for example, the roughly 50,000 km^2 Vasyugane Swamp in the Ob River basin in Tomsk province in the West Siberian Plain. The swamp is roughly 2 percent of the whole area of peat bogs of the world, and it is at significant risk from pollution from growing oil and gas production. Other river systems—the Pechora and the North Dvina in Europe—experience the same massive spring freshets and downstream swampiness.

Central Asian regions presented special challenges to the Kremlin in reworking the landscape and incorporating local people and practices. Hero projects were central to these efforts, especially irrigation systems to provide water for agriculture. The Soviet republics and now nations of Kazakhstan, Kyrgyzstan, Tajikistan, Turkmenistan, and Uzbekistan were part of the Silk Road that brought people, goods, and ideas from China, Western and Southern Asia, and Europe together. Largely inhabited by nomads, it was the focus of Soviet efforts to modernize Muslim peoples (and lands) by forcing them to settle into collective farms and move to burgeoning cities that accompanied industrialization. The Soviets also foisted extensive waterworks and transport infrastructure to help the republics serve Moscow's demands for cotton, fruit, and vegetables.[18]

Central Asia is largely desert, and cotton production strongly relies on irrigation. More than 80 percent of arable land in Kyrgyzstan, Tajikistan, Turkmenistan, and Uzbekistan is irrigated; Kazakhstan, with its wheat-based crop production, irrigates only 7 percent of its arable land. A major desert, the Karakum, occupies about 70 percent, or 350,000 km^2, of the area of Turkmenistan. The Kyzylkum Desert in Kazakhstan, Uzbekistan, and Turkmenistan covers about 298,000 km^2. A major chapter in the pursuit of the collectivization of agriculture involved extensive efforts to irrigate these lands. It led to the death and displacement of millions of people and environmental degradation felt to this day. This can be seen in the fate of the Aral Sea. The Aral Sea drainage basin encompasses Uzbekistan and parts of Tajikistan, Turkmenistan, Kyrgyzstan, Kazakhstan, Afghanistan, and Iran. Formerly the fourth largest lake in the world with an area of 68,000 km^2, the Aral Sea has been shrinking since the 1960s after the rivers that fed it were diverted by Soviet irrigation projects. By 1997, it had declined to 10 percent of its original size, splitting into four lakes.

The vast Far East region that stretches from Lake Baikal to the Pacific Ocean, comprising all of Eastern Siberia, and from Vladivostok to Kamchatka and the Bering Strait refused to cooperate with the Kremlin's plans because of its distance from the Kremlin, low population densities, geography, and weather. This made it difficult to impose hero projects on resources. The Far East comprises one-third of Russian territory, but has only six million inhabitants—4 percent of the total population. It remains a wilderness in the minds of Muscovites who wish to enjoy its great resources of fish, oil, natural gas, forests, iron ore, coal, gold, silver, lead, zinc, and diamonds from afar; Russia produces about one-fifth of the world's diamonds, many from Sakha (the largest administrative unit of the Far East, called Yakutia under Soviet power from 1923), which has 82 percent of Russia's diamonds, 17 percent of its gold, 61 percent of its uranium, and 82 percent of its antimony. Prisoners of war and gulag internees provided impetus to the region's development from the 1940s onward. It borders China, a site of armed battles in 1969 on Zhenbao Island in the Ussuri River. It includes Kolyma, the notorious gulag camps of the Dal'stroi organization (covered below), one of the largest slave labor organizations in the Communist Party's toolbox of resource extraction. In 2016, Vladimir Putin proposed a Homestead Act to give one hectare of land to anyone who would settle in the Far East so long as he or she lived there for five years. As far as can be determined, very few people took the president up on this offer.

Mountain ranges, too, have been important in the history of the Russian empire as barriers to migration, as sites of conflict, as natural borders to invaders from the south and east, and as sources of significant deposits of minerals, gas, and oil. They include the Caucasus with the nations of Azerbaijan, Armenia, and Georgia, the last of these in conflict with Russia since 2008, and Chechnya, a nation of two wars with Russia (1994–1996 and 1999–2003, bloody, genocidal conflicts that contributed to President Putin's image as a strong leader when he commenced the second war as prime minister); the Verkhoiansk Range in Sakha; and the Altai, Saian, and Yablonoi Mountains on Russia's south Siberia border with Mongolia and China.

To take one mountain range: dividing European from Asian Russia, the Ural Mountains range runs 2,500 km north to south from the Arctic to northwestern Kazakhstan. The range fell to Muscovite expansion in the 1500s. The mountains have been crucial to state power as a resource for centuries.[19] Iron and copper works arose somewhat later, especially during the reign of Peter the Great in the early 1700s; railroads traversed the mountains in the late 1800s; and the Soviets pushed industrialization from a base at Magnitogorsk from the 1930s. Military industry rapidly expanded here in Cheliabinsk, Nizhnii Tagil, and Sverdlovsk during World War II, fed by evacuation of entire factories from the west when Nazi armies attacked, and by displacement and exile of millions of citizens. Major nuclear industries appeared in the Ural Mountains in postwar years, and together with heavy industry they have produced toxic and radioactive waste as their legacies. The mountains hold dozens of valuable ores, coal, and natural gas. Many of the rivers on the western slopes flow ultimately into the Caspian, others through the Pechora River basin into the Arctic.

In Russia, in the extent and fearlessness of hero projects from the steppe of Europe to the tundra of Siberia and the Far North, and to the deserts of Central Asia, Marxist visionaries collaborated with hubristic engineers and confident Party officials to re-engineer nature on a scale as never before. They discouraged, if not precluded, public input through highly centralized political institutions and economic ministries. The result is a scarred landscape of huge concrete structures, displaced people, destroyed ecosystems, and little effort at remediation. Now Putin has called to restart some of the most audacious projects of the Soviet era that were mothballed after the break-up of the USSR: dams in the Arctic and sub-Arctic, reclamation in prairies, interbasin water transfer to deserts in Central Asia and to China, and other megaprojects. In word, hero projects acquired great momentum to move forward toward completion even as regimes changed, leaders arose and fell, and citizens from a peasant country became citizens of an industrial empire.

Technological Momentum

A Tsarist project to use transfer canals to move Siberian river water to Central Asia, modified under Stalin and pushed by 250 construction and engineering firms under Leonid Brezhnev, has returned with a new commodity customer in the twenty-first century—China—prepared to buy Russian water. The rejuvenated Rosatom, based on the USSR's ministry of nuclear weapons and reactors, offers self-aggrandizing pronouncements of dozens of reactor starts and sales abroad; it claims that its nuclear-powered icebreakers and floating power stations, most of Soviet design and heritage, will seamlessly expand the oil and gas industry by making it possible to extract Arctic resources year round no matter the conditions. Vladimir Putin himself has announced plans to complete a thousand-mile-long railroad across the Arctic Circle to complete a "magistral" that commenced construction with gulag prisoners under Stalin in 1945—more than seventy-five years ago. Massive projects like these have been born, born again, and reincarnated over the past century on the Russian landmass. Loren Graham analyzes why Russia has succeeded in big projects, has been a pioneer in many technologies, but is weak is seeing modern technologies diffuse or innovations to gain social acceptance. A major reason is that Russian state has preferred military power over economic improvement, easier-to-manage big projects over potentially more innovative small ones, and political authoritarianism that limits the positive impacts of market forces—were they to exist—and best practices that must be subservient to meeting more immediate plan targets.[20] Of course, as noted in the following chapters, because of the absence of functioning markets and weak tools of economic analysis, and the paramount importance of fulfilling the plan, planners had no way and no desire to calculate potential benefits against cost and risk; resources were free and labor power was effectively free, including that requisitioned for hero projects from the gulag.

The phenomenon of technological momentum explains the persistence of large-scale technologies generally, and of hero projects in Russia specifically, across different political systems, economic circumstances, and wildly different geographies and climes. Owing to their roots in the visions of political leaders and engineers, the enthusiastic response of the public in support of them, and the continuities in ministerial, research, and engineering and political institutions behind them, hero projects have become standard for the Russian setting. After their initial stage of development, some technologies seem to take on a life of their own, in particular big technologies, that makes it difficult to alter their scope and redirect resources allocated to them, let alone to stop and defund them. Their initial purposes—to modernize transportation, industry, and agriculture, accelerate resource extraction, enable commerce, and advance the defense capabilities of the nation—justify them even when economic downturns or political uncertainties raise questions about their efficacy. This "technological momentum" ensures that they continue in some form, gaining resources and investment.[21]

A major impetus to technological momentum has been the challenge of meeting resource needs and industrialization programs, of managing citizens to ensure their presence at worksites, and securing the interests of Moscow in controlling distant territories including those of titular nationalities in the provinces and republics, and indigenes in the Far North, Siberia, and Far East. Already in the early nineteenth century, the Tsarist regime employed expeditions, military colonies, and other endeavors to bring stability and control to the periphery of the empire. A series of expeditions from the mid-eighteenth century brought science and engineering into the effort to secure the vast, sparsely inhabited territories of the Tsarist empire, at the same time identifying extensive resources that were important to the treasury and military. Increasingly, science and technology became embedded in state institutions, most importantly the Imperial Russian Academy of Sciences, later the Soviet Academy. In the Soviet period, R&D (research and development), design, and other institutes and bureaus were founded and grew under the protection of self-interested ministries connected with iron and steel; coal, oil, and gas; construction; transport; and the like.

Technological momentum is most evident in the continuity between institutions and their programs from the Soviet period to the present. The initial creation of Soviet R&D centers, with the Academy of Sciences becoming the central, prestigious location for basic research, has been characterized as "a combination of revolutionary innovation and international borrowing."[22] This suggests that the Tsarist engineering legacy had less to offer the Soviet regime in terms of institutions. But Tsarist specialists advanced ideas and projects that found life quickly in the Soviet setting with the support of the Bolsheviks who embraced big science and engineering. The Academy itself dated to Peter the Great in 1725. For the most part, however, R&D and engineering institutes were a creation of the Soviet period.[23] Still, many of the ideas—and personnel—behind various transport, dam, and other projects of the 1920s and 1930s had pre-revolutionary roots. Soon enough the Soviet Academy was incorporated into the Stalinist industrialization effort in a variety of hero projects, some of them with Tsarist roots: a new Trans-Siberian railroad anointed the Baikal-Amur Magistral (BAM), a series of dams on the Volga and other rivers, and several massive transfer canals. Newly created industrial laboratories and research institutes were joined into the efforts with geological and geographical surveys, hydrological studies, and charting of valuable resources. Various laboratories of Academy institutes became special institutes of the atomic bomb project and the foundation of the nuclear enterprise as the Ministry of Middle Machine Building that has been resurrected in the twenty-first century as Rosatom.

Many hero projects fell by the wayside during World War II, then reappeared in the engineering agenda of an emboldened and victorious leadership seeking to extract resources in a Cold War setting. Each Soviet leader advanced new projects and identified new geographic foci for factories to arise, always claiming the pathbreaking nature of the project, but acknowledging in some ways its roots in an earlier period. For example, engineers provided the Kuibyshev hydroelectric power station with project documentation in the mid-1930s. The project commenced on the eve of World War II, was interrupted by the war, was redesigned and relocated in the late Stalin period, and was completed under Nikita Khrushchev. BAM construction dates from the 1930s as a gulag project but became a "project of the century" under Brezhnev. Stalin subjugated the Arctic, a process that gained scientific certainty in the Brezhnev era as specialists constantly occupied drift stations, and it continues into the twenty-first century under Putin with massive oil, gas, and other operations.

In spite of the tremendous disruptions of world war, revolution, and civil war; the political turmoil of the Russian Revolution, the Stalinist "revolution from above," and the collapse of the USSR; and the always present efforts of the Tsarist, Soviet, and Russian states to shape and control economic development programs for the benefit of the Kremlin, there has thus been tremendous continuity between institutions and individuals in hero project over the past century.

A crucial institution in all regards was the gulag prison system. The gulag gave birth to the White Sea–Baltic Canal and dozens of other waterworks projects. Indeed, over time gulag bosses pushed armies of laborers from the northwest to the central regions of the country, to Siberia, the Far North, and the Far East, seeking newer, bolder projects that consumed prisoners and other resources. Gulag workers were central to efforts to take the frontier, fill the distant reaches of the empire, and prepare for war with capitalist nations by applying a new infrastructure of canals and dams, hydroelectric power stations, roads and railroads, power lines, telecommunications, and entire company towns.[24] Hundreds of thousands of them died in the camps between 1928 and 1953, when the camps began to empty out in an amnesty that commenced after Stalin's death.

A number of gulag organizations exist today as Russian corporations. The gulag administration responsible for canals and dams became the Zhuk Gidroproekt Institute in the 1950s and then RusGidro under Putin The new hydropower stations of RusGidro, born out of gulag construction projects of the 1930s, 1940s and 1950s, whose hero projects Brezhnev pursued in the 1970s and 1980s, are arising again in the tundra to power the extraction of aluminum and generate foreign currency earnings through exports of electricity—and perhaps water, another valuable Russian commodity—to China. One such project for a dam in Yakutia had broad support until perestroika permitted the release of a 1988 environmental impact statement from Siberian scientists that documented its devastating impact, especially on the Evenk people. But in the 1990s and 2000s, as the economic situation of the Evenki worsened owing to inattention from Moscow, RusGidro recognised the opportunity to push the station again, while Russian nationalists and hydrological engineers are seeking related Siberian projects to advance Moscow's interests in the former colonies of Central Asia.[25]

It is not difficult to understand that project and design institutes grow, they receive government contracts, they push projects, the larger the projects the better, and their projects provide their daily bread. Working with officials and educational institutions, they create training programs to produce more engineers, young engineers, raised entirely within cultural, engineering, and political milieus that are in obeisance to hero projects. The engineers come to recognize hero projects as the appropriate way to enhance the standing of their institutes, undergird the power of the nation, gain support from the political authorities for new projects, and earn the approbation of citizens who see vast new chemical combines, steel mills, petrochemical combines, glorious transport magistrals, and Herculean hydro- and nuclear power stations that confirm the technological leadership of the country.

Citizens, of course, are part of technological momentum. The Bolsheviks conceived of the first hero projects in the 1920s and 1930s as precisely the site to bring together and train workers in the tasks of construction and operation of factories and mines, to transform peasants into workers, and inculcate tens of thousands of employees simultaneously in the Marxian faith. In addition, since there could be no unemployment in the USSR, design institutes, construction trusts, and other organizations involved in hero projects could rely on ever new projects. Once one factory was up and running, workers did not become redundant, lose their jobs, and seek employment elsewhere, as under capitalism. Rather, the organizations extended their existence and the employment of those involved to more excavation, more pouring of concrete, and more pushing across the Siberian plain, the northwestern forests, and the southern Steppe toward new combines.[26] Today (see chapter 6), big projects continue to enthrall the masses.

In the 1990s many Soviet projects were mothballed or canceled outright owing to the collapse of the Soviet economy. There was a virtual interregnum in engineering efforts under the Yeltsin presidency brought about by a poverty-stricken government and failed economy. And yet the design institutes behind them managed to stumble along, barely able to heat offices or to hold on to crucial personnel. And when the Russian economy recovered in the 2000s through petrodollars, engineers and officials were prepared to embark again on large-scale resource development projects. The Russian Federation has resumed a number of large-scale projects through corporations and ministries reborn from Soviet ones, using them as a symbol of state power, economic strength, and the enlightened leadership of Vladimir Putin.

The nuclear enterprise is, in a way, a self-contained hero project whose grand designs have filled seventy years of Russian history. At present, floating reactors are being built because of the technological momentum of design bureaus and engineering firms. One of the leading institutes for floating stations, the design bureau OKBM Afrikantov, has Cold War roots. Since the 1960s its specialists have finished a series of designs, and participated in the construction of hundreds of reactors and steam-generating plants. Under President Putin it has recovered from budget cuts and mothballed programs in the 1990s. The Afrikantov design bureau now employs about 4,000 people, including over 1,600 design engineers, technologists and test engineers, including twenty of them upon whom Putin bestowed the title "Honored Engineer of the Russian Federation."

Another manifestation of technological momentum—and in this case a kind of cultural momentum—is the identification of Rosatom, the nuclear ministry, as a kind of twenty-first century Glavsevmorput (Main Administration of the Norther Sea Route, founded in the 1930s). Rosatom has claimed leadership in solving the problems of exploitation of oil, gas, and rare metals, and enabling reliable shipping within Russia and to the growing economies of Asia including China and Asia. One of its divisions, Atomflot, responsible for nuclear icebreakers, in this regard acts as an "infrastructure company" tying together pipelines, coal and copper mines, canals, ports, polar airports, and ships.

To take another example of continuity over time, projects, and regimes, Stalin insisted on using tens of thousands of gulag prisoners to lay a polar railroad to bring the Pechora River basin, Ural Mountain region, and West Siberian oil, gas, coal, and ore into state hands. The railroad would terminate at a port in the Ob River delta at Cape Kamenny, then to be served by the Great Northern Sea Route. Stalin's railroad, known as the "Road of Death." Stalin's polar railroad was subsequently turned eastward with the flick of a pen on a map to the Yenisei River with a terminus at the lumber town Igarka, itself a gulag-based lumbering city, because of engineering surveys that belatedly showed the impossibility of building at Cape Kamenny. Putin has called for the completion of the railroad to supplement oil and gas infrastructure on the Yamal Peninsula, and in May 2016 from his Kremlin office he opened a new gas terminal at Cape Kamenny by video link at the "Arctic Gates" facility.

Whatever the Tsars and their advisers lacked in vision, determination, and well-funded government programs to force the economic development of the landscape, the commissars made up for in tons, kilowatts, cubic meters, and armies of workers. They adopted hero projects as the centerpiece of development efforts through a series of five-year plans beginning from the late 1920s. Officials assumed that, unlike under capitalism, socialist planning would avoid duplication of effort; would rationally distribute goods and services, capital, and labor; and would provide proper incentives to managers and workers to fulfill targets. They insisted that a scientific approach based on socialist methods and productive relations enabled the promulgation of targets inconceivable under capitalism. Engineers, for their part, assumed, like many engineers in other systems, that were they to encounter technical challenges, supply problems, or other difficulties they would find technological solutions. Yet of course the system did not function perfectly, nothing close to it, for a variety of reasons. These reasons included the undervaluation of natural resources in the pricing system that led to profligate waste and overuse, the constant push to reach superhuman production targets, the development of a planning system that had little flexibility to distribute necessary resources of labor and capital, and the treatment of all regions and ecosystems, and their natural and mineral resources, as roughly equivalent and malleable according to planners' preferences.

To put it directly, party officials, planners, and engineers set out through hero projects to exploit natural and mineral wealth and created armies of workers to tap it, manage it, and overlay it with infrastructure. They approached these tasks with homogenizing visions and machines across all time zones no matter the climate, topology, and geography through such Moscow-based organizations as Gosstroi, Gossnab, Gosstandart (the State Construction Committee, State Technical Supply Committee, and State Standards Committee, respectively), Gidroproekt, and others, and through powerful central design institutes with branches in other cities and republics that followed Kremlin patterns.[27] The institutes and the projects they imposed upon the landscape acquired great technological momentum, for when they finished one task, there was always another river to dam, mine to sink, or train line to lay. They moved historically and geographically, as it were, across the landscape from the northwest to the east and south, and to the east again, always in search of new projects, at times shedding personnel that became the kernel of other design institutes and construction organizations.

In its explanatory power to illuminate the resurgence of Soviet-style development projects, technological momentum covers many of the features of the theory of path dependency where present decisions are dependent on previous decisions or past experiences. Path dependence exists when a feature of the economy (institutions, technical standards, or patterns of economic development) have been formed by past actions. In other words, history matters in technological change, even when in a given setting there has been rapid and significant political change, for example, regime change—as in the abdication of the Tsar in 1917 or the collapse of the USSR in 1991.[28] In this book we will consider the important historical political factors that have led to embrace of hero projects. The continuities and critical features include: institutes, organizations, and design bureaus; authoritarian political structures and ministries (previously called commissariats) that have limited public participation in technology assessment; and the existence of the very physical structures and materials—dams and rails, concrete and steel, bridges and reactors, girders and uranium—that require maintenance, demand further development, and serve as templates for new projects.

The Cultural Meanings and Costs of Big Technology

As a history of the megaprojects, this book considers the relationship between projects and citizens on three levels. The first is their employment experiences as miners, concrete pourers, construction workers, bulldozer operators, and so on; as gulag prisoners; as family members who lived near the construction sites and mines and whose daily lives reflected the desiderata of production; as Communist Youth League (Komsomol) members enthralled by the lure of heroism and glorious target fulfillment; and as local people including indigenes whose lives were forever changed by the flooding of their lands by magnificent concrete dams, by the despoliation of their ways of life by the raising of factories, the bulldozing of overburden, and the boring and tunneling that accompanies new construction.

A second is how citizens perceive the projects—the ideological purposes of factories, railroads, bridges, nuclear power stations, and other glorious large-scale technologies beyond the narrower technical ends they serve. Russian citizens, not only the leaders, have accepted large-scale technologies both for their technical purposes (of transport, mining, oil and gas production, electrical power generation, and so on) because they feed and house them, and importantly for their symbolic meaning (of demonstrating the physical achievements of the nation, the power of its scientists and engineers, the glories of its leaders, and so on). That is, technologies have "display value," precisely symbolic, ideological, and cultural purposes that are in many cases as important as their engineering ends. The list of such technologies includes skyscrapers and highways, bridges and dams, canals and power systems, and, later, rockets and reactors.[29] The competition to be the first or the best, or to have poured more concrete faster, or to tame rivers for electrical power, irrigation, and flood control—and so on and on—shaped a number of decisions, especially, and not surprisingly in such areas of military importance as aeronautics and rocketry. The display value of technology is a phenomenon across the globe. Brazil's leaders brought hydropower stations to Amazonia not only to extract resources but to indicate the benefits of the modern world to citizens. Americans came to see in technology proof of the glorious civilizing mission in the transcontinental railway (1860s), economic prowess, scientific excellence, and "democracy on the march" in the Tennessee Valley Authority (TVA) dams (1930s–present), its massive new highways (1950s–present), and its space program that put a man on the moon by the end of the 1960s.[30] The Chinese leaders, similarly, see the Three Gorges Dam, bullet trains, and other large-scale technologies as potent symbols of the might of the nation.

The experience of people in the Russian empire has been much the same, if the effort to demonstrate the symbolic meaning of hero projects more obvious, direct, and public. In coffee table books; biographies of heroic engineers, bold builders, and visionary politicians; in ubiquitous posters that celebrate—or call for—always increasing industrial production; in annual holidays named for industrial laborers and public awards given to leading managers and honored workers; and even in postage stamps, Russian society has linked hero projects with the public good. That Russia's leaders to this day see great value in presenting technological achievements as evidence of world scientific leadership, military security, and a reflection of the fact that their nation-building choices have borne fruit, should not be surprising. The display value of technology was clearly in the minds of Soviet leaders already in the 1930s when they orchestrated a series of "firsts" with airplanes and their heroic pilots—flying to the North Pole, over the North Pole, and the huge, eight-engine *Maxim Gorky* airplane (1934) that crashed over Moscow into the Sokol neighborhood killing all forty-eight people on board (the *Maxim Gorky* has been immortalized in stone in the city's famous Novodevichy Cemetery reserved for the nation's leading artistic, creative, scientific, and political lights). Another heroic conquest captured and propagandized in newspapers, on the radio, and in film was a series of Arctic expeditions that showed the heroism and mettle of scientists. A third was the construction of a series of larger and larger hydroelectric power stations and canals whose glories prompted speeches, films, and newspaper articles galore. All these achievements were calculated to demonstrate the legitimacy of the state to the masses. More recently, the Crimean Bridge, erected across the Kerch straits by Putin at a cost of billions of dollars, attempted physically to demonstrate that Crimea, annexed in 2014, was actually an integral part of Russia. The blowing up of several sections of the bridge by unknown actors after Russia's unprovoked attack on Ukraine in 2022 was also more than military in intent, but an assault on Putin's pride, occurring a day after his seventieth birthday.

The USSR was not alone in seeking technological feats as confirmation of the glory of the nation and the caring of the leaders for the masses. Indeed, the USSR and the United States engaged in competition through state-sponsored power generation programs that they claimed were largely for the benefit of the masses. By the 1930s the nations shared the belief that electricity was a panacea for the problems facing each society: imbalances of production, poverty, and the need to demonstrate the legitimacy of the leadership. Electrification programs demonstrated that the nations truly embraced democracy, as indicated by increasing production of and access to electrical power of all citizens—electricity that improved the economic well-being and public health of the people, along the way overcoming poverty and illiteracy. During the Great Depression, the United States embarked on a series of massive construction projects that put millions of unemployed people back to work. This was Franklin Delano Roosevelt's (FDR) "New Deal" with the American people. From the Bonneville Power Administration on the Columbia River in Washington state, with its now thirteen major dams, to the Boulder Dam (renamed Hoover Dam in 1947) on the border between Nevada and Arizona, built between 1931 and 1935, to the TVA, these projects contributed to ending unemployment.

A third way to consider the important relationship between citizens and big technology is environmental concerns and immediate social impacts. Tautologically, big technologies require environmental impacts in the extensive, violent processes of excavation, drilling, and using explosives, in pouring concrete, framing structures, and pushing nature and people aside. In the construction and operation of mines and smelters, forestry roads, rails across the taiga, irrigation and reclamation projects, and in engineered rivers, big technologies permanently alter the landscape, destroy entire ecosystems, and through extensive pollution ensure that those impacts bleed far beyond immediate sites of activity. The negative environmental impacts of hero projects are immediately clear. Many other impacts will be unclear for years, although it is possible to offer scenarios of their destructive capacity based on past experience, especially with consideration of the administrative and political obstacles to a more vigorous assessment of negative environmental impacts and ways to lessen, if not prevent them. Thus, the reader will sense implicit—and occasionally explicit—evaluation of these costs and risks, and they have not abated into the twenty-first century.

These impacts impose significant costs on the workers involved in hero projects and their families, not only through pollution, but through questionable worker safety practices and accidents. Indeed because of the projects, citizens' health is under threat from heavy metals, dangerous wastes, chemicals, ionizing radiation, and pesticides that bear down on them from all sides. In the embrace of big science and technology, the nation's leaders, specialists, and citizens in Russia, indeed in any society, accept a certain amount of risk, and they see the immediate benefits of projects in jobs. This book considers the risks and benefits of hero projects for Russia's citizens in light of the extensive pollution, the industrial accidents, and so on.

This book is not about whether capitalism is rapacious and profligate in use of resources, or whether capitalist industry is highly polluting. It is. It is not about the huge social costs of industrialization in the capitalist West. To be sure, the worker in the Ruhrgebeit in Germany; in Chicago, Detroit, and Pittsburgh in the United States; and in Liverpool and Manchester, England, toiled for low wages in dangerous conditions at risk of life and limb. The focus here is the Russian empire, where these same frightful costs of hero projects were clearly in evidence.

Accidents have acquired special meaning in Russian history, often being seen as an inevitable but necessary cost of conquering the land mass and pushing the country forward toward higher industrial productivity. In the 1930s, Stalin drove Arctic explorers to open the Northern Sea Route with ships and icebreakers in many cases inadequate to the task. When the *Cheliuskin*, a Danish vessel equipped with steel plates on its hull to serve, poorly, as an icebreaker, was caught in the ice and sank, the nation learned of the heroic *Cheliuskintsy* who overcame frigid isolation in a very public rescue—while leading members of the crew were later arrested and shipped off to the gulag for "wrecking." The Chernobyl disaster in 1986 required a battle against mortal radiation by hundreds of thousands of "liquidators." The authorities, claiming erroneously that everything was in control, forced the remaining three reactors, damaged with radiation, into operation only six months later, and we are still learning the consequences of the accident for the environment and people.[31] The Saiano-Shushenskaia hydroelectric power station disaster in August 2009 killed seventy-five people, with Putin showing remorse for the victims, but insisting that electricity must flow; one unit was up and running in March of the next year to power aluminum smelters.[32]

This attitude about safety, accidents, and pollution holds even during regime change, where the mistakes of the past become the property of the present, and still leaders refuse to allocate sufficient resources to remediation. To take one example: the Russian Arctic Ocean is the site of significant radioactive waste and fallout, and not only at Soviet Navy bases from the Kola Peninsula to Vladivostok for submarines and other nuclear vessels, but at other facilities for handling facilities for waste, fissile materials, and spent fuel. Over recent years, greater awareness of the extent of this dangerous problem has grown, but the post-Soviet *Russian* authorities at first tried to prosecute whistleblowers for espionage for publicizing this dangerous legacy, and have still not authorized sufficient action or funding to deal with the problem. In fact, on the shelf to the east of the Novaia Zemlia archipelago the buried radioactive wastes total over 2,400 kCi; it is also an area where the Soviets carried out nearly 100 nuclear explosions from 1955 to 1962.[33]

The Russian empire, of course, is not alone in facing a number of challenges in managing risk in the name of public health. As Ulrich Beck has argued, the pursuit of industrialized modernity and the wealth it produced was accompanied by the production of risks. Pollution, toxins, radiation, and associated risks have become normal occurrences. Whereas before, people assumed these risks might have a technological solution, Beck argued, the risks themselves have become essential to modernity. While societies are more dependent on technology, growing awareness of risk has led other groups to advance rational arguments about the dangers of the modern world in the forms of nongovernmental organizations, lay expertise, and so on.[34]

But the response of successive Russian governments has been to deny problems and silence critics. The first show trials in the USSR—the Shakhty and Industrial Party Affairs—involved engineers who were prosecuted in part for criticizing the social costs of Stalin's first hero projects. In the Khrushchev and Brezhnev eras, while awareness of environmental problems was no longer a crime against the state, there were limited avenues for citizens and scientists to worry about the environmental and social costs of big development projects.[35] During the rule of Mikhail Gorbachev (1985–1991), independence movements broke out in Ukraine, the Baltic countries, and elsewhere that were connected in part with the belief among local people that the republics had been economically exploited by Moscow, and also that unsafe technologies—polluting factories, the Chernobyl reactors in Ukraine, failed irrigation projects—had been foisted on them. Demonstrations and investigations boiled over only after glasnost.

The Putin administration has returned to the tradition of strict control, systematically quieting opposition to big and risky projects, limiting discussion of their social and economic costs, and emasculating NGOs that draw attention to questions of justice, safety, and efficacy that remain an important part of the natural order of business in other countries. The Russian government supports big investment in new projects, not in upkeep, repair, treatment facilities, nor in legislation or enforcement of laws to address the environmental challenges of ongoing economic development projects.

Leaders intend to secure military, geopolitical, and economic advantage through the sale of commodities from Arctic oil and gas, Siberian forests and fossil fuels, and even water from Siberia's great rivers, and environmental laws interfere with this. Ecological understandings enter their considerations in a formal way only, while social concerns about workers, housing, public health, safety, and so on often appear only as political communications of concern or when de rigueur because of such technogenic disasters as floods, fires, and explosions.

Hero Projects

The result is *Hero Projects*: large-scale infrastructure of oil and gas, roads, railroads, and bridges, canals and other waterworks, and nuclear power and hydroelectric power stations with great meaning for the state in terms of its political power and public legitimacy. Across the last century—even more than a century—hero projects have served to strengthen the Russian empire, give the Kremlin control over resources and landmass, and use economic development programs to accelerate settlement of distant regions and force the pace of urbanization. They move ahead with great momentum even when accidents, pollution, and social disruptions are sometimes the result.

Hero Projects is an exploration of empire, technology and resources, of centralized power and natural and mineral wealth, a history of state-sponsored projects. It analyzes the importance of these projects within the closed political culture of a nation with aspirations of a scientific superpower. The Kremlin will push onward, and under Putin with the determination to return to Soviet-era projects in scale and location, with similar political values, institutions, and public tropes to accompany their operation.

The economic and political pressures of each era had a significant impact on hero projects, and each Russian leader from Lenin to Stalin to Brezhnev to Putin shaped them according to his own understandings of the needs of the nation. The leaders understandably pursued infrastructural and development projects that supported state power and resource development, and they established peninsulas of modernity across vast oceans of territory. The projects were run and directed from the Kremlin, whether through commissariats and ministries or today's state corporations. Engineering projects arose and were completed, or proposed and fell, owing to budgetary pressures, or the desire of each leader to put his imprint on the economy. Yet the projects had surprising momentum over the decades, conceived in one decade, even in the Tsarist period, often disappearing into planning offices and design bureaus, then reappearing in a new incarnation, for example, BAM or the new polar magistral. A major difference has been that, in the twenty-first century, market labor institutions ensure the supply of workers. In the Soviet period, state control of production, whether common workers or gulag prisoners, ensured supply of laborers to the various projects. Yet the belief persists among the oligarchs that one can get by with coerced, under-paid manpower.

Thus, Lenin embraced big projects as a panacea to overcome the techno-logical backwardness of the nation. Stalin set in motion the rapid industrial-ization of the USSR through the five-year plans to secure the nation against military threat from without and enemies within, at the same time creating an army of compliant workers. This development model persisted over the decades. Under Nikita Khrushchev (1954–1964) and Leonid Brezhnev (1964–1985), the effort to control resources in service of the Kremlin ex-panded north and east into the Arctic and Siberia. Massive ministries put their design institutes and construction organizations to work in pushing further into the tundra and taiga. After an interregnum in engineering projects under the Yeltsin presidency in the 1990s brought about by a poverty-stricken government and failed economy, the Russian Federation has resumed a number of large-scale projects through corporations and ministries reborn from Soviet ones, using them as a symbol of state power, economic strength, and enlightened leadership. Indeed, Putin continues to find value for the Kremlin in megaprojects that in many ways reflect Soviet approaches, plans, and dreams.

These trends become clear in the following chapters. Chapter 1 covers the railroads—among the earliest major infrastructural projects in the empire. From the Tsar's Trans-Siberian Railroad, to the TurkSib (Turkmenistan-Siberian) project of the late 1920s, to Stalin's gulag transport system intended to secure resources and punish prisoners, the rails grew out from Moscow to the north and northeast toward the Pechora River basin. They included BAM, an unfinished trans-Siberian route from the 1930s that remained un-finished although claimed otherwise under Brezhnev.

Of course, when many people think of Russia, they think of oil and gas. Chapter 1 continues with discussion of railroads and other infrastructure dedicated to the newly hatched and self-proclaimed "megaprojects of the century" to control the Arctic and to move petroleum toward refineries and demand in Central Russia. Megaproject railroads, pipelines, pumping stations, and other infrastructure figure mightily in the plans of the Russian state, in particular in the Gazprom menagerie of oil and gas facilities throughout the Arctic, and those of Novatek, one of the largest natural gas companies in the world, on the Yamal Peninsula, itself a 700 km long territory that extends into the Arctic Ocean. The companies of oligarchic state capitalism in Russia treat these lands as their fiefdoms, building as needed to extract gas, claiming to do so in an environmentally sound fashion yet keeping out journalists and scientists who might discover otherwise, pushing the Nenets and Khanty reindeer pastoralists aside, and they build railroads to secure the space.[36] Petrochemical pollution is visible from space, but gas extraction is an unforgiving taskmaster. Looking northward in the twenty-first century, therefore, one can only feel a kind of fatalism in the fact that Putin and his advisors, oligarchs, and *siloviki* (members of the administration who have come from the security forces, military and police) have embraced projects for resource development similar to those of the Soviet era, including roads, railroads, and pipelines to enhance state power and enrich Kremlin coffers.[37]

In chapter 2 I discuss the history of coal mining in the Russian empire. Mines are dirty and dangerous. Since the extractive industry is crucial to Russia's long-range economic plans, miners have fared poorly, in particular coal miners. They are lowly paid, at great risk to health, life, and limb along with those in Ukraine, China, and Turkey, and seemingly cannot escape their gulag legacy of dangerous working conditions and unfeeling bosses. Gulag prisoners hauled coal, iron, copper, platinum, diamond, and gold out of the earth from mines in Central Asia, Siberia, the Arctic, and the Far East. The mining settlements became company towns dedicated to a specific ore or nearby smelter or furnace, and were often glorified as production utopias.[38] Vasilii Azhaev, himself a prisoner in the 1930s, glorified the infamous Kolyma mines in the Stalin Prize–winning *Far from Moscow* (1950). But Varlam Shalamov was closer to the truth in depicting the murderous, if mundane, daily life of gulag prisoners who extracted gold and built logging roads in his *Kolyma Tales*.

These mines remain crucial to the state, as chapter 2 explores. Mines powered Stalinist industrialization, Arctic conquest, and Siberian assimilation. They have always been hazardous, violent, and filthy places to work or live, especially since gulag prisoners opened a large number of them.[39] Mines continue to provide coal to Russia's factories and cities in new economic circumstances, controlled by oligarchs and serving both domestic and international markets. Many of the Stalin-era ore deposit remain open, with miners increasingly using such brute force and highly polluting methods as open pit technologies, as a result of which they live, breathe, and raise children on the edge of environmental catastrophe: the huge pits, and the rivers and lakes nearby, offer municipal and recreational water laden with heavy metals, sulfur, and ash. Tailings fill every imaginable gully, and slag heaps rise above schools and stores, and even the homes of the nouveau riche. Coal is notorious for its public health and visual impacts on the quality of life, especially in the Kuznetsk Basin (Kuzbass).

Chapter 3 considers waterworks—dams, canals, irrigation systems—across Russian space and time. Building from projects inspired and conceived by Tsarist engineers, waterworks grew in size, scope, and unconstrained visions. Starting from gulag earth moving, dam erecting, and canal excavating operations into post-Stalinist engineering operations, water workers have maintained their authority and filled their coffers with rubles, while their projects facilitate the Kremlin's century-long march along Russia's massive river basins for transport, electricity, municipal, and other purposes into the twenty-first century. Big engineering projects have been reborn under Putin. In the current engineering and political atmosphere, the Siberian rivers diversion project, conceived as a hatchery of Russian colonization in the projects of nineteenth-century nationalists, that involved 250 different ministerial and engineering organizations in the Brezhnev era may be starting anew. Tabled under Gorbachev as far too risky, even for Kremlin leaders, it has gained the attention of Moscow's oligarchs who see water, too, as a commodity.

High-tech hero projects have also served the Kremlin. Chapter 4 considers the nuclear enterprise in Russia today through historical analysis of a variety of big technologies: reactors, icebreakers, and other nuclear-powered devices. The powerful enterprise "Rosatom" is critically important to Russian geopolitical interests, economic power, and self-image. According to national leaders, Rosatom, the inheritor of civilian and military programs of the Soviet nuclear ministry, "Minsredmash," will protect Arctic regions from growing foreign competition and encroachment. Rosatom will power the development of oil and gas, nickel, copper, and platinum, and will also complete the unfinished tasks of the opening the northern sea route to year round commerce.[40] Russia's leaders frequently tout Rosatom activities as a reminder of the fact that the nation remains a scientific superpower in the post–Cold War world. Toward these ends, Rosatom has both embarked on ambitious new nuclear power programs and resurrected and reshaped Soviet-era ones.

Chapter 5 takes as a point of departure, like so many Russian businessmen and tourists hoping to get to Crimea, and now Russian citizens trying to escape the war coming to it, the recently completed multibillion-dollar Crimean Bridge. Having seized Crimea in 2014, the Putin government faced a series of intractable and costly problems to stabilize its illegal land grab that violated the Budapest Memorandum to 1994 that Russia itself signed. Water, electricity, and freight by rail and truck now trickle into Crimea from Ukraine across the 3–5 km wide Isthmus of Perekop. Ukraine has cut all of the flows substantially, including much of the freshwater that comes to Crimea from the Dniepr River into the North Crimea Canal. But bridges served military purposes on the Russian landmass for decades, as this chapter explores in the buildup to the Crimean Bridge.

If the roots of many of Putin's projects are in fact in Soviet technological designs, then memory of them goes only so far. In contemporary political culture it is unfashionable to remember that many of these projects—the canals that still ship freight, trains that carry passengers, dams that transform water into electricity, and the like—have roots in the gulag slave camp system of the Stalin era. After Stalin's death, those projects and the design institutes that built them were sanitized of these memories, and few people speak about them today. In fact, Russian holidays, prizes, commemorative publications, stamps, and first-day covers all gloss over the great human and environmental costs of the Soviet development model. At the same time, the Putin administration has emasculated or outlawed NGOs that are dedicated to fighting preserving the memory of those people who were repressed and murdered by the Stalinist regime, including the NGO "Memorial" that won the 2022 Nobel Peace Prize for its efforts.

Indeed, as discussed in the final chapter of this book, Russian leaders— and many citizens, judging by polls and surveys—have great nostalgia for the Soviet era in terms of the authority of rulers, the power of the state, cultural traditions against the decadence of the west, and especially achievements in science and technology. They recall that Soviets were first to tie a reactor to the civilian electrical grid in 1954, the first in space with Sputnik in 1957 and Yuri Gagarin in 1961, and created the laser, among many other achievements. They secured tremendous international prestige and national pride. Through various earth-moving, nuclei-splitting, and resource-extracting organizations and companies, Russia has resumed Soviet-like projects to demonstrate that it remains a technological superpower. Like Soviet leaders, the president uses photo opportunities to demonstrate his industrial acumen and power over nature, and the administration has reintroduced special Soviet holidays to celebrate atomic workers and cosmonautics.

In a word, megaprojects—large-scale engineering works that have been built and continue to be built across eleven times zones of Russia—are dedicated to supplying the Kremlin with wealth and power. Hero projects reflect the paradox of a glorious tradition of engineering excellence combined with brute force approaches to exploit natural resources. Through an increasingly closed system, political leaders, government bureaucrats, and owners and managers of state corporations and privatized utilities, construction companies, and oil and gas firms, are pushing ahead across the landscape and waterways to control the nation's mineral and natural wealth. State inspection and regulatory agencies have become captured by the industries they are meant to regulate. Leaders today, as they did under the Tsars and the Bolsheviks, have no doubt that state power requires hero projects to subjugate the great Russian landmass to the whim of the Kremlin.

1

Rails and Resources[*]

Massive engineering projects have been central to the Tsarist, Soviet, and current Russian state governments. They enabled the development of the economy in regions distant from Moscow that officials perceived to be empty of people. They provided access to extensive natural resources of forests, furs, and fish; coal, oil, and gas; and multitudinous mineral resources. They were crucial for military reasons—to deliver supplies and troops. In the absence of a large entrepreneurial class in the Tsarist period, the state had to assume the role of kick-starting and funding projects. In the Soviet period, capitalists were declared class enemies and eliminated; the state was the force behind development. And in contemporary Russia, oligarchs in and connected with a powerful state have assumed the role of innovators and promoters—through petrodollars. Even with state support and the pressures of economic necessity, over the past one hundred years railroad construction has moved in fits and starts, in the Soviet period with rail investments competing with other demands of the mass industrialization effort and relying heavily on gulag slave labor for construction. Later, Communist Party leaders required mass campaigns to exhort disinterested laborers, and in contemporary Russia projects move ahead only when connected with the resource needs of the state—if using well-paid shift workers. We can see these continuities and differences clearly in transportation projects, in particular the railroad, and the building projects of Tsar Nicholas II and Joseph Stalin—the Tsar's Trans-Siberian Railway and Stalin's uncompleted Polar "Magistral." Will there be another attempt at a polar railroad route in the 2020s?

Many of these features of railroad construction are part of world history. The railroad, the steamship, and other transportation marvels of the industrial age spread across the globe in the early nineteenth century and captured the imagination of visionaries, patriots, military specialists, and citizens. British inventors and capitalists spoke of the contribution of a transport revolution to industry and empire, with London becoming the center of commerce domestically and abroad, and contributing to profound cultural and social impacts as a result at home and abroad as an imperial power.[1] In the

Hero Projects. Paul R. Josephson, Oxford University Press. © Oxford University Press 2024.
DOI: 10.1093/oso/9780197698396.003.0002

United States, too, from the days that Robert Fulton and others launched steamships along rivers as far west as the Mississippi, commerce and power simultaneously expanded, giving rise to the notion that steam was the key to the nation's future. American entrepreneurs urged public and private inventors to build canals linking cities and rural regions for commerce. Next, steam railroads and ships facilitated the industrial revolution that closed the distance between countryside and city, and finally rail was laid linking the Atlantic and Pacific coast that confirmed the Manifest Destiny of the world's leading industrial nation to control the continent.[2]

In Russia, in the absence of the interest of bankers and government officials, public visionaries, entrepreneurs, and engineers engaged state and society to sell a transport revolution to the nation, as the efforts to modernize transport in the Tsarist empire lagged behind those of other nations in the industrial world. In part, Tsarist officials feared modern transport. The institution of serfdom involved an ideology of passive immobility. It tied peasants to the land and prevented the accumulation of sufficient capital to underwrite improvements in the economy and transportation. Worried about a mobile, landless peasantry, or a nascent, migrant working class, when the Tsarist government emancipated the serfs in 1861 it found other ways to keep them tied to the land by indebting them and making them seek the permission of local communes to leave their communities.[3] But by the end of the nineteenth century, even the plodding government understood the need to expand its transport network and approved the building of the Trans-Siberian railroad to assimilate Siberia, foster mobility and commerce, and improve military transport to counter Japanese encroachment in the Far East. In spite of being pushed by Minister of Finance Sergei Witte, government funding, however, lagged between the needs of the railroad, and the state had to turn to French investors to find financial support the railroad and other projects.

Like the Bolsheviks, the current administration in Russia worries about mobility and control, seeking both to speed the extraction of mineral wealth and the delivery of commodities, yet to shepherd citizens and their ideas in concert with state development programs. Once the Bolsheviks took power in 1917, they rapidly expanded the railroad network. But whether the "Turksib" railroad from Turkestan to West Siberia; a second trans-Siberian route, BAM, to the Far East; Stalin's unfinished Polar Magistral; or Gazprom's contemporary network of railroads and pipelines in the Arctic, all of these "projects of the century" suffer a dichotomous existence: they are magisterial yet costly, romantic yet poorly built, extensive and heroic, yet dangerously decrepit from the moment they open, and, it must be acknowledged, most of them were built with convicts or had roots in forced labor, and were decades late in completion.[4]

The history of freight in the former Soviet Union is the history of moving coal, oil, gas, mineral ore, and iron and steel bars, plates, girders, rebar, and other metallurgical products. If in 1913, such heavy loads comprised roughly 25 percent of the total along Tsarist rails, then by the 1960s, 60 percent of Soviet freight was fossil fuels and minerals. It is not surprising in the modern Russian resource state that the national rail system continues to expand to support oil, gas, and coal extraction, not passengers, although it moves slowly and is focused on regions where extraction is of major of importance to the generation of wealth important to the Kremlin.

The oligarchs of oil and gas companies are the prime movers of contemporary Russian rail projects, and private investment may be crucial to their completion. But without the bureaucracies, equipment, permits, media control, and largesse of the Kremlin, and without massive reserves of gas and oil, the rails would languish in the tundra. As Rosneft, Gazprom, Novatek, and other massive corporations identify deposits, they develop infrastructure to extract it, and they push aside indigenes, who pay with lost cultural heritage and polluted environment.[5] The Russian government has funded a massive new project "Ural Industrial—Ural Polar" that includes a new railway to speed resource exploitation, a major component of which is an east-west railroad across the Arctic Circle to speed resource exploitation.

Railroads thus are tools to meet state priorities of economic growth through resource development, by laying infrastructure over regions perceived to be empty of people, accelerating the settlement of distant regions, and enhancing military security. Even if long ago the state abandoned the practice of building the rail system on the backs of prisoners, it still embraces this technology at the expense of public and environmental health. Perhaps the vast geographies and difficult climates and terrains required state-dominated efforts to implement control over the strategic peripheries of the empire. Yet reliance on state organizations, state corporations, and state initiatives cannot help continuing the costly tradition of costly and unfinished hero projects even as leaders declare them to be unparalleled in the construction annals of world history.

Oil as Bounty, Prisoners as Ballast

Into the late Stalin period, Russian rails were ill-conceived and ill-fated, hurried to incompletion and dangerous to workers, passengers and freight alike. The railroads were intended to extend the horizon. They were a technological solution to the fact that Russian rivers, largely, flow north and south, and could serve trade and communication, but obviously had seasonal limitations, and linking them from west to east, from the major industrial cities of Leningrad, Moscow, Ekaterinburg, and Novosibirsk by canal or road was a laborious and expensive process in the face of climatological and geological challenges. Railroads would solve transportation problems and would also trigger exploration of mineral deposits and exploitation of known reserves.

Tsarist railroad projects lagged in construction because of unclear government priorities. Russia annexed Azerbaijan from Persia in 1806 and began to exploit Baku oil in the Caspian Sea beginning in the 1850s, with the assistance of well-known entrepreneurs and specialists. The chemist Dmitrii Mendeleev, who contributed to the development of processing and transport industries for Baku oil, visited wells in Titusville, Pennsylvania, in the 1870s to understand the international aspects of oil production and brought his knowledge to bear on Baku production.[6] The Nobel brothers, Robert and Alfred, entered the Baku industry at the same time. They built pipelines financed by European capital to pump oil from Baku over the Caucasus Mountains to Batumi on the Black Sea. When fully operational, the pipeline had sixteen pumping stations and, spanning roughly 830 km, was the longest pipeline in the world at that time. The Batumi-Tbilisi-Baku Railway could not keep up with the large amounts of oil being transported across the Caucasus Mountains by the pipeline. The government sought to delay the expansion of the pipeline because it threatened its profits from the Trans-Caucasian Railway, but it did not redouble the effort to complete the railway, only efforts to interfere with the Nobel pipeline.[7]

Russian politicians and entrepreneurs succeeded in building the Trans-Siberian Railroad, the longest ever built, a transportation feat of significance comparable to the Panama and Suez Canals in roughly the same era. They carried out the project from 1891 to 1904, although some variant of the project had been discussed for decades. The delays in forging ahead had to do with ministerial rivalries, with some officials thinking the railroad was too expensive, and others disagreeing on its path across Siberia. Ultimately, the railroad was built quickly under adverse conditions through the leadership of Sergei Witte. It was, like its Soviet heirs, a project intended to expand the empire and secure its borders, in this case against Japanese and Chinese Far Eastern influence.[8] The railroad suffered from substandard quality, bribery, corruption, and theft of materials that resulted in many places to a single track of light rails being laid, and in sharp curves, inadequate ballast, and thousands of accidents. A seven-day trip often took six weeks.[9]

Even though the Tsarist empire had built 50,000 km of rail by the 1905 revolution and 80,000 km by 1917, these lines were still insufficient to meet the needs of an industrializing country, especially with the pressures of supply and troop movements during the Great War.[10] On the eve of the war, Russia annually produced five million tons of pig-iron, four million tons of iron and steel, much of it in the Donbas in Ukraine, forty millions tons of coal, and ten million tons of petroleum, and it exported about twelve million tons of grain annually. The railroad was entirely inadequate to handle this freight in addition to troops, military equipment, and other requirements of war, as well as the growing and overwhelming numbers of passengers who came from households displaced by the war, especially peasants who were fleeing their farms with their animals and machinery. In addition, 80 percent of locomotives and wagons were destroyed between the start of the war and the end of the Civil War in 1920, and a quickly built railroad from Petrograd to Murmansk in 1916—built in part with prison labor—hardly met the needs of shipping war materiel, foodstuffs, and heating fuel to Petrograd or the front.[11] German and Austrian prisoners were used on the 1,000 km Murmansk stretch, establishing an excellent precedent for the Bolshevik use of prisoners to lay rails through the taiga and across the tundra.[12] Bottlenecks on the Tsarist rail system that prevented food, coal, and wood from reaching cities, along with desertions, inflation, and incompetent leadership, contributed to the spontaneous February Revolution in Petrograd in 1917 by starving and cold residents of the Russian capital. The Tsar was forced to abdicate.[13]

The Bolsheviks did not permit a reoccurrence of anarchy along the rails, recognizing their military significance. Indeed, the Bolsheviks relied upon railroad workers and unions for support, and they were crucial to the success of the revolution in securing key transit points and keeping entire cities in Bolshevik hands. Control of the rails—so highly centralized in its organization through Moscow through a series of hubs—enabled the Soviets to deny the White Armies supplies of materiel, food, and troops. Having recognized the importance of the railroads to their victories in the Civil War, the Bolsheviks set to expand the national system. By the mid-1920s, building on those rail projects with Tsarist roots, planners and engineers set forth a series of new lines to extend Bolshevik authority to the east, north, and south, including the "Turksib" line, from Tashkent to Barnaul in central Siberia, one of the first Soviet hero projects. The authorities underlined its importance by announcing to great fanfare that it had been completed early in the first five-year plan.[14]

The idea of a second trans-Siberian route, the forerunner of BAM, likely was advanced in 1906 after the critical failure to transport adequate supplies and soldiers to the Far East during Russo-Japanese War (1904–1905). BAM got little traction because of the focus of the Tsar and his advisors on the continuing political and social turmoil in Petersburg and Moscow after the 1905 Revolution and the overriding costs of the war. Paradoxically, the idea of assimilation of the Lake Baikal region and Far East with the railroad arose with rebels against Tsardom, the Decembrists, who were exiled to Siberia in the late 1820s. Somewhat later, in 1888, members of the Russian Technological Society discussed such a Lake Baikal–Amur route. In 1889, Colonel Nikolai Voloshinov, a tireless researcher of Siberia, led a detachment from the Trans-Siberian Railroad to the Muia River in Buriatia along the path of what would mirror the future route of BAM, but he came to the conclusion that the technical challenges of building it were insurmountable.[15]

The failure to complete BAM until eighty years after construction commenced should concern Kremlin planners and the Russian rail administration today in their ongoing efforts to lay rail for a new polar magistral and other Arctic projects. The Russian Rail Company cannot even force existing trains to move with modern speeds and on schedule along long-completed lines. Yet in the mid-1920s, recognizing Bolshevik enthusiasm for big construction projects, engineers and scientists renewed their calls to build BAM from Taishet near the Biriusa River in Irkutsk province to Okhotsk on the Pacific Ocean. In 1924 the government's Council on Labor and Defense approved a plan for construction of rail lines that included the outlines of a "second Transsib," and in 1926 a division of railroad troops began carrying out topographical surveys for the future rail. In 1930, Dal'kraikom, the Far Eastern Bolshevik party committee of a massive administrative unit that stretched from Vladivostok and Kamchatka along the entire coast to the Bering Straits, proposed BAM, apparently for the first time with that acronym, to the Central Committee of the Communist Party and Supreme Economic Council. By the end of 1931 the Council of Ministers had passed a resolution to build the new railroad in the next three years. They claimed that freight would move in Stalinist fashion—heroically and ahead of schedule—by the end of 1935, and its construction was intended to parallel that of other Stalinist gulag hero projects like the White Sea–Baltic Canal.[16]

In many ways, Bolshevik railway visionaries were like their counterparts in the capitalist West. The world's engineers offer profoundly optimistic claims for construction projects. Their confidence is part of standard operating procedure. They are trained problem solvers and believe in the omnipotence of the laws of nature and in their power to apply them to complete construction projects by specific—and optimistic—target dates. It is also universally part of engineering practice to create planning documents that simultaneously serve as sales proposals to gain government support and financial backing. Just as inevitably, cost overruns and construction delays follow. In spite of the conviction that the Soviet planning system would—in a supremely predictable and rational fashion—avoid this engineering malady, it was no better than capitalist ones in avoiding cost overruns and delays, and perhaps worse.

In the event, construction on BAM commenced in the mid-1930s with gulag prisoners in Camp "BAMlag" forced to toil under the fist of Commandant Naftali Frenkel.[17] As soon as construction began, officials recognized they had neither the machinery nor the armies of laborers they required to move quickly across the landscape laying track. They had planned for 25,000 men and controlled in all 2,500. As a result, the Council of Ministers transferred responsibility of construction from the Commissariat of Transportation to the OGPU, the forerunner of the dreaded secret police, the NKVD (the People's Commissariat of Internal Affairs), and its successor KGB (the Committee for State Security), in October 1932, with battalions of prisoners coming from as far away as the Belbaltlag camp in Karelia responsible for the soon-to-be-completed White Sea–Baltic Canal. The push for BAM was connected with Japan's annexation of Manchuria in 1931 and Stalin's accurate belief that the USSR faced growing military threats in the Far East.[18]

BAMlag was one of the largest divisions of the gulag. Like Glavsevmorput, the Administration of the Northern Sea Route that ruled along the Arctic Sea coast—and Gazprom in the twenty-first century—BAMlag enveloped a massive territory, from Chita to Ussuriisk, roughly 2,000 km. By 1934 more than 100,000 prisoners cleared forest, poured ballast, and lay track for BAMlag; in all the massive construction organization consisted of nearly 300,000 slave laborers, guards, and civilian specialists. Absent modern equipment, the prisoners used sledgehammers, shovels, and wheelbarrows to carve out the route. They erected rudimentary barracks and offices for officers, guards, and engineers while they lived in sieve-like tents. They were permitted to stretch barbed wire along the route to keep themselves in, stoke bonfires to keep warm, and toil by lanterns to see through the icy darkness.[19]

The OGPU leadership ostensibly wanted healthy prisoners for difficult work in horrible conditions that traversed several time zones, and through forest, swamp, and granite mountains. But as for all gulag projects, so for BAM the slave laborers faced both the dangers and impossibilities of digging foundation, pouring ballast, and blasting tunnels in unforgiving environments and geology, and the daily risks of miserable food, leaky and crowded housing, and rags instead of work clothes. Even if prisoners were selected in "good health," by the time they got to the camps after an eight-week journey in cramped, unheated wagons without food or respite, they were ill-equipped to survive, let alone work. The challenges of work on the BAM were aggravated by the fact that the roadbed had to be built in sparsely populated and unexplored areas. In these conditions, even emergency deliveries of supplies and equipment took two to three months. Workers arrived, but many went AWOL, easily walking away through gaping holes in the barbed wire and leaving construction in disarray. There was little food as a direct consequence of the collapse of collective farms; many workers were peasants who had fled from collectivization and the famine resulting from it in Ukraine in the first place. The political officers pushed workers as hard as they could, singling out "doubters, slackers, panic-mongers and opportunists" who had to be "cast out of the ranks of the builders of BAM." Seeking to accelerate the pace of construction, they cheered the uninspired prisoners on with such slogans as, "Down with the doubt, hesitation, sadness, and fear of challenges!" and "Onward with glorious labor!" But plans were fulfilled, if at all, by only 25 percent.[20]

Naftali Frenkel, an odious person, if successful gulag boss, was sent to get BAMlag precisely because of his willingness to work according to party dictates of cruelty and plan fulfillment. Frenkel had crawled as a prisoner out of the Urschleim of the very first gulag camp installed at the Solovetskii Monastery on a White Sea, often called simply "Solovki," to become one of the leaders and organizers of Belbaltlag, and whose career Vasilii Grossman captured in *Life and Fate* (1960):

At the beginning of NEP Frenkel built the Odessa Engine Plant in Odessa.
In the mid-twenties, he was arrested and sent to Solovki. Sitting in the

Solovetskii camp, Frankel gave Stalin a brilliant project. The project, with the economic and technical justifications offered in detail, spoke about the utilization of huge masses of prisoners to build roads, dams, hydropower stations, artificial reservoirs. The master praised this thought. The ease of labor that consecrated easily the prisoners' mouths and their hard labor, and the labor of shovels, picks, axes and saws, "intruded into twentieth century." The camp world began to absorb progress, it attracted into its orbit locomotives, excavators, bulldozers, saws and turbines, cutting machines, a huge automobile and tractor park. The camp world mastered freight and communications, aviation, radio and intercoms, machine tools, the modern system of ore enrichment; the camp world designed, planned, and sketched, gave rise to mines, factories, to new seas, and gigantic power stations. It developed rapidly, and the old penal system seemed funny and touching, like children's blocks.[21]

For Frenkel, prisoners were the building blocks of BAM. Building on the nascent tradition of using slave labor to push major transport technologies across the landscape, Frenkel ordered—and received—more and more detachments of prisoners each month. The authorities ordered machinery and equipment to BAMlag to augment repair shops, tools depots, and agricultural plots, but it was not enough to help the poorly dressed, badly fed men as they laid rail through the open, unassimilated territory of mountains, rivers, swamps, ravines, permafrost, and wetlands. If the bosses had taken into consideration the true nature of terrain and climate, the prisoners might have worked effectively as many as one hundred days per year. But Frenkel had them out in the elements year round, eighteen hours per day. They dropped from malaria, rheumatism, respiratory and gastrointestinal infections, and snow blindness. Somehow by the end of 1937 the prisoners had finished the second of five sections of BAM—from Karymskaia to Kharbarovsk.[22]

One typical BAMLag guard, Ivan Petrovich Chistiakov, left a diary in which he described how he was drafted into the camp at what seemed like the ends of the earth, and certainly not of his own free will, nor of any desire to march prisoners under guard to construction sites each day. He hated the harsh climate, the miserable living conditions, the chilling-to-the-bone cold, the absence of a banya (bathhouse), the constant colds and afflictions. Nights brought discomfort, the impossibility of sleep, screams, and even murder. He realized whom he was required to guard and why they tried to escape at any opportunity since they were treated like filth and the guards them-selves were lousy, dirty, and cold. The camp directors did not provide fire-wood, even when temps reached −50° C. One of Chistiakov's responsibilities was to gather the prisoners and read to them out loud recent reports from newspapers of the party leadership's great accomplishments.[23] He most cer-tainly would have preferred being a shift worker on a drill rig in the Barents Sea in 2015, where he might have felt some reverence for the president of Russia—and certainly would have been paid more.

In 1938 construction of the western part of BAM from Taishet to Bratsk began, and in 1939 preparatory work started for the section from Komsomol'sk-na-Amure, itself a shipbuilding city established in the early 1930s by gulag prisoners to the coast. Russia had essentially settled the Amur River basin, the world's tenth longest river, in the mid-to-late nineteenth century. Now, as the border between China and Russia, it gained immense strategic importance. But in 1942, many of the operations associated with BAM were moved to the Volga River region in connection with the defense of Stalingrad, and BAM was mothballed until the Brezhnev years. Even along the roughly 400 km of the line they managed to complete, all shipments ceased, although in 1943 the State Defense Committee ordered rapid con-struction from Komsomol'sk-na-Amure to Soviet Harbor (Sovetskaia Gavan') in case of war with Japan, and with the help of lend-lease equip-ment from the United States that arrived in July 1945, one month before the Soviet declaration of war on Japan, the line commenced modest shipments. A few stations opened and several short sections that were completed in the 1950s permitted construction of small hydropower stations and power lines nearby.

Rails into the Arctic

The Bolsheviks pushed rails in the 1930s not only along the southern frontier of the empire, but into the sub-Arctic and Arctic northern regions as part of military-strategic plans. The northern rails served the need to secure stra-tegic minerals. Only 1 percent of Russia's industrial production was located in the entire north in 1912, and it consisted mostly of lumber. Stalin hoped to force industrial development northward and tap growing known reserves of mineral ore with his gulag crews. Stalin used the "Kirov" railroad (the one that the Tsar had built to Murmansk in World War I using prisoners of war) to settle and exploit Kola Peninsula resources, eventually opening apatite, nickel, and copper enrichment factories and smelters in the Arctic Circle.

Frightening dark and damp forests, tundra with hillocks, and permafrost, swamps, rivers, and creeks all presented a barrier to construction to mining sites, with long distances between inhabited points, and transport by foot, sled, reindeer, and occasionally horse to support rail construction. For these reasons, the Bolsheviks resolved to order prison labor to lay the Northern Pechora railroad, from Arkhangelsk province to the Ob River delta, 1,100 km as the crow flies to the northeast. The railroad facilitated transport of coal and ore in the Pechora River basin, west of the Ural Mountains. The Pechora River, by mean annual discharge the third largest river in Europe, flows west and north through the Komi and Nenets Autonomous Republics, through Naryan Mar, the capital of the latter, into the Arctic Ocean.

The gulag was the general contractor, prison guard, and economic instance responsible for bringing such big projects as the Northern Pechora rail line to completion. A major gulag construction firm, Sevzheldorlag (the Northern Railway Labor Camp), undertook most of this rail project. Sevzheldorlag camp bosses wore many hats across the vast region and therefore had an insatiable appetite for prisoners. Sevzheldorlag laid the Kotlas-Vorkuta line at 728 km, finished the Konosha-Kotlas line, and expanded the capacity of the Vel'sk-Kotlas-Kozhva line in Arkhangelsk province. These rails by and large served forestry industry that was brought into its own through axes wielded by gulag prisoners. Sevzheldorlag built the Mechanical Factory in Kniazhpogost in the Komi Republic and the Kotlas Bridge Factory, as well as brick, lumber and paper, and other facilities. The camp population ranged from 25,000 prisoners at its founding, to 85,000 on January 1, 1941, and 28,000 when it was closed in 1950.[24]

Sevzheldorlag divisions were spread along the construction line, and in the absence of heavy machinery, bodies were used to fulfill the plan. Gulag bosses secured a steady stream of "employees" because of the very high mortality rate and low productivity of the prisoners. If the government had provided adequate food and medical care, then productivity of labor would have been higher and costs lower. But instead of incentives for workers, the authorities used the machinery of arrest and prosecution. They gathered prisoners by the thousands and shipped them out in transport wagons. Many of the men arrived at the major distribution point, in Kotlas, a major lumber and mill outpost, already dead. They literally fell out of wagons and were buried in unmarked mass graves that were rediscovered only in the 1990s. Sevzheldorlag was home to a great many well-known people; aircraft designer Andrei Korolev got an eight-year sentence, and he may have spent a short time in Sevzheldorlag before being shipped to a special engineers' camp (a so-called *sharashka*) before rising to the position of head designer of the Soviet space program.[25] The entire region is dotted with cemeteries, burial grounds, and unmarked graves that the NGO Memorial and other groups have strived to turn into monuments of the horrible repression.[26]

On November 7, 1940, as usual a day to commemorate the Bolshevik Revolution through the dedication of a new factory or other project completed heroically, railway traffic on the Pechora railroad opened from Kotlas to Kniazhpogost—on the future Kotlas to Vorkuta railway—and on Christmas Day, December 25, 1940, it opened from Kotlas to Pechora. As always, because of the use of prisoners and inadequate access to materials, this finished railroad suffered under its own weight. In spite of the official opening, the railroad demanded constant repairs. Roadbed running along swamps deformed during spring thaws, while temporary wooden bridges rotted. In one case an entire embankment, fortified with sand in the winter, disappeared with the spring freshet into a river. The railroad lacked signals and communications, while the absence of terminals, waysides, and passenger halls, let alone any other social amenities, indicated that the railroad served Moscow, not the citizen. Even locomotives had to beg for water from rudimentary pumps and wells. After the Nazi invasion in June 1941 and the impending loss of the Donbas coal fields in southeast Ukraine, Moscow officials insisted on Arctic coal more than ever, and prisoners, *zeks* in Soviet slang, made it possible. On December 28, 1941, the first "coal train" left Vorkuta to Kotlas and then Moscow. In the middle of summer 1942, the North Pechora line entered regular operation. In establishing a patchwork of rails over twenty some years, Sevzheldorlag served the tundra and taiga, facilitating transport of lumber, coal, and other resources important to the state.

Illuminating the Dark Roots of Russia's Twenty-first Century Railroads

Originally seen at least somewhat as an instrument of rehabilitation and re-education of sinners into upright Soviet citizens, the authorities appreciated gulag camps most of all as a crude economic tool. Stalinist leaders, *chekists*, police, and party officials and planners created hundreds of camps, primarily along the northern tier of the nation, to build roads, railroads, and other infrastructure, and mining, forestry, and other operations. The vast network of camps existed on the foundation of cheap labor and rudimentary technology. These emaciated and poorly dressed *zeks*—citizens accused of treason and counterrevolution, prisoners of war from the mid-1940s, and other innocents—built northeastward toward Salekhard, another gulag city built at first to incarcerate religious Old Believers, but rapidly becoming a vital port on the Ob River to handle mineral ore and diamonds mined nearby. The Ob River, the seventh longest river in the world, flows from the Altai Mountains, northward across the Siberian plane through the Khanti-Mansi Autonomous region of oil and gas production and into the Arctic Ocean, to Labytnangi near the coast.

Currently, the nearest railway to Salekhard is at Labytnangi (on the Salekhard-Igarka Railway), 20 km (12 mi.) northwest on the opposite side of the river Ob. In 2021 there was still no bridge over the Ob River, creating a daily bottleneck for a ferry at the spot—or a long wait for a polar freeze in the autumn to use the river surface itself as an ice bridge. To save money and time, and fearful of the havoc the river and weather might play on the bridge supports, Russian engineers have relied for centuries on ice bridges—frozen rivers themselves—even for such strategic objects as a northern railroad, with ferries carrying traffic across rivers in summer months. The trick is to remove snow, which serves as an insulator on the water's surface to allow the ice to freeze hard. Salekhard town fathers have been waiting for decades for steel and cement to arrive to build an Ob Bridge from Labytnangi to Salekhard an alternative to seasonal, if rock-hard ice. Perhaps that bridge will be built as part of the reborn Polar Magistral, now called the Northern Latitudinal Railway (NLR), which will complete a 700 km long railroad connecting Ob-Salekhard-Sadym-Nadym-Novy Urengoy-Korotchayevo in a project begun in the late 1940s. Local officials are selling the bridge as a key to a yet-to-be-born tourism industry. One official was certain that the nearby mountains, waterfalls, and the Jade Valley, accessible in some unclear post-socialist future by a rail-automobile bridge, would attract the tourist, "allow him to fly to the Arctic in two hours from Moscow, see the culture of the peoples of the North, taste the national cuisine and go on a hike."[27] Unfortunately, the price of Ob Bridge is now forecast at greater than $1 billion; budget, blueprints, and engineering approval have yet to arrive from Moscow; and Putin got the bridge he wanted after annexing Crimea in 2014 from Krasnodar to the Crimea Peninsula.

Hero projects based on slave labor were standard fare. As they moved through the taiga and across the tundra in the bitter cold and polar nights, *zeks* cleared forest, flattened hillocks, poured ballast, and secured rails that serve the Russian empire to this day. The results of their labor—the railroads, and the factories, mines, power stations, and forestry operations that arose next to them—were symbols of Stalinist achievement that were glorified in prison newspapers and national press. Virtually all long-distance passenger trains in Russia today use track originally laid by *zeks*. How could citizens even know of the murderous roots of the rail system when the authorities constantly celebrated railway construction without mentioning them as a glorious achievement of an advanced civilization? The state popularized and propagandized the projects in the press, literature, art, posters, and stamps, and it continues to publish commemorative issues and coffee table books on this history in the twenty-first century.

Contemporary rails rely also on Stalin's military conquests in Central Europe and the Baltic states. The rails were built by and used to murder Polish officers and members of the intelligentsia of newly subjugated Baltic states—from Estonia, Latvia, and Lithuania, and other East European socialist nations. Stalin's bloody polar railroads were directly connected to the Katyn Forest massacre of tens of thousands of Polish officers by the NKVD in 1940 under the order of secret police chief Lavrenty Beria.[28] Stalin and Hitler tacitly agreed to divide Eastern Europe after signing the Molotov-Ribbentrop Non-Aggression Pact in August 1939. The Soviet Red Army then invaded Poland. After the partition of Poland, on October 22, 1939, Moscow secretly ordered the heads of POW camps and processing points to transfer the officers, refugees, and other individuals from Central Poland to Western Belarus and Ukraine, and to round up officers, "spies," police, and members of political parties for dispatch.[29] A day later, an order directed the creation of Starobelsk and Kozelsk camps to receive officers and leading officials, and required registration and interrogation of each prisoner as quickly as possible. Within a week, Moscow stipulated not to release any "doctor-officers." Medical personnel might otherwise have been subject to prisoner exchange. But Beria and Stalin determined that they were officers, period, and therefore an exchange of prisoners would not be permitted.[30]

Sometime in March 1940, Beria wrote Stalin with a proposal to shoot Polish officers, gendarmes, police, and other "spies." He explained that the NKVD had uncovered counterrevolutionaries and other "sworn enemies of Soviet power who were inclined to envy of the Soviet order." The NKVD held nearly 15,000 prisoners in these camps, including 300 generals, colonels, and majors, most of whom the NKVD now murdered with impunity.[31] In April and May 1940, after these murders, tens of thousands of other Poles, thought to be the cream of the Polish intelligentsia, were exiled into the gulag—to Karabusk, Zaporozhsk, and Nikopol, at least 8,000 of them to the Far North, to the Komi Autonomous Republic to work on the North Pechora railroad.[32] Other gulag camps connected with other ministries arose on the tundra, for example, those of Narkomchermet, the ministry of ferrous metallurgy, that sought iron ore. Perhaps a total of 30,000 Czechs, Poles, and even former Red Army officers who were purged themselves fell out of wagons in Kotlas and into service of Sevzheldorlag and other gulag organizations.[33]

After the war *zeks* rebuilt Soviet railroads. The Nazis destroyed 65,000 km of rail, 4,100 stations, 317 depots, and thousands of bridges. The railroad recovered slowly over two decades owing to shortage of capital; the Ministry of Railway Transportation retired the last steam locomotive of the pre-revolutionary epoch only in 1966.[34]

The Polar Railroad

On a cold Kremlin night in 1947, Joseph Stalin gathered his closest advisors to set forth another bold project, a trans-polar railroad, to connect Moscow, Leningrad, and the industrial heartland with Arctic resources and military bases. Stalin intended the railroad, with ports on the Arctic Ocean and Siberian rivers, to meet growing domestic demand for minerals and especially coal, and also the international foreign policy goal of protecting the motherland from attack over the North Pole, the Allied interventions in Arkhangelsk and Siberia in 1918 at the end of the Great War still on his mind. Surveyors had produced only cursory blueprints for the Polar Magistral, but Stalin insisted to Kliment Voroshilov, a marshal of the Red Army, Viacheslav Molotov, his minister of foreign affairs, and Beria that construction begin immediately. The authorities shipped tens of thousands of slave laborers from the just-completed Kotlas-Vorkuta railroad toward the Yamal Peninsula and the Ob River Delta to push a rail line to Salekhard, and then beyond, another 370 km, to a harbor on the western side of the delta at desolate Cape Kamenny. Construction was two years in hand before engineers reported to Stalin that Cape Kamenny could not serve as a deepwater harbor. A new resolution established the site for the port instead on the Yenisei River near

Igarka, a gulag village dedicated to lumber.[35] And so Stalin ordered the railroad to be turned to the south, across the Urals and some 1,250 km to the east. This was the epitome of rational Stalinist planning.

The project cost, according to one estimate, 43 billion rubles and was never finished. Like many of the other such projects, the Polar Rail had historical roots. Already Tsarist noblemen had proposed building an Ob-Enisei River Canal in 1797. The idea of a Great Northern Railway arose again in the sketches of the northern artist Aleksandr Borisov, who accompanied Sergei Witte, the father of the Trans-Siberian Railroad, north to Murmansk in 1894, and in 1915 painted *The Ob' River—Murmansk Railroad*, and the jurist Viktor Voblyi, who had worked on the Pechora Railroad. But it required a powerful state enamored of technology and unconcerned about human and environmental costs to push ideas into practice. In February 1947 the government formed a Northern Design-Prospecting Expedition. A few weeks later, the Council of Ministers ordered the NKVD to build a Salekhard-Chum railroad. From May 1, surveying and construction began.[36]

Two years later, at a January 1949 tête-à-tête in the Kremlin, Stalin, Beria, and Frenkel determined to wind down the unsuccessful effort to drive *zeks* into the Yamal Peninsula with shovels, end efforts to lay a rail to Cape Kamenny, and instead turn east toward the lower reaches of the Yenisei River and Igarka. Two new camp administrations were formed: 501, with a base in Salekhard with responsibility from Labytnangi to the Pur River, and 503, based at Igarka built from Pur to Igarka.[37] In a country whose industrial might had to be rebuilt after the war, there were not enough rails to go the distance, so here and there they used old rails that had already served their time on different railways dating to the 1910s, some of them even manufactured in Nizhnii Tagil' in the Demidovskii Factory in the previous century.[38]

Such failures in engineering works as the Cape Kamenny harbor and railroad did little to dampen the enthusiasm for hero projects, the reason being that by the postwar years gulag operations had grown in reach, size, and momentum, creating a series of powerful construction divisions, each with its own focus and its own momentum. The only question seemed to be whether the authorities could requisition more bodies for each new project. As their camps overspread the nation, gulag administrators created a series of divisions that reflected its entirely economic purposes: oil and gas, construction, dams, canals and other waterworks, and roads and railroads. If administrators and party officials claimed that the gulag was created not only to punish, but to re-educate—or to "reforge"—people, the camps were

primarily and always a brutal economic tool.[39] Acquiring great bureaucratic momentum, division bosses sought or accepted responsibility for new
projects, and always welcomed or requisitioned more bodies to dig, grade,
excavate, fell, saw, burn, burry, extricate, crush, carry, transport, and rework
natural and mineral resources.

One of those divisions built precisely railroads. GULZhDS (Glavnoe
Upravlenie Lagerei Zheleznodorozhnogo Stroitel'stva, the Main
Administration of Camps for Railway Construction), was organized in
1940 under the direction of Frenkel, and it was responsible for 501, 503, and
many other major rail projects.[40] Frenkel's deputy director, V. A. Barabanov,
was head of construction for the polar magistral. Barabanov had the perfect pedigree with twenty years' experience in running camps and building
massive earthen projects. He himself got drunk with other OGPU agents
in 1934, there was a shooting, he was expelled from the party, served six
months in prison, then sent to the Pechora region with his family to run a
camp, becoming in 1935 the commandant of Ukhtpechlag. From here he was
appointed a mine director, sent to the Far East to take on another camp di-
rectorship, and then turned to using *zeks* for in the oil business in the Far
North, and finally headed the labor camp for the Tsimlianskoe Waterworks
of the Volga-Don Canal that was built as part of the Stalin Plan for the
Transformation of Nature (see below). According to some reminiscences, he
was kinder than other camp commandants, realizing that a given project's
success required at least measured coercion of prisoners.[41] Barabanov was
arrested with Beria in June 1953 and sentenced to death by firing squad, but
he was released after meeting personally with Nikita Khrushchev. He then
took a job in the editorial office of *Izvestiia* and died peacefully in Moscow in
1964, having served the empire well in a variety of construction and extractive capacities.

Stalin's ruthless "project of the century," if bold, demonstrated the typical failings of the Soviet system: its claim for efficient use of resources, yet
spending men and steel rapaciously; its avoidance of duplication of effort, yet
a daily litany of requests for still more labor and capital inputs; and its declaration that, like every other construction effort, its fruits were for the benefit
of the new Soviet man and woman, but in fact served only Communist Party
men (and the occasional woman) in Moscow. The polar railroad became
known as the Road of Death for the 50,000 prisoners whose bones figuratively served as railroad ties. When Stalin died, there were likely 2.26 million
people in the gulag, over one-tenth of them prisoners in GULZhDS.

Having abandoned the goal to build to the Ob River delta, GULZhDS administrators turned toward Igarka, but again with incomplete blueprints and surveys; with the administration tight on funding, they decided to build one line, with sidings every 10 to 15 km to allow trains to pass. To save time and money, they did not build permanent bridges over the Ob and Yenisei but used ferries in the summer and ice bridges in the winter. The Stalinist "science of practice" to verify the strength of the ice bridges was inexact and inhuman. In the frigid autumn of 1949, they laid ties and rails across the Ob River 7 km from Labytnangi to Salekhard. They needed a daredevil to try out the ice bridge, and there was none among the civilian engineers. "He who rides the locomotive—he will be a free man," the head of the construction brigade declared. They found a volunteer among the prisoners. At first things went well, but in the middle of the river the ice began to break up. The prisoner/engineer looked out the cabin with fearful consternation, but somehow the rails held on to the ties and he made it to the other side, and therefore arrived a free man. As for the other "science" of construction: the prisoners built wooden structures over the smaller rivers and creeks that quickly rotted. Excavation was done by largely by hand, shovel, and pickaxe because there were few trucks and seldom wheelbarrows.

In a relatively short time, 501 and 503 met in the tundra. The two railroads were joined with a kind of "golden spike" ceremony that mimicked the meaning of the joining of the west and east links of the first US transcontinental railroad at Promontory Summit, Utah, in 1869: here was the tethering of Arctic resources to Moscow. The gulag bosses reported to Stalin about this new victory of socialist labor over hostile nature on November 7, the thirty-second anniversary of the Bolshevik Revolution. Traffic opened from Salekhard to Nadym in August 1952. By 1953 the roadbed had been laid almost to Pur and some of the rails put down. On the eastern part, under 503, things went quite poorly, however; only about 200 km was ready for rails, while the 150 km section between Pur and Taz was planned for construction beginning in 1954. Indeed, only some twenty years later would telegraph/telephone lines reach such places as the Taimyr Peninsula to established contact with the rest of the world other than by radio.[42]

Within three weeks of his death in March 1953, Stalin's successors stopped the Polar Magistral dead in its tracks. Less than half complete, its remnants of rusty rails, locomotives, and wagons have become a curiosity for amateur *kraevedy* (admirers of local lore) and hikers who, through photographs and travelogues of the rusting carcasses of locomotives and twisted rails, now overgrown with larch and covered with the detritus of Arctic weather, document the human and environmental costs of Stalin's relentless determination to subjugate nature and people to state power. Throughout the nation, gulag bosses struggled to hold on to their prisoners and projects for a few more years after Stalin died, and at a few strategic mines ordered more of them, even after Stalin was interred in the Kremlin wall and Nikita Khrushchev had begun to empty the camps. In another cruelty of the Stalinist system, many of the freed *zeks* had to wait for the short navigation season when the Ob and Irtysh melted to journey south and back to their families. According to some estimates, 50,000 prisoners and an equal number of "volunteers" killed time in the tundra for four or five months for the summer to come so they could return to Soviet civilization.[43]

Different sections of the railroad suffered different fates. The section from Chum to Labytnangi entered regular operation in 1955, while the fully finished line Salekhard-Nadym was discarded, although until the 1990s linemen used handcars to move about. The section from Pur (Korotchaevo today) to Nadym found rebirth under the Ministry of Oil and Gas in the 1970s, and in the 1980s the ministry helped build a line from Tiumen in the south to Korotchaevo. Oil and gas helped also open the stretch from Korotchaevo to Novy Urengoi (formerly Iangel'naia). On the eastern section, the rails were ripped up in 1964 and melted down in Norilsk, perhaps for use as girders. From the Taz River to Ermakovo, one of the most difficult spots to reach, the railroad, buildings, depot, and four "OV" locomotives of pre-revolutionary manufacture, one of thousands built from 1890 to 1915, one of which brought Lenin from Gorky City to his processing and entombment in the Red Square mausoleum, have rusted in place. Scores of wagons and flatbed cars sit there, too, on sidings. Fifteen km from Dolgoe, guard towers and barbed wire commemorate the hero project.[44]

Any horror at the scale and inhumanity of the Soviet penal system for its exploitation of human labor should be tempered by noting that British colonialists in India, the Belgian atrocities in Congo, and the French subjugation of Algeria all involved harsh, warlike application of civilizing hero projects in transport, smelting, and extraction forward with great human and environmental cruelty. Indeed, across the American South, simultaneous in some cases with the Stalin years, state officials authorized prison commandants to lease men, often African Americans, into desperate situations, "under the sway of programs for railroad and industrial construction, agricultural development, and road building," reaping huge profits without paying expenses, using "hapless and often innocent individuals to rebuild the infrastructure."[45] Chains, dogs, guns, the absence of inspection, and the scarcity of provisions made life in these chain gangs no better than the gulag. Like Stalin's prisoners, the men were moved about where needed, kept in cages or behind bars, exposed to the weather, and considered expendable.[46] None of the prisoners—Congolese, Indians, Algerians, Americans, or Soviets—were "reforged."

Igarka, Arctic Conquest, and the Soviet Imagination

A number of significant continuities exist in engineering projects of the Soviet era and those of Russia today, in particular the use of media to advance the essentially heroic features of projects in the public mind. In a throwback to the Soviet practice of introducing big engineering projects to the public through radio broadcasts and TV shows, documentary films, and newspapers and magazines, so in contemporary Russia the major industrial leaders—Gazprom, Rosatom, RUSAL—have become adept at pushing hero projects in various glossy formats and publications. All the Arctic development companies have press offices that produce brochures and publish webpages with photographs, human interest stories, and snippets of environmental testimonies that are intended to indicate the integrity of the operations, their environmental soundness, and their upstanding treatment of workers and indigenes. Gazprom draws attention to its superior health and public safety record, its social concerns, and its ever-growing drilling and pumping operations in two such journals, *Gazprom* and *Gazovaia promyshlennost'*.[47] Similarly, the powerful appeal for a new Polar Magistral to tame the Arctic filled a recent volume published by the Ministry of Transport.[48] Stalin's polar railroad was publicized, too, in the genre of a children's book, although obviously without direct reference to the role of the gulag either in the railroad or in the creation of production cities along the route.

Soviet efforts to play up the great achievements of various construction projects at times admitted the role of prison labor but played up the redemptive aspects of internment, never the cruel, murderous conditions of life. Most gulag projects remained secret, at most the subject of furtive whispers as the government determined to classify almost every construction project, factory, and "object" as classified information. Displaying private photographs of the metro, canals, and railroads, even if shown to a closed group of friends, risked prison for publishing state secrets. Paradoxically, the state simultaneously glorified its "hero projects," from the Dniepr hydroelectric power station and Magnitogorsk steel mills in the 1930s, to the Stalin Plan to transform nature in the late 1940s, and to Brezhnev's BAM, most often without referring to prison labor. Journalists, writers, painters, and photographers traveled the country, gathering stories of common workers *cum* heroes who, following the enlightened leadership of the Party and Stalin, erected factories from the ground up, freed resources from the bowels of the earth, and created an unassailable socialist fortress. One of the early examples of a genre that came to be known as "socialist realism" was Fedor Gladkov's *Cement* (1925), in which the protagonist, Gleb Chumalov, manages to get a cement factory, stripped of its machinery, operating again—with the help of both female and male workers—in the name of communism. Just a few years later, by the time of Stalin, the atmosphere for the celebration of hero projects was a strange mix of secrecy and fear engendered by the terror of the camps balanced by literary and mass media popularization of the great construction effort.

A major example of this genre, *Belomorsko-Baltiiskii Kanal im. Stalina* (White Sea-Baltic Canal, 1934), was the product of an authors' collective under the leadership of Maksim Gorky. It celebrated the newly opened White Sea–Baltic Canal but fully ignored its great human costs and its technical failure. Gorky and his coauthors instead sought to indicate that great achievements were possible in such a short time under Stalin's visionary leadership, and how prisoners had been re-educated, learning the extent of their political mistakes and of their ignorant rejection of Soviet power.[49] The authors asserted on the basis of selective use of secret police documents that the prisoners had understood the errors of their ways. The authors did not discuss the facts that 70,000 people, working entirely with hand tools and wheelbarrows, died of exposure and hunger during two years of construction, and that the canal, completed months ahead of schedule, was too shallow to be of use for modern shipping. This did not prevent the great Stalin and his entourage from being photographed proudly beaming in the reflection of his hero projects whenever they were commemorated.[50]

A few years later, Stalin's Polar Magistral found indirect glorification in a paean to its future terminus on the Yenisei River, the lumber town of Igarka built by prisoners, in a children's book, also promoted by Gorky. Igarka, born of gulag camps and forestry resources, 650 km inland on the Yenisei River and 100 km north of the Arctic Circle, was rapidly transformed into a port after the demise of the Cape Kamenny project. Igarka was fueled by the

Stalinist five-year plans with an influx of kulak exiles and *zeks*. It continued to grow with the deportation of 5,000 to 10,000 Lithuanians after World War II, at least 1,000 of whom died on arrival. Igarka grew to some 18,000 residents in 1989 on the eve of the collapse of the USSR, and now hosts 6,000 people, engaged in lumber mill activities and wood product exports.

On the path to celebrating its infamy, Gorky encouraged schoolchildren in Igarka to write a book about their city's history. They had written him to confess their pride in Igarka and their discomfit in its reputation as a far-away and empty place; they had no comments about *zeks* around them. Gorky addressed these children, largely Young Pioneers of the Communist Party, as "future doctors, engineers, tank drivers, poets, pilots, teachers, artists, inventors, and geologists!" In a few years, he was convinced, when their upbringing by the harsh climate was completed in their transformation into "iron Komsmoltsy (Communist Youth Leaguers)," that they would go forward to work and study, and would see the vast expanses of the nation, "its gigantic factories, colossal electrical power stations, cotton plantations of Central Asia." Gorky closed his letter urging the young pioneers to compile a book to show the world the glories of living in Igarkap.[51]

And so they wrote *My iz Igarki* (We Are from Igarka). Leaving no doubt about the crucial symbolism of their book, the government published the first edition in 25,000 copies, and it included on its frontispiece a photo of Gorky and Stalin discussing, no doubt, the glories of Soviet socialist realist literature. The book celebrated a city of high culture that had come into existence only a few years earlier, a city that provided an outpost for Siberian lumber products and that enabled the great Northern Sea Route to reach the thinly settled taiga and tundra. It praised the work of cultural and political officers who had journeyed into the tundra to educate the indigenes about the new, "red law," about Moscow, and about Comrade Stalin. The nomads, the children asserted, called these emissaries of modernity the "people of truth." The truth of modernization of indigenes was much different: unsettling to culture, destructive of their ways of life.[52] But the north had come alive with huge factories, roads, and mines, and had established such "foreposts of culture in the far north" as Igarka. Each spring the float brought massive logs to its mills. Amber-colored planks dried in the sun of the huge lumberyards. A local journalist and writer, Anatolii Klimov, ensured that five editions in a total of 160,000 copies saw light in the polar nights.[53] By the time of the book's publication, many of the adults in the city connected with it had been repressed, and only two copies were to be found in Igarka itself.[54]

Trains Move Slowly—as Planned

The Tsar's projects became the projects of Bolshevik commissars. Stalin's projects became Leonid Brezhnev's projects. Brezhnev (Soviet leader 1964–1982) determined to restart and finish BAM within his lifetime. In the technological glow of his leadership, the Communist Party called BAM another "project of the century" to gain priorities in allocation of capital and manpower. This crucial benefit did not help. BAM was officially finished in 1983, and again "officially" in 1991. Yet it remains in the early 2020s inadequate to the tasks of timely transport of freight and passengers. Enthusiastic workers who flocked to the construction site found miserable living conditions. Scores of boomtowns that arose along the route have become ghost towns, and unemployment along BAM remains high. And so, Vladimir Putin will finish BAM with billions of rubles of investment to meet the needs of the resource state. In February 2019 he declared that the freight capacity of BAM would be increased 1.5 times to 210 million tons by 2025. How could this strategic hero project, important to three Russia leaders, fail so markedly?

Brezhnev sought to extend Moscow's reach through heavy investment in Siberian resource development and infrastructure from the Ural Mountains to the Pacific Coast. While known perhaps more for his efforts to improve the agricultural situation and his later Food Program (1982), Brezhnev also pushed the modern technologies of extraction and cultural assimilation to the ends of the empire, that is, in various "all-union" campaigns and large-scale projects that were paradigmatic for the USSR's economic development model. He supported the rapid expansion of the nuclear power program, too. Already in 1958 as central committee secretary responsible for the military industrial complex, he energetically toured armaments, nuclear, and space facilities as far as Perm in the Ural Mountains and the Chkalov Aviation Factory in Novosibirsk.

When he returned by train twenty years later as a self-satisfied general party secretary to take in his accomplishments in Siberia and the Far East, the frail man was no longer a visionary, had to be physically supported, and the authorities everywhere stocked Potemkin villages of consumer goods displays at train stations to convince the stumbling old man that his food program was working. While known for presiding over the "time of stagnation," some of Brezhnev's supporters fondly recall the certainty of his rule—and the facts that the economy grew twofold during his two decades, government expenses on social programs increased threefold, consumer goods production increased 2.5 times, housing construction reached 60 million km[2] per year, and so on. As for beloved industry, Siberian oil and gas finally were being assimilated, oil and gas pipeline systems were built, and so on.[55]

Yet Siberia demanded not only investment from the emperor, but also his special attention for programs to move forward. The political culture of Soviet development required the general secretary to make pronouncements and claims, and to insist on projects and their completion. When Brezhnev toured Novosibirsk in 1972 with the secretary of the Novosibirsk provincial party committee, Fedor Goriachev, he seemed worried about the level of investment needed for Siberian industry, yet did not quite agree with the latter's insistence·on investment in social capital, in particular to see a subway system built in the burgeoning city of 1.3 million people, the fourth largest in the USSR. When he returned to Siberia in March 1978, taking the Trans-Siberian Railroad all the way to Vladivostok, he saw to it that the agitprop officials produced a photo album and film of his "personal account" of travels and enlightened, populist leadership style, *Vsegda s narodom* (Always with the People, 1978), and he agreed that a metro must be built; construction commenced in 1979.[56] He continued along the Trans-Siberian railroad, weak and in ill health, to Tiumen, Omsk, Krasnoiarsk, Irkutsk, Chita, Khabarovsk, Komsomol'sk-na-Amur, and Vladivostok, along with the minister of defense, Dmitri Ustinov, perhaps as his drinking partner, to celebrate the filling up of empty spaces.[57]

Branch industrial and academy scientific organizations responded to the Brezhnev Siberian initiative with vigorous research efforts. Guri Marchuk, then chairman of the Siberian division of the Academy of Sciences and later the Academy's last president in Moscow, advanced a "strategy of scientific investigation" for the eastern regions of the country in fulfillment of the tenth and subsequent five-year plans. The tenth five-year plan included the goal of an increase in production in Siberia 1.5 times higher than for the rest of the country. The scale and tempo of economic assimilation of Siberia and its increasing role in the country would be solved through some thirty programs for the "complex utilization of natural and mineral resources," including the formation of territorial production complexes. The "Siberia" program, under the direction of oil specialist Andrei Trofimuk and economist Abel Aganbegian, later an advisor to Mikhail Gorbachev, required the massive expansion of oil and gas facilities, with the entire increment in national oil production coming from Siberia, as well as 90 percent of the increase in gas production and 80 percent of coal. Researchers had already identified new deposits in Tomsk and Novosibirsk regions, and they set out to develop them; they are still developing them.[58]

Brezhnev apparently understood the challenges facing the nation in Siberian development. In his report to the Twenty-third Party Congress in March 1966, he noted the geographical maldistribution of the productive forces, resources, people, and industry, and called in the next five-year plan to pursue series of crucial economic and social decisions to bring workers to the task of assimilation of the vast, underdeveloped empty spaces of the Soviet empire east of the Ural Mountains. But by the end of the Soviet period, the "Siberian problem" had only grown worse. The frontier remained a frontier: something like 70 percent of industry and population were located in the European USSR, while Siberia and the Far East remained what officials considered to be an empty expanse of resources, and none of campaigns or incentives to attract more settlers—higher wages, cheap housing, paid vacations, medals and awards—had resulted in higher labor productivity or completed hero projects. Without access to gulag prisoners, officials in Moscow ministries struggled with the "Siberia" project as an endless, expensive, and expansive endeavor.[59] Brezhnev may have understood some of these challenges when he determined to rekindle BAM as the major instrument of Siberian resource development, but he did not solve them.

In 1967 the government and Communist Party authorized renewed design and survey work for BAM, leaving little doubt that it would be completed in the Brezhnev incarnation. The plans set a target of ten years to build 3,145 km from Ust'-Kut (on the Lena River) to Komsomol'sk-na-Amur, plus a second line at 680 km utilizing the already built Taishet-Lena section, and one track at 400 km to connect BAM-Tynda-Berkakit. In March 1974, in Almaty, Kazakhstan, Brezhnev showed that he was a man of the future, not of the failed Virgin Lands campaign of the 1950s to plow under pasture and meadow in the northern Caucasus, in Western Siberia, and in Northern Kazakhstan, by shifting attention to BAM and proclaiming it "the most important project" of the current five-year plan. By the Twenty-fifth Party Congress in 1976, he was prepared to call BAM a "project of the century."[60]

Over the long years of construction, BAM employed a total of around two million volunteers, workers, and engineers who joined out of romance or high salary or fascination with the project or, as in the case of student and Communist Youth League (Komsomol) brigades, the need to get summer spending money. Many individuals stayed on to live in towns and villages that arose owing to the construction only to see their livelihoods disappear in the economic ruin in the 1990s. BAM cost billions of rubles, trillions in today's budget, or perhaps nearly $40 billion—and in fact it was not finished until the Northern Muiskii Tunnel at 15 km in length was opened in 2001. The project of the century was 4,300 km long, crossed eleven great rivers, required construction of 2,230 large and small bridges, passing through more than 200 stations and junctions, and more than 60 cities and towns, and left scars, pollution, and building materials and equipment behind. Unfortunately, BAM also led to music and song, for example Oskar Felt'sman and Robert Rozhdestvenskii's "Do You Hear? Time Is Sounding 'BAM'!" and "In the Vastness of the Steep Grades—'BAM'!"[61] and "A Train Is Running along BAM" (Rozhdestvenskii and Shainskii) with the immortal lyrics:

> Across the distances and the years,
> Steadily and sternly,
> Trains run along BAM,
> The railway works.[62]

BAM gained new importance for Soviet leaders in the 1960s, in part because of the sharpening conflict with China, but mostly to assimilate the massive cooper, fossil fuel, polymetals, and other resources of Irkutsk and Amur regions, Buriatia, Zabaikal, Iakutiia, and Khabarovsk region, with ten territorial production complexes to be formed along the route. There was even some talk of sending BAM northward toward Iakutsk, Magadan, Chukotka, and Kamchatka. BAM, like the White Sea–Baltic Canal and Igarka, became a mass campaign in newspapers, books, and brochures, publications that never indicated the gulag roots of the project. The grandiose "Komsomol" (Communist Youth League) project attracted tens of thousands of volunteers. The new residents of the construction encampments that arose along the tracks raised colorful apartment buildings to distinguish them from the drab, gray buildings endemic to Soviet urbanity, and hung banners and street signs to capture the aesthetic styles of the republics or cities from whence they came. Tynda, the so-called capital of BAM, was built by Muscovites who named their streets after Moscow streets (Arbat, Krasnaia Presnia, and so on); Urgal, another city, by Ukrainians, saw houses ornamented with traditional Ukrainian decorations; and so on other cities by Estonians, Latvians, and others.[63] In September 1984 the authorities decided to celebrate completion of BAM with a golden spike ceremony at Balbukhta led by workers who "could not hide their tears of joy." The project produced its usual heroes of socialist labor, and 43,000 workers received medals.[64]

At the turn of the twenty-first century, Hill and Gaddy examined the costs of the Soviet efforts to plan for Siberian conquest, the hardships of climate that made this difficult, and the absence of employment migration to Siberia to undertake the effort. They noted the extensive subsidies required. They suggested it would be much less expensive to avoid building extensive urban infrastructure, but to rely on shift workers, for example, as is standard in the world's oil and gas industries and has been adopted by Gazprom and Rosneft today. They suggested that the only economically sound approach was to move workers toward Europe to downsize Siberia, and to move the unemployed and pensioners from the Far North to the center. Even with BAM, Siberia remained empty and massive, without infrastructure, without larger urban areas and without connections between centers and markets.[65]

The deliberate policies to facilitate expansion and settlement of Siberia as a frontier had failed. It did not work with Tsarist military expeditions, hunters seeking furs, or peasants desiring farmland, nor did it accelerate naturally with industrialization and urbanization in the nineteenth century. The Soviets pushed again in the 1930s into the Arctic regions under the Main Administration for the Northern Sea Route, Glavsevmorput,[66] and after World War II with the rise of the Cold War military-industrial complex, and efforts to fill the tundra accelerated under Brezhnev. The Soviets used such instruments as five-year plans, gulag organizations, public proselytization, and campaigns, for example, as all-union Komsomol construction sites. But the infrastructure lagged and there was little connection between it across the taiga and tundra.[67] I remember meeting an oil worker from Tiumen in an Akademgorodok hotel in 1989 who had been flown in 1,300 km by helicopter for a short, vacation weekend. Now railroads have begun to find their way across the tundra, and shiftwork has replaced full-time employment, but they are powered by oil, gas, and their oligarchic owners.

Overlaying the Peninsula with the Yamal "Megaproject"

If Stalin could not force Siberian and Arctic development to completion with cold, starving *zeks*, and if the niceties of campaign development with more enthusiastic workers under Brezhnev produced only grudging and slowing economic growth, then perhaps the resource oligarchs of the twenty-first century may succeed because of pipelines of petrodollars. Indeed, Gazprom has assumed the role as builder of railroads and other infrastructure for its self-proclaimed megaprojects, especially on the Yamal Peninsula as it pumps its way through vast gas and oil deposits. How much of these funds will ultimately benefit Russian society is another matter, for Gazprom has determined to push aside local people—Nenets reindeer herders and others—and to lay waste to the tundra.

Pipelines and railroads will cover the Yamal Peninsula and beyond because of the economic and military importance of these spaces to the Russian government. No less than Stalin's "hero projects" and Brezhnev's "projects of the century," the Putin regime sees the Yamal Peninsula not as an ecosystem or a place where traditional societies and industrial workers might coexist, although the webpages of all of the corporations with extractive interests indicates that ecology and society are first thoughts, but as a "megaproject"— the next incarnation of the "hero project" and the "project of the century." The infrastructure of the gas industry grows like a malignancy, with the Kremlin watching in approval.

As its handlers note, the megaproject "Yamal" has no "analogues in level of complexity." The Yamal region has a terribly harsh climate, permafrost, and yet in the summer is covered with lakes, swamps, and rivers that restrict areas where industrial facilities can be located, and inhabited by swarms of ravenous mosquitoes whose six weeks of life could populate a Dracula film. Gazprom insists it has and will carry out exploitation safely, effectively, and with some innovative technology, often developed in its own scientific research institutes. Officials claim they can drill to 700 m and even to 2,000 m, but avoid disruptions by bringing wellheads closer together in the bush from 40 m distance from each other to 15–20 m, to minimize the area of diversion and the volumes of engineering preparation for wells, access roads, and other infrastructure, while ensuring the necessary level of industrial safety through fully automated and redundant safety systems.[68] In addition to wells, there are pipelines. For example, in 2012 the gas pipeline "Baranenkogo-Ukhta" entered operation and at the beginning of 2017 the pipeline "Bovanenkogo-Ukhta 2" did as well.

Railroads and resources are central to the Yamal megaproject. Gazprom has laid a series of major railways from Obskaia and Salekhard to its various LNG and other facilities on the peninsula, at great cost, and perhaps at great graft. One such line is the Obskaia-Bovanenkovo railroad that opened in 2011 and "ensures year-round, fast, cost-effective and all-weather delivery of technical equipment, construction materials and personnel to Yamal fields in the harsh Arctic climate." Previously, Arctic cargo arrived by sea through the Kharasavey port. But this limited deliveries in size and to summer months and would have made the Yamal gas fields impossible to build in a reasonable time. The railroad runs 572 km from Obskaia station to Karskaia (and 525 km to the Bovanenkovo station), and "includes 5 stations, 12 passing loops, and 70 bridges with a total length of more than 12 kilometers."[69]

Gazprom and railroad engineers employed a variety of techniques to protect permafrost, swamps, and other ecosystems. All construction occurred in subzero temperatures "with a view to protect the ecosystem and preserve the load-bearing capacity of permafrost.... The railroad embankment was made from damp silty sand, which solidifies under low temperatures. A unique multi-layered heat insulation system was developed and employed to ensure roadbed stability in summer: expanded polystyrene was laid over frozen sand and geotextile reinforcements were installed."[70] Seven thousand, five hundred men toiled on the railroad. Construction on the Obskaia-Bovanenkovo railroad line commenced in February 2010 and included bridges, distribution lines, and communication facilities, with shift workers handling −55° C. temperatures, blizzards, snow drifts, and permafrost. They completed bridges that totaled 12 km in length across the Yamal Peninsula.[71]

One of the most challenging steps in taking the tundra was the Iuribei River Bridge, the longest bridge north of the Arctic Circle at nearly 4 km. According to its Gazprom builders and designers, the Iuribei Bridge meets all environmental standards to build on permafrost, avoid disruptions of the tundra, and deal with the surprisingly significant seasonal changes. It has two main spans of 150 m (490 ft.), on top of which it is much wider than the river width, as it must be because in the spring melt torrents of water spread across the plain rather than being absorbed in permafrost. To raise the bridge, they used custom-made off-road skidders that delivered 70-ton girder-type bridge sections and 110 pillars that were sunk 30 to 60 m into the ground.[72] The *Iuribei* is also the name of an icebreaking tugboat that works the new port of Sabetta that was built for handling natural gas.

Gazprom insists it will limit environmental and cultural impacts through small industrial sites, closed water supply systems, constant monitoring, special transit areas for reindeer (and herders) through industrial objects, and so on.[73] It enunciates its intentions to be the leading company in the world in environmental quality, replacing pipelines that are not up to its standards, using contemporary computer monitoring equipment and drones, and pursuing early replacement of still functioning pipelines as part of a "Clean Territory" program (since 2010). This has enabled Gazprom managers to claim that the company has reduced accident risk by roughly one-quarter annually since 2010.[74]

In fact, Gazprom's environmental record is poor, and given the breakneck speed of development, the safety standards for Russian hero projects, and the powerful and unforgiving nature of the "Yamal" megaproject, the expectation must be that environment and local people will pay high costs for polar railroads and pipelines. One study in 2013 indicated at least seventy major environmental hotspots of mining (gold, platinum), electrical energy, coal, oil and gas, including terminals, pipelines, factories, and prospecting across Sakha (Yakutia) and Kamchatka alone.[75] Yamal development has similar if not greater costs. Indeed, a variety of technogenic phenomena have a particularly poignant negative impact on the health of indigenous ethnic groups, especially heavy metal contamination (cadmium, lead, nickel, and chromium).[76] Oil sheens on land and lakes indicate haphazard leaks. Bodies of water are in particularly poor condition, especially in the petroleum regions of the tundra, with high levels of pollution in the Nenets and Yamal-Nenets Autonomous, Murmansk, and Arkhangelsk regions. Those in the Yamalo-Nenets Autonomous region exceed various toxic chemical norms by 2.5 to 5 times. In the Nenets Autonomous region, nearly three-quarters of water samples do not meet national standards for microbiological parameters. Entire regions have excessive levels of sulphur dioxide and heightened risk of cancer from exposure to benzopyrene. Arctic soils have been particularly degraded.[77]

There are far more data available to judge the environmental impacts of hero projects for the period after the collapse of the USSR than before; Soviet data were often classified. But it has become increasingly challenging to locate information—environmental impact statements, data, and so on—under the increasingly restrictive Putin administration and its ongoing effort to silence environmental NGOs. In addition, Russian researchers have been lax in the study of environmental problems in a variety of areas. For example, their work on the biomonitoring of persistent organic pollutants (POPs) and metals in biota and human tissues on the territory of the Russian Arctic have been relatively limited during the last forty years; for several Russian Arctic regions there are no data. The overwhelming majority of recent studies have been carried out within the framework of international projects with co-financing, assistance, and contributions from the foreign colleagues and partners which will likely dry up because of sanctions imposed on Russia because of Russia's war on Ukraine.[78]

Still, it is possible to document the dozens of spills, small and large, across the Yamal Peninsula. These leaks, spillages and accidents, and long-term damage to various ecosystems of the megaproject should have been expected given the experience of the Alaska pipeline. In Alaska, megafauna (elk and bear) have suffered significant population losses, and promised attempts to reclaim construction areas have failed.[79] Similarly, the lakes of the Yamal region suffer from acidification due to the effect of the atmospheric deposition of emissions that largely originate in local sources of nitrogen and sulphur, although there is some air-mass transport from the western and northwestern industrialized areas of Northern Europe and European Russia; the high level of lead contamination in lakes depends on the degree of their sulphate acidification.[80] Other lakes in the vicinity of the Gazprom Bovanenkovo airport receive untreated sewage from the airport, for example, the nearby Lake Ngarka-Neradsalyato, since the local water treatment plant works intermittently, and Gazprom officials have not let inspectors to examine the situation because they need special permits to use Gazprom roads. The company has obfuscated requests of the prosecutor's office, county departments, and the national environmental inspectorate, Rosprirodnadzor, for documentation. Gazprom controls the disposition of and access to vast land holdings with impunity.[81]

More troubling for hero projects has been the steady encroachment of Russian explorers, naturalists, and settlers from the nineteenth century to the present on local peoples. Nenets reindeer herders have borne the burden of gas development on the Yamal Peninsula. Stalinist cultural emissaries were determined to tie indigenes to five-year plans. Since that time, the increasing pace of Arctic industrialization on these and other northern peoples have put traditional lifestyles under permanent threat. In a battle between industry and profit, on the one hand, and preservation of ways of life, on the other, the herders have little voice when resource managers in Moscow set production targets. There are at least 280,000 reindeer on the peninsula tended by more than 5,000 Nenets. But in a place with 23 percent of the world's known reserves of gas and 60 percent of Russia's, the Yamal Peninsula has become a place of "meeting and competition of at first sight incompatible technologies of reindeer breeding and gas-extraction." This is because the two longest roads that cross the peninsula are the nomadic herding paths that have existed for centuries and the newly built railroad from the mainland to Bovanenkovo.

If the Nenets seek to preserve a traditional rhythm of migration and pasture use, then industry forces them to change in line with its needs for extraction and transport. No matter Gazprom's claims to ensure preservation of culture and nature, the gas fields make Nenets herding and breeding of reindeer impossible.[82] Stalin's polar magistral and Gazprom's Yamal railroad look alike on maps—and they are alike in terms of human and environmental costs. Lines appear, they crisscross the tundra, and there are few signs of people, reindeer, lakes, or swamps except as an afterthought.

In keeping with Stalin's and Brezhnev's devotion to extraction, Gazprom is loyal only to gas, not to passengers and other locals. On June 1, 2015, the company closed part of the Novyi Urengoi-Yamburg line on the peninsula that had operated since the 1980s on which local people came to rely for many supplies. It was built for Gazprom after its decision to turn to the shift method to exploit the rich Yamburgskoe deposits. Not only shift workers, but all sorts of other Yamal residents used it. Regional officials were upset by the sudden appearance of another "railroad cemetery," a place discarded with rails and wagons left to rust, although not in the way that Stalin's polar railroad was suddenly abandoned with the *zeks* left to find their own way home. In this case, nothing could be done, as it was a private rail. This was typical of Gazprom traditions to assimilate colossal amounts of money at a site, and then dump the ballast. Gazprom workers appeared out of nowhere, built compressor stations, drilled into the tundra, laid track, welded pipelines, and left, and the reindeer could not get around the railroad tracks to their food. In any event, Gazprom "Urengoi" announced that trains from kilometer marker 12 ("Evaiakha") to Yamburg (220 km) had ceased operation. One reason for doing so was the risk of a serious accident since, in fact, the line had operated in a "temporary regime" since 1986, and Gazprom had long before given up on finishing the line, let alone carrying out repairs at a cost of $36 million.[83]

The condition of Russian rails from the bed up to the wagons has always been a concern, from improper ballast and poorly tempered steel, to rotted bridge and supports, and to the challenges, even after decades of experience, of building across the tundra. Specialists at the Melnikov Permafrost Institute and other specialized research centers have long worried about safety and quality. They have documented why Russian freight trains have to move at a frozen snail's pace across the Arctic. The deformation of roadways and bridges is a fact of life. And slave laborers could hardly have been expected to give their all to working for Stalin. Conditions will only get worse with global warming and the melting of the permafrost, as massive piles sway and ballast slides. Some segments of Arctic rails have had to reduce their capacity to 30 percent to serve coal and passengers.[84]

BAM, Oil, Gas, and the Arctic Dream

Traveling by train in the former Soviet Union in the 1990s, I saw the decay of the railroad system: scheduled trains arbitrarily canceled, failing service on local and national routes and nary new construction, insufficient repairs, rickety, old wagons, and train stations in disrepair and filled with garbage that had become a site of crime and sad, helpless homeless folk. People stopped buying their tickets and rode for free. But in the 2000s, I saw improvements—special public-private express trains, better ticket control, the presence of more janitors and guards at stations—in a system still inadequate to the needs of the nation, especially when compared with the advances and improvements in the rail system of Gazprom in the Far North, let alone trains in the European Union, China, and Japan. Many regions still lack regular train service, like the United States, where the US Congress has permitted, indeed encouraged, passenger rail traffic to shrink and die, and safety remains a significant problem. In Russia, efforts to modernize nonetheless go forward with the installation of electronic ticketing, and the acquisition slowly, but surely, of new locomotives and wagons. On the other hand, in the Russian Federation over the past twenty-five years the nation has built only as many kilometers of rails as the USSR built in an average year, a total of 400 km, with the longest stretches from Kizliar to Karlan Iurt (53 km, likely to facilitate troop movements in Dagestan), Kochkoma-Ledmozero (132 km, in Karelia), Iaiva-Solikamsk (48 km to tie together salt and other mineral deposits of chemical industries), Adler–Roza Hutor (48 km, to serve the Sochi Olympics and a ski resort), Vakhitovo–Kazan Aeroport (22 km), and the Severomuiskii Tunnel and approaches (30 km).

And what is the significance of the Severomuiskii Tunnel? It was opened in 2003, finally completing BAM, the project of the century, twenty years after the official celebratory dedication of Brezhnev's great project. Preliminary work on the 15 km long tunnel commenced in 1975. The tunnel went through or over nearly impenetrable rock, traversed four major faults with seismicity to 9 on the Richter scale, and encountered rivers of underground water, some under high pressure. In September 1979, workers broke into a fault that opened a 12,000 m^3 underground lake, required construction of a drainage tunnel, and delayed work for eighteen months. When it became clear that the tunnel would not be completed in time for the planned official opening of the BAM in 1984, a 28 km bypass was built during 1982–1983 with a 4 percent grade and limited traffic to 15 km/hour. Seven years later, a new bypass of 54 km was completed (with a 2 percent grade), but it required auxiliary engines to push trains up steep sections and took 2.5 hours to cross (at 20 km/hour). It had tight curves, viaducts, two tunnels, and was costly to maintain. Step by step to overcome these nagging problems and significant obstacles, the workers bored the Severomuiskii Tunnel, taking over a quarter century, with a series of accidents that took fifty-seven human lives. And to top it off, the tunnel was bored for only one track. The costly BAM project, begun with slave labor, interrupted by war, and begun again in the 1970s, thus was finished seventy years later, with significant environmental impacts on flora, fauna, forests, prairies, meadows, river basins, and valleys, not to mention upon the people who lived along the route, and still without tracks in both directions.[85] Russian leaders and engineers would not be deterred!

BAM, the Trans-Siberian Railroad, and a new Polar Magistral have renewed importance to Russia's political leaders and oligarchs in the twenty-first century. Since the rails move coal, gas, ore, lumber, and so on, they must run well. Yet the Soviet legacy of poor roadbed and ballast, rails of low quality, multitudinous sidings, and tortuous passes impinges on any hopes of increasing the amount or speed of freight. On top of this, the people who built BAM, so called veterans of Brezhnev's project of the century, find themselves ignored by the nation to live in the shadow of a dozen or so trains that pass through their ghost towns each day.

In keeping with the Soviet tradition of public greetings to workers at special objects, on July 8, 2014, on the occasion of the fortieth anniversary of the Baikal-Amur Tynda railway station, Putin congratulated the Tyndinians—also by teleconference. Tynda, often called the "capital" of BAM, is 560 km northwest of Blagoveshchensk, the administrative seat of the Amur region, and currently has 36,000 residents, down from its peak of 67,000 in 1989, a population drawn largely from the influx of Moscow Komsomol enthusiasts called to complete BAM. Putin called the workers at the Tynda stadium construction site that will someday be cleared of its dilapidated barracks for the local employees and their families finally to move into nice apartments. He placed a second phone call to the Taksimo-Lodya Ferry terminal. He praised the dedication and labor of the workers. He said, "Today, the Baikal-Amur Mainline is an important, integral part of the country's unified transport system, a key link in the economic development of vast areas rich in valuable mineral resources, energy and forest resources. Life itself has convincingly proved the demand for this strategic highway for Siberia and the Far East, for the whole country. Therefore, further development of the Baikal-Amur Mainline, increase of its throughput capacity and comprehensive modernization of infrastructure are on the agenda."[86] The real occasion of his phone calls may have been to take some credit for newly opened apartment buildings intended for roughly 2,000 residents.

The residents thanked Putin for arranging the new, bright, comfortable housing, informing him by teleconference that "You are a man of your word!" Putin acknowledged that much remained to be done to address "social issues" of those who built the BAM. "The country certainly owes you a debt," the president said. Being a man of all the people, able to satisfy all requests, and most important being able to cut through red tape and corruption, Putin promised more. A young boy approached the microphone. He said, "There are a lot of children in the neighborhood who are keen on sports. Give us an indoor sports complex." Putin responded, "We will solve this issue."[87] As far as can be determined, there is no sports center to this day.

What did he mean by further development? One project is "BAM-2," as the press refers to it, intended to increase freight capacities significantly on the Baikal-Amur and Trans-Siberian railways for freight moving to the seaports and border crossings of the Far East by the mid-2020s.[88] By freight, government officials apparently mean coal, but also other commodities to take advantage of growing and regular exports including of natural gas and to meet growing demands of the Asian-Pacific region. Natural gas to China may be a major volume along the rails until a pipeline opens sometime in the 2020s.[89]

Already in 2012, Putin raised the possibility of turning the Ministry of Regional Development into a state corporation because of what he called its unsatisfactory work in the modernization of Siberian and Arctic railroads. "Unsatisfactory" was an understatement, in that freight was at only one-sixth of the target. At a meeting of the state council he said, "The most important condition for the development of the region is the creation of transport infrastructure and (power) generating capacities. Already now more than 100 million tons of cargo have been designated for shipment via the Baikal-Amur Mainline, while its capacity is only about 16 million tons," he acknowledged. He simultaneously urged that power lines be built along BAM and the Trans-Siberian Railway.[90] The Russian Railways (RZhD) president Vladimir Yakunin promised that his company would do its part, but he has asked Putin for supplementary funding to modernize BAM, in addition to 150 billion rubles (roughly $2.4 billion) already allocated for Siberian rail projects.[91] Toward the ends of upgrading BAM, the authorities have apparently decided to employ prison convicts; they are already using convicts to clean up toxic spills and other environmental disasters in Arctic regions. According to *Moscow News*, "Amid labor shortages Russian government officials have discussed plans to use prison labor for major construction projects but they insist there are no plans to revive the Stalin-era Gulag practice."[92]

Completing Stalin's Railroad

Roads, railroads, and canals change the landscape of the mind and of nature. The rights of way for roads and railroads cut across and through forests, prairies, and meadows, along river basins, across ridges. They have, by now, well-known impacts on ecosystems, flora, and fauna. They reshape the contours of the land and interrupt feeding, migratory, predatory, mating, and other practices—of humans and other fauna alike. Transport technologies interrupt and alter ways of life in lands and territories opened through these transportation technologies, in large part because they consciously reflect the economic, political, and military beliefs of their promoters that require uncomfortable changes in the attitudes and lifestyles of local residents.[93]

Simultaneously, railroads are a major force of modernization, a symbol of industrial civilization, a major tool of the conquest of the frontier, of spaces considered to be empty of people, or at least empty of important people, but filled with resources important to the state. And, of course, megacorporations, like megaprojects, confirm the overriding financial interests of state officials in big extractive and transport technologies. The Russian government will not be deterred from increasing gas flows by permafrost or Nenets herders or sanctions or market fluctuations or NGOs or a railroad with one track, sidings, terrible grades, and frightening tunnels.

In all events, Russia freight moves like a troika-drawn sleigh with the horses pulling at different gaits. Tungsten, platinum, nickel, copper, coal, and oil and gas wait at sidings and loading docks to be hauled. This mirrors a problem during the 1930s under Stalin and the 1970s under Brezhnev, when congestion became so severe that factories were at times forced to slow production. Putin has pressured the transportation industry—the railroads and the shipping industry—to prevent these bottlenecks. To avoid them, he promoted the expansion of railroads in the Arctic as part of the "global conception of the development of the Northern Sea Route." The basic idea is to complete Stalin's Polar Magistral. In 2005 Putin announced the "Ural Industrial–Ural Polar" project to guarantee the development of a rich mineral-ore resource corridor—specifically a railroad—through the Arctic Urals. Putin's project, now renamed the Northern Latitudinal Railway, has struggled with technical and financial problems, and there are few results to show.[94]

The NLR is more ambitious than Stalin's polar route. First, the 170 km long Bovanenkovo-Sabetta section to carry gas condensate, oil, LPG distillate, and supply and construction cargoes on the Yamal Peninsula has been added to the original railroad. The northernmost railway in Russia, whose design was completed in 2015 by the engineering institute Lengiprotrans with a target of completion by 2022, will not be finished until 2030. Second, ground approaches to the ports of Dudinka and Igarka on the Northern Sea Route and the creation of a railway connection to Norilsk will allow access to the raw material areas of the Far North all year round.[95] The NLR will likely include a railway bridge over the Ob River, with elected officials of the Yamal Nenets Autonomous Region asking that an automobile roadway be added to it.[96] Only survey work and geological expeditions had been conducted and, judging by the relative silence in the Russian media, it will be years before construction truly starts.

But there are signs that NLR may be completed. President Putin likely relished the moment when he, unlike Stalin, could indeed open the Cape Kamenny port in May 2016. At the terminus of Stalin's dreams, Gazprom commissioned a fully automated, turbine gas-powered pumping station called "Arctic Gates"; Putin ceremoniously started the flow by telelink from the Kremlin by pushing a button on his desk.[97] Gazprom CEO Alexey Miller and Gazprom Neft CEO Alexander Diukov both were present on site for the festivities. Putin gave the order to commence the loading of Novoportovskoe oil onto a tanker. Since the sea along the coast is no more than 11 m deep, as Stalin's advisors belatedly discovered, the oil-loading terminal, with a capacity of 8.5 million tons annually and year round operation, had to be located 3.5 km from shore.[98]

The palpable connections of the Tsarist, Soviet, and Russian rail heritage are present in today's special luxury trains that literally call on the past to generate business and enthusiasm for the future. One is the famous *Red Arrow* express from Moscow to St. Petersburg that is referred to as the "80+ year icon of the Russian Railways. This luxury sleeper train first started its regular service in 1931 and since then it has only been interrupted for 2 years (from 1941 to 1943) during the Siege of Leningrad." There was another direct overnight train, the *Leo Tolstoy*, that is "the best way to travel between Moscow and Helsinki in terms of price, safety and comfort. It started to run in 1975 being the first overnight train traveling at a speed of over 120 kmh. Now the Tolstoy offers modern compartments and excellent service covering the distance of 1108 km in just 14 hours that makes a journey onboard the Tolstoy an unforgettable experience in itself."[99] Or, 80 km/hour, according to the conventions of long division. And if the Trans-Siberian intrigues you, "There is a luxury Trans-Siberian railway train as well as several Trans-Siberian railway private train options available offering fixed date departures. These trains are only available to tourists and so can offer a schedule that allows you to visit more stops along the Trans-Siberian route than is possible to do on the public trains."[100]

The Russian Railway Company (RZhD) runs the third longest network of rail in the world behind the United States and China at 87,000 km, about a third the length of that in the United States, but with twice the area to serve. This means there is essentially no railroad reaching two-thirds of the nation, precisely that region of natural, mineral, and hydrocarbon wealth, from Western Siberia to the Far East, especially in northern regions, and much of the existing system requires significant repairs, expansion, and upgrading, even if named after the author Tolstoy or in honor of Stalin's Moscow-Leningrad express, the *Red Arrow*. Russia's railroads have always been intended primarily to ensure east-west transport. Only decrepit rails have resulted from a 120-year effort to build them using slave labor, or with laborers in the post-Stalin period high on enthusiasm but low on equipment and budget. Current Russian leaders hope that a public-private effort will finally complete several of the most technically challenging efforts in the Arctic and Siberia. But Russia lives—and moves slowly—according to always changing schedules of megaprojects advanced, canceled, and advanced again by the Tsars, commissars, and oligarchs.

2

Mines and Magnates[*]

In August 1935, the Ukrainian miner Aleksei Stakhanov jackhammered 102 tons of coal in under six hours, an achievement documented in the Soviet press as fourteen times his established quota. Within years, other miners broke his record and other industries adopted "Stakhanovism" to push production levels higher—in light industry, automotive, fishing, railroad, agriculture, and other sectors of the economy.[1] In the absence of capital inputs and material incentives for laborers, Stakhanovism served the Party leaders well by increasing productivity of labor and melding workers to the tasks of building socialism with enthusiasm, even if many workers resented the overachieving Stakhanov for making their lives harder by altering expectations of *their* output ever upward. The movement was abandoned after Stalin's death and later shown to be a sham. But the fact that the coal industry first adopted Stakhanovism points to another crucial consideration: the critical place of fossil fuels in the USSR's economy and its identity as an energy power. Although Russian oil and gas have the attention of the world in the twenty-first century, coal retains its position as fuel for Russian economic growth and as an export commodity, especially in Siberian open pit mines in the Kuznetsk Basin ("Kuzbass"). The miners, laboring more and more often in vast open strip mines, suffer through poor wages and environmental conditions in a crisis situation, getting none of the recognition that Aleksei Stakhanov captured.

In spite of the glory of Stakhanov, and the glory and gritty devotion of hundreds of thousands of miners worldwide, mining is a nasty business, involving digging and excavating, bulldozing and shearing, exploding and dumping, and the deaths of thousands of workers in frightful and dangerous conditions. Even after the beginnings of state intervention to regulate mines for safety purposes and to keep small children out of them in the nineteenth century, and the promulgation of laws in the second half of the twentieth century to insist on some measure of environmental protections, stipulate fines, and occasionally force reclamation, it has remained a violent process, an extensive large-scale technology involving vast stretches of geography.

Hero Projects. Paul R. Josephson, Oxford University Press. © Oxford University Press 2024.
DOI: 10.1093/oso/9780197698396.003.0003

Mining is earth and rock: water, runoff, and the accompanying heavy metals, arsenic, and other potential pollutants; gases and ominous dusts and particulates; and miners. Mining requires picks, hammers, and shovels; jackhammers and compressors; bulldozers and excavators; explosives; and still more miners. As the industry modernized, mining remained rudimentary in its means of assault on ore. Its major forms are shafts and open-cast or strip mines with extensive overburden removal, in many cases the removal of entire mountaintops with the overburden dumped into valleys, streams, and rivers below spreading earth, rock, heavy metals, and air pollutants farther into nearby villages and towns where miners and their families live.[2]

Coal was crucial to make iron and thus was sustenance for the belated industrialization of the USSR. Coal-powered thermal and electrical power stations impelled burgeoning industries and cities forward as the Bolsheviks completed the proletarian revolution. Bessemer production required coal, too. Many of the first mines were rudimentary shafts, with humans and horses providing the power to hack out coal. Most Soviet mines were filled with gulag prisoners through the early 1950s. Coal and coal miners and their families made a name for such "mono-cities" (company towns) as Kemerovo, Anzhero-Sudzhensk, Leninsk-Kuznetskii, Prokopievsk, and Vorkuta, if not for themselves. In the 1960s, following the work of mono-profile engineering and design institutes dedicated to mining and enrichment, the mines became increasingly mechanized and large scale, and eventually, following world trends, employed open-cast or strip mine extraction. While mining employs around 1 percent of the global labor force, it generates 8 percent of fatal accidents worldwide, some 12,000 annually, and Russia's mines, along with Chinese, South African, Turkish, and Ukrainian mines, have among the highest in fatality and injury rates; typically, however, open-cast or strip mines are vastly safer than underground mines.

Mine bosses in the USSR declined to provide adequate safety protections for Russian, Ukrainian, and Kazakh miners until after decades of Soviet power. The protections should have included pumps to remove water, ventilation systems to circulate fresh air, helmets, and other equipment. (In nineteenth-century mines, water was lifted or pumped out by steam power; as for ventilation, early coal mines often employed a furnace at the bottom of a shaft that created a draft to ventilate the mine.[3]) Instead, mine bosses—and their Party and ministerial bosses—forced the pace of mining. Brute force political institutions—laws against strikes, for example—were a central part of the machines and processes that brought coal to the surface. Owing to overriding state interest in coal, the state protected coal from social reformers to exploit coal fields wherever deposits to exploit appeared: in Siberia's Kuzbass, in the Arctic, in Ukraine's Donbas. Authoritarian mining policies aimed at keeping mines open and ignored even modest efforts to improve safety margins. This explains why both free men and gulag prisoners, who formed a large share of the overall mining labor force, worked in conditions worse than those of workers in capitalist mines, and it explains the belated application of more "scientific approaches" to mine safety and operation even though coal industry research institutes dated to the time of Catherine the Great in the late eighteenth century.

Whereas elsewhere in the world, coal gave working-class people and unions power and became, through labor actions, a catalyst for democracy, coal has never been a force for democracy in Tsarist, Soviet, or post-Soviet Russia. It has been a source of power to Stalin, to Khrushchev, and Brezhnev, and again to Putin, although at moments miners pushed for fulfillment of the social contract, if not for more democracy.[4] Coal shook Mikhail Gorbachev's attempts to reform the USSR when his policies of glasnost and perestroika led to national miners' strikes against the state. But it is an easily obtainable energy, whether through poorly organized workers, gulag prisoners, or even in an increasingly mechanized industry with still exploited, poorly paid workers.

The Kremlin's insatiable need for coal and oil was reflected in the determination to extend imperial control over fossil fuels in Chechnya, Kazakhstan, Siberia, and the Arctic regions. Ultimately, the USSR realized 20 percent of the world's coal production primarily from such major deposits in the Don, Kuznetsk, Karaganda, and Pechora basins. In the 1970s such "objective" factors as the increasing depth of mining work, the eating up of rich deposits, and the need to establish enterprises in difficult-to-reach regions led to higher costs and labor supply challenges. By 1985, expenses on mining and extraction and transport of mineral ore and fossil fuels consumed a massive share of national GDP.[5] The state subsidized the industry, and the Putin administration is still subsidizing fossil fuels, not unlike the US government with its massive direct and indirect subsidies of tens of billions of dollars to hydrocarbon industries.

This chapter considers the history of coal mining in the USSR and its migration in workers' bodies, party doctrines, engineering conceptions, and gulag camps from smaller, rudimentary shafts in deposits in the European part of the empire to huge open-cast mines in Siberia, stimulated in large part by the postwar determination to develop energy resources far from vulnerable western borders. Throughout this history from the Tsarist era to present-day Russia, mining has remained a violent practice, dangerous to miners and their families, and destructive to the environment no matter the promises of reclamation. Mining is inherently a megaproject that requires access to vast deposits, removal of millions of tons of overburden, and the treatment of workers as expendable, including the families of workers who live in proximity to the dangers, dusts, and din. Coal fed the Bolsheviks' dreams, stoked Stalin's iron and steel mills, supported Brezhnev's fossil fuel regime, and in the twenty-first century continues to support oligarchs of Russia. As a result, miners are denied fundamental rights to strike, to earn a decent wage, to return alive from the shafts and strip mines at the end of the day, and to find a safe clean environment in which to raise children. Stakhanov has never been their hero.

From the Tsars' Mines to Stalin's Camps

The journey of coal miners to the Kuzbass began under Catherine the Great (1762–1796). The Tsarist government supported prospecting and mining as it did other natural resource development to enhance the power of the Tsarist regime and enrich the state treasury. In this case, under Catherine, in 1773, the Higher Mining School, later the Mining Institute, opened in St. Petersburg. Most of the major powers began to back mining schools around the late eighteenth to nineteenth centuries. After industrialization, it was evident that coal, iron, copper, and other metals were vital constituents of any powerful nation or empire. For the Mining Institute, then as now, it is a state institution that requires students to wear military uniforms to display their dual allegiances to coal and the state. Alfred J. Rieber writes, "The marriage of technology and central state power had a natural attraction for Peter the Great and his successors, particularly Paul I, Alexander I and Nicholas I," all of whom had a military education and appreciated the achievements of the engineers of France.[6] Into the nineteenth century the Mining Institute sponsored extensive expeditions under the Imperial Academy of Sciences and later the Geological Committee of Mining Department whose officials studied potential deposits from the European part of country to the Kuzbass to the Far East and Pacific Coast and to Central Asia. Coal mining yielded only 121,000 tons in 1860 but reached 12 million tons in 1900 and 35 million in 1916. This was twenty times less than in the United States, fourteen times less than England, and six times less than Germany, but it was crucial to Russia's industrialization.[7]

Soviet economic planners accelerated the turn to coal. They found it easier to locate, extract, and transport coal than oil, and better to burn it than Vladimir Lenin's beloved peat, from both calorific and other points of view. Lenin supported peat engineers to develop new processes to cut it from bogs. He was considered infallible, so his ignorance of peat's low energy content and inadequacy as an industrial fuel was accepted. He created a Main Peat Committee and the Commission for Hydraulic Peat Extraction under it. He approved extra rations to people connected with the committee as part of an effort to protect "bourgeois specialists" from starvation in the first years of Bolshevik power. He ordered a film to be made on hydraulic peat extraction.[8] Lenin told Bertrand Russell of his fascination with peat—which he saw, together with electrification—as the keys to building communism. Lenin worried to Russell about the peasant question but was confident that electrification of industry over ten years would secure peasant support. Russell recalled, "He spoke with enthusiasm, as they all do, of the great scheme for generating electrical power by means of peat."[9] This fascination with fuel was not extraordinary. In 1924 a British engineer claimed that coal was the pinnacle of modernity. He called coal "fundamental to the civilization of the present era." The high level of civilization in Great Britain rested on coal, this engineer observed, while Italy, with limited resources, had a population "of low intelligence and low standards of living." The cause was not "the degeneracy of the Latin stock" but an economic crisis at the root of which was low power production.[10]

In service of coal, after the Revolution in 1917 the Soviets opened or expanded existing mining academies and institutes in Moscow, Kharkiv, and Krivyi Rog, and the Mekhanbor in Petrograd (1920). Mining departments of branch (applied science) institutes or at mines themselves opened in Novocherkassk in Rostov Province, Vladivostok on the Pacific Ocean, Tbilisi and Baku in the Caucasus, and Tashkent, Uzbekistan. The Council of Ministers (Sovnarkom) created a geological administration to identify new deposits and manage them, with Bolshevik party planners determined to each massive coal deposit.

Soon after Lenin's death, and on the basis of newly completed mining studies, party officials set about planning to exploit the Kuzbass in southwestern Siberia, the Karaganda deposit in central Kazakhstan, and the

Pechora River basin in northwest Russia, and parts of the Nenets and Komi regions into mining and industrial centers, a process that accelerated with Stalin's five-year plans. Already in 1930, the Party had decided to invest in the creation of the Ural-Kuzbass coal-metallurgical base. The Kuzbass had been known from the time of Peter the Great but was exploited only from second half of nineteenth century near Anzhero-Sudzhensk, and later along the Trans-Siberian Railroad. By 1940, the share of Kuzbass in nation coal production reached 14 percent. Generally, Stalin's five-year plans forced the pace of survey and prospecting, and World War II gave greater impetus to Kuzbass mining as a region far from the war front when production grew 1.3 times. Open pit mining began from 1943, with mines reaching 200 to 600 m in depth. Highly mechanized coal enterprises in the Kuzbass at the Raspadskaia, Pervomaiskaia, and Zyrianovskaia mines appeared significantly later.[11]

Slave labor was important to establishing a coal industry in the USSR, especially in clearing forest, laying roads and rail, digging shafts, and removing overburden; many of Russia's mining companies have roots in the gulag.[12] Stalin provided real impetus to gulag mines, in particular in Siberia. He visited Siberia secretly for seventeen days at the beginning of 1928. His trip convinced him that the kulaks—somewhat wealthier peasants—were a real obstacle to well-functioning agriculture and that the New Economic Policy of Lenin, with its relaxation of laws against profit-making enterprises, needed to be abandoned. He determined to collectivize agriculture and to pursue breakneck industrialization. He believed that he had to show a firm hand among Party, communist youth league, and secret police leaders, and that only he was capable of breaking the will of any remaining opposition through violence and repression. In visits with officials in Novosibirsk, Barnaul, Rubtsovsk, Omsk, and Krasnoiarsk, he urged them to be as tough as nails. He threatened those who disagreed on the pace and scale of industrialization with jail. He insisted upon acceleration of confiscations of food, especially corn and grain from the peasantry. He wanted workers to feed industry and the cities. Eleven months later, "dekulakization" had led to the forced exile of two million people, many of whom were exiled to the periphery of the empire to establish mines and factories, and it led also to the murder and starvation of many innocent individuals.[13] Industrialization, collectivization, and the gulag were the signposts of Stalinism, and kulaks provided coal.

In autumn 1929, eighteen months after Stalin's visit, the authorities created a Siberian labor camp, SibULON, called Siblag from 1935, with its headquarters rotating from Novosibirsk to Mariinsk several times, before finally settling in Mariinsk, a town in Kemerovo region where the Trans-Siberian Railroad crosses the Kiya River, in 1943. The camps, filled with kulaks and other exiles, carried out primarily mining and forestry work, with rail construction also a crucial component of both industries. Siblag's domain stretched from the Irtysh River in the west to the Yenisei River in the east, but its center was along the Trans-Siberian Railroad from Novosibirsk to Mariinsk, Taiga, Iurga, to the Iaia with its major sand and gravel quarries, coke and petrochemical factories, and lumber mills, and to Suslovo, a logging zone dotted with small camps of approximately 500 to 1,000 prisoners each. Siblag subcontracted with industrial and light industry commissariats (later called "ministries") to mine coal, erect brick and textile factories, establish fish processing plants, open metal fabrication operations, and lay railroads, in particular a trunk line, the Gornoshorsk railroad, from Tomsk northward into the taiga.[14] Already in 1930, Siblag and its Far East counterpart, Dal'ULON, later Dalstroi, together held nearly a quarter of all Soviet prisoners; these were massive economic commissariats as much as they were slave labor camps.

Thousands and thousands of prisoners arrived in boxcar convoys, one train after the other, to engage in the construction and mining frenzy. The main transit points of Novosibirsk, Tomsk, Mariinsk, Krasnoiarsk, Irkutsk, and Khabarovsk became dumping grounds for skin and bones, centers of filth, unbearable hunger, disease, epidemics, infection, and death. In Krasnoiarsk, bureaucrats reported, "The prisoners eat all sorts of scum, husks, hooves and other rubbish. The incidence of malnutrition among prisoners has increased. Brought to production places they drop from exhaustion."[15]

The murder of Leningrad Party leader Sergei Kirov on December 1, 1934, and the resulting well-orchestrated "Leningrad affair," the rooting out of an alleged conspiracy against Stalin and the state, led to tens of thousands of arrests. This was accompanied by a new wave of repression against peasants, exiles, intellectuals, party officials, minority nationalities (Balts, Poles, Volga Germans, Kalmyks), and others, with many of these thousands of innocent people ending up in mines. Chaos resulted at the overwhelmed transit points and in the camps. As of January 1, 1936, 69,000 prisoners found themselves spread among twenty-two departments of Siblag, of whom 45 percent were peasants, 14 percent workers, and 22 percent "hostile class elements," most of whom were accused of counterrevolutionary activity (17 percent) and lesser numbers of social-harmful elements, crimes against state property, espionage, and so on.[16] Between 1936 and 1938, during the Great Terror, the number of prisoners of Siblag expanded so rapidly that the authorities could not handle their processing; the camps were pitched hells of disease and starvation.

One Shadganov, who survived the horror of the Mariinskii transfer point in January–May 1938, recalled that his camp consisted of one building designated for 250–300 men, but that the entire camp held roughly 17,000 men who were exposed to the elements. They built *zemlianki* (underground earthen bunkers) heated if at all with rudimentary wood stoves that spread smoke over the prisoners. People filled the bunks—wooden planks—three across, then filled in under the bunks and in the narrow spaces between them. One could not move without stepping on someone's arms or legs. No one wanted to move; the temperatures reached –40° C. There were Turkmen, Azeris, Tatars, Mordovians, and "homelanders" from Moscow and Leningrad. Clothing was in tatters. There were no bowls or knives. The sorry *zeks* formed a long queue to wait for soup of frozen potatoes and something that could not even pass for bologna. The *zeks* held out their caps and galoshes to carry their food. One winter, the plague hit, potatoes disappeared, and there was no water. People ate bloody snow. The weakest could not make it to the latrine. Dysentery raged. Dozens died every day. The planks for coffins ran out, so they built a shed and stacked the corpses inside. Perhaps ten thousand people died in this one camp from January to May. Shadganov's memories are confirmed by archival documents that show how the authorities did not learn the horrific lessons of 1938 and repeated them in 1941 and again after the war.[17]

Coal benefited from this large-scale mayhem by providing the industry with thousands of unpaid laborers. The first prison camps in the Kuzbass appeared in 1926–1928, but many more prisoners arrived in the 1930s, especially at the Gornoshorsk Labor Camp that was dedicated to railroads. Prisoners set to building the Mundybash-Tashtagol railroad in 1934; the line was later extended from Mundybash to Novokuznetsk to help bring supplies to burgeoning metallurgical facilities there. A sintering and ore-dressing plant of the Kuznetsk Metallurgical Combine was built later in Mundybash. From April 1938, Gornoshorsklag took on other regional rail construction projects. The mortality rate at this camp reached 25–27 percent. The prisoners starved as they wrestled with shovels and wheelbarrows. German prisoners of war came in another wave, and also some 16,000 "Volga" Germans, Soviet citizens whose relatives had emigrated to the region in the eighteenth century but were interned as enemies, and also thousands of Tatars murderously expelled from Crimea by Stalin. After the war the government authorities cruelly jailed Soviet citizens and soldiers who had been caught behind enemy lines, were repatriated at war's end, were briefly treated as heroes, but now were called spies and traitors for having seen the West.[18]

Peasant exiles were crucial to the labor supply, and their appearance marked a new stage in the assimilation of Ural region, Western Siberia, and Eastern Siberia coal and the eventual establishment of the megacomplex of the Ural-Kuznetsk Combine. The growing scale and tempos of industry demanded more coal, and therefore mining always demanded more labor. In the Kuzbass during the first five-year plan (1928–1932), twenty-four mines entered operation whose output grew from 3 million to 9.7 million tons at "Black Mountain," "November 7th," "Pioneer," "Communist Youth Leaguer," and other mines that were often named for communist heroes or institutions, if not nearby towns. Stalin proudly named mines after himself and his close allies: Voroshilov, Kalinin, Kaganovich, and Molotov. Twenty large-scale operations that gained similar honorable names opened during the second five-year plan (1932–1937). Workers began to excavate at other big deposits: "Severnaia" in Kemerovo, "Kapital'naia" in Kiselevsk, and "Baidaevskaia" in Stalinsk, all of which in one form or another are still operating. By 1937, Kuzbass provided 75 percent of all coal in Siberia.[19]

Kulaks, "enemies of the people," and "wreckers" were exiled to far regions of the country without any legal or even quasi-legal procedures. They occupied the largest single group of workers in Kuzbass until the dissolution of the gulag. Eventually one-fifth of the miners were women. By September 1933, Kuzbassugol' already had 41,500 prisoners, or 40 percent of its total labor force. At several mines the percentage of forced laborers among all workers in 1933 reached 65–77 percent, for example, the Povarnikha and Maneikha mines in Prokopevsk. As always, they lived in unfinished barracks through which the snow and wind blew. They worked twelve-hour days, and many of them perished.[20] In a perversity of the Soviet system, in 1948 the Supreme Soviet recognized roughly 2,000 gulag prisoners with such honorary prizes as "Master of Coal," "Honorary Miner," and even "Stakhanovite." For Stalin, coal was political prisoners.[21]

The Science and Ideology of Forced Mining

If the mines could count on labor inputs, they were undercapitalized. One of the reasons for the continuing lag on a technical level of Russian mines into the twenty-first century, and the poor level of safety and environmental concern, may be the historical weakness of mining R&D and the difficulty in changing patterns and processes that have prevailed since the 1920s. While there exist a series of first-rate branch research institutes whose engineers contributed to mining science, the overriding interest of the studies has been to get the coal out of the ground as quickly as possible. The leading *Gornyi zhurnal* (Mining Journal, essentially 1825–present) had no regular section for environmental, mine safety, and similar topics until the 1990s. Rather, rubrics and articles were concerned with identification of deposits, expansion of mining, and ore enrichment, and the journal spun off a series of other publications dedicated to production, most of which are still published: *Ugol* (Coal, 1925–), *Tsvetnye metally* (Non-ferrous Metals, 1930–), *Stal'* (Steel, 1931–), and *Obogashchenie rud* (Enrichment of Ores, 1956–). The fact that engineers and students in the state-sponsored Mining Institute in St. Petersburg wear uniforms to this day indicates the mindset that they serve the state and that their rank depends on getting coal out of the bowels of the earth. It was, it must be noted, at the Mining Institute where Vladimir Putin defended his candidate of science degree thesis on the importance of state control of mineral and fossil fuel resources (see chapter 6).

A struggle between miners, engineers, and the Bolsheviks in the 1920s in the Donbas region of Eastern Ukraine set the tone for the future relationship between state power, technology, and coal that was temporarily settled in the first Stalinist show trial, the Shakhty (Mining) Affair, in 1928.[22] It is this region where renegade Russian proxy armies from 2014, and the Russian army itself from 2022 have sought to seize control of Ukrainian territory in pursuit of Putin's persistent and cynical attempts to expand the Russian empire. The mines in the Donbas that contributed to making Ukraine the third largest coal producer in Europe tend to have thin seams, run very deep, carry lots of methane, and are among the most unsafe in the world to this day.

The Donbas has been the site of political conflict between the Kremlin and the miners since the 1920s. In November 1923, miners in Shakhty ("Mine") in Rostov region, perhaps expecting the support of the Bolshevik workers' state that had promised that the proletariat would control the means of production, went on strike to demand better conditions of work, increased wages, improved safety regulations, and workers' control of the enterprises. Ten thousand miners descended on the building of the State Pedagogical University that the secret police, at that time called the OGPU, had commandeered. Armed soldiers met them with live fire, many strikers were wounded, and how many were killed is not clear. Unrest subsided with a change in administrative leadership, and worker-manager-party relations stayed calm until May 1927 when strikes again broke out in response to newly imposed daily mining norms, food shortages, and real wages falling by a half. The mines were in miserable shape, too, since the managers did not care sufficiently about safety; they were damp, often flooded, and a series of explosions had rocked the mines. Bribery of officials and theft of equipment put the miners are greater risk. Stalin ordered an end to labor unrest. The authorities arrested hundreds of strikers, and while some of them were eventually released, scores of others were exiled for crimes against the state.

The Shakhty Affair involved engineers more than workers. Through the show trial, Stalin and the Communist Party leadership and managers informed all engineers that they were the arbiter of the scientific truth in establishing plan targets and allocating (insufficient) labor and capital resources toward plan fulfillment. In preparation for the trial, the OGPU identified fifty-three individuals, largely "bourgeois specialists," and accused them of "counterrevolution," a nebulous term used with increasing frequency over the next decade. The specialists also faced charges of "wrecking" the coal industry by interfering with the achievement of production targets, which were hugely inflated in any event. The choreographed attack on the specialists indicated that the state would not tolerate interference in the establishment of rational plan targets from experts but would insist on superhuman targets. The riveting show trial took place in Moscow from May 18 to July 6, 1928. One hundred twenty journalists covered the spectacle. The goal was to blame endemic failures on the industrial front to meet target plans and find appropriate scapegoats (not planners and officials!). The charges included ties with spy rings and foreign counterrevolutionary organizations, and theft, bribery, and mismanagement. The investigators coerced and browbeat prisoners into incriminating confessions and into incriminating others. Twenty engineers admitted their guilt, eleven were sentenced to death, and five were shot.

The innovative, proletarian, Soviet science that arose at this juncture under Stalin was supposed to facilitate industrialization, change the social order, and increase coal production—and all other production—without the labor violence and engineering uncertainty that prevailed in the capitalist system. Under Stalin, production would benefit the common man and woman, or the New Soviet Man and Soviet Woman, on the foundation of scientific production that had been fixed through research in branch industry institutes. Proletarian specialists would study the "objective conditions" of the productive forces in megacomplexes, then force the earth to give its riches to the proletariat. No longer would so-called bourgeois specialists direct the slow tempo of research for the benefit of the owning classes, nor would they be permitted to sit in their offices far from practice to engage in "ivory-tower reasoning." All this resulted in the rapid increase in the number of branch industry institutes representing all fields of twentieth-century technology: smelting, mining, ball bearings, electrification, heat engineering, hydrology, and so on. The expansion of engineering research and development was effective to an extent in increasing output, but the Shakhty Affair indicated that proletarian science was constrained in its focus to increasing production and finding deposits, not necessarily in promoting cutting-edge, innovative research, and certainly not on industrial hygiene.

Branch institutes in every sector only rarely managed to accelerate innovations in the economy for several reasons. Perhaps the most important was the presence of strong ministerial barriers and rivalries between universities, branch laboratories, and Academy institutes, with prestige going to the latter. This frequently left the branch research institutes scientifically and qualitatively as poor second cousins of Academy centers. Another reason was the hesitance of factory managers to embrace innovations that might be effective in fulfilling plan targets down the road, but in the short term might lead to production shortfalls as managers, engineers, and workers figured out how best to employ new techniques, devices, tools, machines, and processes. Because of their fear of financial punishments—or, as we have seen, fear of arrest for sabotage—managers were loath to take risk.

The Donbas continues to be a source of battle over memory, safety, and nation in the twenty-first century. First, only in the year 2000—seventy years later!—did the General Prosecutor's Office of the Russian Federation overturn the convictions of and rehabilitate the forty-nine defendants of the Shakhty Affair owing to falsified evidence and the innocence of all parties. Second, the Donbas mines remain among the most unsafe in the world and the region also one of persistent and extensive environmental problems. Third, war between Ukraine and Russia broke out in the region in 2014. With the support of Russian troops, self-proclaimed independent republics have appeared in the Donbas, based in the cities of Lugansk and Donetsk, and the mines have deteriorated in production and safety. Apparently, Kremlin oligarchs believe that they own Donbas mines in the twenty-first century.

Pushing the Coal Empire after the World War

Strategic considerations—the outbreak of World War II—provided impetus to the development of coal mining far from European industrial centers and from the Donbas as they were quickly overrun by Nazi armies. The "front" required coal. One wartime slogan was "Everything for the Front!" At the outbreak of the war, as rapidly as possible, the authorities stepped up coal mining in the Arctic, Siberian, and other regions. This required redoubled efforts to expand mines with gulag prisoners in Siberia, in particular at sites along the Trans-Siberian Railroad, and to restart projects for rails and roads to gain access to mines in the Kuzbass. As workers went to the front, and *zeks* were in demand everywhere, other personnel rushed to fill mines. After the war, as leaders struggled to come to grips with the phenomenal costs of rebuilding Ukraine, Belarus, and the Caucasus, Stalin and his advisors nonetheless diverted scarce labor and capital to Siberia to ensure access to strategic resources far from the nation's borders. The program had Arctic components, sub-Artic programs, and Siberian projects including mining and metallurgical combines.

Proletarian science enabled the rapid expansion of Siberian coal operations. At the end of the 1920s in southwestern Siberia's Kuzbass there were but eleven relatively small mines. Uneducated laborers toiled mostly by hand in the absence of mechanized processes and safety standards. The Soviets were determined to establish and operate their own modern mines without the assistance of foreign firms that had dominated the industry before the Revolution, and to that end opened such new technical institutes as the Siberian Physical Technical Institute and Sibgiproshakht, which opened in 1929 as the Siberian branch of the Kharkiv Design Institute "Giproshakht."

Sibgiproshakht, a research enterprise whose corridors produced applied research to locate coal, build shafts, design pits, and accelerate extraction under severe Siberian conditions, grew rapidly in the postwar years, establishing branches in other coal towns that later became independent institutes: Kuzbassgiproshakht and Karagandagiproshakht. Its personnel designed open pit mining operations. On the basis of the work of these institutes, a number of major mines opened. In May 1954 the Council of Ministers approved the formation of the Kedrovsk, Khorosheborsk, Gramoteinsk, NovoBachatsk, Novosergeevsk, and Svobodnyi mines—mostly open pit facilities—and in all, ten new mines in the 1950s. By 1967, in celebration of the fiftieth anniversary of the Great October Socialist Revolution, Sibgiproshakht had seen the opening of the "Kuzbasskar'emgol'" Combine with sixteen open pit mines, some of which are still operating with a total output of over 21 million tons per year.[23] Scientifically designed mines and craters came to dominate vast stretches of the Siberian plain.

Science was crucial in opening Siberia in the immediate aftermath of the war. At the beginning of 1946, representatives of the Irkutsk provincial party and central executive committees joined local scholars in calling for the Communist Party Central Committee and the Council of Ministers in Moscow to authorize a conference on the study of the productive forces of the region and nearby parts of Eastern Siberia, and to consider the organization of an Irkutsk Branch of the Academy of Sciences to chart resources and organize their development. Irkutsk, then a provincial city on the Angara River and not far from Lake Baikal, eventually became an industrial center with the completion of the Bratsk Hydropower Station in 1958 and the expansion of the Irkut Aviation Factory (established in 1932). But in the late 1940s in Irkutsk there were insufficient hotel rooms, let alone school dormitories, to house scientists and officials, and a ration card system still prevailed in the country that made feeding conference attendees a challenge. With emergency budgetary support from Moscow, and the requisitioning of local laborers, the organizers of the conference managed to upgrade the hotel and dorm rooms, construct meeting halls and a dining facility, and even resurrect a rudimentary local transport system to serve attendees. The first Irkutsk tram started running just in time for the conference, although the system had been approved three years earlier in 1945.[24]

In August 1947 the Council for the Study of Productive Forces (SOPS, a direct descendant of KEPS, the Tsarist institution formed in 1916 to chart resources in support of the Great War effort) gathered scientists, planners, and party officials in Irkutsk to consider the extent of Siberian resources and how to exploit them systematically, in particular its fossil fuels. Specialists were determined to transform the region into an industrial machine, especially for the chemical, metallurgical, and mining branches of the economy. They discussed a general vision in decades hence to rely on hydroelectricity to power burgeoning industries. But for now, the participants saw coal as the way to power new smelters, manufactories, and other facilities in the Krasnoiarsk-Enisei, Ust-Kut, and Irkutsk regions. A twelve-volume report resulted from the conference.[25]

Energy production and especially electrical energy were central among conference attendees to visions of nature transformed into a vast, coal-power industrial complex serving state ends. A. V. Vinter, a leading hydrological engineer and head of the Dniepr Hydroelectric Power project, and his colleague V. I. Veitz advanced just such a view at the Irkutsk conference in their talk on energy resources of Eastern Siberia.[26] They emphasized the importance of taming energy resources as the key to Siberian grandeur. They pointed to the example of the Leninist GOELRO state electrification program and the Stalinist five-year plans of the 1930s as what could be accomplished in a command economy. They advanced bold ideas to increase Siberian energy production manyfold toward the end of aluminum, copper, calcium carbide, and petrochemical production. They acknowledged that low population density and labor shortages were a real brake on development, but they proposed focusing resources on energy-intensive industries, not on creating better living conditions for workers and their families, and apparently they supposed this would be sufficient to serve as a magnet for workers. They insisted, "In spite of the grandiosity of these plans it must be underlined that they are only the first stage of the broad assimilation of energy resources and of the productive forces of Eastern Siberia." The British witer H. G. Wells, they reminded attendees, called GOELRO a "great fantasy." But in socialist Russia, everything was possible.[27]

In 1948, SOPS followed up with a meeting on the Kuzbass that addressed similar questions with the goal of turning its coal into electricity, and the Kuzbass into production center for such energy-intensive metals as aluminum and titanium, and for petrochemicals and electrochemicals. The Kuzbass's extensive coal, coking coal, iron, rare metals, and forest resources made this, in the minds of planners, not a pipedream, but a smokestack dream of real pipes and mines. At the conclusion of the meeting the participants voted unanimously to organize a branch of the Academy of Sciences in Irkutsk, and promised that from this perch scientists would contribute to Siberian development. In actuality, the task of creating a new division of the Academy presented significant challenges of staffing and facilities: there were no empty buildings for offices and laboratories, no apartments for employees, and few qualified local researchers or students.

In Moscow and in budget-conscience GOSPLAN, the state planning agency, regional scientists encountered quite a few opponents to the idea of opening an eastern branch of the Academy of Sciences in Irkutsk, on top of which specialists in Moscow, Leningrad, and elsewhere refused to move to Irkutsk because they saw only isolation and poor living conditions in a regional backwater. Fortunately, the president of the Academy of Sciences, Sergei Vavilov, physicist and brother of Nikolai, the world-class biologist who died of starvation in a gulag camp in 1942 because of his support of modern genetics, supported the endeavor. Already in February 1949, institutes of geology, energetics, and chemistry, and biological and geographical-economic sectors opened with a handful of employees, and they immediately began to recruit graduate students, a number of whom later became its leading scientists, including G. I. Galazii of the Limnological Institute involved in the study of Lake Baikal. But all did not go smoothly, especially with administrative leadership and the quality of facilities. The geologist S. S. Smirnov died before he could occupy the position of branch chairman. Another possible choice for director, Vinter, who had played a major role in the 1947 conference, and who had participated in site selection for the future Irkutsk hydropower station, was not designated for unknown reasons. Vasilii Zvonkov, a naval engineer, who was appointed director in the middle of 1950, himself lived in Moscow, commuted to Irkutsk only a few times, stayed about a month in total, and asked to be relieved of the burden in order to remain in Moscow.[28]

In the event, however, as part of the Khrushchev-era enthusiasm for expansion of the scientific enterprise network nationwide, the branch itself grew quickly with the addition of the Baikal Limnological Station and the Irkutsk Magnetic-Ionosphere and Seismic Station. A decade later, the branch had 468 scientific and technical personnel, over a fifth of whom with advanced degrees. The Irkutsk branch research menu grew to include liquid fuels and catalysis, organic synthesis; ferrous and non-ferrous metallurgy, including new alloys and enrichment processes; phenols and nitrogen compounds; production of such energy intensive products as aluminum (with major bauxite deposits in nearby Bratsk, but also in Krasnoiarsk, Novokuznetsk, Achinsk and Saian areas)[29]; machine building, especially for the chemical industry and mining; and, of course, coal.[30] Irkutsk's star would be short-lived because of its narrow focus on applied research, and especially because of the establishment of a vital, new city of science, Akademgorodok, built outside of Novosibirsk in the late 1950s, that quickly surpassed the Irkutsk branch in scientific excellence.

Empire Building through Territorial
Production Complexes

Russia has long been cursed by a geographical resource-industry disjunction. The most extensive deposits of mineral resources as a rule sit far from industrial and other urban centers, while existing, nearby sites were quickly exhausted. For example, the development of industry in the Ural Mountains with extensive deposits of iron ore led ultimately to the denuding of forests with profligate use of timber for charcoal; as part of a nascent industrial revolution in the Russian empire, the Donbas then began to be exploited for the iron industry, and a pattern of high costs due to transport long distances commenced. One solution was to build costly transport infrastructure from the points of extraction and felling to industrial facilities far away. Gulag labor was a cruel, but inefficient solution. Soviet planners never truly figured out how to judge among competing possibilities in the resource-labor-capital conundrum. The result was European infrastructure and industry that required modernization and expansion, Siberian infrastructure and industry that begged to be built and encountered challenges in attracting workers to unfinished factories and to the unfinished workers' villages around them, and an economic and planning system that could not make efficient choices among various approaches. One scholar noted in the 1980s, "The industrial development of Siberia is lagging considerably behind the planned rates. It is taking place under the stamp of a policy of devoting all efforts to the forced development of the fuel-energy complex. But this is being achieved at the expense of an increasing lag in manufacturing industry and the infrastructure. Investment activity in the region is aggravating the disproportions in the industrial structure and slowing the development of production that is vitally necessary for the region."[31]

The Soviet economy was a planned economy with planners' preferences clearly indicated in one-year, five-year, and other plans. In spite of being planned, and in spite of claims that it was efficient or would overcome capitalist inefficiencies and waste, and in spite of periods of tremendous economic growth, it was noteworthy for its plodding stagnancy and its limited innovative capacities especially in the last years of Soviet rule. Some commissariats—later ministries—were powerful and well run, but most others not as effectively and lacking the capital and labor inputs of their ministerial rivals. Over time, the authorities tinkered with the system, hoping to improve its innovative strength and performance, and they hoped that feeding huge amounts of fossil fuels into the open mouths of smelters, boilers, and furnaces would overcome all other problems. This promoted only profligate use of fuels and extensive pollution. Khrushchev's Sovnarkhoz reforms were a failed attempt to build or help stimulate closer relationships among sectors of the economy in regions rather than in an industry.[32]

In another attempt to find a solution to the geographical disjunction between various resources, labor, and capital, Soviet planners in the 1960s turned to the creation of territorial production complexes (TPKs), a kind of regional megaproject that was never as big as the sum of its parts. In theory, TPKs would promote diversification of the economy, interrelations between its sectors, and territorial unity.[33] As Lonsdale noted a few years later, the TPK was intended to take advantage of regional grouping and proximities of the entirely planned economy. He suggested that the roots of the approach in the thinking of some Soviet specialists was in GOELRO, which Soviet specialists saw as a group of interrelated economic activities based on the processing of some raw material and utilizing a particular energy source.[34] TPKs were introduced almost exclusively in Siberia and involved some fuel or extractive industry and some production operation or energy, for example, the Bratsk TPK of hydroelectricity and aluminum, the Saian TPK, also for aluminum, and KATEK, the Kansk-Achinsk TPK of coal, iron ore and metallurgy, and thermal power stations at Krasnoiarsk. The TPKs arose to great fanfare but suffered from the typical challenges of the planned economy: labor shortages, underinvestment in heavy machinery, and confusion about how precisely regional organization would overcome technological lags, bottlenecks in supply, and bureaucratic barriers. Officials pushed harder from the time of the Twenty-fifth Party Congress in 1976 to see TPKs come to fruition. But the gains from the agglomeration of production never resulted in significantly higher productivity. Technical economies of scale and benefits from the joint use of transportation and support activities, social infrastructure, joint services, provision of housing, and social infrastructure did not materialize as promised.[35]

An obstacle to the success of TPKs and other big projects was precisely lack of communications, services, and labor since their focus was "the development of the virtually uninhabited regions of Siberia." The relative abundance of energy resources or ore could not overcome underdeveloped settlement structures, and the remnants of the now-closed gulag camps along the rails could hardly be expected to serve any purpose. Urban structures got no further than studies, for example, those by specialists at the Akademgorodok

Institute of Economics and Organization of Industrial Production;[36] recall that BAM workers are still waiting for the conveniences of daily life in the cities and towns along the route. Today the oil, gas, and other industries hope that the shift-method of labor in the Arctic regions will be a panacea for the problems of lack of infrastructure. Unfortunately for coal, from the point of view of labor and capital, company towns remain the approach in the Kuzbass, and the towns seem unable or unwilling to modernize, provide better social services, or deal with extensive pollution.

Planners approved a major TPK for Kansk-Achinsk coal and metallurgical facilities in Krasnoiarsk region. KATEK, located to the east of the Kuzbass, was typical for its massive scale, local social impacts, and environmental disruptions. KATEK stretched 800 km, covered 50,000 km², or roughly the size of the states of New Hampshire and Vermont together, and it ranged in width from 50 to 250 km, enveloping parts of the Irkutsk, Kemerovo, and mostly Krasnoiarsk regions, making the notion of "regional focus" rather absurd. It included such industrial cities as Krasnoiarsk, Kansk, Achinsk, and Sharypovo, a town of 37,000 on the western border of Krasnoiarsk region known from 1984 to 1988 as "Chernenko" after Konstantin Chernenko, the decrepit short-term general secretary of the USSR for thirteen months in 1984–1985, who was born there. Chernenko died after brief rule, when already quite weak, his demise perhaps brought on by food poisoning from eating smoked fish.

The Yenisei River divides the Kuzbass into the western or Chulym-Enisei basin and the eastern or Kansk basin. In the 1960s, geologists estimated its coal reserves at 140 billion tons. The two main centers of mining activity were Nazarovo and Irsha-Borodino. By 2017, KATEK included twenty-four active or recently exploited coal deposits, some of which reached 800 m in depth. Yet recently a number of them have been mothballed, and only the Berezovskoe and Borodinskoe are actively exploited. The advantage of KATEK coal over that of the Kuzbass is a much lower ash content—12 percent versus 30 percent—and lower sulfur. There are some problems, for example, a high concentration of refractory calcium oxide in coal-bearing rock—to 42 percent. Soviet scientists were also worried about impacts on soil, air, forests, and water quality, and urged two rather than the four mines proposed.[37]

The authorities developed KATEK beginning in the late 1970s for two major reasons: first, the reliance of much of Siberia on hydroelectricity that led to regional shortages and brownouts in drought years, and second, plans to expand markedly Siberian petrochemical, wood, and other industries that required new sources of electricity. But expansion of KATEK ran into the problems again of labor shortfalls, limited capital investment, low-quality coals, and underdeveloped infrastructure.[38] If in the 1980s there was some promise KATEK power could overcome stagnant regional economic growth, then in the 1990s during the crisis dissolution of the USSR it became prime territory for the post-Soviet corporate raiders to become wealthy oligarchs. They were able to organize steel and aluminum production in close cooperation with newly privatized fossil fuel and hydroelectric power facilities—and to enrich themselves.

KATEK coal itself engendered monstrous operations. For example, two conveyers capable of transporting 4,400 tons of coal per hour ran to the Berezovskaia electric power station in Sharypovo, 14 km away from the basin. Originally 1,600 MW, with its first two units coming on line in 1987 and 1991, the Berezovskaia power station was redesigned at 2,400 MW through three units of 800 MW each, and earned a prize in the "Russian Organization of High Social Effectiveness" competition, a prize unparalleled in world experience. Berezovskaia's 370 m tall chimney is the tallest industrial object in Russia. But apparently it is not too effective; a fire of unknown origins damaged the third block in February 2016, following another fire in December, and unit 3 was not operational again until spring 2021, with repairs reaching $500 million.[39]

More efficient and massive post-Soviet coal machines arrived at Siberian mines only in the twenty-first century. They include boring machines, bulldozers, and trucks with a capacity of 100,000 to 200,000 tons. They dig the coal out of Sharypovo with one of the most massive earth openers ever constructed, the ERSHRD-5250 "excavator rotary stepping-rail mining" shovel with two dozen buckets that are fixed on the rotor wheel of a giant self-propelled machine that can scoop 5,250 m^3 of coal per hour. The length of the boom of this type of excavator allows it to process seams up to 30 m in height. The ERSHRD-5250 is the great-great-grandson of the ERD-1600 that crawled out of the earth in Ordzhonikidze, Ukraine, in 1963, produced by the Novokramatorskii Machine-building Factory (NKMZ). NKMZ, which opened in 1934 under Sergo Ordzhonikidze, minister of heavy industry, built other special machinery, for example, for spacecraft and bridges. There are four ERSHRD-5250s used in Ordzhonikidze, Krasnoiarsk, Ekibastuz, and Rudnyi (Ukraine).[40] The city name "Ordzhonikidze" signified the glory of big machines; it was named after Ordzhonikidze, a long-term Bolshevik

who joined Stalin's inner circle and, as commissar, oversaw the implementation of the first five-year plans. But he refused to join in the frenzy to identify
"wreckers" and other enemies, and in February 1937 shot himself at home.
At least big machines came to KATEK in the twenty-first century. Miners
in Russia generally were forced to use rudimentary equipment and toil in
dangerous conditions from the time of Ordzhonikidze. Their frustration
over wages and safety that had unsettled Shakhty in the 1920s boiled over
in Siberia in the 1980s with strikes that slowed Gorbachev's efforts to reform
the USSR.

Megacoal and State Power under Gorbachev and Yeltsin

In July 1989, just after the first free elections in seventy years to the Supreme
Soviet, the USSR's legislative body, coal miners in Siberia struck to protest a
lack of soap, low pay, inadequate benefits, poor equipment, and dangerous
work conditions. In the winter of 1991 they struck again, demanding Mikhail
Gorbachev's resignation. Since they provided coal to the state, they had
great economic power and could lead people in some cities to freeze or sit in
darkness without electricity. Since they represented the proletarian alliance
between the Party and the worker, they threatened the legitimacy of what
remained of Communist Party rule.[41] And many people knew that cold,
hunger, and lack of fuel had brought down the Tsarist regime 1917.

Indeed, in strikes of 1989 and beyond, miners in essence rejected Soviet
social contract. As soon as wages, already low, no longer met the needs of
miners and their families, as inflation swallowed their hopes, and as glasnost
encouraged their boldness to speak up about the dangers of working in the
mines and the lack of concern for their health and safety generally by mine
managers and environmental officials, the miners went on strike. In all, some
400,000 miners across the USSR took over mines, occupied city squares,
and demanded economic reforms. They forced Gorbachev to meet their
demands for higher wages and better work conditions. Miners in both Russia
and Ukraine joined the revolt, leading to "the downfall of the Communist
Party and the Soviet state."[42] (The Chernobyl disaster was another signpost of
the terminal ills of the Soviet development model and its technological ethos
of production at any cost and safety if time permitted.)

If striking coal miners presented a problem for the Gorbachev administration, then so too did growing awareness of the public health, safety, and

environmental problems that plagued big industry, including coal. Although it was far from alone in visible manifestations of health and safety violations, it may have been the most unrepentant of scofflaw industries of the USSR with its ruptured earth, unsightly rip rap, dangerous runoff, toxic tailings, and alchemical emissions. At the end of the 1940s the mines were relatively small and underground, and proximate environmental degradation was mainly from runoff, disposal of rip rap and tailings—not considering air pollution, particulate, and acid rain. But open pit mining meant hundreds and thousands of hectares of scarred earth opened to the rain, wind, and sun. For the small mines, periodic reclamation commenced in the 1960s. For open pit mines, reclamation was supposed to commence in the late 1980s, but as capital and other investment funds were shifted to oil and gas, the coal industry lost any interest in reclamation.

The rise to power of Gorbachev and perestroika contributed to the spread of informal environmental movements and to the promulgation of reformist environmental legislation. This led to some progress in dealing with the nation's public health and pollution problems, and to forcing at least some circumspection in industry even in such polluted areas as the Kuzbass. Yet it took pressure from miners striking about economic issues to generate public awareness of the social and environmental costs of Soviet coal mining combines. When the economy began to falter, the coal industry focused its budgets on salary payments but then cut those, too, and strikes reverberated throughout the industry in 1989, with 140 mines closed from Donetsk to Kuznetsk. The strikes showed the limits of Gorbachev's ability to shape the future direction of perestroika.[43]

Miners from Kemerovo in the Kuzbass gathered in the central square to protest, and they were joined by miners from Mezhdurechensk, Tisul', and other coal towns. They wanted pay. They also demanded the creation of a nature preserve (in Russian, *zapovednik*) nearby. The authorities in Moscow responded with full support, realizing that the nature preserve might be the easiest demand to meet. From outside the region they appointed Andrei Andreevich Vasilchenko, an ornithologist well known in scientific and government circles, to lead the effort to establish a zapovednik.[44]

The zapovednik "Kuznetskii Alatau" in Kemerovo region sits amid the most densely populated and industrial area of Russia beyond the Ural Mountains, in the midst of open pit coal mines, discarded piles of overburden, and other filth connected with the explosive violence and excavation of mines. The zapovednik comprises about 5 percent of the Kuzbass yet cannot compensate for that violence to the surrounding cities, towns, and communities. The determination to establish it in an area rich with coal, metal, forestry, gold, and other important resources arose among state officials who felt growing pressure from local inhabitants and environmental activists to provide clean water to workers and their families, and where else might clean water be protected if not in a nature preserve? In 1984, a professor of zoology at Kemerovo University, T. N. Gagina, began discussions with colleagues and officials about establishing a preserve in the mountains. She herself was deeply familiar with the region, having led several expeditions into the still unspoiled areas of the region.[45] In January 1984 the administration of hunting affairs of the region received a letter from central authorities precisely about creating several different kinds of nature preserves in the nation between 1985 and 2000, and perhaps one in Kemerovo region. Supporters pushed the idea of a park of no fewer than 400,000 hectares as crucial to clean water supplies to residents that would simultaneously permit preservation and remediation of river sources, mountainous swamps, and taiga. Even with orders from the center to push forward, the provincial authorities refused to act. Into 1989, clear-cutting of forests and other degradation continued, with officials in Zapsibgeology (a prospecting company), Zapsibzoloto (a gold mining operation), forestry employees, and even local journalists in opposition to the zapovednik seeing jobs as more important than environment.[46] Eventually, and ironically, the collapse of the coal industry facilitated the creation of park.

After the dissolution of the Soviet Union in 1991, the economic situation of miners deteriorated further, as it did for all Russian citizens who faced skyrocketing inflation, consumer goods shortages, and the like. Boris Yeltsin had taken advantage of the 1989 strike to build his authority, and then another 1991 strike to weaken Gorbachev further. But in the mid-1990s, after the breakup of the USSR and the creation of an independent Russian Federation, now as president of the Russian Federation, Yeltsin himself felt the brunt of the miners' actions. From 1992 through strikes and strike threats, miners gained concessions from the government that somewhat softened their job losses and falling living standards. The miners had mass support in social circles and in the government that enabled them successfully to push their special situation.[47] Then, in 1995, "215 of Russia's 235 mines closed in a culmination of protests that began in Rostov, where miners and their families live in miserable conditions, often with no heat or running water." This was the very region where Stalin orchestrated the Shakhty

Affair to eradicate alleged foreign, technocratic wrecking in the industry. A year later, in 1996, strikes shook the nation again. At one point nearly half a million Russian coal miners were on strike to demand $200 million in unpaid wages; one million coal miners in Ukraine who were owed $367 million in back pay also went on strike. The strikes extended to perhaps three-quarters of the mines in Russia, from Kemerovo in Siberia and to Vorkuta in the Arctic. The workers also demanded that the government pay overdue subsidies to the mines, although industry owed the mines money, not the government.[48]

The Yeltsin government pursued market reforms including mass privatization in most industries. An exception was coal; it could operate only with massive subsidization. The state assumed control and ownership of the coal industry in the state-run Rosugol company, closed loss-making mines, and cut subsidies. This led to improvement in the industry and made it attractive to investors. By 2001, "some 77% of coal output was accounted for by private operators," especially from surface mines in Siberia. Still, the industry had limited resources and minuscule tax revenues, and it could hardly provide a safety net to anyone on pension, let alone raise wages.[49] In this financial environment, private owners and bosses established fiefdoms of coal. Coal was mined to support state power for the Tsars, the Bolsheviks, and the Soviet industrial bosses. Now it became Putin's coal with the help of such people as the governor of Kemerovo province, Aman Tuleev, who served as governor for over twenty years until 2018.

The Khanate of the Kuzbass

The Russian Federation produces a sixth of its energy from coal. Russia has the second largest reserves of coal in the world behind the United States, and Russia is the sixth largest producer of coal in the world, much of it coming Kuzbass and Kansk-Achinsk regions of Siberia. In the 1990s, coal production plummeted from a high over 400 million tons annually to under 300 million tons annually; in the 2010s, it has risen again, reaching 385 million tons in 2016. Many of those tons are designated for export, as gas, nuclear, and hydroelectricity replace coal power production domestically. Open pit mines provide 60 percent of the total. Most of the coal moves toward the coasts on railroad. This is an old industry, undercapitalized, highly polluting, and with a high accident rate.

Because of the great importance to Russia and to the Soviet Union of oil and gas to domestic and international energy policy, foreign currency earnings, and so on, many people have lost sight of the fact that coal was the first fossil fuel to draw the nation's leaders' attention. Under President Vladimir Putin, such former Soviet ministries as those connected with oil and gas have been reborn as several of the world's major, most highly capitalized, and most powerful corporations as Gazprom, Rosneft, and Novatek.[50] Because of the visibility of Russian oil and gas—from ubiquitous Gazprom insignias that are the Coca-Cola of Kremlin corporatism, to its importance in heating European homes and powering European industry, to its centrality to the conflicts with Ukraine over (energy) independence—the importance of coal to Russian economic and other plans remains obscure.

The Kuzbass, one of the largest coalfields of the world, affords mystically beautiful vistas in the Tom River basin between the Kuznetsk Alatau and Salair mountain ranges. The fields cover about 26,000 km^2, with reserves in excess of 300 billion tons, dozens of workable anthracite and rich coking coal seams, some up to 15 m thick, and in places reaching 40 m. The coals are low in sulfur, if high in ash. Known since the early eighteenth century, industrial mining of the deposits began during Stalin's first five-year plan when coal development was accompanied by the creation of an industrial area, the Ural-Kuznetsk combine for iron and steel, especially at Magnitogorsk, built "heroically" in the 1930s, and at Novokuznetsk (from 1932 to 1961 called "Stalinsk" after the man of steel), a coal town of about a half million inhabitants.[51] Lead, zinc, tin, copper, and mercury deposits exist in the adjoining Altai region. Factories to mill and process the ore have risen throughout the region, never giving relief to the exhausted landscape and its inhabitants. All the major towns—Novokuznetsk, Kemerovo, Anzhero-Sudzhensk, Kemerovo, Leninsk-Kuznetsky, Prokopyevsk, Osinniki, and Kiselyovsk—support coking coal, or other potentially hazardous products in the manufacture of plastics, fertilizers, and pharmaceutical goods.

The megacompany Kuzbasrazrevsugol, one of the largest coal operations in the world, grew up here out of the disarray of the breakup of the USSR. Another massive Russian company with gulag roots, it officially entered the pantheon of post-Stalinist state companies in May 1964 when the Council of Ministers of the RSFSR founded Kuzbasskarerugol, which united all open pit coal mines in the basin—then thirteen active quarries, a series of auxiliary enterprises, and 14,000 employees. By 1974, the mega-enterprise united forty-nine enterprises and organizations connected with open pit mining including seventeen sites that employed 36,443 people, and mining settlements—company towns—with the entire suite of apartment buildings, stores, hospitals, schools, and so on that characterized Soviet and post-Soviet industrial company towns.

The low environmental quality of life in the Kuzbass from the Soviet era into the present reflected the desideratum of coal. The area looks, tastes, and smells of coal. Enormous quarries and pits spread across a lunar landscape at depths up to 200 m, hiding vistas and obscuring the zapovednik. Today, even in neighborhoods where there are big houses owned by the nouveau riche, overburden has been pushed into ugly grey-brown mounds by bulldozers and steam shovels where it abuts backyards. But the nouveau riche support the local politicians and coal mining for bringing them wealth.

The politics of the Kemerovo coal basin in the twenty-first century, what might be called "resource extraction authoritarianism," is the same kind of politics that protects oligarchic wealth and limits manifestations of civic culture at the national level. Some observers referred to the region's former governor, Aman Tuleev, as "the most effective governor in Siberia," others as "the Kuzbass Khanate," for managing to keep miners quiet, if not content, and certainly not permitting them to go on strike, even as they faced a deadly, dangerous job. Only a March 25, 2018, fire in a shopping mall that killed at least sixty people, most of them children, forced Tuleev to resign from office after a quarter century of service, although he was forgiven for his sins by Putin just two days later with a seat in the Kemerovo region legislature, becoming its speaker, and was also appointed rector of the Kuzbass Regional Institute of Professional Education.

Tuleev, a Turkmen born in 1944 in Krasnovodsk (now called Turkmenbaşy, a city that serves the petrochemical industry on the Caspian Sea), cut his teeth on coal and railroads. From 1973 to 1978 he was head of the Mezhdurechensk rail station, and from 1988 head of the Kemerovo railway, one of the largest in the USSR, whose major freight is coal. In 1990 he was elected to the Supreme Soviet of the RSFSR and became chair of the Kemerovo regional council of deputies. His selection by President Yeltsin in July 1997 to head the regional administration was connected with rising social protest of miners and repeated wildcat strikes. In October 1997, Tuleev was elected governor of Kemerovo oblast, the first time voters in Kemerovo elected a governor; until then governors had been appointed by the president. Tuleev won 94.6 percent of the votes cast. He ran against two token opposition candidates to ensure that he would not infringe the electoral law by running unopposed. Tuleev was a populist who advocated increased state investment in industry and tax relief for small businesses. His real raison d'être is to defend coal interests. In 2015, Tuleev won re-election with 96.69 percent of the vote, an all-Russian record.[52]

Tuleev ran for the presidency of Russia in 1991, 1996, and 2000, in 1991 receiving 6.81 percent of the vote. In 2000 he won 2.95 percent of the vote, in the Kemerovo region roughly 50 percent, higher than even Putin. In July 1999 he refused an award of honor from Yeltsin, saying in principle that he had to reject such an award from a leader who had dragged the country into poverty. In September 2000, however, he accepted the award from Putin, showing loyalty to a different kind of man with a more authoritarian style of leadership—and a deeper appreciation of coal. He has been rewarded again and again by the president for his efforts. In elections to the parliament in 1999 Tuleev ran as a communist, although in Kuzbass he already supported the forerunners of Putin's United Russia party. In 2003 he headed the United Russia party in Kemerovo. In 2005, Putin extended Tuleev's term to 2010 and Tuleev officially entered Putin's party United Russia.

Tuleev proselytizes coal, even as the public health and environmental dangers of open pit mining grow. Output increases, miserly salaries help workers meet daily needs, but little more, yet very few people protest expanding operations. It seems that only residents in villages under direct threat from expansion of mining operations speak out. One activist, Sergei Sheremeteev from Alekseevka, succeeded in stopping the Bungurskii-Severnii Excavation Company from blasting operations less than 1 km away from a residential area that sent rock chunks into people's gardens. Apanas, on the taiga, was also saved. Sheremeteev and his group lay down in front of Caterpillars and dump trucks to stop loading coal. They wrote protest letters. Others tried to organize during Putin's Year of the Environment (2016) to protect the surroundings by planting trees around the edge of an old mine and releasing carp into the water that fills it. Anton Lementuev, a mining engineer and coordinator of the environmental NGO Ekodefense!, says that locals have grown increasingly angry about mining operations and have organized protests in Novokuznetsk, the tiny village of Gavrilovka, and elsewhere. But coal, tradition, jobs, and home heating overwhelm the opposition. Of the region's 2.5 million inhabitants, 150,000 are employed by mines. Others serve the mines indirectly as van and bus operators, cooks, and the like. As in Soviet times, managers ignore rules, regulations, and formalities, and push to keep operations expanding; local and national environmental, mining, and technical inspectorates are weak, disinterested, or captured by the interests they are meant to regulate.[53]

For Tuleev, coal is god. If he were Fedor Gladkov, the author of the first socialist realist novel, *Cement* (1925), then he would likely write a book called *Open-Pit Mine*. Tuleev has earned a series of degrees and honorary degrees, and he is the lead author of dozens of publications, some of which he many have helped write, but like any Soviet leader he was able to insist on being a coauthor by virtue of his leadership positions.[54] As such, he is a tireless author. He completed his doctoral dissertation on "Political Leadership: Regional Specificities and Mechanisms of Realization"; he is an academician of the International Academy of Informatization, an honorary professor of the Academy of Applied Sciences, and the author of several books: *The Long Echo of the Putsch* (1992), *Power in the Hands of Man . . . and Man in the Hands of Power* (1993), *The Price of Illusions* (1995), *Fatherland: My Pain* (1995), *Judge Yourself* (1996), and *Overcoming* (2009), among others. For his service to the fatherland he has received several Orders for Service before the Fatherland; an Order of Alexander Nevsky, given to civil servants with more than twenty years of meritorious service; and other honors. Kemerovo Region is landlocked, yet Tuleev's coal activities earned him the Medal of the 300th Anniversary of the Russian Navy.

In February 2016, Tuleev rejected any argument that Russia move away from coal: "You can't get rid of coal: it has been, is and will continue to be one of humanity's most precious resources." On the eve of Miners' Day in August 2016, he repeated the ash and smokescreen mantra that jobs, not profits, were the key: "We have all had to make a colossal effort to turn Kuzbass from a jobless hole into Russia's industrial backbone. For the last 20 years, our coal industry has gone through a complete cycle of rejuvenation, and has changed from a failing sector subsidized by the government to an economically effective one and become the first wholly privately-owned sector of the Russian economy."[55]

And coal is crucial to the Russian empire beyond Kemerovo. The Russian authorities have resurrected a series of Soviet-era holidays and competitions to infect workers with feelings of patriotism, or perhaps ennui, and to support such bureaucrats as Tuleev. In July 2017, miners from Nazarovo in Krasnoiarsk region in Borodino participated in the All-Russian Competition of Professional Trade of Workers of the Coal Industry in the "Coal Miners' Olympiad of 2017." Such reborn Soviet-style Olympiads, contests, special days, and honors for workers in various industries and fields are a significant feature of political culture in Putin's Russia. In this case, representing the Siberian Coal Energy Company, the miners celebrated the seventieth anniversary of the Day of the Miner. Some four hundred of the best representatives of the industry from seven regions of Russia from the Kuzbass to Vladivostok participated. The Nazarovo representatives won awards as the best excavator operators in all of Russia.[56]

Tuleev's removal as governor in March 2018 had nothing to do with his cavalier attitudes about coal miners' rights, but with his insensitive comments after a fire in the "Cherry" mall in which sixty-four people died because of faulty construction, blocked emergency exits, and other signs of corruption and criminal negligence. A few days after the fire some three thousand parents, friends, and sympathizers gathered to march Kemerovo, a city of a half million people, demanding straight answers about how the tragedy had occurred and a public apology from the authorities. In response, Tuleev criticized the protestors for spreading rumors and upsetting the quiet city. He accused them of spreading false information about the death toll. He also disputed the size of the demonstration. He longed for the passivity of the miners, calling these protestors—miners, their families, friends, mourners all—provocateurs and troublemakers.[57]

Tuleev and his administration have often been linked to corruption and payoffs, even if nothing has ever been proven. But the Kremlin insisted he resign after this shameful behavior over the "Cherry" mall protests. Perhaps only the deaths of children could frighten the aged man. During the late 1990s amid his rise to power, Tuleev had warned the federal police that someone was following his car. He claimed his office was bugged. He kept his curtains tightly drawn and the outside door to his government office locked. His behavior was a recognition that the Kemerovo region was "a hotbed of organized crime, and one of his advisers was gunned down on the doorstep of his Moscow apartment." Tuleev presided over what he called the most dangerous region in Russia: in 1998, eighteen local business leaders were murdered, and fifteen coal mine managers had also been killed in the previous five years. By Tuleev's estimate, 60 percent of the mines had fallen into the hands of organized criminals.[58] No wonder Tuleev was happy to be a part of the relatively calm disposition of managing coal resources in the Putin era. Payoffs and threats had given way to a more stable kind of resource management. Today he can enjoy the fruits of coal from a position as parliamentarian—still far from the dangers of the mines.

Coal is mega-corporations. Nine major companies now handle most of Russia's coal, many of them in the Kuzbass which supplies over half of Russia's coal, with one-eighth from the Kansk-Achinsk basin (Table 2.1). The coal industry is nearly entirely privately owned, although it receives government sudsidies. These are massive coal corporations. The second largest, Kuzbassrazrezugol, was privatized in 2003. In 2017 it administered eleven coal seams or outcrops and one mine (Baikaimskaia), while exploiting seventeen deposits.[59] Apparently it has sufficient reserves to stay in operation at least another fifty years. Its open pit mines use line shovels, diesel shovels, and also massive BelAZ trucks of 27-, 42-, 75-, 110-ton and gargantuan 200-ton capacity produced by the Ural Turbomotor Factory.[60] Profitable and active, the company has sought to expand its technological base and to underwrite development of production infrastructure in the region. Kuzbassrazrezugol and five other coal companies of the Erunakovsk deposit opened a new electrified railway line to tie deposits to railway mainlines that permitted a two-thirds' increase in freight in 2003, which suggests that gas, oil, and coal companies will always be able to build infrastructure to exploit fossil fuels.[61]

In its scale, expanse, importance to Moscow, and impacts on local people and environment, Kuzbass coal mining has thus been a paradigmatic hero project. In the 2000s and 2010s the Kuzbass economy grew by 1.5 times and industrial production increased twofold because of Tsar coal. In 2007 the Kuzbass was first region in Siberia and tenth in Russia in level of investment. To Tuleev and others, coal remains critical to the Kuzbass in the twenty-first century even if in world markets coal is dying a slow death.[62]

Table 2.1 Major Russian Federation coal companies

Arktikugol (Spitsberg)
Zarechnaya (Kemerovo)
Kuzbassrazrezugol (Kemerovo)
Mechel (Southern Kuzbass)
Raspadskaya (Mezhdurechensk)
Siberian Anthracite (Iskitim)
Siberian Business Union (Kemerovo)
Siberian Coal Energy Company (Krasnoiarsk)
Vorkutaugol (Vorkuta)
Yakutugol (Neryungri, Yakutia)

No Clean Coal

But if coal is crucial to Russia's energy balance, then it is a blight on the atmosphere, climate, and countryside. As Slivyak notes, "Over 170 power plants in Russia run on coal. More than 80 percent of these plants are over 20 years old, and some have an electrical efficiency of only 23 percent."[63] These operating specifications would lead coal plants anywhere else in the world to shut down. Russian analysts have been fully aware of the industry's inefficiencies and environmental costs for decades. Danil Aleksandrovich Dodin, who studied the geology and minerology of the Arctic from 1958 and participated in the development of massive deposits on the territory of the Norilsk Industrial Region, wrote in his last years about the insatiable appetite of mining and processing companies for ore, the anthropogenic impact of mining technology, and the nature of the Soviet development model as contributors to the extensive environmental degradation of the Arctic landscape. Dodin wishfully argued for the creation of "ecologically clean little-waste closed system [resource-saving] technologies." He called for modern, ecologically pure territorial-industrial centers.[64] This was an unexpected argument for someone with coal in his bloodstream. Dodin, born in Leningrad in 1935, was evacuated with his parents to Stalinsk after the Nazi attack, where his brother, Lev, a world-renowned dramatist and producer, was born. The family returned to Leningrad at the end of the war in 1945. Dodin graduated from the Mining Institute in 1958—wearing an institute military uniform with all other graduates—and joined the Institute of Geology of the Arctic (today, the All-Russian Scientific Institute of Oceanology). A leading specialist in mineralogy, geology, and petrology, he lived for many years in Norilsk and became chairman of the coordinating counsel of the "Russian Platinum" scientific group in the Academy. He participated in thirty-three Arctic expeditions, twenty-nine of which he himself organized, including one to the Talkhansk and Oktiabrsk sulfide platinum-copper-nickel deposits.

Dodin pointed out that the Russian Arctic is crucial for many minerals in short supply—chrome, titanium, and gold—and hence will continue as a strategic region for the Kremlin well into the twenty-first century. Various trusts throughout the Arctic regions and elsewhere worked at full bore: in Kovdorsk, Norilsk, Deputatsk, Iultinsk, as well as on thousands of gas wells and oil derricks. He noted that precisely the increase in nickel and copper production at Norilsk in the 1970s and 1980s led to the expansion of the Northern Sea Route and required year-round navigation that tied together the big technologies of transport and excavation. But, he observed, Russia lagged significantly in the assimilation of high technology to develop these resources intensively instead of wasteful and extensively. Dodin wrote, "Precisely the harmonic combination of mineral ore basis, environment, and cultural aesthetic inheritance of the small peoples of the North define the future of northern territories and the Russian Federation as a whole."[65]

Yet how could coal mining or coking be other than a highly polluting process? Coke making is the carbonization of coal (reducing coal to its carbon content) in a coke battery at high temperature without oxygen. This causes such impurities present in the coal as hydrogen, oxygen, nitrogen, and sulfur to be released, so that they can be collected or burned off. (Coke ovens produce toxic air pollutants, or air toxics, that "are known or suspected to cause cancer and other health problems."[66]) To take reliable figures where they exist, coke production in the United States increased steadily between 1880 and the early 1950s, peaking at 72 million tons in 1951. In 1976, the United States ranked second in the world in coke production, producing 52.9 million tons, or about 14.4 percent of world production. In 1984, it was estimated that 330,000 to 3.5 million pounds of coke oven emissions were produced annually in the United States. Although the by-product process is designed to collect the volatile materials given off during the coking process, emissions escape because of structural defects around the doors or charging lids, improper use of engineering controls, improper work practices, and insufficient engineering controls, permitting dangerous carcinogens to enter the workplace and beyond.[67] Coal burning produces the most air pollution deaths in China.[68] In the USSR, coke production was 117 million tons in 1962 and around 67 million tons in 1980; further, pollution controls were significantly less than in the United States, and with unclear but no doubt significant impact on public health.[69]

Because of the concentration of mining and metallurgical enterprises that operate in Russia on Soviet-era technology, cities in these coal mining regions are among the most polluted in the nation. Take Krasnoiarsk region, known for its nickel, cobalt, diamonds, and copper, but also for its production of one-sixth of the nation's coal. Perhaps 80 percent of Krasnoiarsk region industrial production is concentrated in four mono-cities that emit hundreds of thousands of tons of air pollution annually and are at the top of a list of the most polluting cities in the nation: Krasnoiarsk, Norilsk (the nickel city with massive pollution problems[70]), Achinsk (a number of industries, but known for alumina), and Kansk. The most polluting enterprises are not only among the largest, but also the oldest, most energy-intensive, and most prone to fire and explosion, even if they have changed their names in the new Russia: the Norilsk Mining Metallurgical Combine, the Yenisei Chemical Combine, the Achinsk Alumina Refinery, and the Achinsk Petroleum Refining Factory.[71] Technogenic air pollution is one of the leading factors causing poor public health. Filthy inversions plague regional cities. Sanitary (exclusion or buffer) zones of forest have themselves disappeared in the name of apartment construction or have died out from acidic runoff and air pollution.

As for coal: huge open pit mines have scarred the earth far and wide. Brute force technology for excavation and processing was so efficient that it shoveled up trace deposits while removing entire mountaintops and polluting entire valleys. Enrichment facilities promptly extracted ore from the thin deposits and disposed of the rest. Vast hills of tailings and rip rap piled up, then slowly leached heavy metals into the environment. In the haste to remove overburden and extract ore, the mining concerns destroyed ecosystems and accelerated erosion, processes that Tim LeCain, in a study of copper mining in the United States, calls "mass destruction," and he means in particular the ability of big machines to excavate great amounts of ore, even if low-grade, followed by using concentrators and smelters to get the metal out of the rock.[72] In the American West, private agribusinesses, mining, timber, other resource extraction industries came to control vast sections of the land that they engineered with impunity. High-pressure water cannons washed away the earth, followed by the use of such poisonous substances as mercury to trap such valuable metals as gold that poisoned the land. This led, in California, to an active environmental movement in response to the agro-industrial despoliation of the nineteenth century.[73] In Russia, mining machines and processes to suck wealth from the ground retain nineteenth-century avarice and twentieth-century brute power, and nascent public environmental movements to tame the machines have been silenced by state interests.

Russian government efforts to strengthen environmental laws and increase enforcement efforts lag, while modest efforts to involve the public in environmental decision-making have been stultified by attacks on NGOs and by the co-optation of the environmental sentiments by powerful industrial PR offices that represent major industries from coal to nuclear power.[74] The efforts of PR offices may represent a sincere attempt to educate the public about the nature of the technology at hand, its safety features, and how the enterprise manages risk. But they often can be superficial and seem largely to represent propaganda or PR performance. One such attempt was the program "Children's Siberian Ecological Expedition" (2010) under the theme "Begin with Your Own Home," which sought to educate impressionable minds that the coal companies cared about the environment.[75] Yet it is difficult to produce, let alone raise, healthy children when your home is the Kuzbass and the nearby forests consist of slag contaminated by heavy metals. Recognizing the need to give up to three hundred children of miners something to celebrate, Kuzbassrazrezugol provides a small allotment to summer camps for children, in 2018 some $500,000 (31 million RUR).[76]

And sometimes their parents don't return from work. The mines are among the most unsafe in the world. Raspadskaia in Mezhdurechensk ("Between Two Rivers"), the largest underground coal mine in Russia producing 10 percent of the country's coking coal, has a long history of accidents and of management ignoring safety measures. In March 2001, a methane explosion killed four miners and injured six; the mine was shut down for two weeks in 2008 due to safety violations; a worker was killed when part of the mine collapsed in January 2010. All of this pointed to the May 2010 disaster. On May 8–9, 2010, two explosions killed 91 and injured 99 minors, destroying most shafts and filling the mine with water. A second methane explosion four hours later destroyed ventilation system and rescue was suspended— nineteen of those killed were rescuers sent into the mine. Fires continued for over two weeks. A commission blamed both managers and miners who apparently failed to note signs of the impending explosion.[77] Boris Nemtsov, a viable opponent to President Putin before his assassination not far from the Kremlin in February 2015, called for demonstrations in support of mining safety and democracy.

Methane explosions ripped through the Zyryanovskaia mine in Novokuznetsk in December 1997, killing more than 30 miners; in January 1998 an explosion at the Tsentralnaia mine Vorkuta killed 27 miners; in April 2004 a gas explosion at the Taizhina mine in Kemerovo region killed 45 miners; in March 2007 a methane gas explosion killed at least 78 people in the Ulyanovskaia coal mine Novokuznetsk; and so on. Every year another explosion or fire kills miners, mostly in the Kemerovo region, but everywhere where coal mines operate: in Vorkuta in February 2016, another 36 miners killed by a series of explosions.

The government has been intolerant of strikes even in protest of fatal accidents. If in 1989, Gorbachev was unwilling or unable to call in troops to put down the miners' strike, then in May 2010, in the face of tragedy, the government was less tolerant of civil unrest. President Dmitrii Medvedev, who appeared at Raspadskaia that May to console the victims' families, sent Prime Minister Putin to lead the rescue mission and secured large financial payments to the families of the killed and injured miners. Yet the government arrested twenty-eight miner-demonstrators who refused to disperse. Ultimately, Governor Tuleev met with the protesters and agreed with some of their demands. What had the miners demanded? On May 16, the "Union of Kuznetsk Basin Residents" issued an appeal to the Russian president to release the detained miners in Mezhdurechensk, increase minimum salaries threefold, stop persecution of an independent trade union, withdraw police forces brought in from other regions, and set monthly meetings of the town administration with the residents. They published their appeals in such blogs as *Golos Kuzbassa* (Voice of the Kuzbass); Nina Ostanina, the communist state duma deputy from the region, supported them.

Voice of the Kuzbass activists publicized the strikes that spread throughout the region. Dozens, in some cases hundreds, of miners fearlessly protested against megamines. They called for the formation of an independent union in Kemerovo, not one tied to state power. They welcomed the fact that "all of our brothers who were held earlier have been released" without charges. Yet they were angered that no recognized political organization had supported them. The miners issued the following demands. First, that memorial services be held across the nation for the miners killed in the disaster, with moments of silence to light candles in front of municipal buildings. Second, they called for all criminal investigations against the miners to be ended, and that bureaucrats issue monthly reports about measures taken to improve safety. They did not want revolution; they did not ask for it. They wanted support for the miners and their families and quick results on safety.[78]

But the authoritarian politics in the Russian resource empire did not permit the expansion of trade union movements, and the protests faded, as did the miners' anger and bewilderment, perhaps because the company was successful in buying off future protests with payments of $33,000 to each dead miner's family. In August 2012, a chapel opened in Mezhdurechensk in memory of the victims, dedicated to St. Barbara, the patron saint of saint of armorers, artillerymen, military engineers, miners, and others who work with explosives. The chapel, near the city part at the intersection of 50th Anniversary of the Komsomol Prospect and Cosmonaut Street, street names that date to the Soviet period, is a cruciform shape. A mosaic icon of St. Barbara, who prayed for miners in the hours before her own death, adorns the main façade, and inside is a carved oak iconostas with eleven icons and a memorial marble plaque with the names of those killed in the Raspadskaia Mine disaster.[79]

Despite No Respite, No Reclamation

Massive mining systems do not permit attention to environmental conditions. Across the globe, thousands of square kilometers of land have been chewed up; tailings have been dumped willy-nilly into ravines, lakes, and valleys; surface and ground water carry away heavy metals; and foul air wafts beyond borders in carcinogenic forms or as acid rain. In Siberia the conditions are critical. Virtually all industry operates factories with pre-historic filters and other forms of rudimentary pollution control. Open pit mining, which does not require ventilation, is an especially coercive force. It destroys environmental stability through erosion, removal, and pollution of surrounding soils, and it destroys families.[80] Even reclamation may not help. Recultivation is not a simple matter of filling massive pits, covering shafts, and planting ground cover.

Reclamation requires great expense and uninterrupted effort in damaged areas that extend to the horizon. It requires engineering, forestry, agricultural, and other measures to resurrect the productivity of the land. Yet how do you return industrialized landscapes into cultural ones? Is it sufficient to apply liberally truckloads of good soil and then drive way? What of the creation of roads and pathways, the regulation of hydrological regimes including those of rivers, creeks, and canals? What will the creation of drainage and catchment systems accomplish? Even the best of efforts cannot guarantee a return to biological stability, let alone any full future utilization, especially when the owners of the land, the coal companies, have run roughshod over the Siberian landscape for over a hundred years, when in many sub-Arctic region trees grow very slowly, so that it would be decades to re-establish forests, even with good soil, and complex ecological interactions are generally devastated and impossible to reestablish in any human-scale times. "Reclamation," even in the United States or other "environmentally" advanced nations, often just means planting some sort of vegetation, not necessarily restoring anything like the ecosystems destroyed.

And, indeed, the oligarchs do not care about reclamation. In Russia in the 1990s there were no funds whatsoever for reclamation as the economy tanked; reclaiming the land had been an afterthought in earlier periods. In the Kuzbass in the eighth five-year plan (1966–1970) only 190 hectares per year were recultivated, and by the twelfth five-year-plan (1986–1990) no more than 500 hectares per year in the Kuzbass. According to one estimate, out of 85,000 hectares to be reclaimed, only 18,000 hectares—less than a fifth—were eventually reclaimed, the lowest percentage of any region in the country except Vorkuta at the Arctic Circle. At this rate, another century would be required to finish reclamation, while more and more open pit mining continually adds to the total. The State Program for the Environment to 2005 set a target for Kuzbass of reclaiming 1,000 hectares per year. This target, too, did not come close to being realized.[81]

Even more, bandit mines have appeared. In September 2010 the Russian investigative department for economic crimes uncovered four illegal mines producing on the order of 6,000 tons of coal every two weeks. The losses of coal are in the tens of millions of rubles. The police created in June 2011 a "Coal Spetsnaz" (Spetsnaz = "special operations," a kind of Coal Swat team). According to one report, between 2007 and 2010 hundreds of these illegal operations were liquidated.[82] Yet these efforts do not lead to reclamation, only to the shutdown of smaller, illegal mines.

In the absence of federal or regional support for reclamation and cleanup, for safe operation or pollution control, and with the government in fact seeking to quiet dissent, local residents themselves have stepped up to stop pit mine operation, even if it means that jobs will disappear. They do not consider their protests inappropriate or illegal, but simply wish to attract the attention of local, municipal, and regional authorities to prevent in the future any further opening of open-pit mines near inhabited villages. One mine recently opened on the outskirts of three nearby villages, Korotkovo, Khakhalino, and Mencherep. The residents wanted to save their children from exposure to noise and dust, heavy metals, methane gas, and the drumbeat of nearby explosions, nothing more. But the mines swallowed up more earth and exposed more and more people to dangerous pollution. The protestors lamented the fact that always the companies remove overburden, take their profit, and move on without recultivation, while the local people are stuck, cannot move on, and are not relocated.[83] This has been the economic development path for over a century: exploit ore, dump the overburden and tailings, ship off the coal, take the profits to Moscow, and leave the workers behind.

The Belovsk Reservoir near Mencherep long allowed local people to rest, swim, and sun. One local resident, Maria Sataeva, said, "It is our park region.

Of course, it's not Sochi, or Crimea, but nonetheless. There is nothing better in the Kuzbass."[84] The locals call the Belovsk reservoir at 13.6 km^2, formed on a tributary of the Ob River, the Inya River, the Belovskoe Sea or the "Pearl of Kuzbass." The reservoir opened in 1964 to feed the Belovskaia GRES.[85] After the announcement of plans to locate an open pit mine near the "sea," activists posted a change.org petition urging opposition to a decision of the Federal Agency for Mining of the Siberian Federal Region to allow seizure of four sizable nearby four parcels for mining.[86] The petition noted that a miserable ecological situation already existed because of the Belovskaia electrical power station (begin construction 1956, opened 1964, at 1,260 MW that provides energy to Kemerovo, Novokuznetsk, Belovo, and other towns), and the presence of eight mines already located within 20 to 30 km of the reservoir that were slowly encroaching on the last remaining recreational sites. Local residents already suffered from unexpected oncological and respiratory diseases, and to open a mine 500 m from the reservoir zone, near the "Golden Sand" beach and a children's sport camp, with a few remaining pastures and meadows nearby, made sense only to coal magnates. The petitioners pointed to fact that Putin himself advanced the right to live in comfort as a goal of his the national "year of ecology."[87]

The Putin administration has not been shy about shutting down most avenues of protest by controlling media outlets and by strictly limiting any protest with threats and arrests and opaque laws. Certain kinds of protest persist, especially if they involve a "petition to the Tsar"—or to the commissars or oligarchs. In the nineteenth century, many citizens of the empire came to believe that the Tsar was a decent man who cared for his subjects. The injustices and inequalities, they believed, were because of unfaithful bureaucrats and evil noblemen. If they approached the Tsar directly as petitioners, they thought, then their situation might be rectified. This view of things met its demise on Bloody Sunday in January 22, 1905, when imperial guards in Petersburg fired on petitioners led by Father Gregory Gapon, who wished to deliver a complaint about the grievances to Tsar Nicholas II at the Winter Palace. Perhaps a thousand people were killed, wounded, or trampled in the event that destroyed the myth of the caring Tsar.

Many Russian citizens believe that President Putin can intervene to rectify problems they face because of a corrupt government, and indeed Putin makes certain during an emergency, such a natural disaster as a flood or forest fire, or a major accident, to assure the public that he is in control and will order his subordinates to fix things without delay. Many of them seem to think he, too, is a decent man, and in a series of public forums, some of them televised, he presents the image of a busy man, but one who is concerned about the average citizen. Like their Tsarist predecessors, citizens want to believe that, if only they could contact Putin directly, submit a petition to him, or write a letter to him, then their problems with bureaucracy, red tape, and unfeeling officials would be overcome. In provincial Russia, judging from press coverage, they apparently also think that if only the president knew about the extensive pollution and scofflaw businesspeople, then he could rectify local problems. President Putin's national call-in press conferences where citizens ask questions of the leader give some substance to that belief. But in practice, not much changes. Putin clearly believes that Russia's strength comes from ore, not citizens. The extractive industry, the hero project, the project of the century, the megaproject, and the open pit mine are still what matters most to the Russian government.

Yet Achinsk residents have not been shy about expressing their worries on the environmental dangers they face in daily life. On September 28, 2015, they began to circulate a petition to President Putin and simultaneously to the Minister of Natural Resources and Gospotrebnadzor in the name of all citizens to address the ecological disaster of the city. Among other things, a fire had knocked electrofilters out of operation, but the Achinsk Alumina Refinery (AGK) did not shut down its furnaces, instead seeking to keep the money coming in and the orders going out. A dangerous white dust spread over the territory, with impacts on nature and public health. The petitioners asked Putin immediately to force the combine to shut down the dangerous atmospheric releases and to hold the directors of RUSAL, the world's second largest aluminum company, run by Oleg Deripaska, personally responsible.[88] Deripaska, a close friend of Putin, a powerful and wealthy oligarch, was under US sanctions because of the Russian annexation of Crimea. The sanctions were lifted by the administration of Donald Trump; one aspect of the deal to lift sanctions allowed Deripaska to transfer millions of dollars of his wealth to his children as part of a divorce agreement with his wife. Another curious event quickly followed: in May 2019, RUSAL announced a $200 million investment in an aluminum rolling mill in Richland, Kentucky, the state of Republican Senate Majority Leader Mitch McConnell. All this may of course be coincidence.

In any event, the press office of the AGK disputed any great danger to the residents of Achinsk, claiming that the accident had shut down the filters for only a short time, and that production resumed with discharges within established norms, including those for inorganic particulate. The PR office pointed out that the factory was replacing outdated equipment at 250 million rubles in 2015 (a paltry $4.2 million for such a wealthy and well-known polluter) and double the amount in 2016. The residents collected 2,500 signatures in protest, and the pollution continued.[89]

On the whole, contemporary Russian approaches to resource development resemble those of the Soviet era in the disregard for, or studied inattention to, workers' living situation and safety. One of the last major independent NGOs, Ekodefense!, has long struggled against the spiraling environmental disaster and social disintegration in the region, especially after the signing of the Paris climate accords of 2016, noting that "the mining industry has been in decline for several years." In changing political conditions that favor them, local coal producers are ignoring laws to save money. They do not follow environmental regulations, and they refuse to maintain infrastructure. Indeed, open pit mining means to "save a fortune on infrastructure."[90] Yet in a crucial way they are quite different from Soviet managers: they no longer pay for new housing developments or assist in retraining and relocating workers, and they are miserly in support of citizens' infrastructural needs generally. The market prevails for salaries, public transport, and comfort, while authoritarian approaches have reappeared in terms of weak regulation and disinterest in the environment.

Far from the Kremlin

A major reason for the preeminence of coal over the simple needs of workers and their families and the environment is distance from the Kremlin. The distance is multifaceted: geographical, climatic, political, economic in terms of investment priorities, and legally in terms of enforcement and investigation practices. The Putin administration is content with a local khan so long as he keeps the coal miners quiet and produces coke for industry and export. Russia has significant environmental problems, as is well known, with some regions worse off than others, especially in or near the so-called monocities (company towns) that arose in the Soviet period and have maintained their devotion to ore extraction. The thought that the nation has enough space to handle pollution by simply putting it aside certainly helps maintain these monocities as the tailings and slang pile higher and deeper on their outskirts.

Coal's human, environmental, and economic costs are borne most of all locally, even if coal is an international commodity and is burned in boilers and ovens elsewhere. Russia's Kuzbass, central to future export plans and national energy strategies, offers its coal at great distances to users at home and abroad. The Pechora Basin, in second place in Russia in terms of known reserves with 210 billion tons of high quality and calorific value coal, a significant part of which is coked, faces extreme climate, low population densities, forces of deindustrialization, and poor infrastructure as obstacles to development. Kansk-Achinsk basin coal reserves are estimated at 600 billion tons.[91]

Densities of population and industry exacerbate serious problems in the Kuzbass: 70 percent of the population and virtually all industry and mines are located in just 30 percent of the territory. The entire Kemerovo region has become a mining-metallurgical hero combine. There are simply too many enterprises in the region, almost 1,500 of them, and the state body to regulate them, Goskomekologiia (the State Committee on Ecology) of Kemerovo, is not up to the task. It monitors: 21 enterprises of ferrous and nonferrous metallurgy, 126 coal-mining and coal-processing enterprises, 18 thermal-power engineering facilities, 10 chemical enterprises, 83 machine-building and metal-working plants, 184 construction-industry enterprises, and 308 enterprises of rail and motor transport and road services, as well as agricultural, food, light industry, and furniture enterprises and numerous steam heating plants, all concentrated within 95,700 km^2.[92]

As a result, the rivers of the Kuzbass run green, brown, and black. Over 1.5 million tons of pollutants and roughly 0.5 million m^3 of contaminated effluents annually fill the Kuzbass. Slag and runoff have fouled the Tom River, flowing through Mezhdurechensk, Novokuznetsk, and Kemerovo.[93] Water quality is well below safety norms. Petroleum products, phenols, metal compounds, ammonium, and nitrites are major problems; as mining increases, water demand and pollution also increase in the major rivers of the region, the Tom, Inya, Chulym, and Chumysh Rivers basins. Over 100 million m^3 of wastewater from the districts of Belovo, Leninsk-Kuznetsky, Guryevsk, and Promyshlennov were discharged into the Inya River in a recent year, of which 90 percent was treated, but ultimately only 10,000 m^3 met standards. Together with wastewaters, 125,000 tons of pollutants were discharged into the rivers of the basin, including 249 tons of toxins and 20,562 tons of pollutants with reduced toxicity.[94] Discharges of solids of all sorts exceed safety levels 2 to 34 times from mines near the Big Bachat, Bungurska, Aba, Olzheras, Kondoma, and Garshina Rivers.[95] All these rivers link to the Ob

River basin as tributaries of its upper reaches. To put it another way, the coal industry discharges almost 60 percent of untreated waters into Kuzbass water bodies. More wastewater is to be expected: when mines are closed, they are flooded, and this water will likely discharge into surface and subsurface water streams.

According to Slivyak, "Each year, 360 million cubic metres of air are blown into Russian underground mines, and over 200 million tonnes of water are pumped out. At open-cast mines, between 300 million and 350 million tonnes of rock are shifted into waste dumps. With open-cast mining, solid particles—inorganic dust containing silicon dioxide, coal ash and black carbon (soot)—are the main pollutants. In the Kemerovo Region alone every year, over 1.5 million tonnes of pollutants are emitted into the atmosphere, and over half a million cubic metres of polluted wastewater are discharged. A 2011 report on the state of the environment in the region estimates that the average concentrations of harmful air pollutants were two or three times higher than the allowable maximum in Russia. On a number of occasions, they exceeded these limits by as much as 18 times."[96] And as if these environmental concerns weren't bad enough: Ukrainian mines have become a site of military conflict between Russia and Ukraine, with Russian-backed separatists threatening to flood the Yunkom coal mine in the occupied Donbas, the site of a Soviet peaceful nuclear explosion in 1979, with danger because of radioactivity entering the drinking water of thousands of Ukrainians in Russia-controlled eastern Ukraine.[97]

In Putin's Russia, such regions as the Kuzbass will continue to suffer extensive pollution, public health risks, and industrial safety problems owing to coal's persistence as a state hero project. The proximity and cheapness of coal for local people in the coal basins means that most homes use it for heating, too, and there is no interest or investment capital to lay natural gas pipelines to replace coal; pipelines are needed to earn Euros by pumping gas and liquid west to Europe, although Europe will wean itself from Putin's gas in response to his brutal invasion of Ukraine. Similarly, the wealthier European part of Russia gets its heat and electricity in greater shares from gas and nuclear power—and those lucky citizens breathe somewhat cleaner air and drink somewhat more potable water.

The Kremlin loves coal, it has loved coal for over a century, and it shows no interest in giving up its rich fields. Coal is ultimately a rather simple, if violent, large-scale technology. The industry builds on rich deposits, and it opens mines nearby to rivers for transport and processing purposes, or builds railroads, for twenty-five years using gulag prisoners, and later employing pliant and cowed workers. Its directors have always been closely tied to the Kremlin. The continued development of coal combines in Siberia means further environmental degradation and the loss of social safety nets for exploited workers and their families. Little has changed since the Bolsheviks started tapping Siberian coal through hero projects a century ago.

ILLUSTRATIONS PART I

Hero projects—large-scale technological systems—have been the centerpiece of Soviet and post-Soviet Russian development projects for over a century—from the Tsars and the commissars to the oligarchs, and from Vladimir Lenin to Vladimir Putin. They have centered on extractive industries—coal, oil and gas, copper, nickel and platinum; transport; waterworks; and such high-technology areas as atomic energy and space. Hero projects, "projects of the century," and megaprojects, as they have been called by successive Russian leaders, and by the appreciative masses, served the strategic, economic, political, and cultural functions of transforming the nation into a superpower, extending the horizons of state control, and molding citizens into conscious workers engaged in joint, often heroic, efforts to create a glorious, modern empire.

Yet hero projects have had significant environmental and social costs, leaving a scarred landscape behind. They have forced workers, peasants, and indigenes into a resource empire dominated by the Kremlin and for the benefit of the Kremlin. Russian leaders, from Lenin to Stalin and Brezhnev, claimed that hero projects were essential to protect the country from enemies both within the country and at its borders. They relied on slave labor in the gulag to build much of the extractive infrastructure, or simple coercion, or exhortations to toil for the state. After the gulag camps closed, citizens continued to work, but with stagnant wages, and they faced shortages in housing, food, and social services in return as payment.

Russia remains a resource empire, whose leaders and engineers entertain hubristic visions of power and glory based on extraction of its wealth. Its leaders seek to build railways across the Arctic Circle and dredge canals to siphon off water from its great Siberian rivers for export to customers in Central Asia and China. It invests fully in the infrastructure of Arctic assimilation. It extracts oil, gas, diamonds, and gold to power the engine of economic and military strength. It has become an empire of technological paradox, of oil derricks and pipelines, but polluted waters and displaced people; of rockets and reactors, yet hardly functional roads and railroads; of fantastical canals, yet inefficient irrigation networks and persistent floods; of nuclear power stations and dreams of a journey to Mars—perhaps to claim as Russia's—but which uses hero projects to pursue imperial claims to land and resources from Europe to the Pacific and from Central Asia to the North Pole.

Railroads Extended the Empire, Moved Troops, and Facilitated Commerce

Coal and Hero Projects. Gulag prisoners ("*zeks*") interned in the Sevzheldorlag (the Northern Railway Labor Camp), one of scores of camps across the nation, built the Kotlas-Vorkuta Line in Northwest Russia to enable forestry and coal operations. Sevzheldorlag shipped coal from the Pechora basin to feed the Red Army in World War II after Ukraine's Donetsk basin coal region had fallen to the Nazis, cutting off that strategic supply to the front. Sevzheldorlag held 85,000 *zeks* at its maximum in 1941 and closed in 1950.

Image 1 *Zeks* in a series of smaller camps laid track from Kotlas 800 km to the northeast to the coal mining town of Vorkuta in the Pechora Basin. As *zeks* in other camps, these men in the Kniazhpogost outpost toiled as lumberjacks to produce wood for ties and bridges. Source: Archives of the Komi Republic.

BAM—the Baikal-Amur Mainline Railroad.

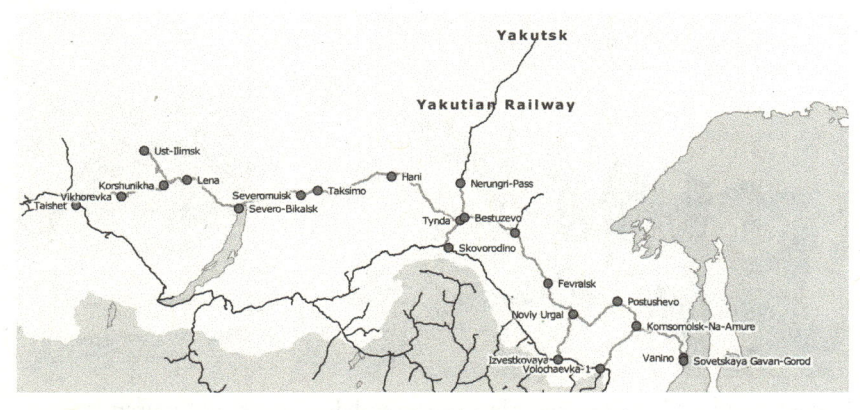

Image 2 BAM, a never-completed railroad hero project of gulag laborers under Joseph Stalin, and a "project of the century" of Leonid Brezhnev, was intended to open Siberia to further economic development and meet strategic defense needs of the USSR, and to augment the Trans-Siberian railroad built at the turn of the previous century. BAM ran from Taishet to Soviet Gavan' (Harbor) on the Pacific. The authorities declared it completed in the 1980s, but the last segments opened around 2003, and it many places it still has only one track, while freight speeds in a number of regions are under 50 km/hour. Source: Wikimedia Commons.

Stalin's Polar Magistral (Arctic Railroad). "The Road of Death."

Images 3 and 4 Gulag prisoners laid rails—and died in tens of thousands—on Stalin's polar railroad (late 1940s—abandoned weeks after Stalin's death in 1953). This "hero project" lacked not only properly paid, clothed, and fed workers, but ballast, rails, and lumber. It remained far from completion when halted. It has become a site of investigation by curious tourists. Vladimir Putin supports plans to restart and finish Stalin's last railroad, now called the Northern Lateral Railroad, but financial and other obstacles have so far blocked any progress. Source: Archives of the Komi Republic.

Arctic Oil and Gas: Twenty-first-Century Heroes.

Images 5, 6, and 7 The city of Novyi Urengoi, established in 1973 in the Yamalo-Nenets Autonomous Region in the northern West Siberia Basin, has the world's second largest natural gas field with 10 trillion m³. In January 2013, Prime Minister Dmitry Medvedev visited the Zapoliar'noe gas treatment installation, 220 km from Novyi Urengoi. The megaproject infrastructure of wellheads, compressors, pipelines, railroads, and roads enables Moscow to control Arctic oil and gas. Source: Russian Postal Service; Office of the President of the Russian Federation.

Images 8 and 9 Hero projects subjugated both Arctic lands and Arctic people. The Nenets people who engage in nomadic reindeer herding in the Taimyr, Yamal, and other regions of the Arctic—and other indigenes—have long been considered "quaint" for their lifestyle. This 1933 postal issue, on the eve of Stalin's violent effort to force the Nenets into collective reindeer farms to secure the fur and meat of reindeer for the proletariat, and because of the belief that people of the north were hostile to communism, captures this view of the "simple" Nenets people, while a 2005 stamp shows a solitary Nenets teepee in an Arctic landscape of cities, fisheries, and gas operations under the gaze of the powerful Slavic conqueror. Source: Russian Postal Service.

Coal Mining. Fossil Fuels for the Kremlin.

Images 10 and 11 Soviet postage stamps celebrated the glories of labor. A series of 1948 issues commemorates the "Day of the Miner," one of many such holidays and other trappings of Soviet customs that have been resurrected in the Putin era to maintain pride in the imperial Russian effort. Another stamp (1958) urges miners, guided by small lamps, to raise production from 496 million to over 600 million tons of coal production by 1965 in the Seventh Five-Year Plan. To this day, miners toil in dangerous conditions at low wages with few rights, and they hardly share in the profits of their efforts. Source: Russian Postal Service.

Kuzbass Coal Mining. Osinnikovskii Mine in 1987.

Image 12 The Kuznetsk Basin (Kuzbass) is one of the largest coal mining areas in Russia at 26,000 km^2, with deposits estimated at 725 billion tons. The Osinnikovskii Mine in Kemerovo region sits in a landscape of black riprap and overburden. It is the site of extensive pollution and hardship for the miners and their families, yet calorific importance to the empire. The miners have struggled, both under Soviet power and in Russia today, for higher wages, safer conditions, safe water, and reclamation of ravaged lands, but are essentially forbidden to strike. National strikes in 1989 during the Gorbachev era were a sign that the social contract between the state and the miners had failed. The importance of coal for the Russian leaders has remained from Catherine the Great to Stalin and to Putin. Source: Wikimedia Commons.

The Gulag in Service of Hero Projects. Waterworks, railroads, forestry operations, smelters—built by slave laborers—especially in weakly settled regions of the Arctic and sub-Arctic north, Siberia and the Far East.

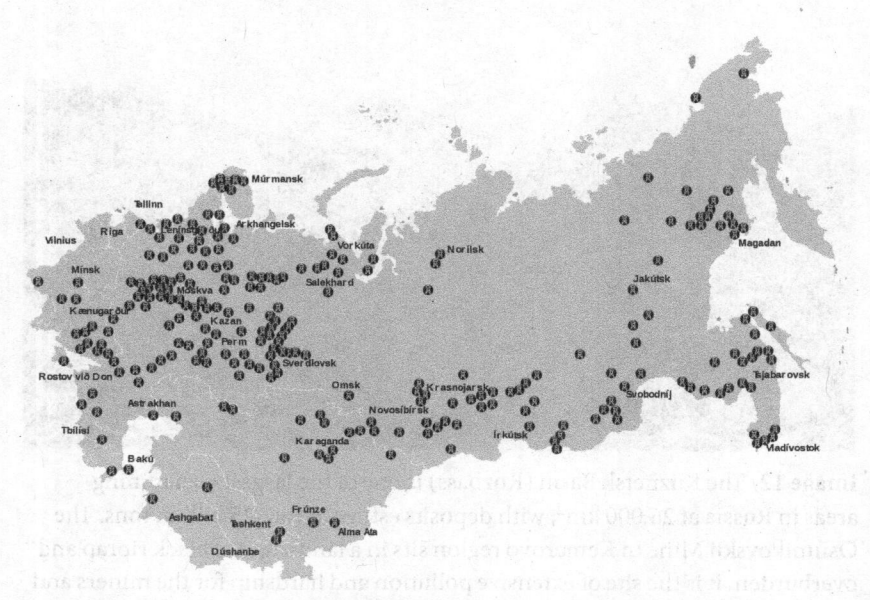

Image 13 From the 1930s, authorities used the gulag camps to accelerate the efforts at the control and subjugation of resources with armies of poorly fed and attired prisoners (referred to in slang as *zeks*) being shipped to thinly settled regions to break the tundra and fell the taiga. The gulag grew to include waterworks, forestry, rail, and other divisions. The gulag gave birth to the White Sea–Baltic Canal in Karelia and dozens of other waterworks projects that filled the nation from west to east over time. Indeed, gulag bosses pushed the *zeks* from the northwest to the central regions of the country to Siberia, the Far North, and the Far East, occupying other regions, undertaking other projects, and consuming more prisoners. Gulag workers were central to efforts to take the frontier, fill the distant reaches of the empire, build infrastructure, extract coal and other ore, raise smelters, and prepare for war with capitalist nations. Hundreds of thousands of them died in the camps between 1928 and 1953, when the camps began to empty out in an amnesty that commenced after Stalin's death. A number of Russian corporations and agencies have roots as gulag organizations, for example, the gulag administration responsible for canals and dams that became the Zhuk Gidroproekt Institute in the 1950s and then Rusgidro under Putin. Source: Wikimedia Commons.

Gulag Canals: The Moscow-Volga Canal.

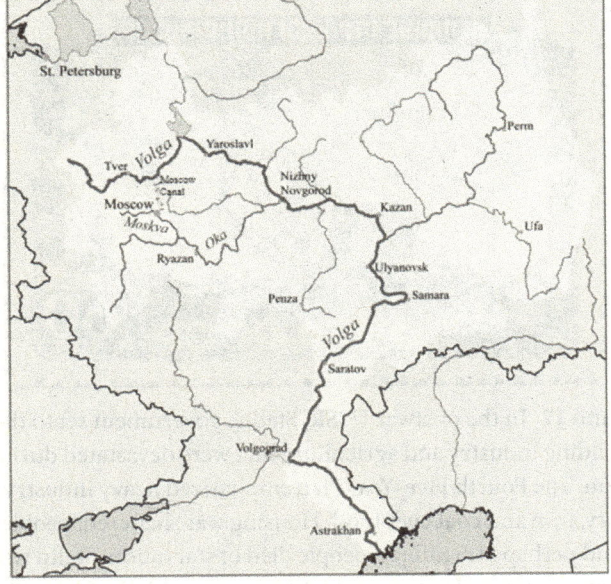

Images 14 and 15 The Moscow-Volga Canal (1932–1937), Stalin's second hero project after the White Sea–Baltic Canal, and one that used prisoners exported from the White Sea region to Moscow, was intended to link Moscow with the greatest river in Europe, the Volga, known as the Mother of Russia, and to guarantee water for municipal and industrial purposes of the capital of the glorious socialist nation. This 1947 stamp was issued on the thirtieth anniversary of the Russian Revolution. Source: Russian Postal Service.

The Stalin Plan to Transform Nature (1948).

Images 16 and 17   In the postwar USSR, Stalin's government set to the massive task of rebuilding industry and agriculture that were devastated during the Nazi invasion. The Fourth Five-Year Plan emphasized heavy industry over light industry, iron and coal over food. Housing was shattered, people lived in rubble, and perhaps 1.5 million people died of starvation. Stalin would not rest, setting in motion a plan to rebuild nature itself with the Stalin Plan for the Transformation of Nature (1948). The goal of the plan was to incorporate all of the major central Russian riverways into a transportation, hydroelectric, and irrigation machine—that would eventually extend through other canals and rivers to Leningrad (St. Petersburg) and to the Black Sea. The plan included "forest defense belts"—70,000 km of trees planted in bands up to 300 m in width—to protect fields from hot winds, and a series of other hero projects—dams, canals, and so on. These post office issues celebrate the forest defense belts and the Main Turkmen Canal in Turkmenistan (1950—and abandoned as abject failure in 1954 after Stalin's death). Only 5,000 km of forest defense belts were ever planted. Source: Russian Postal Service.

3

Water and Empire[*]

—Чем дальше в лес, тем больше ГЕС.
—The farther into the forest, the bigger the hydropower station.[1]

Water is a valuable commodity, and it will likely grow in importance in the twenty-first century in response to climate change, population growth, and other factors. Agriculture consumes four-fifths of the water in the United States; about 8 percent of this is for irrigation agriculture. Water scarcity is becoming a growing problem in the European Union. China likely has sufficient water resources to continue on its path of economic expansion through the twenty-first century, but 80 percent of that water is in southern parts of the country, while substantial amounts of water are needed for industry and agriculture in the north; its $62 billion South North Water Transfer Project (SNWTP) will divert 44.8 billion m^3 of water annually to the population centers of the drier north by linking China's four main rivers—the Yangtze, Yellow River, Huaihe, and Haihe—through three diversion canals. In addition, China is negotiating a project with Russia to sell water from its Altai region that would be pumped and prodded through transfer canals into the Ningxia and Shanxi regions.

In fact, Russia, the commodity state par excellence, has engaged in preliminary talks with China about the sale of Siberian river water through as-yet-to-be-designed, but no doubt frightfully expensive, transfer canals. Ambitious waterworks projects are paradigmatic for Russia and have had a place for several hundred years. Tsarist engineers advanced dam, canal, and transfer projects to accelerate industrialization, resource assimilation, and settlement. Under the Soviets, the projects took off in number and grandeur through massive ministries that commanded equally massive budgets, branch research institutes, construction operations, and the complete authority of the Communist Party to alter river basins. The descendants of those ministries and design institutes have begun to assemble a portfolio of

Hero Projects. Paul R. Josephson, Oxford University Press. © Oxford University Press 2024.
DOI: 10.1093/oso/9780197698396.003.0004

similarly ambitious projects in Russia in the twenty-first century. Working with transportation, resource extraction, and other state bodies, they embrace hero projects to enhance Russia's role as a resource state.

The impressive list of Russian waterworks projects covers all kinds of engineering projects in every geography and climate imaginable: dams, canals, hydroelectric power stations, irrigation systems, and reclamation projects; above the Arctic Circle, in arid Central Asia, and in the deep frosts of Siberia. Russia has long been a major world power in civil engineering works, in construction and pouring concrete, and in putting large organizations into motion to achieve state ends. First advanced by Tsarist engineers, promoted by the state during the Lenin years, forced upon the landscape during the Stalin years with the establishment of research firms and constructions trusts and the spread of the gulag, and assuming all-union proportions in the postwar years, water projects were as central to Soviet self-notions of legitimacy, state power, and modernity as space and atomic energy. Waterworks demonstrated to citizens from all walks of life the glories of state power and modern science. Waterworks were crucial to rapid industrialization, collectivization, and agriculture. They served transport. They generated electricity. The provided water to burgeoning cities. They celebrated despots whose names and massive statues adorned them, for example, that of Stalin towering 37 m over the Moscow Canal.

If big engineering projects fell on hard times after the breakup of the USSR, under President Vladimir Putin they have been reborn. They include rekindled efforts to raise hydroelectric power stations on Siberian rivers to increase vastly the nation's electrical power generation capacity—and to serve aluminum, petrochemical, and other industries. Russia has recaptured the verve of the Soviet period, and many of the institutes, ministries, and state corporations connected with these efforts have recaptured the momentum of their predecessor Soviet design institutes, ministries, and construction firms. Noteworthy are the efforts of the state hydroelectric power agency, RusGidro, to complete some of the world's largest stations on Siberian rivers that were mothballed in the Soviet era, and to embark on new ones, including interbasin transfer projects to Central Asia and China. While the government is committed to these projects, it faces significant financial obstacles to achieving them and growing concerns about their social and environmental costs. It has not paid sufficient attention to the need for upkeep, renovation, or removal of increasingly decrepit Soviet-era waterworks. The aging of dams and other concrete structures is a fact of life everywhere, but Russian officials will need to be very attentive to this critical problem, as the accident at the Saiano-Shushensk hydroelectric power station (hereafter "GES," the Russian acronym) in August 2009 indicates. At the same time, surprisingly, many Russian citizens have inadequate access to safe water. Yet the projects are so important to the nation's leaders that they reject public opposition to any of them. While expensive, often environmentally unsound with unheeded negative social impacts, and, as many citizens worry, unnecessary, leaders insist that waterworks go ahead. The projects have acquired nearly unstoppable momentum because of their symbolic, political, and strategic nature, and because many supporters believe they will recreate the technological glories of Soviet power.

Waterworks after the Russian Revolution

There is a seamlessness to the history of canals, dams, and reclamation projects from Tsarist to contemporary times. The projects are timeless testimony to the achievements of a modernizing society, its workers, its engineers, and its bosses. At first the projects were small-scale and utopian in their conception and in the accompanying certainty that dams and canals would lead directly to revolutionary changes in the socialist economy and society. The waterworks grew larger and larger as armies of laborers were dedicated to them. If the projects were touted as a matter of the entire people, they were in fact the physical manifestation of the ability of an authoritarian regime to command resources of labor and capital to enhance its power, and they served symbolically to enhance the legitimacy of the state. From the 1920s to the 1960s, the authorities forced the projects from the center to the periphery to power resource extraction for the Kremlin, meet the strategic interests of the state, and secure the empire against enemies.

Lenin was a technological utopian. He believed that the production of copious amounts of electricity would enable the rapid construction of communist society in short order. In 1920, Lenin promoted a fifteen-year State Plan for the Electrification of Russia (in Russian known as GOLERO), with Gleb Krzhizhanovsky its first director who later served as head of the State Planning Agency, GOSPLAN. Lenin considered GOELRO a kind of "second party program." GOELRO was based on a system of central production and distribution stations (largely peat and increasingly hydroelectricity) serving eight districts. GOELRO would overcome extremely low capacity in comparison with Europe and the United States, and magically transform labor, agriculture, and society through socialist productive relations.[2]

In the 1920s under the leadership of engineers trained in the Tsarist era, and with technology imported from the United States and Europe, the Bolsheviks built several flagship GES that served as kind of a blueprint for future decades and projects. Lenin personally joined GOELRO engineers in approving the first modern facility, the Volkhovsk station northwest of St. Petersburg, whose machine-hall, visible from the St. Petersburg–Murmansk train that passes by, has almost a Bauhaus aesthetics; Lenin died before its completion in 1926.[3] Officials made the project a priority, requisitioning what they might from as far away as Siberia as Soviet industry struggled to recover from war and revolution. Construction dragged on for over five years, and it consumed 16,000 tons of iron, 80,000 tons of cement, five million bricks, and 40,000 m^3 of stone.[4] In a paradoxical combination of men armed with rudimentary tools, technological lag, and naïve enthusiasm, the construction site resembled many of the other later Soviet sites as engineers, party officials, unskilled workers, and political prisoners from burgeoning gulag camps moved across the landscape from river basin to river basin, and from the northwest to the Volga River and then to Siberian rivers with increasingly powerful, but still inadequate, machinery and equipment. The fact that the authorities designated the project a priority also became paradigmatic for Soviet and post-Soviet waterworks. Hero projects that had the Kremlin's attention received the nation's labor and capital inputs as needed.

Even with Lenin's support of new construction projects to build "electrified communism," many projects faltered in the early years. Some faltered because of lack of funding. Others could be no more than the dreams of engineers under conditions of political anarchy, civil war, and economic free fall; the empire's production reached 1914 levels again only in 1926. Still others failed because of vigilant—overly vigilant—secret police who saw enemies everywhere, including among Tsarist engineers. They saw these people as untrustworthy enemies, even if Lenin urged and personally ordered cooperation with them. The experience of Georgii Konstantinovich Rizenkampf, a visionary engineer whose own dream was the establishment of irrigated fields in Central Asia that extended to the horizon and opened agriculture in the desert—and which incorporated Muslim peoples into the nation through modern technology—indicates the challenges of pursuing waterworks in the early Soviet republic.[5]

Rizenkampf was international in his roots, and this ensured he was always suspect to secret police (Cheka) officers. Born in 1886 in Yerevan, Armenia, Rizenkampf lost his father at two; his mother remarried a lieutenant general (Rizenkampf) who adopted him. He entered Petersburg Institute of Communications Engineering. Specializing in hydrotechnology and water transport, he went to Germany, Austria, Switzerland, and Italy for study and to observe hydrotechnological works. Upon graduation he was sent to the Technical Department of the Caucasus Mountains Regional Communications division. In 1910 he returned to Petersburg to audit classes at the university and work in the Ministry of Interior, where he carried out research on irrigation projects in the Caucasus and Turkestan, and he developed a scheme for irrigation in the Hungry Steppe in Kazakhstan; with his assistance an irrigation system main canal opened in October 1913. In 1915 he was transferred to the Ministry of the Interior, where he created an administration for hydrotechnological studies to serve the needs of the Army of the Northern Front and also worked at the Petrograd Polytechnic Institute and the Institute of Means of Communication.

Like a number of other Tsarist specialists who carried their engineering enthusiasm forward into the Soviet period, no matter the politics of the Bolsheviks or their mistrust of Tsarist specialists, in 1918 Rizenkampf turned to Lenin with a report on the state of irrigation in Turkestan and appended a project for a new scheme. Lenin indeed paid sincere attention to oceanographers, foresters, hydrologists, Arctic explorers, and "bourgeois specialists" generally, and he supported their efforts directly on many occasions, signing slips of paper in his office with a handwritten proclamation that the scientist in question merited unquestioned support in the given project, and directing the appropriate commissariat to follow through. A May 17, 1918, decree of the Sovnarkom (Council of Ministers) created a Special Administration of Irrigation of Turkestan (IRTUR) under Rizenkampf's direction that turned quickly to onsite surveys. If IRTUR was intended to develop irrigation in the Hungry Steppe of Samarkand region, the Kurgan Steppe of Fergana Region, and fill a reservoir on the Zeravshan River to expand local cotton textile industry, all in a revolutionary fashion, and all as approved by decree of the Supreme Economic Council (VSNKh) with Lenin's imprimatur, then someone forgot to tell the vigilant local secret police. Samara chekists, unfamiliar with the equipment that was shipped from Moscow to Turkestan, invented some kind of counterrevolutionary activities surrounding IRTUR. In November 1918 some 200 personnel, with roughly 1,000 family members, arrived in Samara and took rooms in the Grand Hotel on Soviet Street. The commandants of the municipal Cheka arrived, cursorily inspected Lenin's work order, rejected the paperwork, and instead incarcerated the entire irrigation team, even secretaries and cooks, Rizenkampf among them.

Rizenkampf's protests got nowhere. The Cheka interrogated everyone and confiscated all the expeditionary property, but never charged the team with any crime, although hoping to prove they were some kind of anti-Soviet organization that intended to join up with the monarchist Whites. Only a month later, after two explicit orders from Lenin, did the Chekists begin to release the irrigationists. In late February, three months after the affair began, the Chekists admitted that no kind of "counterrevolutionary activity" had been established. Still, they kept several men in Butyrsk Prison into 1920. Rizenkampf continued work in IRTUR and helped organize Turkestan University with an engineering-melioration and irrigation department as a professor. Unfortunately, the IRTUR experience set a precedent for the arbitrary behavior of the Cheka, NKVD, and KGB, such as that with the Shakhty Affair later in the decade (see chapter 2): they could arrest with impunity; took perverse interest in suspecting the loyalty specialists, engineers, and technologists working in industrial enterprises, waterworks, and on the railroad; and in spite of written requirements that they follow written rules and keep written records, they did not. IRTUR left Samara and in August 1919 transferred all of its irrigation projects to VSNKh, which caused irrigation projects to slow to a trickle, while Rizenkampf became a consultant on Turkestan.[6]

Yet Rizenkampf was a fearless irrigator. In 1921 he published *Trans-Caspian Canal* about a proposed canal route from the source of the Amudarya River in Afghanistan to the west, across irrigation systems of the Murgab and Tedzhena, then along a railway line through Ashkhabad and Kyzylarvat to the Caspian Sea—a distance of more than 1,300 km and a clear fantasy in the 1920s, not the least from the point of view of finances. In the meantime, reclamation specialists from the Institute of Means of Communication succeeded in expanding cotton culture from 250,000 to 350,000 hectares in the Hungry Steppe on the left bank Syrdarya River further to the north. These projects, like the Tsars' military settlements and the Soviets' railroads, were intended to bring in thousands of Slavic agriculturalists to settle and work.[7]

Rizenkampf remained in hot water the rest of his life.[8] From 1924 to 1929, Rizenkampf refined his irrigation projects with a new scheme using the Syrdarya River. He was then arrested, like many other engineers, in 1929 as part of a national scandal of show trials for wrecking and anti-Soviet activity, received a three-year term, and was sent to work as an engineer on the first great Stalinist hero project, the White Sea–Baltic Canal. Released in 1932, he next headed a Special Central Bureau of Gidroenergoproekt that advanced a general plan to reconstruct the Volga, the "Big Volga," including organization of irrigation, a massive project interrupted by World War II and realized to a great extent by the time of Stalin's death in 1953. But Rizenkampf was arrested again, in Moscow, in 1941 or 1942, was sentenced to ten years in the Temnikovskii camp, and died in 1943; his skills as an irrigation engineer had been used instead to fell trees and lay railroad tracks for Stalin.[9]

Waterworks in the Stalin Era

Stalin intended to remake nature through waterworks. He saw natural barriers of climate, season, geography, and topography as obstacles to state priorities no less than people he believed were enemies of the state—so-called wreckers, Trotskyites, counterrevolutionaries, spies, and a host of other evil nemeses. From the commencement of rapid industrialization and collectivization of agriculture at the end of the 1920s, the Communist Party pursued geoengineering projects that grew in scale over the decades and extended the geographic reach of the state to the periphery of the empire, enabled access to previously remote, if rich resources, and secured their transportation, all with a goal of creating a unitary, centrally controlled economy. The resulting waterworks construction fury was among the greatest in world history, rivaling those in the American West, and the more contemporary efforts of China, Brazil, and India.[10] While a number of authors have covered the Stalin period, it bears discussing two important points here briefly: the gulag roots of many of the waterworks, and the increasing grandeur and reach of these so-called hero projects.[11] The first projects generally commenced in the northwest of the nation and were then designated for the center of the great landmass—the rivers of central Russia and Ukraine—before being forced to the Arctic, Siberia, and Central Asia with vast armies of prisoners.

Soviet waterworks projects originated in gulag labor camps in the early 1930s; many of them grew precisely out of the operations of the White Sea–Baltic Canal (1931–1933). The OGPU-NKVD (secret police) administrations ordered equipment, personnel, and prisoners from the canal to the next major project, the Moscow-Volga Canal (1932–1937). By the late 1930s, Stalin's secret police commanded huge numbers of prisoners in bold and massive projects that dominated the horizon and commanded resources from Europe to the Pacific. The heartless slave labor bureaucracies were transformed into legitimate, public organizations in the post-Stalin era, and have found new inspiration in the twenty-first century as RusGidro, which is equally heartless but flows along on paid workers.

In *Oriental Despotism* (1957), Karl Wittfogel analyzed "hydraulic civilizations" that he believed predominated in Eastern Asia, wherein states that relied heavily on irrigation required substantial and centralized control of resources, and that this resulted in an absolutist managerial state. He noted the frequent use of forced labor in these civilizations.[12] Stalin's empire according to these criteria was such a hydraulic civilization.

Let us remember in the United States, as well, that engineers and policymakers pressed the nation to tame water resources. Like the Soviets, they equated hydroelectricity with democracy. In the 1930s, as part of the New Deal, and as part of a global fascination with electricity and a way to put people back to work during the Great Depression, the US government supported a rapid increase in the size and reach of the power grid to bring electricity to the masses and especially to poor folk. How much of this was a universal utopian embrace of electricity, how much a direct response to Soviet electrification programs "in the name of the toiling masses," how much of it was the need to respond to citizens with concrete proof that government cared for them during the horrors of unemployment, poverty, and hunger during the Great Depression are important questions to ponder. But the fact is that planners assumed electricity would magically solve the problems of the Great Depression and strengthen democracy itself.[13] Other US projects—the Central Valley agricultural system in California, the engineered Columbia River basin of hydroelectricity, agribusiness irrigation and plutonium production—share the features of promises of enlightenment of the masses and their magical lifting from poverty and backwardness.[14] In China, too, a series of costly, massive and environmentally questionable hydropower stations (e.g., Three Gorges Dam), interbasin transfer projects, and irrigation systems, and in Australia, the Snowy Mountains scheme, all of which were set forth as economically viable, demonstrate that Stalin's projects were not the result of the machinations of a madman but standard fare for big twentieth-century projects.[15]

Whatever the historiographic debates, Stalin's hydraulic civilization was built by an authoritarian government that employed armies of slave laborers. Stalin pushed the nation to build waterworks that would out-illuminate and out-flow those in the United States. After the interruption in projects by World War II, Stalin insisted on an even bolder construction effort of canals to link the nation into a gigantic transportation network and a hydroelectrical factory with stepped dams on major rivers, especially along the Volga River, in his Stalin Plan for the Transformation of Nature (1948) culminating in the Kuibyshev GES, at the time of its completion in 1957 the largest dam in the world.

After Stalin's death most of the gulag administrations that had carried out construction of roads, railroads, canals, and dams were reconstituted as legitimate Soviet design institutes, construction firms, and other industrial objects, and many of them have found a post-Soviet incarnation as quasi-public state corporations; the giant gulag hydroelectric and melioration organization became the Zhuk Gidroproekt Design Institute in Moscow, named after its first director, a former camp prisoner and later NKVD colonel, Sergei Zhuk. Gidroproekt became RusGidro after the breakup of the USSR.

Some of the projects advanced by design organizations and ministries boggle the mind. Gidroproekt proposed a dam on the Bering Sea to connect Chukotka and Alaska; a cascade of twelve dams on the Yenisei River, to some extent still under development, all far from consumer or industrial demand; diversion of waters from the Danube to the Dnipro; the Lower Lena hydroelectric power station at Tiksi, not far from the Laptev Sea, a structure 118 m tall (a forty-story building!) with a reservoir stretching 1,694 km south into Yakutia rated at 28 GW, larger than China's Three Gorges Dam; and a dam across the Strait of Gibraltar.[16] Gidroproekt engineers and other hydro-apologists in India, China, Vietnam, Brazil, and elsewhere still tout hydroelectricity for low-cost electricity; positive impacts on microclimates by moderating extremes; improvements in transport over rapids and by increasing navigable length; irrigation; and a general increase in the economic well-being of the nation.

Whatever the economic benefits and their symbolic promise, Stalinist projects were completed precisely because of the requisitioning of slave laborers, tens of thousands of whom died, and they were horrifically costly in other ways, too: to entire families and children orphaned by the state because their parents had been arrested, and to the environment. Yet to make the slaves' achievements palatable, the prisoners—while rarely discussed publicly—were treated as if renewed and reformed by their labor, and having been "reforged" as good citizens, and their works were sometimes immortalized in literary and photographic books, in postage stamps, and other works of art and culture. Thus, these cultural artifacts that stood tall as the achievements of the concrete pourers did not even hint at the mud, din, and disorder of construction sites, let alone the wasting away, starving to death, and murders of these men and women. Instead, waterworks hero projects unfailingly documented Stalin's leadership, and that of the party behind him, as well as unflinchingly heroic efforts to secure the economic and strategic interests of the proletarian state. In an NKDV publication on the Moscow-Volga Canal, the frontispiece shows "Comrade Stalin at the Perevinskii Lock (summer 1936)" (p. 5). The caption notes, "The construction of the Moscow-Volga Canal is the second link in the matter of realization of the genius idea of the leader of the people Comrade Stalin—the radical reconstruction of water routes of the Soviet country." The Moscow-Volga Canal far exceeded the Panama Canal in length, earthen works, and concrete poured; in its magnificent, ornate locks, dams, pumping stations, eight hydroelectrical units; and in its seven reservoirs.[17]

As befitting a proletarian canal, a special aesthetics existed for these and other Soviet projects that is absent in Putin's projects today. To be sure, the locks and dams served the same technical tasks of transport, freight, and shipping. But in furnishings and message, the passenger halls of riverboat stations served and glorified the worker and emphasized the grandeur and omniscience of state power. The Moscow-Volga Canal main Khimki port station had classical terraces and galleries with gracious views of the waters, unlike anything in capitalism, its designers claimed. It was a "historical architectural site" with broad steps, and a high steeple that resembled overall a ship.[18] The construction projects were accompanied by the penning of such wondrous agitation songs as "My Canal," "I Am Prepared!," and "Song of the Concrete Pourers!"[19] The authorities admitted some effort to rehabilitate those condemned to build the canals. Ida Averbakh, daughter of Leopold, who had been head of the Russian Association of Proletarian Writers (RAPP) in the 1920s, and who wrote a paean to slave labor on the White Sea–Baltic Canal with Maxim Gorky in 1934, only to be ostracized and condemned, wrote her own volume on rehabilitation through labor for the Moscow-Volga Canal.[20] For her efforts, like her husband, Genrich Iagoda, head of NKVD for two years until his arrest in 1938, she was shot. In all, 23,000 prisoners died in the Dmitrovlag camp dedicated to building the Moscow-Volga Canal.

Of course, the real reason for these great waterworks was economic: collectivization of agriculture, rapid industrialization, urbanization, and military preparedness would all be enhanced and accelerated. Water was needed as a foundation for amalgamated farms, to feed burgeoning cities, to support mining, metallurgical, and other works. Canals and irrigation found significant response in Central Asian agriculture already in the late 1920s as forced collectivization of nomadic peoples commenced, and continued into the 1980s as in an ill-fated effort to create cotton and fruit culture in deserts 2,300 km to the south for the benefit of the Kremlin. In May 1932 the Supreme Economic Council voted to study the transfer of Amudarya River water toward the Caspian Sea for irrigation purposes. This project commenced in fits and starts as the Main Turkmen Canal and then the Karakum Canal over the next fifty years, with evaporation and salination of water leading to the devastation of the river and the destruction of the Aral Sea.[21] Needing some visible evidence of the friendship of Soviet peoples and success at river diversion, in the late 1930s the authorities ordered the Great Stalin Fergana Canal to be built. This canal ran through the Fergana Valley some 280 km through Uzbekistan and 60 km in Tadzhikistan, and was built in forty-five days in 1939–1940 as a "people's construction site" employing the labor of 160,000 collective farmers—Uzbeks and Tajiks who had just been forced into collective farms—using hand tools in the effort. It took water from the Syrdarya River for cotton irrigation.[22] In the 1950s it was reconstructed to widen and deepen, but it never functioned as intended.

At the Eighteenth Party Congress in March 1939 the Communist Party determined to build a cascade of modern dams on the Volga River. By 1940, engineers were planning how to defend waterworks from invaders. And at the breakout of World War II the Volga dams, the Volga-Don Canal, and the Central Asian canal projects were all put on hold and many of their resources, including men, were transferred to the front for the military effort.[23] The Volga cascade had to wait until the late 1940s. Ultimately, few preparations were undertaken to forestall destruction of most GES in the European USSR when the Nazis attacked—many of them were dynamited by the Soviets themselves to deny the Nazis war booty and electricity.

The Stalin Plan of 1948

After the devastation of World War II, the Communist Party determined to rebuild heavy industry without delay, and accelerate construction of a new, more powerful Soviet Union including with the creation of glorious waterworks more ambitious and extensive than those planned and unfinished in the 1930s. The cascades of dams would power a burgeoning military sector, including nuclear weapons facilities. Levels of investment in housing or the food industry that might have shown the "advantages" of the socialist system for the worker over the capitalist system were forced to wait for decades after Stalin's death.

The Nazi armies destroyed much of the industrial infrastructure of the European USSR during World War II. On top of this, Stalin and military leaders determined to prevent any resources from falling into Nazi hands. They ordered the evacuation of strategic industrial and military sites, if possible, all rolling stock, all engines and wagons, all fuel and grain, all farm animals, and any other raw materials. Still, almost 32,000 industrial enterprises were destroyed during the Nazi invasion.[24] What they could not withdraw, the Soviets themselves destroyed with explosives or fire, including buildings, public records, monuments, homes, dams, locks, and factories— and including the Dnipro hydroelectric power station.[25]

(In autumn 2022 Ukrainian president Volodymyr Zelenskyy publicly accused Russia of plotting to blow up the 350 MW Nova Kakhovka dam [1956] on the Dnipro River with a total reservoir volume of 18.2 km^3 of water, and indeed on their cowardly retreat from Kherson region in October 2022, Russian soldiers booby-trapped the dam and caused some damage. In June 2023 Russian armies blew up the dam, emptying the reservoir, sending the tumult of water downstream, inundating cities, killing people, pets, and farm animals. The reservoir's waters cool the Zaporizhzhia nuclear power station, the largest nuclear power plant in Europe, its waters feed urban centers in the Dnipro River basin, and the reservoir irrigates large areas of southern Ukraine and northern Crimea that Russia annexed in 2015. The fact that Russia would consider employing the same diabolical tactics to destroy Ukrainian people and land that the Soviets had used to deny the Nazis eighty years earlier revealed again the absurdity of Putin's justification of his war on Ukraine based on the brazenly false claim of the need to eliminate Nazis in Kyiv.)

In 1946 the government passed the fourth five-year plan for the rebuilding the socialist economy, and followed this with resolutions to stimulate the construction and modernization of hydroelectricity. In October 1948 the Communist Party unanimously passed the Stalin Plan for the Transformation of Nature.[26] According to the propaganda of the time, nature itself would be subject to the Party's dictates.[27] The Stalin Plan was in fact one program dedicated to improving agricultural performance in the European part of the country and in particular the steppe region of the south. It then became connected with a series of related projects to transform and remodel nature in the USSR, some of which, including the 1948 Plan, became known as "hero projects." In this way the Stalin Plan was more than the 1948 decision alone with its focus on the European USSR, but part of a larger program of economic, scientific, and cultural construction. I use the term "Stalin Plan" as shorthand for this entire series of dam, reservoir, canal, forestry, roadway, and other construction projects, some of which dated to the 1930s, and others of which required significant investments and institutional expansion even to begin in the years following the promulgation of the Plan.[28] In any event, the hero system of survey, design, and construction was established and would hold to the present: study a river's hydrology, topology, flow characteristics, and so on; move from data analysis as quickly as *zeks* permitted toward a series of flood control, water storage, power generation, and irrigation scenarios; almost simultaneously join ministries, design institutes, geological organizations, and construction firms together in the effort; and requisition the labor and capital needed to develop a river basin fully, usually without plans to provide long-term housing, stores, schools, or hospitals. Move eastward into Siberia and repeat.

As Evgenii Burdin notes, the original decision to build Kuibyshev GES was taken in 1937, and already during the construction of the Moscow-Volga canal engineers, surveyors, and geologists under Sergei Zhuk conducted site surveys for the future dam. They re-gathered in Samara, where IRTUR had met its demise, to design the facility that would maximize electrical energy production, improve shipping along the Volga and its tributaries, guarantee extensive irrigation, and be accompanied by the construction of railroad and automobile bridges across the Volga. By 1937, some work had been accomplished in preparation to build two stations, one at 1.2 million kW at the Zhiguli Rapids and the second at 1.4 million kW not far from Samara. In 1940 the authorities established the Moscow Design Administration of Glavgidrostroi, a gulag design organization that worked with transport, fishing, forestry, and other organizations to pursue the dams. "Elektrosila," the largest manufacturer of turbines in the USSR, was joined into the project along with a number of scientific research organizations and universities.[29]

The government and Party passed resolution No. 1339 on August 10, 1937, to build the Kuibyshev hydroelectric complex; the war ended any nascent site preparation. The government published a new resolution to build the Kuibyshev power station only on August 21, 1950, and at a different site. The Stalin Plan itself was a belated response to droughts in 1946 in Ukraine, the Northern Caucasus, Black Earth, Volga, West Siberia, and Kazakh regions in 1946 that contributed, along with Stalin's investment policies that favored industry over agriculture policies, to famine in 1946 that reached its peak in August 1947 and caused at least one million deaths. Construction on the Volga-Don Canal actually predated the Stalin Plan by six months, and itself dated in designs to 1944, and in the popular press to an article in *Tekhnika-Molodezhi* (Technology for Youth!) in 1938. All of these projects were gulag projects and many of the lead engineering and design institutes were gulag organizations.[30]

For its waterworks projects the secret police ultimately established a special division, as it did for railway work and other "branches" of prison industry, in this case the Main Administration of Prisons of Hydrotechnical Construction of the NKVD (GULGTS) in September 1940 that by 1951 held almost 200,000 men. GULGTS worked on repairs and widening of Volga-Baltic and Northern Dvina Routes; rebuilding the Sukhona River; erecting GES on the White Sea–Baltic Canal and at a nearby aluminum combine; and so on. GULGTS and its successor, Gidroproekt, built the Kuibyshev GES.

No sooner had the tide turned at the Battle of Stalingrad (August 1942–February 1943) in the Red Army's favor than the first teams of geologists and surveyors appeared on the Volga River under the direction of Zhuk to select the site and begin planning for the Kuibyshev GES. After the war, they determined to move the site 80 km higher than Kuibyshev along the Volga in part for cost considerations near Stavropol-on-the-Volga (now Tolyatti, a city of 700,000 inhabitants, named after the Italian Communist Palmero Togliatti, and site of the AvtoVAZ factory [1966] run in cooperation with Fiat to build the small, proletarian and underpowered "Lada" vehicle). The poverty-stricken USSR, in the full fever of reconstruction, required attention to food, housing, and light industry, but instead focused on heavy industry, military, and waterworks: the Kuibyshev GES, the South Ukraine Canal, the Main Turkmen Canal, the Northern Crimean Canal, and others.

In connection with the Stalin Plan, an armada of earth movers, canal diggers, concrete pourers, lumberjacks, carpenters, aggregate mixers, explosive experts, and others was unleashed on the Volga River, on its tributaries, on the steppe, and in the forests to turn European Russia into a natural machine. On the Volga they built a total of eight GES over the decades; they planted 5,000 km of forest defense belts (of 70,000 km planned); they irrigated millions of hectares of land. When they finished it (in 1958), the Kuibyshev GES was the largest station in the world and accelerated the powering up of the city of Tolyatti (based on the Kuneevskii Gulag Camp) and the Lada Automobile Factory.[31] All these projects took resources away from the countryside, the provinces, and from any other region where the leadership could not fathom immediate strategic returns. One engineer claimed—in 1949— that 8,500 collective farms, 1,500 machine tractor stations, and 6,000 collective farms had been electrified. Yet the rudimentary power stations providing power to rural farms ranged from 10 to 50 kW in capacity, most were only 20kW, and in fact most farms had no more than a few light bulbs.[32] The point was big projects; large-scale technologies to secure the nation and develop its natural, mineral, and agricultural resources; and to establish, in part through these technologies, control over all citizens in service of the state.

The Kuibyshev GES was a hero project par excellence in its seemingly autonomous ability to command resources. The main construction organization, Kuibyshevgidrostroi, filled up with prisoners who were corralled in Volgolag, Samarlag, and Kuneevlag and other labor camps. The dam required aggregate and concrete and mixing factories; railroads, lumber and ties; roadways and asphalt; conduit, piping, electrical wiring; power lines and towers; a thermal power station; and growing village and municipal demands, structures, stores, hospitals, and so on. The prisoners worked in three shifts, around the clock, 12,000 to 15,000 prisoners at a time, with 2,000 to 3,000 free "volunteers" and specialists joining them. Hundreds of them perished in accidents during construction of the massive foundation pit; the Kuibyshev GES was known to some people as the "fraternal grave." Granted, many *zeks* were able to work off their terms through "exemplary" labor, but why were they in prison in the first place? Did the award of Order of the Red Banner of Labor at the Kuibyshev works to fifteen *zeks* give them joy in their service to the state and convince them the sacrifices of their lives and those of their friends and families were worth it? Political prisoners remained suspect; some gulag camps were closed only in March 1958—and many prisoners were transferred directly into the prison system of the Ministry of Justice.[33]

Colonial Hydraulic Landscapes: The Main Turkmen and Karakum Canals

Central Asian waterworks deserve mention for three reasons: first, those waterworks projects were the epitome of the use of state power to exploit the periphery of the empire in service of the Kremlin; second, a daring, indeed unfettered hubris of these projects persists in the minds of Russia's engineers—and those of Uzbekistan, Tajikistan, and Turkmenistan who were trained in Soviet design institutes and who maintain their enthusiasm about Soviet-scale waterworks—into the twenty-first century; and third, Russia, as a commodity nation, is engaged with these now independent nations in the twenty-first century to develop irrigation projects with Russian water.[34] In pursuit of cotton (and other cash crop) production, the Russian colonists, convinced of their technological superiority, pursued irrigation and other projects that instead destroyed local environments and communities. The Central Asia projects were, and therefore in many ways remain, colonial hydraulic landscapes.

The Main Turkmen Canal was built for irrigation, to drain the waters of the Syrdarya and Amudarya Rivers, dampen the Caspian lowlands, and create cotton and fruit cultures. In fulfilling the dream of watering the Caspian lowlands, Soviet engineers completed the dream of nineteenth-century explorers, nationalists, and settlers to settle and exploit Central Asian territories, develop agro-industrial complexes, and meet the interests of Central Asian leaders and commodity traders. As was typical for many of the Central Asia projects, the canal was a failure even before it was canceled— immediately upon Stalin's death. Water evaporated from it or seeped in the ground, weeds grew and swampland developed, and when abandoned it was clear that, even using one-quarter of the Amudarya's water, hundreds of thousands of hectares of land would never see any water, as the canal in places had slowed to a trickle. Thus, the engineers turned instead to the Karakum Canal, an equally wasteful enterprise that was completed only after thirty years of misplaced investment. The opening and operation of the Karakum Canal left behind one of the signature failures of Soviet hero projects: the destruction of the Aral Sea, where the rivers at one time had finished their desert journey. Starved for water, the Aral Sea has become a parched graveyard of engineering hubris and has transformed into four much smaller lakes that are at risk to evaporate.[35]

Russian explorers began extensive study of the Aral-Caspian basin in the 1870s.[36] A series of military expeditions were responsible for geographical study. The geographers paid special attention to the old riverbed of the Amudarya-Uzboi and the Karakum and Kyzylkum deserts. General N. G. Stoletov, whose brother was a leading physicist, led an 1874 expedition to the Caspian and Aral Seas, with 100 attendants and specialists, and 25 infantrymen. Other expeditions focused on the eastern shore of the Caspian Sea, the Mangyshlak peninsula, where a mothballed breeder reactor sits that produced both electricity and desalinated water for a burgeoning petrochemical industry, and in particular the lower reaches of the Amudarya to ascertain shipping prospects upstream to Bukhara. Together these expeditions added to physico-geographic, geological, meteorological, biological, and soil science knowledge of the region, and reinforced the belief that this was a "hostile" environment that must be tamed by military and scientific force before being settled by Slavs. Russia took control of these lands through annexation (primarily from England). From this point, various Tsarist and later Soviet explorers, scientists, and officers thought about the possibility of irrigation to make the land and people less hostile.[37]

More than 70 percent of the territory of Turkmenistan can be used only for pasture for camels and sheep, and oases occupy 2.5 to 3.0 percent of the land, while nonetheless agriculture earns three-fifths of the republic's revenues. Most agriculture relies on irrigation, deltas, valley rivers, and mountain ravines. Soviet writers asserted that while many nomads suffered along with their animals in the capitalist past, under socialist conditions with state and collective farms, the farmers and their animals would flourish; state support and state-provided water would make good and green what Tsarist engineers left brown and dry.[38]

To transform the situation from one of aridity and exploitation of nomads and peasants under capitalism into a garden of Edenic proletarian freedom, gulag hero projects filled Soviet Central Asia from the late 1920s, from the 100 km long Bassaga-Kerkinskii Canal (1929) that involved tens of thousands of pastoralists forced into construction, to the Great Fergana Canal of the late 1930s that involved hundreds of thousands of people forced into unfamiliar construction sites, to the Main Turkmen Canal, and to the Karakum Canal, 1954–1988, a failed project after thirty years of effort.

The Main Turkmen Canal should have been laid from the Amudarya River to Krasnovodsk on the shore of the Caspian (now Turkmenbashi, where Coal

Khan Tuleev was born), and was supposed to be the second longest in the world at 1,200 km. But the Party could not find adequate funds or laborers for the project. Of six variations for the project, one of which dated to the 1890s, the authorities chose a variant provided by the Central Asian Melioration Institute, Sredazgiprovod. The design indicated a width of 100 m across and 6–7 m deep, and it included 10,000 km of major and distribution canals, 2,000 reservoirs, and three GES at 100,000 kW to irrigate roughly 1.3 million hectares of land and feed 7 million hectares of pasture in the middle of the Karakum Desert. Of course, such a design meant huge amounts of water, very high rates of evaporation, and rapid salination of soils. Shipping was also envisaged between the Volga and Amudarya to unite the Aral with the Caspian, Azov, Black and Baltic Seas, and eventually with the Arctic Ocean, to create during Stalin's rule the world's largest river machine in sheer size and capacity that stretched from Central Asia to Europe. Engineers calculated the need to requisition 5,000 dump trucks, 2,000 bulldozers and excavators, and fourteen suction dredges. In the tradition of Volkhovsk and other early hero projects, it was a "matter of all the people, a site of all-union significance" to be completed by 1957. While Moscow would be the main beneficiary, the entire nation gladly sent the project building materials, trucks, equipment, graders, and books. Newspapers regularly published hundreds of letters from volunteers wishing to work at the "hero project."[39]

No sooner had construction on the canal begun, than at a scientific conference of the All-Union Geographic Society on March 27, 1951, one specialist raised the problem of the declining level of the Aral Sea as a result of decreased river flow, the shrinking of the surface area by 15,000 to 20,000 km^2, its volume by 700 km^3, the water level by 6–7 m, and an increase in salinity by 1.5 gram/liter, although he confidently suggested these negative impacts would be manifested only 200 to 300 years in the future.[40] But Stalin's projects never lacked for the determination or the prisoners to build them in the face of bad engineering news. For the Turkmen Canal, the gulag majors and colonels established two camps: Karakumlag in Nukus, and Takhiatashlag, the former with seven divisions, one of which was for the construction outside of Krasnovodsk on the southern part of the canal with 7,300 workers, engineers, and military construction workers. The noble goals of the canal were cotton culture, reclamation of land in Karakalpakiia and Karakum, and inland water shipping from the Volga to the Amudarya. Stalin himself was said to be involved in the planning and carrying out of construction. One journalist said of him, "He was very proud of the fact that he was not only the all-powerful commander of the fate of men, but of nature itself!"[41] This set a high water mark for later Soviet and Russian leaders to emulate.

So important was Stalin to the Main Turkmen Canal that secret police chief Beria felt free to order its cancellation within a few days of his boss's death. Beria also ordered cessation of the Volga-Baltic Route, the Volga-Ural Canal, the polar railroad, and other hero projects as impossible without the will of Stalin. On April 8, 1954, the Ministry of Agriculture created a commission to liquidate the Main Turkmen Canal; the commission met over two years and spent 130,000 rubles but could not figure out what equipment left behind to rust, rot, and burn under the sun, let alone with the canal bed.

Under Khrushchev, construction of a Central Asian irrigation systems commenced again with the Karakum Canal that had little in common with the previous design. It went from the southern Amudarya to the west in the direction of the Kopet-Daga Mountains, and then north along the Ashkabad-Krasnovodsk railroad—but only for irrigation, not shipping along its 1,445 km length, yet it was finished only in 1988 at 1,300 km long.[42] As usual in the Soviet system where production values outweighed those of comfort, laborers arrived before the work sites were ready for them; builders lived in tents in temperatures ranging from −30° to +30° C. Some of the lucky workers slept in prefabricated units, trailers, or mud-brick houses, but no one had electricity and food was of low quality. Thirst, dysentery, and malaria landed many of them in the hospital. The canal suffered through decades of supply bottlenecks, and from waste, loss, rusting of machinery, and theft.[43] Without proper equipment or adequate labor, the engineers built the canal using an "original method," by first using bulldozers, graders, and steam shovels to open a small section roughly 15 km long, fill it with water, and then bring in huge suction dredges to widen and deepen the canal, using the temporary canal for water, transport, and other needs. To facilitate this approach, many builders were shifted to barracks floating on barges and had floating machine shops.[44] Soon flora, fauna, and civilization moved up to the shores of the canal—birds, for example, that changed their migratory patterns, rested, and even wintered in new wetlands along the canal. The specialists watched as the soil became supersaturated with salt. Excavation lagged, equipment lagged, concrete production lagged.[45] If communism was Soviet power plus electrification, then in the desert communism was concrete, rust, and highly saline irrigation water. For a while, at least, the canal permitted irrigation of

1 million hectares of land for cotton, fruits, and vegetables, and municipal water supply.

The canals were not coercively forced on Central Asian nations and people, but in many cases were welcomed as engines of economic development and symbols of scientific modernity. In the twenty-first century officials and engineers in those countries still count on Soviet-style waterworks like transfer canals as crucial to the national economies. The republics opened branch engineering institutes of Moscow and Leningrad research centers in their own major cities that were staffed by local people who were often trained in Russia, for example, the Institute of Water Problems and Hydrotechnology of the Academy of Sciences of the Uzbek Republic in Tashkent, which after the collapse of the USSR added "Ecology" to the institute's name. Local elites fostered the establishment, with Moscow's support, of entire republican Academies of Sciences. These academies, whose institutes focused on ways to exploit local resources, were established beginning in the war years. Some of the impetus for the academies came during World War II when many Russian and Ukrainian specialists were evacuated from rapidly approaching Nazi armies and who served as the seeds of new institutions. The Cold War provided another push as the union republics joined in the battle against American science and imperialism. Local scientists relished membership as academicians and corresponding members that confirmed their expertise and gave them prestige and status at home and in Moscow. Ultimately, the Soviets founded Academies of Science in Kyrgyzstan (1943), Uzbekistan (1943), Turkmenistan (1951) Kazakhstan (1946), and Tajikistan (1951).

At the Twentieth Party Congress of the Communist Party on February 16, 1956, known for Nikita Khrushchev's secret speech that condemned Stalinism, Sukhan Babaev, first party secretary of the Turkmen Republic, referred to the centrality of waterworks to Central Asian futures, noting that "for centuries the Turkmen people have dreamed about 'big water.' In the years of the five-year plans in the republic, owing to the constant care of the Party massive hydrotechnical works have been built. . . . The republic is covered with a new network of irrigation works. At present the largest in the country, the Karakum Canal is being built, and work will be carried out on the Sara-Iazinsk and second Tedzhenskoe Reservoirs." In his address Babaev acknowledged great achievements in canal construction but also criticized the slow pace of construction.[46] Babaev had training in hydraulic engineering, so likely knew what he was talking about. He was later purged from the party for Stalinist practices.

The current elites of Central Asian nations—Tajikistan, Uzbekistan, Kyrgyzstan—and their predecessors were weaned on irrigation water, and they made their wealth on the control of cotton and fruit sales. If the Tajik, Kyrgyz, and Uzbek nomads were compelled to modernize in the 1920s and 1930s, to abandon pastoralism and nomadism, and worst of all forced into difficult and dangerous settlement in permanent homes, then the new leaders cultivated by the Bolsheviks were sedentary and agronomical, like modern cotton culture itself. They invested in waterworks as the only path to transform their nations into worthy partners in the socialist empire of big and little brothers through production of agricultural and industrial goods and services for distant markets. They willingly embraced the modern scientific enterprise that underpinned the technological wonder world of hero waterworks, and many of them support Russian projects in Siberia and Central Asia into the twenty-first century, including that for a massive transfer canal from the far-off Ob and Irtysh river basins to ensure water for their crops and people.

Waterworkers Subdue Siberian Rivers

During the Khrushchev era (1953–1964), geoengineering organizations came into their own. No longer quasi-secret gulag armies of earth-moving machines and emaciated prisoners, they became reputable design and engineering firms with access to construction machinery and men, and they had the full-throated endorsement of government and party organizations to change the landscape for the better. Local party organizations welcomed small-scale dams, flood control projects, and low-powered hydroelectrical power stations in the effort to democratize waterworks so that not only Moscow benefited. Regional officials were thrilled to see their dreams of greater investment in their cities and in the nearby countryside realized, in part with new waterworks. All the same, hero projects continued to be large-scale, and the ministers and their ministries who made money on nature transformation projects embraced massive investment in their organizations by pursuing massive projects. In this way Gidroproekt, Lengidroproekt, Lengiprovodkhoz, and a variety of other inland water transport and shipbuilding organizations poured water on the Soviet countryside—or siphoned it away, increasingly in such big projects as Central Asian canals and Siberian hydroelectric power stations. The most audacious project involved a multibillion dollar effort to transport water from Siberian rivers to Europe and Central Asia through massive transfer canals.

With European rivers largely tamed, the engineers and policymakers turned their attention to the Siberian Ob, Yenisei, and Angara rivers as part of the general effort to develop Siberian resources, and they are still pondering how to rework these rivers in the twenty-first century. Hero projects were intended to turn each river basin into a kind of integrated machine with dams and hydropower stations creating massive impoundments—reservoirs—to improve transport, generate electricity, control flooding, and enable irrigation where appropriate. Other technologies—roads and railroads, smelters and forest operations—accompanied the construction of GES. The experiences of two hero rivers, the Ob and Angara, reveal the challenges of planners, engineers, and workers in reworking river basins.

For the Angara, complex riverine development had fateful consequences for Lake Baikal by accelerating its industrial transformation, too, by tying the basin's forests to pulp and paper mills and the lake's fisheries into part of the national supply chain. The Angara runs 1,779 km, and its basin holds 38,000 different rivers and streams. The dams have changed the ice regime, increasing its cover and reach, and altered flora and fauna. The shorelines have been damaged. The sharp decline in open water and increased ice thickness have lowered the number of wintering birds fourfold. Siltation and algal blooms are growing, spawning areas have disappeared, and millions of cubic meters of wood have sunk into the depths of the river.[47] Where once flowed a majestic and clean river, now exist dams and highly polluting metallurgical and aluminum enterprises.

The transformation of the Angara River relied initially on the gulag. To push eastward into Siberia and northward into the Arctic, the authorities initially filled the Angara gulag camp (1947–1960), consisting of fifty-six settlements and sub-camps along a 300 km stretch of the Taishet-Bratsk-Lena railroad. They forced some 30,000 *zeks* into railway, civil engineering, forestry, and industrial activities including smelting. In Irkutsk region the Ozernyi and Ilimsk special camps occupied geographically one of the largest camp complexes in the USSR, filling the territory between Taishet and Bratsk. Gulag prisoners worked at the Bratsk GES at the end of the 1950s, when the prisoners were transferred into the Ministry of Justice system to continue as project laborers into the early 1960s.[48] The Kitoisk camp (1947–1961) that reached 59,000 prisoners in 1952 built petrochemical facilities in Angarsk, an oil-refining city of roughly a quarter million people on the Trans-Siberian

Railroad. Rosneft now owns the Angarsk Petrochemical Company, which was commissioned in 1955, and today is one of the largest refineries in Russia, a major petroleum product supplier in Siberia and the Far East that produces more than 200 types of products.[49] The Bodaibinsk camp (1947–1954) extracted gold from nearby hills, using some 7,000 prisoners, while the Usolsk camp (1949–1953), with 1,600 men, built mining equipment. Of course, the western section of BAM was the largest employer for the *zeks* (Taishet—Bratsk—Lena) in connection with Taishetstroi, Angarstroi, the Western Administration of BAM Construction, a Japanese POW camp, Tiashetlag, Angarlag, and Ozerlag.[50]

Engineers ultimately erected five GES, with a sixth planned, on the Angara River to put it into the service of forestry, aluminum, and petrochemical products: the Irkutsk (660 MW, 1956), Bratsk (5,000 MW, 1971), Ust-Ilimsk (3,800 MW, 1978), Boguchansk (3,000 MW, 2015), and Motyginsk (planned). The stations have displaced countless people and inundated tens of thousands of hectares of land. From its sources at the single outflow of Lake Baikal, the Angara River thus itself became a hero project. For some engineers, this was not enough, and they suggested using of 20,000 tons of explosives along that outflow to permit millions of cubic meters of lake water to pour downstream to generate several millions additional megawatts of electricity in the downstream GES. This did not occur, but such hubristic thinking was evident in the decisions to make Baikal an integral part of the river, primarily through building pulp and paper mills on Baikal's shores from the mid-1950s. The intense economic activity on Lake Baikal, the "jewel" of Siberia, the largest freshwater lake in the world by volume, with 1,500 endemic species, has had a lasting negative impact on flora and fauna.[51] Together these projects transformed Irkutsk, only 100 km downstream from Baikal, from a provincial town into a major scientific, educational, and industrial city of aluminum and petrochemicals. When BAM passed along the norther shore of Lake Baikal in the 1970s, it stimulated further regional development. Not only the Angara River, but all of Irkutsk region—and soon Siberia itself—became a big project.

The story for each Siberian dam is the same: envisaging a massive project, engineers, surveyors, and geologists arrived, made calculations, returned to design institutes, came up with plans and blueprints, and got to work. The plan involved ordering labor and materials; identifying sites for aggregate and a new cement factory; erecting support infrastructure including roads and railroads; ousting local people from land to be inundated; and building apartments for them to live, often in worse circumstances, or at least that is how the local people felt, and always with great delay, and never with stores, schools, or hospitals until later.

The Ob River GES, more modest than Angara dams, came together as a concrete sluice dam, an earthen and concrete impoundment, and a shipping canal with a three-chamber lock, with a 1,070 km^2 reservoir, 200 km long and up to 17 km wide, that inundated scores of villages and towns. Its construction required the ousting of around 30,000 people and demolishing over 30,000 structures, and flooded over 80,000 hectares of land. Railroad bridges, roads, and other facilities had to be rebuilt in new locations, with hundreds of kilometers of new roadways and telephone and telegraph lines.[52]

The workers and *zeks* began arriving at the site of the future Ob GES in the late 1940s, where miserable conditions greeted them. They lived in drafty tents if they were lucky. One eyewitness, Taisia Kozlenko, recalled that there was a huge peat bog where they planned to build the dam. Engineers decided to pump out the water, freeze the peat, and then with explosions excavate the stuff. People worked in freezing water shift after shift, twenty-four hours per day. Sometimes they got vodka and warm meals. Excavators submerged, trucks and other vehicles sank in muddy ruts.[53] Eventually they transferred roughly 12 million m^3 of peat, earth, and rock into the earthen dam. On top of this, when they began to close the dam, the weather took a turn for the worse with powerful winds, pontoon bridges were pulled away, and in fact the breach grew wider. By the time they finally sealed the dam, Khrushchev had grown so angry about costs that he ordered the road along the top of the dam to be limited to 4 m—or to one-way traffic. But taking advantage of an innovation in the Soviet construction industry—ugly and inexpensively produced prefabricated concrete forms—the engineers came up with a design to lay the panels end to end for an uneven if 10 m wide road.[54] For hydropower stations, one thing is clear: even in times of peace or in places that do not fit Wittfogel's notion of hydraulic civilizations, there was great violence to surrounding communities, especially to the oustees who lost their homes and memories under water, whether in China, Brazil, the United States, India, the USSR, or elsewhere.

The Need for Repairs and Remediation in the Post-Soviet Era

During the Yeltsin presidency (1991–2000), repairs and upkeep on dams, sluices, and other facilities lagged in the absence of budget support, and many Soviet-era waterworks began to weep and decay. All of this led to some circumspection whether the Soviet approaches to nature engineering had produced desirable economic and environmental outcomes. The Russian countryside is dotted with scores of small waterworks, mostly modest power stations, that have begun their return to nature as the concrete melts and the metal rusts.

A series of federal programs dating to the 1990s attempted to deal with the problems of operation and maintenance of aging Soviet infrastructure from dams to canals to other industrial objects, some with greater success than others. Take the example of the Volga-Don Canal: by 1996 freight had shrunk by 80 percent since 1983. Several state programs to consider the problem involved complex research of the situation and also repair of locks and some renovation works: "Internal Waterways (1996–2000)," "Modernization of the Transport System of Russia (2000–2010)," and "The Development of the Transport System of Russia (2010–2015)."[55]

Yet rather than repairs, the federal programs encouraged engineers to advance hubristic projects anew. There have been discussions about a second Volga-Don Canal (Volgodon-2) to complement Stalin's original canal that would ostensibly benefit oil and gas tankers. Engineers have advanced the Volgodon-2 Canal to relieve anticipated increased freight loads on the existing canal. In their designs the new canal could use the already existing Varvarovskoe, Berezlavskoe, and Skatovskoe reservoirs with their high throughput capacity. But they acknowledge challenges to the new canal. First, the Volga-Don Canal is already pumped with water from the Don, and Volgodon-2 would have to be filled from Don water, too. But the water balance of the Don has been negative for a long time, and this is a threat to other Don needs and its ecology. Engineers suggest that it may be possible to take advantage of another project started in the 1980s just above Volgograd, near the village Erzovka. Builders conducted preliminary excavation for a new canal and began building the largest pumping station in Europe—to feed the Don with Volga water. In any event, then prime minister Dmitrii Medvedev endorsed Volgodon-2 in 2008.[56] Still, a local historian of the canal, Anatolii Chalykh, points out that it would be cheaper and safer to build a pipeline to handle increasing oil and gas exports, and he believes that Volgodon-2 will not help but must be compared with the construction of the Panama, Suez, and Volga-Don-1 canals with their tens of thousands of victims lost in construction.[57] The engineers seem not to understand that, in siphoning water from one region, they create water deficits in another region. They then plan to solve the deficit by pumping water from another basin—and then another project to pump it back, and none of them talks about impacts on ecosystems. They stand instead at the water trough of government funding with their buckets waiting.

On top of this, Russia faces a plague of the collapse of small GES. It is impossible to figure out how many GES the Soviets built, but they seem never to have found a river they could not dam. They dammed them north and south, from the Arctic to Kazakhstan. Many stations long ago reached the end of their usefulness because of siltation that should have been included in calculations, inadequate repair budgets, aging, and floods. The decrepit concrete impoundments have become sites for curiosity seekers, hikers, nude swimmers, and weekend bacchanalia. Some people still argue that energy production that takes advantage of the "gifts" of nature from small rivers may be effective in isolated regions where there is nevertheless relatively constant demand, and therefore repair or building of small stations with new turbines and generators could easily satisfy rural villages in a sustainable way without oil, gas, and coal.[58]

Small-scale hydroelectric power stations appeared like mushrooms as part of GOELRO, but their real golden age was from 1948 to 1962 until the era of "giants" and economies of massive scale commenced on Siberian rivers. Party organs propagandized local efforts while reparations from Austria and Germany brought high-quality machinery and equipment for these small GES. Yet suddenly the vast majority of stations were abandoned in the 1980s and industry stopped repairing them. Of 246 stations in the northwest of Russia, only a few dozen remain in anything close to operable condition. The regional energy company, Lenenergo, has refused to keep track of these stations (many of which, to be sure, were deep in the countryside), and there were few, if any, government programs to support them. Lenenergo officials ordered the stations and the buildings locked up, and the dams began slowly but surely to collapse.[59]

The example of Leningrad region reveals the both the promise and problems associated with small GES. According to the Lengidroproekt design institute, of forty-two small stations in Leningrad region only two were in operation, and another twenty-one might be rebuilt reasonable at cost, although sixteen were in a hopeless state. The entire northwest region reveals a similar picture of small GES with few in operation. In Karelia eight or nine operated of roughly fifty built, in Arkhangelsk region roughly eighty still operated, although of how many was unclear, and in Vologda,

Novgorod, and Pskov provinces the same picture of uncertainty and decay held.[60]

Leningrad policymakers and frustrated engineers from Lengidroproekt have been nostalgic about small GES since late in the Yeltsin era, in part because of cost considerations. The institute's chief engineer, Vladimir Lvovskii, determined that the stations he has examined would require from 3 to 10 million rubles ($100,000 to $350,000 at that time) each to bring back on line. Three years of research showed there were thirty-eight small stations at 120 to 720 kW in various stages of disrepair. Only one operated: in Kingiseppskii region the Luzhskii Fish Hatchery had gotten the Ivanovskaia station operating at its own cost. Lvovskii was certain that investment possibilities would grow as electricity grew in cost, at the same time that inflation made fuel for thermal stations (oil, gas, coal) more expensive. But hydroelectricity in the energy balance of Leningrad region never had a significant role versus thermal stations and especially after the building of Leningrad Atomic Energy Station, initially at 4,000 MW, and because of relatively gentle relief.[61] In the absence of capital investment from local businesspeople or the central government that was wedded to big power, "small is beautiful" had no promise except to weekend skinny dippers.

Not only the need for repairs plagues many Soviet-era waterworks. There is also significant pollution that threatens waterways in the Russian Federation, and rather than focus resources on this problem, the authorities advance other new projects. Unfortunately, a dangerous petrochemical sheen covers Russian waterworks past and present. Reports of oil spills and leaks that endanger waterways fill the media in every region of the Russian Federation. Every year, oil, toxic metals, and PCBs enter waterways along with massive floods whose frequency seems to be on the increase on dammed rivers everywhere. In Tomsk, an underwater pipeline ruptured and required emergency cleanup.[62] An oil leak into the Tula River that reached the Ob in September 2013 may have been related paradoxically to riverbed cleanup. Other sources of pollution include landfill leaks and storm run-off. Many Russian rivers have dead zones. Fish have left smaller tributaries for main rivers in search of food. Pollution has killed off all but the hardy ones.[63] Rubbish litters the banks of most rivers and lakes, where trash washes up upon the shore; dacha latrines and public restrooms lack septic systems.[64]

The response of the government has been still more hydroprojects and still new development programs in sensitive areas, without any cleanup or repair of the Soviet legacy. Industrial and forestry pressures bear down on the land

and rivers. The Zalesovskii Nature Preserve in the Altai, a large relic forest with many endangered species listed in the *Red Book of Russia*, is under threat because of large deposits of cement, gold, and bauxite that businesses covet. The gold is along the Berd River (which flows into the Ob). The firm "Nedra" ("Subsoil" in Russian, but I prefer to translate it as "bowels") has asked permission to cut 30 percent of nearby forest and to mine gold using bulldozers, excavators, and KamAz trucks to remove peat to 6 m depth—with catastrophic impact on streams and hydrological regime generally. This would repeat with brute force the destruction of hills and valleys in California in its gold mining days. The Maslianinskii and Iskitimsk areas already suffer water shortages. More floods will result with the vegetation and peat removed. The turbidity of water is already skyrocketing. And the Ob River will continue its transformation from a waterway into an industrial hero project from its source and tributaries to its Arctic delta now overlaid with pipes and railways.[65]

Siberian River Diversion

If Putin proceeds with a Siberian River diversion canal, a project conceived in the nineteenth century and pursued avidly since the late 1960s, he may remember that Stalin intended four massive canals before his death, of which three were built, the White Sea-Baltic, 1931–1933; Volga-Moscow, 1932–1938; and Volga-Don, 1948–1953. These projects, only partially successful from technical points of view, were extremely costly from environmental perspectives, and could be built only because of reliance on slave laborers. Today's waterworks projects will be much more costly than those of the Stalin era because of the need to use free laborers, more extravagant designs, and geographical location in Central and Northern Siberia with its lack of infrastructure and labor market. But abundant water calls the Kremlin, and it seems that Putin, too, is enamored of hero projects.

Four of Siberia's rivers rank among the top twenty-five in the world in terms of annual outflow, among them in twenty-second place the Ob-Irtysh Rivers that drain a basin of nearly three million km^2 and whose flow averages 12,500 m/s. To many hydraulic engineers, that water flows uselessly into the Arctic Ocean. Couldn't it better serve man—or at least the men in Moscow and the presidents of the Central Asian states—through irrigation or hydroelectricity? Already in the mid-nineteenth century, nationalists thought about how to supplement military conquest with installation of modern technology and settlement of Russian peasants to control the empire. At the turn of the century the Tsarist engineer Ia. G. Demchenko presented a proposal for an "inland Siberia Sea" to the Imperial Russian Geographical Society; Siberian waters—arriving in Central Asia—would permit Russian peasants to establish their agriculture and culture and facilitate the incorporation of Muslims—Uzbeks, Tajiks, and others—into the empire.[66]

Specialists took advantage of Bolshevik interest in big projects to raise the diversion project a number of times. In 1949 a government commission approved a proposal to divert Siberian water into the Aral Sea, but it died in 1951, not so much from concerns about environmental damage, but because of great costs that might slow the other hero projects of the Stalin Plan. With the expansion of agriculture in Kazakhstan and other Central Asian republics, Siberian river diversion again found support in the late Khrushchev period. Under Brezhnev in 1968 a large number of bureaucracies and research institutes joined the task of building a canal to transfer 25 km^3 per year, rising in subsequent project variants to 75 to 100 km^3 per year, and considering using water not only from the Ob River basin but the Yenisei River as well, under the slogan, "Give good clean water to the fraternal people of Central Asia."[67] During perestroika, in 1986, the Communist Party eventually killed the project as expensive and perhaps foolhardy; a literary journal, *Novyi mir*, under the editorship of Sergei Zalygin, a former hydrologist and now opponent of the project, was at the forefront of the effort to show how arid the project was—with its ballooning costs and absurd promises.[68]

The roots of Siberian diversion may be in speculations of geographers and explorers in the late 1700s who discussed the joining the Ob and Yenisei Rivers through a canal. Later parties of engineers examined the prospects but gave up upon seeing many physical difficulties, low population densities, and high costs. In 1873 a Yenisei merchant, Funtusov, allocated 8,000 rubles for research on a roadway that is now the Ob-Yenisei Canal. After fits and starts, this small canal opened in 1891. It could handle only small ships, and construction often faltered because of lack of funds, and also because of the completion of the Trans-Siberian Railroad and the Great War that drew attention elsewhere. In 1918 the Whites destroyed both the locks and the road along the canal. During World War II, three paddlewheel steamships and a small cutter passed though the canal with great difficulties. The canal has become overgrown and a memory of failed dreams; many of the local people today along its banks are Old Believers who arrived in the 1930s to escape religious repression. But the history of Siberian river diversion is a history of a project of fantasies that will not die.[69]

If Demchenko's proposal was dismissed as foolhardy and impossible, then Mikhail Tsunts and Mitrofan Davydov advanced a bolder project for a Siberian Sea in the Stalin era.[70] Davydov and Tsunts noted how in the mid-1920s two such projects to provide water to Central Asia involved the transfer of water from the Irtysh River to the Turgai Steppe. They believed that the projects were "naïve" in crucial aspects but properly drew attention to the far off rivers of Siberia as a key to the transformation of southern deserts into agricultural regions. How could they transfer water to the Aral-Caspian lowlands? Davydov set his eyes on both the Ob and Yenisei rivers. On the Ob, lower than the confluence with the Irtysh, a 78 m high dam would flood the surrounding lands and create a gigantic artificial Siberian Sea (Ob Reservoir) at 250,000 km^2, four times larger than the Aral Sea, submerging largely swamps, brush, and scraggly forest. The Siberian Sea would occupy the watershed between Western Siberia and the Aral-Caspian lowland at a geological obstacle, the so-called Turgai gates. Davydov, Tsunts, and other engineers proposed "simply" opening the "lock" of this gate by building a canal between the basins that might be around 800 km in length. Ob River water would flow, voilà, into the sunbaked arid steppe, "spring days" would arrive, the land would turn green with grass and flowers, and hundreds of billions of cubic meters of Siberian water would irrigate over 40 million hectares of land, creating a "gigantic oasis." There would be rice, cotton, and beet plantations, gardens, vineyards, lemon and orange groves. And what if the lowlands also received water from the Yenisei, too, with its billions of superfluous cubic kilometers of water that flowed uselessly into the Arctic Ocean? Downstream from the mouth of the Tunguska River, where Rusgidro construction crews in the 2020s are preparing to build a massive dam, engineers would build a second dam and create another reservoir, a second Siberian Sea, from which the water would flow into a tributary of the Ob—the Ket River and thus join with the first Siberian Sea.[71] The prospects were apparently limitless.

At the same time that engineers were laying Karakum canals, a series of scientific organizations, already realizing they had overestimated the stocks of water available for their extremely thirsty visions of an agricultural renaissance in Central Asia, and underestimating how much of it they would lose to evaporation and leakage, turned to the study of the transfer of Siberian water into Central Asia to augment the flow of the Syrdarya and Amudarya. Engineers could rely on an audience for these projects because of growing concern about food shortages in the nation that might be addressed through melioration.[72] The Siberia project gathered momentum slowly, however, because of the great expenses of the Stalin Plan for the Transformation of Nature. Yet soon after the death of Stalin, the Siberian river interbasin transfer project took off precisely because of increasing water demands and growing population, while canals that had drained the Amudarya and Syrdarya could suck no more out of them. As early as 1958, Chafik Chokin, the great Kazakh energy specialist and briefly president of the Kazakh Academy of Sciences, raised the issue of interbasin transfers from Siberia to Central Asia and Kazakhstan to solve the problem of the Aral Sea. For almost twenty years at his Institute of Energetics, Chokin pushed a project that in 1978 his institute presented to Soviet Ministry of Waterworks (Minvodkhoz SSSR).

A series of all-union conferences addressed Siberian water plans in 1961 and 1965 in Novosibirsk, 1962 in Tashkent, and 1967 in Moscow and Almaty, while water melioration programs spread through Moldova, Belarus, southern Ukraine, and elsewhere and institutes in these republics contributed studies to the national project. Indeed, after a 1968 plenary session of the Central Committee, GOSPLAN, the Academy of Sciences, and other organizations, the Party issued instructions to develop a final project for interbasin transfer, and already in May 1970 a Party resolution confirmed the go-ahead for the Ninth Five-Year Plan (1971–1975) that involved the diversion project of canals and reservoirs, ostensibly without significant inundation of adjacent lands, with a series of powerful pumping stations, and with energy generated for the pumps through new GES built on the same rivers so as not to siphon the electrons away from existing power stations that were needed by aluminum and petrochemical industries. Engineers estimated that by 1985 the first Siberian waters would flow into Central Asia, with the entire project completed by 2000. A massive feeder canal longer than 1,000 km, up to 300 m wide, and 15 m deep was indicated, with other feeder canals perhaps totaling another 1,500 km, with their own attendant pumping stations, dams, with holding ponds for industrial and agricultural purposes, and with excavation in part through peaceful nuclear explosions to accelerate the work and lower the costs, although several studies indicated potential dangers here, for example, explosions not far from natural gas deposits, whose conflagration would be a real disaster, not to mention the possibility of radioactive fallout and leaks into groundwater.[73]

As a sign of the hopes that engineers put into their Siberian canal, in the early 1970s the water engineers opened the Irytsh-Karaganda Canal at 458 km in length to help irrigate Kazakh land. But if the canal suggested to hydrologists unlimited possibilities of future designs to re-engineer nature, it never came close to functioning as designed and instead resembled the White Sea–Baltic Canal in its inefficiencies and hydrological failings: the canal never carried water or freight at design levels. The canal, at 20–40 m wide and 5–7 m deep, and consisting of eleven locks, 22 pumping stations, two reserve reservoirs and 17 bridges, siphoned off 75 m^3/s of water for Ekibastuz, a coal town founded by gulag prisoners where writer Aleksandr Solzhenitsyn had served a term, and Karaganda, another massive coal-company town reborn with gulag labor. The canal has needed constant refurbishment since its opening because of evaporation and invasive plants that choke its flow. Still, Kazakh leaders in the early twenty-first century insist that they ought to build another Karaganda canal, at a cost of $3.3 billion, to drink up to 1 billion m^3/year of water from the Irtysh to feed the capital of Kazakhstan, Astana, a growing oil and mineral economy, and to allow the first canal a bit of rest.[74]

For the Siberian canal and sea, all was for naught. No matter the tens of thousands of scientists, engineers, and workers involved, the multitudinous ministries and their institutes and construction bureaus, on August 14, 1986, at a special meeting of the Politburo, Communist Party officials voted to stop all work for economic reasons primarily, but also because of far-reaching public horror about the environmental extravagances of the pyramidical project. At least this project did not have to wait the death of Stalin for his underlings publicly to reject the murderous absurdities of his canals and railroads. Mikhail Gorbachev's glasnost exposed the diversion project for the massive white Siberian mastodon it was.

But the project will not dry up, and to this day many engineers believe that they can save or rebuild the Aral Sea through diversion. Pressures to pursue diversion dreams have their genesis in the belief that the solution to a problem of technological origin is a technological fix. Thus, if canals and diversion from the Amudarya and Syrdarya rivers for cotton and fruit culture contributed to unexpected environmental and social problems, then diversion—additional transfers of water to those basins—can fix them quickly. If the two rivers together at the beginning of the 1950s fed 100 km^3 into the sea per year, now the flow has dropped to a relative trickle of roughly

2–3 km³/year. In 1960 the surface area of the Aral Sea was approximately 66,100 km², but by 1990 was 36,500 km², and it had lost three-quarters of its volume, while the shoreline was 100 to 150 km from its previous borders. It has become in fact four seas. Roughly 45 million people live in the basin of the two rivers—5 million of whom reside in the delta—which is truly a disaster area because of the diversion of water. Respiratory illnesses, rising infant mortality, dust storms, pesticide poisoning, and the destruction of the fishing industry have resulted. The draining of the Amudarya and Syrdarya has led in some places salinity to exceed 60 g/l. Vozrozhdenie Island, home to a top-secret, secure facility where biological weapons were developed and tested, has become a peninsula, more accessible than ever and thus even more dangerous. Filthy, dead. or dying salt flats have replaced the Aral Sea that is surrounded by three deserts—the Kyzylkum, Karakum, and a rock plateau to the west. Locals say soon the sea will become the Aralkum (Aral Desert).

The collapse of the USSR might have saved the Aral Sea. In 1993 the governments of Central Asia created an international fund to protect the Aral Sea, the Intergovernmental Coordinating Water Management Commission and Basin Water Management Joint Organization on the Syrdarya and Amudarya. In 2002 they pushed a program to improve the ecological and socioeconomic situation in the basin through 2010 with UN support. From 2012 to 2015 with a budget of $3.8 million, the UN Aral Sea Program "work[ed] to improve the economic, food, health and environmental security of low-income rural communities of Karakalpakstan" to overcome the destruction of the Aral Sea "due to an unsustainable use of natural resources." The Aral Sea had provided both irrigation and fishing "while nowadays due to the reduced water flow, the fishing industry and related sectors are devastated." The funds will create a network of agroconsultants, equip 150 small farmers from the Baday-Tugay nature reserve with sustainable land-use techniques, train 160 primary health care workers in family and reproductive care, establish a group of seven trainers to assist public authorities, and focus generally on sustainable resource management toward the end of food security. The program is centered at Nukus, Uzbekistan, yet another former gulag camp, to help 130,000 people of the Aral region. The World Bank has joined the effort.[75] Yet a project to save the Aral through diversion of 23 km³ of Siberian rivers, primarily from the Ob, continues to be floated, and supporters are hesitant to recall that diversion of the Amudarya and Syrdarya led to this situation in the first place.

Siberian Rivers for Putin's Engineers

What is the solution to these problems? Energy demand in Russia fell by nearly 25 percent in the 1990s because of the economic crisis that gripped the country; capacity reserves therefore exist, especially in the European part of the nation.[76] Yet, wedded to massive geoengineering projects, the Russian Federation has determined to embark on a future of increased electrical energy capacity and production, perhaps based on nuclear power in the European part of the country, and hydroelectricity in Siberia and the Far East.[77] Russian engineers have thought—since the time of Lenin—that more electricity capacity is a solution to any problem, even a nonexistent one when generating capacity is more than adequate. According to official plans, the government planned to introduce 26,000 MW of new GES by 2020, most of them large-scale, although the plans indicated some effort to build small GES again.[78] Of course, this heroic construction effort that rivaled Stalin's great plan never materialized. But the lure of hero projects remains powerful.

For Siberia and the Far East, massive stations with thousands of megawatts of generation capacity is the chosen engineering path. The Boguchanskaia GES, first proposed in the mid-1970s, with a dam at 96 m tall and 2,690 m in length, a reservoir at 2,326 km², reached full power in 2015. It produces 20 percent of the region's energy, the largest share of that going to the Boguchanskii Aluminum Factory.[79] The government seems determined to move ahead with the Angara Cascade to finish the often-delayed Motyginskaia GES in 2020s. The Nizhneboguchanskaia station, with a reservoir extending 107 km, with forest and agricultural land inundated, with fourteen towns and settlements flooded and erased from history, is also moving ahead in spite of criticism.[80] Many of these stations face the same criticism as past projects of environmental degradation, costs greater than benefit, and intolerable local impacts including violation of local cultures and loss of land. Most stations are being proposed or built in regions of low population densities where those who will pay the costs by being removed from their homes and livelihoods are indigenous peoples. Russia's imperial water dreams to settle and control the interior continue to motivate construction (see Table 3.1).

Not surprisingly, in the commodity state of Russia, interest in the Siberian river diversion project at home and abroad has burst forth again like a political freshet. Islam Karimov, former president of Uzbekistan, proposed

Table 3.1 Siberian and Far East projected hydroelectric facilities

Andiiskoe Koisy (Agvali)	Dagestan	220 and 200 MW
Labinskaia[a]	Krasnodar	pumped storage at 600 MW
Zaramagskie (Ardon R.)	Northern Osetiia	357 and 812 MW
Mokskaia (Vitim R.)	Buriatiia	1,120 MW
Tel'mamskaia (Badibo R.)	Irkutsk region	450 MW
Boguchanskaia		3,000 MW
Nizhneboguchanskaia		660 MW
Motyginskaia (Angara R.)		1,320 MW
Evenkiiskaia (Lower Tunguskaia R.)		8,150 MW
Krapivinskii Works (Tom R.)	Kemerovo	300 MW
Tuvinskaia		1,500 MW
Nizhnebureiskaia (Bureia R.)	Amur	321 MW
Gramatukhinskaia (Zeia R.)	Amur Region	300 MW
Ust-Srednekanskaia (Kolyma R.)	Magadan	570 MW
Kankunskaia (Timpton R.)	Sakha	1,300 MW
Nizhnetimptonskaia (Timpton)	Sakha	800 MW
Sredneuchurskaia (Uchur R.)	Sakha	3,300 MW
Verneaɮdanskaia (Aldan R.)	Sakha	1,000 MW

Source: Government of the Russia Federation, *General'naia skhema razmeshcheniia ob"ektov elektroenergetiki do 2020 goda*, Pasporiazhenie no. 215-r, February 22, 2008 (Moscow: Government of the Russian Federation, 2008), 136. On the environmental costs of the Labinskaia pumped storage station, see V. Makarov, "Pamiatnik ekologicheskoi bezgramotnosti," *Nauka v Sibiri*, no. 49–50 (December 25, 1998), at http://www.nsc.ru/HBC/article.phtml?nid=79&id=23; and Andrei Filimonov, "Stroitel'stvo Labinskoi GAES mozhet stat' prichinoi novogo ekologicheskogo bedstviia," at http://ewnc.org/node/8565.

rejuvenating the project in 1995 and discussed it again in 2001 with President Putin. At the Eleventh Petersburg International Economic Forum in 2007, President Nursultan Nazarbaev of Kazakhstan expressed support for any river basin transfer: "Such strategic projects will decisively bring our countries closer together."[81] Supporters from Kazakhstan and Uzbekistan gained the support of an unlikely ally, former Moscow mayor Iurii Luzhkov, who in January 2002 published an open letter to Putin, outlining the problems of water deficits in the world, focusing on the nations of Central Asia, and asking the president to take the project under his own wing, to form a group of representatives of interested national parties, including scientists, administrators, and bureaucrats, and to order the Ministry of Natural Resources to pursue designs with the appropriate financial, organizational, and scientific measures. Acting like a doctor of hydrology, Luzhkov even penciled in the route of the canal; Luzhkov, who revered Stalin, may have been inspired by the greatest waterworker of all time whose determination to end drought forever through irrigation projects was captured in a famous Communist Party poster that shows the dictator, pencil in hand, drawing a line across a map of Central Asia as the route of a hero project. Local people and geographical obstacles in the way would be brushed aside. Without a doubt, Luzhkov saw Stalin's projects as a way to reconfirm Russian's imperial legacy and meet its foreign policy goals as a commodity power.[82]

Luzhkov, perhaps aspiring to Tolstoyan grandeur, followed his letter to Putin with the publication of *Water and Peace* (*Voda i mir*, 2009), in which he argued forcefully in support of Siberian water for export to bring peace to Central Asia.[83] Making light of the amount of water to be transferred as insignificant to the environment, he wrote of takings of only 5–7 percent of the Ob River's total flow, pumping it up over the Turgai Gates, and sending it thousands of kilometers through canals to state customers in Central Asia to the direct benefit of agriculture. The water would return to Russia as fruit, vegetables, and cotton. He noted that if Central Asia remained without water, then there will be millions of emigrants coming to Russia instead in search of jobs, implying Russia to be an unhappy recipient. Rather, undesirables should stay in the desert, and the fruits of their labor could cross borders without visas. Russian water had become the "oil of the twenty-first century," and Russia should not stand in the way of the flow: "Russia is fully capable to become an exporter of water, and the central Asian governments—exporters of intensively water use products: cotton, fruit, vegetables."[84]

If a hugely costly project whose history and that of other canals suggests will be nearly possible to complete, then already in 2004 the director of a major waterworks company, Soiuzvodoproekt, Igor' Zonn, told *New Scientist* that plans to pursue Siberian river basin transfer were afoot and perhaps already 300 institutes were involved.[85] One can understand Zonn's excitement: the main canal might be 200 m wide and 16 m deep and 2,550 km long, with the construction site, loaded with dump trucks, excavators, cements trucks, aggregate quarries, generators, and multitudinous laborers in places a half kilometer wide—working in concert to pump 27.2 km^3 of water annually southward.[86] That's a lot of jobs, a lot of land, a lot of water and inundation—and a lot of rubles. Central Asian leaders have joined into the growing chorus to quench their thirst. In June 2013 the Ministry of Regional

Development of Kazakhstan, together with the Kazakh Scientific Research and Design Institute of Construction and Architecture, presented a general schema for development of the country that included Siberian river basin transfer of Irtysh water to Kazakhstan—for the simple reason that much of the regional economy, especially Uzbekistan and Turkmenistan, depend on cotton.[87]

Scientific specialists and environmentalists immediately challenged Luzhkov. Andrei Ozharovskii from the NGO Ekozashchita! called diversion "pure recklessness." The chair of the Independent Ecological Expert Review Panel, Vladimir Anikeev, worried about the impact of water diversion on the Arctic Ocean. Zelenyi Mir (Green World) commented on idiocy of the Siberian project in 2002; N. F. Glazovskii noted its "irrational use of water resources," its significant negative environmental impacts, and the fact that it cannot fix the problem of the destruction of the Aral Sea and overuse of chemicals, let alone poor agricultural, water use, and other practices.[88] Other specialists point out that the project would inundate valuable agricultural and forest regions, raise groundwater the entire length of the canal, potentially flood nearby towns and roads, wipe out important fisheries along the Ob River important to local minorities, change the permafrost regime, increase the salinity of the Arctic Ocean, significantly alter the climate and the ice cover in the Ob delta and Kara Sea, and destroy flora and fauna along the transfer canal.[89]

Still others doubt the entire economic rationale of the canal. A corresponding member of the Academy of Sciences, Viktor Danilov-Danilian, deputy director of the Institute of Water Problems, an institute that had been a major supporter of the Brezhnev diversion project, pointed out the canal itself would likely cost on the order of $175 billion to build, while new drip and other irrigation technologies use water more efficiently.[90] But it seems likely that the Russian government is willing to submerge a bit of Russian land if the result is piles of hard currency. If Russia heated Europe with gas until sanctioned and boycotted over its war on Ukraine, then why not feed Central Asia—and China—river water? Soviet patriots saw nothing wrong here. One author noted how Stalin got things done quickly and without the meddling of public naysayers, and his projects used perhaps only 10 percent slave laborers in their workforces. The new canal would save Central Asia, facilitate Siberian transport, finally finish the work that Stalin began with his great canals, and refill the Aral Sea in the process.[91]

The Hydroelectric Chernobyl

While projects go forward to sell Russian water abroad, a Chernobyl-like disaster technological failure at home indicates that the industry is unprepared to complete them safely. In August 2009 the machine hall of a massive power station, the sixth largest in the world on the Yenisei River in Siberia, was destroyed when a 1,700-ton turbine burst through its cover, jumping 15 m into the machine hall, destroying the rest of the station, and killing seventy-seven workers. Was this accident caused by human error? An unfortunate, but rarely occurring accident because of the nature of large-scale technologies? Or was the Saiano-Shushensk disaster the result of Soviet and post-Soviet technological approaches? And is it surprising that the response of the Putin administration would be to identify the guilty, clean up the mess, repair the station as quickly as possible to demonstrate the unstoppable power of leaders, and to power up the aluminum industry, while setting forth with renewed will to build another such four, five, six massive stations on Siberian rivers?

The 6,400 MW Saiano-Shushensk Hydroelectric Power station (hereafter SShGES) typified Soviet projects in a variety of ways. First, it was hatched in the postwar enthusiasm to rebuild the nation from the devastation of the war and the desire to develop Siberian resources rapidly that accompanied the victory over Nazis and Nikita Khrushchev's rise to power. Such hydroelectric complexes that arose on the Angara, Yenisei, and Ob rivers were seen as "epic heroes" whose time had come. In his speech at the Twenty-second Party Congress, Khrushchev noted the "heroes": "In eastern Siberia, along with the Bratsk and Krasnoiarsk GES there are plans on the Angara and Yenisei by 1980 to build such powerful stations as the Saiansk, Ust-Ilimsk, Boguchaiskaia, Yeniseiskaia, Osinovskaia, and Nizhne-Tugunskaia."[92] Every one of these stations has been built, or will be built along the Yenisei according to RusGidro by 2030, no matter the social or environmental costs.

Second, as the largest GES in the USSR, the SShGES generated electricity both to feed the burgeoning aluminum industry and to reiterate to Russian citizens in the twenty-first century the twentieth-century messages of Soviet determination, enlightened Party leadership, and power over nature. Fieldwork, surveys, and mockups for the dam appeared in Leningrad design institutes in the early 1960s. Construction began in quiet Siberian forests that quickly transformed into workers' villages, machine parks, aggregate and concrete factories, and so on. Typically heroic concrete pourers poured more cubic meters of concrete in shorter time spans than were conceivable—except of course in the land of concrete, the USSR.[93] And, according to official history, the station came on line, step by step, as planned beginning in 1978.[94] The station met party and social norms of "socialist obligations" to manufacture, deliver and install turbines.[95] The organ of the local party committee, dam administration, and the local newspaper, *Ogni Saian* (Fires of Saian) celebrated cement factories coming on line that would enable them to produce nearly 700 tons of the wondrous stuff per shift, while the construction of the aggregate sorting factory continued in dark, long winter nights, and devoted workers promised to fulfill socialist obligations even on *subbotniki* ("voluntary" weekend workdays). Brigades of student workers came from Moscow and elsewhere to meet labor shortfalls and fulfill any looming target ahead of schedule. And, of course, the bosses worried sincerely about safety and accidents, although how many accidents happened was never publicized, and of course when they occurred they were blamed on the workers' lack of knowledge of safety rules and the lack of proper organization in the event.[96] The monolithic 245 m high arched gravity dam with ten turbines, over 1 km wide at the top and able to withstand an earthquake even of 7.5 on the Richter scale, closed the Yenisei in 1978.

In two other worrisome ways, however, the SShGES was typical of Soviet accomplishments. First, it opened in fact long after its official dedication. Its history was fraught with delays, poor operation, safety commission interventions, and the reality that local people were shunted aside, like superfluous water molecules, to watch their memories, homes, hopes, and dreams inundated. Only at the height of perestroika, in 1990, did the press report on growing environmental concerns about the station.[97] In fact, from 1978 to 2000 the SShGES operated in fits and starts; there were accidents and cost overruns. In 1979 flooding destroyed the first turbine, in 1985 heavy waters destroyed the spillway, and in 1988 it collapsed again and had to be rebuilt over three years. From 1992 to 1997 the builders had to eliminate high filtration of water through fissures in the concrete. And only in 2000 did a government commission finally permit "industrial exploitation" of the GES, in part to generate investment and replace worn-out equipment. How much of this history contributed to the loss of seventy-seven lives and the cost of at least $1.5 billion to rebuild the station after the August 2009 catastrophe?

Second, there are still debates over what indeed was the ultimate cause of the accident. The official report blames people, not the technology, in part to enable them to justify pushing four turbines of the station back on line already in the following year. Narrowly, the cause was the fatigue and failure of the bolts that held down the turbines, plus the unacceptably low technical responsibility of the people at the station, who, during the project itself, did not make plans for any emergencies.[98] Let us recall that only a half year after the Chernobyl disaster, by November 1986, the remaining Chernobyl reactors units were brought back on line because electricity was the food of Soviet gods, and circumspection does not enter the lexicon of engineers of big objects.

Vladimir Putin made certain to show both resoluteness and sympathy after the accident. He personally guaranteed unprecedentedly large payments to the families of the dead and injured when he visited the site just five days later and ordered that a plan be presented within six weeks to clean up, and to accelerate construction at the Boguchanskaia GES to make up on the energy shortfall during the four years it might take to repair the doomed dam. The payments would be at least $16,000 to the family, free tuition to children under eighteen, and a small fund (of $70 million) for family members suffering from PTSD. The "Parents Committee of the Dead" asked RusGidro for 15 million rubles for each family (almost $85,000), and apparently the company agreed.[99]

Putin publicly lamented losses at the SShGES, but like a good Tsar praised its resurrection as its "second life."[100] He also insisted that the guilty be prosecuted for the accident. Someone was prosecuted, but not the guilty parties. The authorities brought charges against journalist Mikhail Afanas'ev for publishing stories in the web newspaper *Novyi focus* about recovery efforts at the station that the district attorney of Abakan called "slander" for creating panic and for endangering the psychological health of citizens, with the possibility of a three-year sentence. Afanas'ev suggested that the rescue workers might not have done enough to save people who were trapped in air pockets in the machine hall. RusGidro demanded action against him for trying to "make money on the tragedy." Afanas'ev was threatened and beaten for his reporting on a variety of subjects in Khakassia, including this report on SShGES, an attack that left him with a broken jaw. Interior Ministry investigators took his mobile phone, computer, and apartment keys. In the face of mounting public criticism for attacking the messenger, the authorities announced a few days later that they had dropped the charges against him.[101]

The accident itself remains a source of dispute. According to the official version, the cover of the turbine housing failed when many of the 80 bolts holding it down (each 75 mm diameter) broke, and then the 1,697-ton turbine itself was forced up and out by the water, destroying the cover, where-upon torrents of water flooded the machine hall. One theory is that excessive vibrations of the turbine led to the failure, yet after registering the vibrations no one seemed to know what to do because the GES director, Nikolai Nevolko, had left to celebrate his birthday and no one else had the desire or authority to take charge.[102] Yet the bolts seem to have failed gradually, and a close examination of the data does not reveal a precise onset point of the accident; the vibrations of unit 2 did not seem immediately remarkable, and then only for several seconds when suddenly it was impossible to do anything.[103]

These conditions have led others to question the official report and also to worry that the dam itself was at risk. One idea was that there was a powerful water hammer (hydraulic shock) associated with the accident, and after the machine hall calamity neither RusGidro nor emergency ministry personnel was certain the dam itself would remain fully intact. The NGO Plotina.Net! argues there is no way a water hammer could raise a turbine 15 m. The failure of bolts was not a cause, but a result of the accident, and the investigators should be looking for the causes of such a hydraulic impact at the station, for example, blockage of the water conduit with a fallen piece of concrete, or the slamming shut of a gateway from the downstream side.[104]

Nostalgic engineers have their own theories. One specialist, Goldanskii, blamed the accident on the collapse of the USSR. Here was one of the largest GES in the world that produced ~23 billion kW/h annually, designed to with-stand a major earthquake, that preserved the local ecosystems and cultures, and whose 300 km reservoir connected Tuva with the rest of Siberia. It was built before perestroika to produce pure kilowatts, not to serve as a target of rapacious capitalism whose owners sought only profits; the "spineless 'nineties" led to "unprofessional, barbaric" operation of the station. The accident was entirely by human fault: incompetence and the failure to maintain the station, but to enrich billionaires.[105]

The former deputy director of the SShGES, V. I. Babkin, worried that a hydraulic shock remained a possibility—and another catastrophic accident remained a possibility, too, even if a new regime for operating the station has been introduced.[106] The plant's automatic safety system should have shut down the turbines and closed the intake gates on the penstocks at the top of the dam, but turbines 7 and 9 still operated at full speed, in excess of 142 rpm, triggering the crackling short circuits that darkened the plant. Amateur video footage taken downstream at the time of the accident shows bright flashes and a huge explosion in the vicinity of turbines 7 and 9 as a wall of water spews from the structural breach near turbine 2. Environmental cleanup crews attempted to contain the oil spill that stretched 80 kilometers down the Yenisei River and killed 400 tons of fish at trout farms. Over two weeks, 2,000 rescuers removed 5,000 m^3 of debris, pumped out over 2 million m^3 of water, and pulled fourteen survivors from the wreckage.

Perhaps age was the problem. Turbine 2 had been shut down for repairs before, and when brought back into operation, it vibrated at four times the maximum limit, likely stressing the fatigued metal pins holding it in place. After all, unit 2 had come within two months of its thirty-year service. And if unit 2 had been offline until the previous night, then it was brought online to compensate for energy lost because of a fire at another plant. This recalls reactor 4 at Chernobyl that was in the final stages of a shutdown but called back on line to meet a sudden grid shortage, and through a series of operator errors and design faults in the reactor itself exploded the night of April 26, 1986.

The result of all this is that the SShGES came fully back on line within four years. It was needed for aluminum, and the president insisted upon its resurrection. The man who swims with dolphins and explores Baikal by bathysphere, the man with his hands on Russian rivers, Vladimir Putin, returned the station to operation by videolink from Moscow with the control room. Before pressing the button, he noted that from 2007 to 2011 the country had brought on line 12 GW of new power and that in 2012 another 6 GW of startups were forecast. As for Soviet leaders, so for Russian leaders today these "great tempos" of growth gave a powerful impulse to the economic development of Krasnoiarsk region and all Siberia. Putin mentioned that electricity from SShGES would feed stadiums and hospitals and high schools. But most important, "of course," was the Bogunchanskii Aluminum Factory. That was why those in attendance included the vice minister, Arkadii Dvorkovich, the minister of energy, Aleksandr Novak, the leading aluminum oligarch and head of RUSAL, Oleg Deripaska, and the head of Rusgidro, Evgenii Dod. And in fact, RusGidro and RUSAL had provided most of the 90 billion rubles for the repair project.[107] In 2016 the SShGES produced 25.48 billion kW/h of electricity, a record for the station since 1978, and nearly 5 billion kW/h higher than in 2015.[108]

But is there not a risk that other accidents of this magnitude may occur, given the fact that many industrial objects, not to mention the roads, pipelines, transmission towers, and other facilities, have worked too long, serving not only the Soviet past, but the Russian present? One journalist wrote, "Legacy equipment, a blessing for newly privatized companies in the early post-Soviet period, has now become a headache, or worse, for many private Russian companies." They may have facilitated rapid growth in the 1990s and beyond, but now they require substantially more investment for repairs, upgrading, and modernization."[109] Power engineer Viktor Kudryavy stated that "the catastrophe at the Saiano-Shushenskaia HPP is a system failure." Maintenance has fallen behind, research is underfunded, and emergency response agencies are woefully unprepared. According to *Bellona*, "The consequences for the industry are critical: only every seventh HPP [GES] of Russia has a wear of less than 50%, SSHPP [SShGES] has an 86% wear."[110]

Twenty-first-Century Russian Waterworks

The major focus of RusGidro is hero power stations in service of industry, a number of which were mothballed in the construction interregnum of the 1990s, and not smaller stations or their repair. The designs of the Turukhanskaia GES on the lower Tunguska River, a tributary of the Yenisei River, date to the heyday of Brezhnevism in 1978 and an order of the Ministry of Electrification in that year, and were supported by leading specialists including Guri Marchuk, then president of the Soviet Academy of Sciences. Supporters claimed the dam would have minimal impact on reindeer herding and fisheries in the Evenk region, and they asserted that the land to be inundated was not fruitful for agriculture. But a 1988 environmental impact statement from Siberian scientists concluded that the entire project would have a negative impact on the region's inhabitants, and in the period of glasnost and perestroika the project was put on hold.[111]

Yet, in the 1990s and 2000s, as the economic situation of the Evenki worsened owing to inattention from Moscow, RusGidro recognized the opportunity to push the station again, if with a new claim and a new name: the Evenkiiskaia GES (EvGES), of benefit to the way of life of the Evenki. At 120 km from the delta of the Yenisei, and a dam at 200 m high with a reservoir of more than 9,400 km^2, a little smaller than the area of Delaware and Rhode Island combined, it would be one of the largest in Russia. Supporters claimed its importance for economic, defense, and transport reasons, that it would cut down on greenhouse gas pollution, earn millions of rubles annually in taxes, increase the navigation season by 70 to 100 days, eliminate dangers from floods, and raise the quality of life (housing, medicine, education). But a recent survey indicated that most residents of the district anticipate destruction of traditional reindeer herding, a lower quality of life and climate, the inundation of grazing areas and forest, and other negative factors. Nor, ultimately, will they be able to use the electricity produced by the destruction of their ways of life.[112] That electricity is essentially designated for aluminum or export, not for ordinary folk.

Unlike in the Gorbachev era when public protest burst forth over economic, political, and social questions, the Putin administration has developed a number of tools to weaken or silence opposition to its projects, especially since the 2012 elections, and these have told on efforts to slow megaprojects. State corporations have created information centers and PR programs to inform the public about the benefit and safety of their reactors, dams, and pipelines. On top of this, the government now requires NGOs to register as "foreign agents" (which is meant to sound like "spies") if they receive any support from abroad. Another law permits the authorities to remove content from a webpage and prosecute its authors if it promotes "extremism," immorality, or other loosely defined terms, but this seemingly reasonable control has been used generally to stifle free speech. The Federal Agency for State Security (the FSB) interferes directly and regularly with the activities of NGOs that might question the costs and benefits of state-supported projects using this vagueness and relishing its power.[113]

RusGidro used this menu of opportunities in an attempt to silence opponents of the EvGES. Its representatives asked the FSB to prosecute Alexander Kolotov and Aleksei Kolpakov for extremism and "inciting national hatred" for their anti–big dam website, www.plotina.net, and also asked they be charged with anti-government propaganda as foreign agents for WWF, Radio Freedom, and Greenpeace for criticizing the station. Under Stalin the government had used Article 58:10 of the Soviet penal code to charge individuals with "anti-Soviet propaganda and agitation"—a crime punishable with death. The crime of Plotina.Net! activists was to write that the GES would inundate 1 million hectares of land, submerge six villages including the capital of Evenkia, and fill underground nuclear test caverns with water with the danger of spreading radioactivity and degrade permafrost. The Evenkis' pastures, lifestyle, gravesites, and so on would disappear; these assertions, RusGidro representatives claimed, incited hatred of the Evenki. Fortunately, the local district attorney rejected the charges of extremism.[114]

NGOs and environmentalists face a difficult fight in the battle against the stations because of the political and economic power of those who invest in them—Russia's wealthiest men and the companies they own including RusGidro and RUSAL, the world's second largest aluminum company with over 72,000 employees. They have been denied access to environmental impact statements and social plans intended to compensate "oustees" whose livelihoods will be affected. On top of this, in 2007 the federal government passed legislation on environmental impact statements that, in the name of security, have excluded waterworks from state ecological expertise and limited public access to reliable information.[115] In essence, the government has sought fully to constrain public intervention and other dialogue about Russia's environmental, industrial, and resource-intensive future.

What has been the response of Russian citizens to waterworks? If in the Stalin era criticism was muted, and dangerous to the critic, since the Khrushchev era public concerns about environmental degradation have been enunciated in a variety of forums and in a variety of ways. One way to read citizens' responses to riverine engineering projects is through cultural works. Beginning in the 1950s, many authors challenged the authorities over the massive water projects, for example in *Literaturnaia gazeta* over the despoliation of Lake Baikal. Such novels as Leonid Leonov's *Forest* and Valentin Rasputin's *Farewell to Matyora* questioned the environmental and human costs of the Soviet economic development model, while *Novyi mir* under editor Sergei Zalygin in the late 1980s railed against Siberian diversion.[116]

In the twenty-first century, local environmentalists continue to be active in spite of legal obstacles and threats. Angara-185 members have protested long and hard against the construction of the Boguchanskaia GES, a state-sponsored dam to support aluminum, and other waterworks for their impact on Irkutsk region, Krasnoiarsk, and Buriatia.[117] Construction on the 3,000 MWe Boguchanskaia GES commenced in the late 1970s. But as the construction was nearing completion—and many villages had been evacuated—it was put on hold as the USSR collapsed. In 2010, Putin ordered the federal government to subsidize efforts to complete the station. It came online in 2012, nearly thirty years after the original construction commenced in 2012. But the main reason for the GES was to power the Taishet aluminum smelter that alone required 1,000 MW, since the SShGES accident had led to regional electricity shortfalls. RusGidro and RUSAL (Russian Aluminum), not citizens, are the primary beneficiaries.

Based in Ust'-Ilimsk, Angara-185 members took their name from their demand that the new station be built no higher than 185 m, while design engineers produced specifications at 208 m, which would lead to flooding of additional towns and cause other environmental damage. At 185 m tall, flooding would affect only Krasnoiarsk territory—some 600 km along the river—and the capacity would fall to 1,620 MW. At 208 m, the capacity rose to 3,000 MW, but 830 km of the river would be flooded from Ust-Ilimsk to Boguchany, including a number of villages, 7 million m^3 of pine, and 4.5 million m^3 of peat land. Scientists further worried that the tectonics of the river had changed since data were first collected in 1979, and the water mass would affect the seismic regime of the region. Vasilii Korpachev, dean of forestry at the Siberian State Technical University, asserted that timber rot and pollution make the river water poisonous, not only unpotable, and with lowered oxygen content and pH level that leave the lakes (reservoirs) a "dead zone." The federal budget to prepare the basin work zone, 15 billion rubles, was half the annual budget of the region.[118]

According to *Ecologist*, in 2006 the dam "was resuscitated by a consortium of the parasitic businesses that are busy sucking Russia's natural resources dry, aided and abetted by the Russian government, which took upon itself responsibility for clearing the area to be affected, of trees, buildings and people." This was "a moth-eaten idea [that] was wrapped up in a big shiny package and presented to the public as a private-public enterprise—the Combined Power and Water Development Plan for the Lower Angara Area—which would bring the local people a host of benefits: jobs, infrastructure, tax revenue to boost local authority budgets." The plant came on line in 2012, but the region stills suffers in poverty, with oustees who had fished and hunted sent to small provincial towns, "the solid wooden houses of their grandparents in ashes at the bottom of the reservoir." The costs to the local people will rise as the dam reaches its full height of 208 m, and "ten million m^3 of forest over 1,200 km^2 will be flooded." Another station or two may follow, pushed by aluminum and Deripaska.[119]

Hydropower and Nation under Putin

The hero waterworks being advanced in recent years are geared to commodity production and sale, with water itself a potentially major commodity. Russia's rivers demand attention and investment for investment into the safety of existing facilities, cleanup of river basins, and flood control management, not commodity sale alone. Significant flooding seems to be on the increase in Russia in several river basins, and the costs to human life and property are extensive. The great challenges to the Putin administration in responding to them indicate that Russia is no different from any other nation in dealing with natural disasters: the determination to carry out extensive engineering projects in river basins, and not only those of Siberian rivers with their huge volume and massive spring runoff, has resulted in extensive flooding events—not flood control as promised. To reclaim wetlands and build on the Mississippi River flood plain, the US Army Corps of Engineers erected massive control levees. As a result, when floods occur, they cause billions of dollars in damage, and hundred-year events have become fifty-year events, fifty-year events occur every ten years, and so on.

Similarly, in the Altai region of western Siberia, in spring 2014 massive floods washed out bridges and roads, leaving almost 1,000 residents of the villages of Elanda, Tolgoek, Uozhan, and Kuius isolated. At least six died and up to 10,000 people lost their houses. Heavy floods destroyed 230 km of roads, twenty bridges, and electrical infrastructure. Over 200 towns and villages and 40 municipalities were flooded. At least 36,000 people were evacuated.[120] The governor of the Altai region, Alexander Karlin, took a helicopter to view the extensive flooding of the Ob that stretched to the horizon. He saw here and there a house above the water. Hay lay ruined, firewood floated away, basements filled with water, and the government offered aid, a pittance in fact: 10,000 rubles ($300) per person, and if their property had been destroyed they might qualify for another 50,000 or 100,000 rubles ($1,500 to $3,000) after paperwork was filed. Emergency personnel handed out pills and vaccinated against hepatitis A. The Regional Directorate for Entrepreneurship (a kind of Small Business Administration) promised to provide loans.[121] The government also sent in 600 Rospotrebnadzor (the Federal Office for Supervision of Consumer Protection and Welfare Rights) representatives to provide local assistance.[122] Round the clock, some forty mobile teams worked sanitation and disinfestations, building fecal barriers, testing treatment plants, and supplying bottled and tanker water.[123]

Modern governments have the mandate to help in times of crisis. The US Federal Emergency Management Administration (FEMA)—and the George W. Bush administration—faced withering criticism for their poor handling of the Katrina hurricane disaster. Donald Trump's government failed to support American citizens in Puerto Rico after Hurricane Maria, as Trump cruelly made light of the devastation of the island by tossing a roll of paper towels into a crowd. FEMA admitted failure.[124] Soviet and Russian leaders, since the time of Mikhail Gorbachev's tardy initial response to Chernobyl, have tried to be more proactive in their responses to disasters: under Gorbachev the Spitak earthquake in 1988; under Putin and Medvedev, a series of mining accidents and the *Bulgaria* ferry sinking in July 2011 with 128 killed.

President Putin reacted presidentially to the 2014 floods with a televised meeting in the Kremlin, a table of advisors sitting around him. He said:

> We have discussed this issue on numerous occasions. I know that the Emergencies Ministry has joined the efforts recently along with the Defense Ministry. Together with the regional authorities, they have done everything necessary to save lives, avoid major damage and protect people's property as far as it was possible. We have to take all the necessary measures to maintain a normal epidemiological situation in the area considering the dead cattle and cattle burial sites, if any. We should also see how we can help schools, where the finalists are about to take their National Final School Exams. In addition, we should do our utmost to restore the damaged housing and help the people in this difficult situation.

But he called for authority to be vested in Moscow far from the disaster. "Let us listen to reports from the actual locations, and then here in Moscow we will discuss all this with our colleagues and develop a plan of action for the short term." In conclusion, Putin praised the relief effort. "I would like to note that the crisis management system generally performed in a timely fashion and corresponding regional relief centres were set up on time. I would like to thank everyone for their work during the initial stage of the relief effort." Putin urged officials not to become "too satisfied" with their achievements and promised timely assistance and help in restoring lost property.[125]

Scientists also have been actively involved—especially since the Gorbachev era—in drawing attention to the dangers of massive waterworks. Those in Akademgorodok worry about the Ob Reservoir, its health, and the impact of frequent strong winds and waves on its shoreline. The deterioration of reservoirs is a national epidemic owing to siltation, rapid construction, and the failure properly to remove forests, towns, and other material from river basins before inundation, and of course owing to their age. Disagreements among competing interests (timber, transport, fisheries, leisure), climate change, drought, and pollution make things worse.[126] RusGidro, responsible for the Ob GES, often sponsors cleanup of the shorelines.[127]

But cleanup of filth is not enough. The Federal Water Resources Agency and regional governments have developed sustainable-use programs to deal with drought, reservoir levels, and other water use problems, although insufficient funding for these programs is an obstacle. In 2012–2014 only 16.5 km of the entire Kuibyshev system was repaired, although scores of facilities and hundreds of kilometers required support. The allocation was roughly 16 million rubles in 2014 and 40 million rubles by 2020, hardly enough to make a dent.[128]

While water quality may be adequate in some cities, generally poor water management and low standards leave most Russians at risk. Three-fifths of Russians draw water from wells where contamination is often an issue; industrial pollution and agricultural run-off remain significant problems; significant fish kills frequently occur; heavy metals contaminate many water sources; wastewater is poorly treated; and epidemics of cholera, salmonella, typhoid fever, dysentery, and viral hepatitis reappeared in the 1990s. Only 1 percent of all sources of potable water in Russia meet standards of the highest category of quality without needing extra purification. While basins and lakes and rivers, including artificial reservoirs formed to serve industrial needs, are closely monitored for levels of pollution, they remain in a crisis state and a threat to public health. The Beloiarskoe Reservoir, for example, has higher levels than background of radioactive pollution.[129] Built in the 1950s to feed the nearby nuclear power station of the same name, it releases radioisotopes into the water even during the station's normal, safe operation, and independent experts have measured ^{137}Cs (radiocesium) in soils 50 km from the station, and plutonium as well, the closer to the station, the greater the concentration.[130] On top of this, waterworks are deteriorating at a rate that far exceeds the pace of their modernization, repair, or replacement.[131]

Hero waterworks, old and new, ignore citizens. But the massive projects continue to pique the interest of Russian builders, engineers, and policymakers for foreign policy reasons. RusGidro is pushing dams in Vietnam, India, and Egypt—and the colleagues of Russian engineers in those countries have great interest in seeing dams built. Canal builders through and through, Russian officials have expressed interest in working with the Nicaraguan government to build a new canal across the Panama isthmus, although as yet there are no concrete plans, nor concrete poured. Russian officials maintained that Americans opposed the canal for selfish business reasons, while Russia's interests are for a multipolar world and a better transportation system, not a foothold in Central America.[132] Central Asian leaders envy Siberian river water and see transfer canals as a panacea for their agricultural problems. Over the objections of then president Islam Karimov of

Uzbekistan and Nursultan Nazarbaev of Kazakhstan, Putin signed an agreement to build the Verkhnenarynskii cascade of GES on behalf of RusGidro with President Almazbek Atambaev. He claimed the GES would produce jobs and raise the quality of life among the citizens of Kyrgyzstan—which he referred to as a "republic," not independent nation.[133]

China is also becoming a customer for Russian water. Already in 1999, its engineers proposed a canal that would permit takings of water for industry and agriculture from the Uliungur Lake from which the Karamai and Sin'tszian-Uighur regions would be watered—although this project led Chinese and Russian ecologists to protest for destroying the water balance of the entire region. Yet the minister of agriculture of Russia, Aleksandr Tkachev, was inclined to provide water to China. Cost concerns and technical uncertainties would seem sufficient to stop the project dead, but Tkachev observed that superfluous water exists and that it was available for purchase.[134]

Danilov-Danilian, who has been minister of the environment and head of the Institute of Water Problems, saw the minister's comments as dangerous, and the prospects of pumping water from Siberia to China as far-fetched and profligate, its costs inestimable, but certainly trillions of rubles. He notes that there is no "excess water," no matter what bureaucrats say, and that transfers to China will not prevent downstream Ob river floods. He further worries that the Chinese are already draining the source with excessive withholdings from the Irtysh on Chinese territory. Rather than take water from one place to another, it would be best to improve technologies to utilize existing water more efficiently. Otherwise it will take thousands of tons of water (including that to produce chemicals required in irrigation agriculture) to produce one ton of grain. Finally, Danilov-Danilian notes, taking water will hurt Siberian rivers when there are "fallow" years for shipping. He concluded that the entire initiative of the agricultural ministry will lead only to bad things, and the "desire of the government to give our natural wealth to our eastern neighbor will make Russia an ore appurtenance of the always growing China" —forest, oil, gas, and now water.[135]

Russian leaders, engineers, and others have rarely questioned the utility and importance of hero projects that the nation has pursued across different decades and under different leaders. The projects were crucial to the Bolsheviks as symbols of what could be accomplished under socialism. Under Stalin they were transformed into violent attacks on humans and nature as what *must* be accomplished under socialism in a garrison state. When a mature resource state had formed in the postwar years, the canals, dams, and irrigation systems became more hubristic, more wasteful, more socially disruptive, yet even more important to the state, if based ostensibly in scientific study of resources, hydrology, and economic justifications. And in the twenty-first century, when their environmental and social costs have become clear to most observers, the institutions and engineers who grew out of the Soviet legacy continue to pursue large-scale projects, apparently knowing no other way than to force water to obey the state rather than to flow according to the mold of river basins, the desiderata of gravity and hydrology, and the needs of local people. But if a canal has aged, another must be built. If aluminum calls, then dam a Siberian river. The result is that natural disasters plague the nation's water regimes, and the government faces new challenges in dealing with all-the-more-frequent floods and accidents.

Over the decades, the hydrologists' calculations for the benefits of their projects, their utility and longevity, the strength of their concrete, the turbidity of the water, the immediate onset of sedimentation of reservoirs, the impact of changes in the speed, temperature, and salinity of water on the environmental impacts—in all of these calculations, the engineers were either overly optimistic and mistaken from the start. Merely decades later, pumps failed; canal beds leaked; silt filled streams, irrigation channels, and reservoirs; and concrete cracked and melted in the sun. And since the time of the Shakhty Affair they have failed to consider the impact of large-scale technologies on local peoples, lifestyles, and ecosystems. By the time of the breakup of the USSR, many facilities were in critical condition, and ten years later the new Russian government that had inherited them and their managers, experts, and workers from Soviet power realized they could not fully guarantee their safety. One GES experienced catastrophic failure. But the projects have not lost their verve—or support of the state.

One military historian who lamented the fall of Soviet power condemned those who, at the beginning of the 1990s, carried a campaign against the waterworks of the country—canals, locks, GES, and reservoirs that had been built at such great human cost—the labor of prisoners, canals built on bones, Russian cities and villages entombed in the depths of water. He noted that for twenty years, in thousands of articles, dozens of books and films, these critics had discredited these wondrous Soviet achievements. They had forgotten, he declared, the economic growth they brought to the provinces. He noted the "great importance of waterways for Russian history since the rise of [medieval] Rus' and the coming of the Varangians to conquer, trade, impress into military service." He discussed evidence of canals among Russian princes already in medieval Russia; the construction of St. Petersburg; military advances in waterworks that saved the empire in the nineteenth century, for example by taming rapids and enabling military transport; and he referred to great projects, but not concrete results until glorious Soviet power.[136] And he was right. Russian leaders are dam builders and meliorators. Lenin and Stalin were, Khrushchev was, and Brezhnev may have been the meliorator par excellence. And President Putin's government supports a variety of expensive, expansive, and heroic projects, most with Soviet roots, and others new, but just as grandiose.

The tens of thousands of gulag prisoners who perished, the hundreds of villages—and memories—submerged, the failed projects—forgetting these things, we must assume, are small prices to pay for reborn interest in water transfer projects in contemporary Russia. Indeed, Russia still celebrates Day of the Reclamation Specialist (День мелиоратора) on the first Sunday in June, a holiday first established by Soviet government in May 1976.[137] The Federal Agency of Maritime and River Transport has published an entire glossy issue of *Vestnik rosmorrechflota* on "From the Volga to the Enisei" glorifying past projects and advocating preserving and expanding possibilities, including at the White Sea–Baltic, Volga-Don, and Moscow-Volga canals, and even the tiny Novosibirsk GES locks, the only such locks beyond the Urals that were "built in record time."[138] One hopes, given the record, that Russia does not ever attempt to build a new Inland Siberian Sea, let alone in record time. But dreams of hero projects die hard in Russian history.

4

Nuclear Wonderlands

In nuclear technology, too, large-scale, hubristic approaches to the development and diffusion of technologies prevail. This is the case not only for the former Soviet Union, but for the world industry. Nuclear technologies require extensive prospecting and mining operations; massive and dangerous milling, enrichment and fuel fabrication facilities; entire cities devoted to those ends, plus construction and deployment; and hazardous waste and spent-fuel storage facilities. The Soviet and now Russian nuclear enterprise is distinguished by the pursuit of applications deemed too expensive or risky or otherwise inconceivable in other nations: nuclear-powered icebreakers, breeder reactors to generate electricity and produce plutonium, and a variety of other applications.

Yet the promises of nuclear power remain: nuclear medicine; radiation sterilization of food; nuclear rocket ships, airplanes, and floating nuclear power stations; and nuclear-powered oilrigs. All these have seen profound development in Russia. These utopian technologies to enable heating, electrification, and exploitation of taiga and tundra have been resurrected in the twenty-first century, coming from reborn Soviet nuclear institutions. And if many Russian citizens have discomfort about nuclear power because of the Chernobyl disaster and other serious accidents, or because of their knowledge of the extensive pollution of vast regions of the nation—Murmansk province and the Arctic Ocean generally, the Urals region military industry complex, and other poorly managed waste dumps—many others see the "peaceful atom" of nuclear power as a sign of modernity, a source of cheap and clean energy, and an indication that Russia remains a scientific superpower.

Since the rise of "Atoms for Peace" programs in the 1950s to demonstrate to publics across the globe that nuclear power was not only about annihilation in a military attack, physicists and engineers in a number of nations have advanced hopeful visions of the application of nuclear power in energy production, industry, agriculture, and medicine. During the Cold War, many of the applications advanced almost without check in competition with other

Hero Projects. Paul R. Josephson, Oxford University Press. © Oxford University Press 2024.
DOI: 10.1093/oso/9780197698396.003.0005

nations to be first and the most peaceful. Many of the projects, of course, had clearly military significance, such as nuclear rocket ships, airplanes, and even icebreakers—since the reactors for the last of these were in essence submarine reactors, and since the icebreakers served geopolitical purposes of opening and protecting harbors and seas.

Perhaps the most hubristic of the nations in pursuit of nuclear power has been Russia—the former Soviet Union. With physicists occupying nearly unassailable positions of prestige, and with them and political leaders sharing the firm belief that electricity—production of copious amounts of electricity—would secure the empire's glorious future, the nuclear lobby gained broad budgetary and social support. It embarked on ambitious programs to create a network of nuclear power stations throughout the European USSR. Many of these programs have found rebirth in Russia in the twenty-first century.

The powerful enterprise "Rosatom," essentially a self-contained hero project as one of the largest organizations and employers in the nation, is critically important to Russian geopolitical interests, economic power, and self-image. According to national leaders, Rosatom, the inheritor of civilian and military programs of the Soviet nuclear ministry "Minsredmash," will protect Arctic regions from growing foreign competition. It will assist in developing extensive national resources, and perhaps complete the unfinished tasks of the legendary northern shipping route that Stalin's super commissariat, Glavsevmorput, established. Toward these ends, Rosatom has both embarked on ambitious new nuclear power programs and resurrected and reshaped several ambitious Soviet-era ones. These include floating and other mobile nuclear power plants, icebreakers, and third-generation pressurized water reactors (PWRs) and breeder reactors (LMFBRs). Many of these projects have Cold War roots, and they seem to reflect reasonable technological choices given existing scientific and engineering experience, and a vast network of personnel and institutions. These are the projects of a powerful state corporation reborn in the Putin era whose programs reflect the economic interests of the state, geopolitical scientific competition, and nostalgia for the prestige of the Soviet past.

Russian state corporations are noncommercial entities, although with stocks. The state owns the majority of the stock of a state corporation. It is not bound by an "open information" requirement or by bankruptcy laws. This means it does not necessarily follow international accounting standards, although it may. Rather it is rather an opaque organization. Russian state corporations do not report to specific state bodies on their activities, nor can state organs request to see their documentation, financial reports, or other financial information, audit or control the activities of the state corporation, and so on. Many state corporations, for example Rosatom, are conglomerations of companies and can share the funds across units. Generally, the Russian president is the head of the corporation. Starting in 2007 the process of establishing state corporations gathered momentum as President Putin and his advisors pushed parliamentary legislation to establish a series of these organizations: Rosnano, Rosatom, Roskosmos, the latter created in 2015, and most of which represent cutting-edge scientific fields (nanotechnology, nuclear technology, and space). By the beginning of 2008, six of them had been created, with the one established for the Sochi Olympics later disbanded.

Together with state-owned joint stock companies (i.e., those in which the government owns more than 50 percent of the stock), these state corporations give the presidential administration great control over the leading sectors of the economy concerned with resource development (oil, gas, coal, nickel, copper, platinum, and so on) and for "big science" (space, nuclear, nanotechnology). Granted, the Russian president appoints state corporation directors, and they still have a degree of autonomy. But most state corporations have direct Soviet roots, for example those connected with space and nuclear industry. They receive both substantial funding through state budgets and through oligopolistic control of markets, and their power derives in part by the fact that leading officials are closely tied into government circles by personal contacts and by state ownership of the majority shares of the corporations. Rosatom, according to Julian Cooper, "may be one of the best run corporations in Russia, [and] an interesting example of path dependency. I know from talking to business people that they are always impressed by the professionalism of its managers." A visit to its webpage and the kinds of documents and materials available to understand its organization, structure, and business capabilities confirms Cooper's evaluation.[1]

Rosatom's size, power, and range of projects indicates that the nuclear enterprise has recovered from the 1990s when, because of a series of political and economic crises, including massive deficits and inflation, many reactor construction projects were put in mothballs.[2] After the Chernobyl disaster in 1986, leading specialists worried openly about continued operation of the remaining Chernobyl-type RBMK reactors at the Kursk, Smolensk, and Sosnovy Bor (Leningrad) sites, although they eventually kept those stations open. Now, an extensive, state-supported recovery demonstrates the allure and political security of nuclear-powered futures for Russia. By 2007, officials had created Rosatom with capitalization valued at $40 to $50 billion, consisting of 350 enterprises and employing over 190,000 people.[3] As its head for many years, Sergei Kirienko observed that Rosatom was "a recreation of the legendary Minsredmash of the USSR, but in new market conditions."[4] The entire program consists of efforts to create on closed fuel cycle with PWRs and breeder reactors, and to keep the submarine builders of the Cold War in the business of launching floating nuclear reactors of various sorts. Many of the people in Rosatom and its shipping division, Atomflot, see it as a new ministry of the Arctic, capable of powering hydrocarbon development, keeping the Northern Sea Route open, and securing the nation's borders. Through scores of nuclear power stations it will illuminate the taiga and tundra. It is actively selling reactors abroad to Iran, Finland, Bangladesh, Belarus, and elsewhere. Because the history of the Soviet nuclear program— its development, size, various military programs, and in particular its reactors—is well documented[5], this chapter will focus on the programs of Rosatom in the twenty-first century as manifestations of continuity in grandeur, scope, institutions, and visions with the Soviet past.

Reactors in Russia's Electricity Plans to the Mid-Twenty-first Century

Over the next decades, Rosatom intends to build scores of reactors in Russia and abroad at construction and licensing speeds never before encountered in the international industry, and to increase the share of nuclear electrical energy nationally from around 18 percent in 2014 to 50 percent by 2050.[6] The Russian government started planning for rapid expansion of nuclear power capacity in the late 1990s. In July 1998, the Russian government approved the Minatom's "Program for Development of Atomic Energy in the Russian Federation in 1998–2005 and for the Period until 2010." Under this plan, nine reactors would be decommissioned, and sixteen would be brought on line by 2010 including four to produce district heat; during the Soviet period, specialists envisaged these "AST" reactors on the outskirts of major cities to produce steam for housing, industry, and even desalination.[7] Substantial export earnings were also anticipated through the sale of reactors to Finland, Iran, Vietnam, Egypt, and elsewhere, and also of "floating" nuclear power plants to a long list of potential customers, although plans for reactor exports have faltered owing to the Russian attack of Ukraine and the cancellation of orders already by Finland.[8]

By the mid-2000s it was clear that the 1998 program was unrealistic; indeed, only three new reactors came on line in 2001, 2004, and 2010 respectively. This failure did not prevent Rosatom from announcing in October 2006 the plan to bring ten new power units online between 2007 and 2015.[9] Yet this plan appeared reasonable compared to the next Rosatom vision that forecast at least thirty reactors by 2020 (*not* realized), including floating nuclear power stations.[10] In their unlimited confidence, these documents indicate that the Russian nuclear industry has recovered from its self-inflicted wound of Chernobyl, even if the environmental and public health costs of the Chernobyl disaster will be paid out for some time to come. Indeed, Chernobyl is rarely mentioned, or is an afterthought among engineers, although Putin commemorates the disaster annually on its anniversary.[11]

The next-generation VVER 1200 (a pressurized water reactor, or PWR), the flagship nuclear power and the core product of Rosatom's program, features "improved performance across all parameters and a range of additional safety systems preventing radioactive substances from getting out of hermetically sealed containment in cases of emergency." The VVER 1200 has a 20 percent higher power capacity while having a size comparable to VVER 1000, an extended sixty-year service that seems unrealistic given the tremendous heat, pressure, and radiation stresses on reactors; and is apparently earthquake-proof, its designers claim. The VVER 1200 is manufactured by Atommash in Volgodonsk, the resurrected facility intended to produce reactors serially. Yet even if meant to reduce costs and lower the opportunity for worker error in the field, the notion of serial production of reactor components, like automobiles, seems premature.[12] As for RBMKs, the Russians believe they can manage still operating units in safe regime, in spite of the lack of containment, rapidly accumulating spent fuel on site, and inherent instability flaws. With license extensions, Kursk units 1–4 and Leningrad units 1–4 will continue to operate into the late 2020s, and Smolensk 1-3 into the 2030s. Units outside of Russia in Lithuania and Ukraine have been permanently closed, in the former case as a prerequisite for joining the EU, in the latter case because of the Chernobyl disaster.

Breeding Plutonium: A Closed Fuel Cycle

Russia has long pursued liquid metal fast breeder reactors (LMRBRs). Breeders can reduce actinide wastes, in particular plutonium, by consuming them. Breeders transmute ^{238}U that is non-fissile into ^{239}Pu that is fissile. Spent fuel can be reprocessed and used again and again in a reactor, in theory until all the energy in it is extracted, but leaving waste, although the waste decays over hundreds of years, not millions of years as with the actinides. Yet reusing the fuel—closing the fuel cycle—is hardly clean and far more expensive than the open cycle in PWRs, physicists have hesitated to use these alternative fuels for safety reasons, and there is sufficient uranium to power them for decades.

The United States (in the 1970s), France, and Japan (in the 2000s) abandoned commercialization of breeders for fuel cycle, as well as non-proliferation and technical reasons, leaving Russia the world leader in the field.[13] Russian engineers were not worried about breeders and proliferation, and even in the face of significant technical problems have pushed into the twenty-first century to bring on line an industrial prototype. The first Soviet industrial breeder, the BN-350, arose in the desert in the 1970s at Shevchenko (now Aktau), on a Caspian Sea peninsula rich in uranium deposits, oil, and gas. The BN-350 operated from 1972 to 1999 to produce electricity and de-salinate water. Powered with "nuclear" water and electricity, Soviet engineers built chemical and petrochemical industries along with a city to support them. This all became the Mangistauskii Atomic Energy Combine upon Kazakh independence, but it was closed in 1997 because of an international agreement and concerns about its safety, although it had been designed for fifty years of operation.[14] Indeed, breeder reactors have had a checkered history of cost overruns, sodium spills, and fires.

Engineers next pursued the BN-600 reactor, whose first blueprints date to the early 1960s, at the Maiak Chemical Combine, a facility to produce weapons-grade plutonium and also of extensive regional pollution, including of Lake Karachai and the Techa River, sites of some of the world's worst nuclear disasters.[15] They settled instead on construction at the picturesque Belioarsk NPP in the foothills of the Ural Mountains.[16] During the operation of the BN-600, there have been at least twelve cases of ruptures, twenty-seven leaks, five of which with radioactive sodium, fourteen with sodium fires, five because of improper repairs, and in one case a leak of 1,000 kg of sodium;[17] sodium conflagrates in contact with water or oxygen. A series of other accidents has plagued Beloiarsk—both its VVERs and its LMFBRs. In January 1987, BN-600 fuel rods melted. Total radioactivity was about 100,000 Ci; this was a level 4 accident according to the International Nuclear Event Scale, indicating a serious accident with local consequences. In August 1992 an expedition of Goskomchernobyl Russia near BAES observed anomalous concentrations of ^{137}Cs and ^{60}Co. In December 1992, personnel mishandled liquid radioactive wastes leading to spills of 15 m^3 and total radioactivity of 6 mCi; this was a level 3 accident. In September 2000 personnel of Sverdlovenergo mistakenly cut power to the station; three seconds later the BN-600 scrammed, steam was released, and according to an expert commission only several minutes remained before a catastrophic accident would have occurred.[18] The beautiful forests and cooling lake of the BAES station have also not fared well.

In spite of all this, Iurii Kazanskii, who participated in the start-up of the BN-600 in 1980, explained the long break in moving ahead with breeders not because of accidents, but meddling by Green Party activists in a special commission to evaluate the BN-600's safety. He remained convinced that the BN-800 would function properly.[19] It, too, dates to the Soviet era, being designed from 1983 to 1993. Plans to build four BN-800s were stopped after Chernobyl, and only in 1997 did the LMFBR program take off again.[20] This reactor has fans. Iurii Nosov, the main engineer at Beloiarsk, praises it as an "omnivore" for being able to operate on almost any fuel, even that reprocessed from other reactors.[21] After the Russian annexation of Crimea, Aleksandr Shutikov, director of production and operation of NPPs of Rosenergoatom, found another reason to praise the BN-800: it was of national significant because it "can guarantee the energy of Crimea"—some 1,600 km away.[22] Putin put his imprimatur on breeders, claiming that fast reactors are "technically quite feasible," perhaps because he agrees with Kazanskii, who called the BN-800 "a question of the leadership of Russia."[23] Late in 2016, Russian engineers in Zarechnyi began operation of the BN-800. It is no coincidence that Beloiarsk operators pushed to bring the BN-800 on line on December 22, "Day of Energetics," which celebrates Lenin's State Program for Electrification, GOELRO.[24]

Next on the drawing board is the BN-1200 (1200 MW), which is expected to become the mainstay of breeders, with a new design that consumes 50 percent less steel than the BN-800, with the number of primary loop valves reduced from 500 to 90, and total piping 30 percent shorter.[25] When the BN-1200 was announced, the head of Rosenergoatom, Romanov, asserted that three BN-1200s would be online by 2030 in an unheard of fifteen-year construction period, would "enable a closed nuclear fuel cycle," and heralded "a new era in nuclear power engineering."[26] There have been conflicting reports when the BN-1200s will commence construction, let alone how many will be built. In February 2016 the then head of Rosatom, Sergei Kirienko, opined that the fate of the BN-1200 depends on whether they can lower the costs of construction since the BN-600 was more expensive than the VVERs by roughly 30 percent and the BN-800 was more expensive by 16 percent. But in a draft energy strategy up to 2035 published in 2020 the BN-1200 was not included, and judging by technical problems with the BN-800 and resources diverted to the war, perhaps a more likely date is after 2040.[27]

Russian specialists insist that experience with the BN-600 and BN-800 justify moving to serial production of the larger BN-1200s. Beloiarsk director Nikolai Oshkanov acknowledges that there were problems with sodium leaks in the past, but that they have solved this problem, on top of which breeders, he claims, generate less radioactive waste than conventional reactors. He waxes nuclear, "In this case the future of atomic energy will really be radiant (будет действительно светлым)."[28] As for less waste, that is a misleading statement. The hope is that breeders will consume plutonium produced in other reactors. But waste in mining, milling, fuel manufacture, and reprocessing will be extensive and intractable. Breeder reactors are opposed by non-proliferationists of all stripes, not only by Russian ecologists.[29] Alexander Nikitin points out that it is hardly possible to achieve a closed cycle, nor to manufacture fuel without risk at Maiak or Zheleznogorsk, nor prevent more plutonium from finding its way into the environment.[30] There is only the myth of proliferation-resistant technology.[31]

Portable and Floating Nuclear Power Stations

After their initial stage of development, some technologies seem to take on a life of their own, in particular large-scale technologies that make it difficult to influence and steer, let alone to stop and defund them. As noted earlier, this "momentum" ensures that they continue in some form, gaining resources and investment. Technological momentum has surely contributed to the construction of mobile nuclear power stations in the Russian Federation.

Based on submarine reactors of crucial service to Cold War submarine-launched ballistic missiles (SBLMs), developed in Severodvinsk at Sevmash, in St. Petersburg at the Baltic Shipyards, and in a number of powerful de-sign institutes, floating reactors, known by their Russian acronyms as PAES or PATES, can provide electric energy and heat above the Arctic Circle, according to their promoters in almost any bay or inlet, and may be used to desalinate water for potential clients in a series of arid, equatorial coun-tries. Rosatom intends to sell them for $335 million each: China, Algeria, Indonesia, Brazil, Malaysia, Indonesia, Mozambique, Namibia, South Africa, Egypt, Jordan, Kuwait, Vietnam, and others have expressed an in-terest in them. Orders may depend on how well the first PAES, the "Academic Lomonosov," in Pevek, on Chukotka's northern Arctic shore where it was moored in September 2019, twelve years after construction began in St. Petersburg, operates.

Mobile and floating reactors are nothing new, have completely military roots, and were developed in the United States as well. For example, a US sur-plus Liberty Ship, the *Sturgis*, was fitted with a reactor to serve the Panama Canal in the late 1960s and early 1970s, but was moved out of harm's because of fears of a terrorist attack on it.[32] In the USSR, Igor Kurchatov, the head of the Soviet atomic bomb project, energetically pushed the development of mobile reactors, including component atomic power stations that could be parachuted into remote regions and be assembled quickly on site. Nuclear locomotives, also, were explored, both by Soviet and American engineers in the 1950s; the Soviet Ministry of Railways saw nuclear locomotives as a way to avoid electrification of rails in the Arctic, Far East, and Central Asia. Russia's railroaders have not abandoned the lure of the atomic locomotive. In 2011, Russian Railways vice president Valentin Gapanovich announced a joint project with Rosatom to build a nuclear locomotive with a fast-neutron reactor that would be used in the Far North, as well as to provide electricity to small settlements in those areas.[33]

Soviet engineers built several mobile models that moved on flatbed railway cars and tank treads, no doubt intended initially for military purposes in some occupied area or to replace generation capacity destroyed in war. The Belarusian contribution to this genre of devices, the Pamir-630-D, had a 630 kW reactor "hidden" on a tractor-trailer truck within 2 m thick walls; the authorities sent its spent nuclear fuel to the Maiak Chemical Combine for reprocessing only in 2010.[34] Similarly, the Russians developed a project, Volnolom ("Wavebreaker")-3 on the basis of submarine reactors, for the Novaia Zemlia nuclear weapons test site at the end of the 1970s, to provide electricity in the event that US nuclear bombs destroyed electricity infrastructure, with design work continuing into the 1990s.[35] The grandfather of these devices was the TES-3 tank model developed at Obninsk at 1.5 MWe with a PWR that operated from June 1961 until 1965.

Floating reactors thus are nothing new. Yet whether they are necessary or safe remains an open question. Many people criticize PAES precisely because the power units are based on Cold War submarine technology. The floating stations are also vulnerable to weather, tsunamis, and terrorism in ways that land-based facilities are not. But Rosatom remains convinced in PAES safety and efficacy, and no one even suggests cutting this program as unrealistic or unsafe. A recent study at the Massachusetts Institute of Technology confirmed the safety of floating NPPs, albeit with significantly different design and deployment parameters than the PAES (using floating platforms more like oil and gas operations; anchored 22 km off coast where waves are not a significant risk and in relatively deep water; and use of PWRs).[36] Former Rosatom head Kirienko observed after the 2011 Fukushima disaster in Japan, "I know Fukushima has sparked many inflammatory rumors and gossip, including on the floating nuclear plant. Some people say that if a land-based plant could not withstand a tsunami, what would then happen with a waterborne nuclear plant. But nothing will happen. Everything will be just fine."[37] There have been at least forty-five accidents involving atomic apparatuses on "floating installations" in Russia, including at least ten major accidents on Soviet submarines.[38] Everything will be fine.

Floating reactors will be built precisely because Russia can build submarine-inspired reactors and wants to keep building them so that its nuclear shipyards remain nuclear beehives of activity. The Soviet navy had many hundreds of reactors; the Russian navy is still acquiring new designs. And floating reactors will be built because of the technological momentum of design bureaus, engineering firms, and Rosatom itself in the post-Soviet era.

In Russia the demand for PAES seems to be primarily to secure Arctic development. Already in 2007, Kirienko and the president of Sakha (Yakutia), Viacheslav Shtyrov, signed an agreement to invest in PAES to serve its northern regions.[39] Engineers are interminably enthusiastic.[40] At the Kurchatov Institute of Atomic Energy, the birthplace of the Soviet peaceful atom, physicists fully endorse the program of medium-power (and small-power) reactors based on the existence of a strong reactor and machine building industries connected with nuclear submarines and icebreakers. They forecast the size of floating and land-based units from 6 to 100 MW at "small" size, and medium units to 600 MW, produced serially, especially if factories can manufacture the parts and components. Rosatom will offer factory service and repair.[41]

Like other PAES, the 70 MW *Academician Lomonosov*, launched from the Baltic Shipbuilding Yard in June 2017 for fueling in Murmansk,[42] and later tugged to Pevek, near Chukotka on the Eastern Arctic Coast,[43] is affixed to a barge, moored in a bay, and surrounded by buffers against ice and waves. It finally began operation in December 2019. The hope is that the PAES will rejuvenate Pevek as a logistical center of the Northern Sea Route. In general, a PAES barge may have four units, either power plants or desalination plants, or a combination of these applications, plus living quarters for sixty workers. KLT-40 reactors adapted from submarines, each producing 35 MWe with a lifetime of thirty-eight years, will be employed. According to specifications, they will have a relatively repair-free life span of 110,000 hours and should operate continuously without maintenance for periods of up to 9,000 hours in harsh Arctic conditions.[44] Each of perhaps ninety crewmembers who works by shift method, four months on, four months off, will have his own quarters and bathroom. There will also be a sports hall, pool, banya and sauna, library, hair salon, and even bakery "that they say turns out very tasty [bread]."[45] This "sales brochure" assessment of PAES ignores the fact that the *Academician Lomonosov* was hit by significant delays and cost overruns, as have all nuclear projects around the world, since its start in the 1990s, with its final cost three times above original estimate.[46]

As with other such technologies, it is difficult to know precisely how many PAES are planned and when they will appear. Partly, this is because of the typical cost overruns and delays for any nuclear technology, but also because the industry—as any major industry—uses its enthusiastic forecasts to assure clients, including the Russian government, what is possible, and these forecasts change every few years. Rosatom apparently plans to manufacture about a dozen of these units as a first step. In any event, Rosatom brought the floating *Lomonosov* to full power in 2021 to replace the Bilibino ATETs (a thermal electric nuclear station) and Chaunskaia TETs (fossil fuel boiler).[47]

Icebreaker Nostalgia

Russia's nuclear icebreakers are dedicated to opening Arctic resources, serving military bases, and resurrecting Stalin's Glavsevmorput. Like Stalin's public airplane spectacles to demonstrate enlightened leadership and Soviet achievement, so for Russia's current leaders, icebreakers are a kind of techno-logical sublime.[48] They demonstrate control over nature and geography, na-tional will and world leadership at the cutting edge of engineering, and they will enable assimilation of Arctic resources. Russian leaders, businessmen, journalists, and citizens ignore such problems as massive cost overruns, lags in construction, and a series of serious accidents in running the icebreakers, instead celebrating them as a sign of national virility as the preeminent ice-breaker power over Canada, the United States, and other nations. Russian specialists forecast that by 2030 they will have established year-round trans-port to strategic sites along the Russian coast—through the construction of no fewer than forty new icebreakers, a number of them nuclear-powered and run by Atomflot, a division of Rosatom. Big ships and icebreakers also serve to secure the defense of the nation and the legacy of empire bequeathed by Soviet power. On many occasions, Putin has shown up to christen new ships or shipyards (or pipeline pumping stations served by Arctic tankers). In 2007 on board the nuclear icebreaker *Fiftieth Anniversary of Victory*, Putin declared the need to increase the competitiveness of Russian naval freighting, and he emphasized that the Naval Doctrine of the Russian Federation to 2020 employed nuclear icebreakers to be competitive in world markets.[49] Russian officials are sanguine about global warming in that it has led to the rapid melting of polar icecaps and will ease shipping in the Arctic Ocean.

The nuclear icebreaker fleet developed in parallel with domestic nuclear power.[50] The decision to build the first nuclear icebreaker was taken on November 20, 1953, and six years later the *Lenin* was launched on September 5, 1959. A matter of national pride, and a typical all-union hero project, over 500 manufacturing plants and organizations all over the country were in-volved in its building. Its sailors relished gleaming white interiors, polished wood railings, sauna, and swimming pool. Other nuclear vessels joined the caravan beginning in the 1960s and 1970s: *Arktika*, *Siberia*, *Rossiia*, *Sovetskii Soiuz*, and *Iamal* built at the Ordzhonikidze Baltic Plant in Leningrad, and the *Sevmorput'* lighter container ship was built at the Butoma Peninsula Shipyard in Kerch in Crimea that Russian annexed from Ukraine in 2014. The *Taimyr* and *Vaigach* nuclear icebreakers were built at Wärtsilä Marine in Finland (1985–1989) using Soviet equipment and steel, and both were launched on the eve of the breakup of the USSR.

Of six Russian nuclear icebreakers, five were built in the Soviet period and are reaching the end of their service. In August 2008, the fleet was handed over to Atomflot. Atomflot operates four icebreakers with the capacity of

75,000 horsepower (the *Rossiia*, *Sovetskii Soiuz*, *Iamal*, and *50th Anniversary of Victory*), two icebreakers at 50,000 hp (*Taimyr* and *Vaigach*), and a lighter container ship *Sevmorput'* with 40,000 hp. In addition, there are two service ships (*Imandra* and *Lotta*), a special tanker for liquid radioactive waste *Serebrianka* (the *Smolt*), and a vessel for personnel cleanup and dose measurement, *Rosta-1*. The *Arktika*, a second-generation nuclear icebreaker, was retired on October 3, 2008, after thirty-six years of service.

To this day, Russia officials and engineers reminisce about the glories of the *Lenin* icebreaker and its offspring. When referring to competition for Arctic resources, journalists point out that Russia is a full quarter century ahead of the other nations in the icebreaker, if not the space, race—witness the Luna-25 spacecraft that Roscosmos crashed into the moon in August 2023. At the end of the 1950s, "We left the Americans behind and first built a nuclear icebreaker," the chief engineer of the *Lenin* recalled.[51] Yet the *Lenin* had two serious accidents in 1965 and 1967, both of which released significant amounts of radioactivity and required illegal dumping of wastes and reactors at sea.[52] On August 17, 2012, the nation observed the twenty-fifth anniversary of the sailing of the *Arktika* to the North Pole, the world's first surface vessel to do this.[53] This was the celebration of a nuclear icebreaker that was turned into scrap four years earlier. A journalist wrote, "The shutdown of the reactors of the 'Arktika' in no way signifies that the biography of this wondrous ship has closed, for she will be turned into scrap metal."[54]

Nuclear icebreakers remain crucial cultural artifacts. One journalist who writes for *Pravda*, recalled how, early on the morning of August 17, 1977, the authorities announced *Arktika*'s venture to the North Pole. He observed, "The world propaganda effect was roughly that after the flight of Iurii Gagarin. At the northern top of the earth the flag of the USSR was planted. . . . ,I remember that both Soviet central TV stations reported up to the hilt about the details. . . . The mighty Soviet people rejoiced."[55]

To indicate its Soviet heritage, the next new icebreaker to be launched was also christened *Arktika*.[56] Unfortunately, extensive cost overruns and delays plagued this megaproject that, in 2016, finally left the Baltika Shipbuilding drydocks in St. Petersburg for tests in the Gulf of Finland and the loading of the reactor in Murmansk. The *Arktika*, and other icebreakers of the new LK-110Ya new type, will have reactors at 110 MW, are planned to lead caravans of ships year-round, handle ice to 4.3 m in thickness, and have a top speed of 12 knots instead of 6 in the previous generation; the ship was launched in 2022 at two to three times its original $1 billion estimated cost.[57] Yet the

Arktika has suffered a series of commissioning problems: in February 2020 the propulsion motor on the starboard shaft failed during the quayside trials, reducing the vessel's maximum icebreaking capability by about 20 cm; and design problems led to the increase in the *Arktika's* operating draft from the planned 8.7 m (29 ft) to 9.3 m (31 ft), which would prevent it from operating efficiently in such shallow ice-covered river estuaries such as the Gulf of Ob. Putin has demanded investigation of cadres and organization to identify who is responsible for all of these problems. But it may be difficult to find the culprits, since the contractors were personally selected by the ex-head of Rosatom, Sergei Kirienko, who became the first deputy head of the presidential administration.[58]

Nuclear icebreaking engineers have Soviet pedigrees or were trained by Soviet engineers, indicating that Soviet institutions gave significant momentum to their Russian inheritors. Two Soviet-era design bureaus participated in the *Arktika* project, the Afrikantov OKBM, an enterprise of Rosatom founded in 1945 that is now responsible for reactor design and manufacture of reactors for ships, icebreakers, floating nuclear power plants, and fast reactors,[59] and the TsKB "Iceberg" that dates to a 1947 resolution of the Council of Ministers "with the goal to serve the Northern Sea Route with powerful icebreakers and transport fleet for sailing in the Arctic and the transformation of the Northern Sea Route into a normally functioning ship highway."[60]

In 2016, Atomflot helped transit 7 million tons of freight. The head of Atomflot, Viacheslav Ruksha, claimed that in 2021 the tonnage will rise to 40 million and by 2025 to 75 million tons, and will meet the government's target of liquefied natural gas and other freight for 2025 and beyond, especially with the launching of three LK-60 (MW) icebreakers: the "Arktika," "Sibir," and "Ural."[61] The "Sibir'" entered service in January 2022, and the "Ural" underwent successful testing in the Gulf of Finland in October 2022, and awaits now final testing and commissioning. (The "Yakutia" and "Chukotka" are projected to enter service in 2024 and 2026, respectively.) These Project 22220 icebreakers, with twin RITM-200 reactors, were designed to break through 2.8 m thick ice at up to two knots. Planners intend these nuclear icebreakers to clear the ice for continued huge increases in tonnage and speed of freight along the Northern Sea Route. Taking advantage of climate change and recovery from the global economic crisis of 2007-08, in 2017 Atomflot's ships assisted 87 sailings, 48 in the east, 39 in the western regions of the Arctic.[62] Yet the usual failure of Russian plans to meet targets, COVID-19 pandemic, global economic downturn, and Russia's war on Ukraine have together joined to preclude building on the modest freight increases.

Nuclear icebreakers remain artifacts of special political, economic and cultural importance in Russia. The head of third generation icebreaker projects, Roman Chernigovtsev, spoke of the pride of his staff and employees in the fact that only Russia—and only the Baltic Factory—built nuclear icebreakers. Atomflot general director Viacheslav Ruksha added, "Our country possesses a unique fleet of atomic icebreakers . . . that demonstrates our unconditional leadership in this area."[63] According to a recent article, Russia has "always had the largest and most powerful [icebreaker] fleet in the world. In the inheritance from the USSR Russia gained several dozen icebreakers and ships of 'ice class'—e.g., nuclear icebreakers. But time hasn't stood still. The time has come to build new, more contemporary models!" The article concludes, "Russia is ahead, so it was and so it will be."[64] Russia is ahead, and so it will be, because of institutional momentum, nostalgia, geopolitical interests, and national fascination with the Northern Sea Route, and these factors will enable Atomflot and the political leadership to overlook cost and technical challenges to building new icebreakers.

A manifestation of technological momentum—and in this case a kind of cultural momentum—is the identification of Rosatom as a kind of Glavsevmorput of the twenty-first century in solving problems of exploitation of oil, gas, and rare metals, and ensuring commerce and freight along the Arctic Ocean shores to enable Russia to stay ahead of the growing economies of Asia including China.[65] Atomflot in this regard acts as an "infrastructure company" tying together pipelines, mines, canals, ports, polar aviation, and ships through nuclear icebreakers with great economic effect. Atomflot both serves and relies on the state to function because "megaprojects here without the direct participation of the government are impossible."[66] Russia's "Arctic SPG-2" program, to produce liquid natural gas, to keep Arctic shipping lanes open, to escort caravans of tankers, and to feed such clients as China, encompasses precisely the geological survey, shipping, and resource management tasks of Stalin's Glavsevmorput ninety years earlier.[67]

One manifestation of Rosatom's growing role as a kind of Glavsevmorput is Sabetta Port, a joint venture between NOVATEK, Russia's largest independent natural gas producer, and the Russian government. Construction on the port commenced in summer 2013.[68] In November 15, 2017, the icebreaking tug *Yuribey* arrived at Sabetta for winter work, assisted by

Atomflot icebreakers, to ensure the flow of LNG.[69] Sabetta Port centers on a large LNG facility capable of producing 16.5 million tons of LNG per year, while nuclear icebreakers and tugs have become essential parts of this large-scale technology to enable export of LNG year-round by sea. As noted earlier, a 180 km railway line will connect the Bovanenkovo gas fields on the Yamal Peninsula to Sabetta. Atomflot has considered the possibility of building icebreakers powered by LNG instead of reactors because of the Novatek projects in the Kara Sea. These will cost at least €200 million each, although at half the cost of a nuclear icebreaker.[70]

Will Rosatom and Atomflot help realize the dream of complete Arctic assimilation and exploitation that dates to the Stalin era? A dream of resources flowing seamlessly from Arctic climes to Moscow, through ships, and caravans, and pipelines from the Kara and Barents Seas to the industrial heartland and to clients in Europe, and increasingly China and Southeast Asia? Dmitrii Rogozin, chair of the state committee for Arctic development, apparently thinks so. He referred to Rosatom precisely as the operator and administrator of the Northern Sea Route and the territories abutting it, and he envisaged giving Rosatom the responsibilities of a new kind of agency with all sorts of responsibilities over the Arctic.[71]

Polar Bears in the Control Room: Deep Ocean Prospecting and Mars Missions

Russia's nuclear shipbuilding industry has found striking ways to engage the resources of the peaceful atom. After the Cold War, such shipbuilding yards as Zvezdochka and Sevmash in Severodvinsk on the White Sea fell on hard times. The vital and active shipyards let some employees go, while others sought to set up small businesses based on shipyard production units and materials (submarine "crystal" decanters or shiny steel hip flasks, anyone?). Yet most loyal and patriotic employees never lost hope for a variety of peaceful applications that would take advantage of the machine shops, reactor technology, and other components of Cold War manufacture. In the late 1990s some of the factory officials mentioned to me that a number of important military conversions came to mind including nuclear-powered deep water drilling platforms. Of course, the Exxon *Valdez* and Deep Water Horizon disasters came to mind, the former on March 24, 1989, when the huge *Valdez* struck a reef in Alaska's Prince William Sound and spilling

260,000 to 750,000 barrels of crude oil, covering 2,100 km of coastline and 28,000 km^2 of ocean with long-term, significant, and irreversible damage.[72] The explosion and sinking of the Deepwater Horizon offshore drilling rig in April 2010 killed eleven workers and spread oil over hundreds of kilometers of Gulf of Mexico coastlines.[73] The Barents Sea would hardly be easier and safer to drill, and its coastlines are just as fragile and important to world ecology.

The physicists of the Kurchatov Institute and the engineers of Sevmash and Zvezdochka nonetheless have in mind precisely submarine nuclear tankers and nuclear-powered oil drilling platforms to face of the great challenges of drilling and transporting oil and gas in treacherous arctic waters. The Kurchatov Institute remains the leading R&D engine of the nuclear enterprise in Russia. Its specialists, together with those at the All-Union Research Institute of the Oil and Gas Industry (VNIIGAZ), had determined that nuclear power will solve the "grandiose problem of the assimilation of the arctic shelf," by which they mean extracting oil and gas from what may be 30 percent of the world's reserves in conditions of ice and deep ocean. They propose autonomous underwater surveying, extracting, and transportation technology powered by nuclear energy that will be "energy efficient" and with the "smallest risk of negative impact on the environment."[74]

The Kurchatov Institute has an interesting place in the nuclear empire. Founded by its namesake in the 1940s in what was a field in the Moscow city limits ("October Field"), it now dominates basic and applied research of the entire nuclear enterprise. With its central institute in Moscow, it has branches with different research foci in Gatchina, Moscow, Protvino, and St. Petersburg, and its specialists cover a range of topics from nuclear physics to plasma research, to high-energy physics and theoretical physics. Its past president (and president of the Soviet Academy of Sciences), Anatoli Aleksandrov, was a principal designer of the ill-fated RBMK reactor. And its current president, Mikhail Kovalchuk, has direct connections with the Russian president.

Kovalchuk is the scientific director of nanotechnology industrial R&D of the nation's effort in that crucial field. Yet Kovalchuk, a specialist in materials science, was not a full member of Russian Academy of Sciences and therefore was prohibited from being appointed an Academy vice president, an appointment legally required for official designation as nanotechnology tsar. Instead, his was given the title "acting" vice president of the Academy for nanotechnology. Further, because Putin been involved in ongoing efforts to force the Academy to comply more directly with government dictates, rumors circulated that Kovalchuk might become its next president.[75] Despite pressure from Putin, the Academy rejected Kovalchuk's application for full membership in May 2008. Making the situation more curious, Mikhail Kovalchuk may have been drawn into the inner circle of Kremlin politics by his brother, Iurii, who, who became president of Rossiia Bank, and who has gained the imprimatur of "Putin's Purse." Iurii Kovalchuk, Putin, and several other individuals became acquainted through involvement in a kind of gated community of summer homes outside of St. Petersburg, where their acquaintances date back twenty-five years.[76] The nuclear enterprise, nanotechnology, Rossiia Bank, oil and, gas are thus linked through personal connections, big science projects, and wealthy oligarchs. And in any event the Academy of Sciences was subjugated fully to the Putin administration by 2017 including its formerly secret elections to membership, property holdings, and budgets.[77]

Kurchatov specialists cannot rest. They are now advancing other floating and submersible nuclear devices: tankers, gas compressing stations, drilling equipment, and so on. Underwater tankers have been designed by the Malakhit Engineering firm and have living quarters, turbogenerators, icebreaking equipment, and of course nuclear reactors.[78] Another engineering group proposes an underwater LNG tanker at 277,000 T at 260 m in length, and perhaps $600 million in cost.[79]

Not content to drive mobile reactors on the tundra, tug the floating ones into Arctic bays, and send nuclear subs and tankers diving into the ocean, Rosatom has turned its visions to the heavens. Another program, a fantasy judging by the grudging progress in aeronautical applications, is nuclear-powered space research. Intensively for at least twenty years, and intermittently since the 1970s, both the United States and USSR experimented with development of nuclear rocket ships, airplanes, space-based reactors, and nuclear batteries, the outrageously expensive rockets and airports an abject failure, and the Soviets launched at least thirty nuclear powered satellites into space, several of which have burned up upon re-entry into the atmosphere and some radioactivity fell to earth on premature re-entry. Indefatigable in the search for new heights, the Russians nevertheless intend to power a Mars expedition with nuclear power, and they also are designing a reactor for a lunar base that Putin insists will be manned by 2030–2035.[80] As for Mars, Kirienko at one time announced that Rosatom would have a prototype nuclear engine, capable of reaching Mars and bringing cosmonauts back, ready for testing by 2018;[81] it is not ready. Rosatom has already produced an experimental fuel for the Mars reactor to fuel a nuclear propulsion space engine that would, according to Kirienko, shorten the trip to the Red Planet significantly.[82]

From Mars to the moon, from inlets and bays on the Arctic shore to deep sea drilling, and from the usual PWRs and LMFBRs, Rosatom has established a powerful vision for the ubiquitous power of the atom. That power rests on nostalgia for the Soviet era, and the tremendous momentum of the institutes, factories, and design bureaus of the nuclear enterprise that have recovered from the shock of the end of the Cold War and the breakup of the USSR. It counts on the support of a resource state whose president sees exploitation of oil and gas as the key to Russia's strength. And it moves forward with few checks on its programs. Some of the public is skeptical of these hubristic applications, and citizens have essentially been deprived of the right to protest against the nuclear enterprise—and almost everything else—in Putin's Russia. But most of them accept post-Chernobyl nuclear power as safe and important to the nation's energy balance. Whether Rosatom has gained public acquiescence or simply can ignore what it believes are misplaced safety concerns, the nuclear enterprise can and will embrace the largesse of the government as it advances its programs and those of a nuclear-powered resource state.

ILLUSTRATIONS PART II

Floating Reactors. Bringing Power on Nuclear Barges to the Arctic.

Image 18 The *Academician Lomonosov*, the first floating nuclear power station, was tugged from the "Baltika" shipyard in St. Petersburg to Murmansk for fueling and to Pevek, on the Chukotka coast, in August 2019 for power generation, a distance of 10,000 km. Well over cost and long delayed, the station remains a symbol of the hubris of the nation's nuclear corporation, Rosatom, to produce a series of floating reactors to power Arctic resource development. Soviet and Russian planners have coveted the antimony, copper, gold, molybdenum, and other minerals in the Chukotka region, and forced the indigenes of the region, Chukchis, to join in industrial modernization. Rosatom is offering to sell these floating reactors abroad. Source: Wikimedia Commons.

Hero Projects or Forgotten Rural Poverty?

Image 19 The modernity of the *Academician Lomonosov* contrasts sharply
with decrepit infrastructure of Soviet Far East development, much of it initially
carried out in the massive Dalstroi gulag camp. Depicted here is the Bilibino
Bridge near the Bilibino Nuclear Power Plant that was closed down after the
mooring of the *Lomonosov* in Pevek some 400 km away. Moscow's oligarchs
may be rich, and they tout the glories of modern hero projects, but citizens live
in a different landscape and seemingly a different century. Source: Wikimedia
Commons.

Russia: First in Space!

Image 20 Cosmic research—space—was a Soviet hero project crucial in creating the myth of the invincible scientific superpower and the conqueror of all frontiers. The USSR was first in space with Sputnik (1957), the first man in space (Yuri Gagarin, 1961), and the first woman (Valentina Tereshkova, 1963), among other "firsts." Gagarin, who died in an accident in 1968, would have celebrated his fiftieth birthday in 1984, the year of the issue of this stamp. Space remains important to current Russian leaders, who have designated extensive labor and capital resources, including the new Vostochny Cosmodrome, still under construction, to replace that in Kazakhstan lost in the collapse of the USSR. The goal is to return man to space, first to a lunar base and then to Mars. Russian leaders believe that the West, in particular the United States, stole the fruits of Soviet space science in the 1990s on the cheap, and they are determined to re-establish the myths and realities of Russian preeminence in the cosmos. Putin greets each Cosmonautics Day (April 12) with a speech on the glories of Soviet science and of the will of the Russian people to return to their rightful place in the stars. The program, however, has been belabored by delays and failed launches. Source: Russian Postal Service.

Overlaying the Arctic. The Assimilation of Arctic Regions as Megaproject.

Images 21 and 22 The Stalin-era bureaucracy to create and administer a Northern Sea Route from Murmansk to Vladivostok, with all of the requisite scientific surveys, infrastructure, and personnel, called Glavsevmorput, has been reborn in Russia's Atomflot, the nuclear icebreaker company, and Rosatom, the state nuclear corporation, whose technologies will facilitate the breaking of ice, transporting supplies and commodities, and the provision of electricity and industrial heat in floating nuclear power stations. Russia sees the Arctic not only as strategically vital—witness the expansion of the country's military (and nuclear) presence in the north (troops, submarines, hypersonic weapons, and so on)—and economically central to the nation's future, but as its patrimony. Depicted here is a stamp praising the sailors of the *Cheliushkin*, a ship fitted with metal plates to cut through thick ice like an icebreaker to open a year-round sea route. But it was crushed in the ice and sank; its sailors were praised publicly, but many were arrested upon return to Leningrad and Moscow as "wreckers." A second stamp highlights recent efforts to establish national parks in the Arctic under Putin (and ignores the vast quantities of hazardous waste littering the region left there by Russian soldiers and oil workers). Source: Russian Postal Service.

Nuclear Icebreakers from Khrushchev to Putin.

Images 23 and 24 Nuclear icebreakers are an integral part of the megaproject to conquer the entire Arctic, open the Northern Sea Route to year-round shipping, and transform cold, icebound regions into sites of normal industrial operations and resource exploitation. Russian postage stamps explicitly tie today's icebreakers to Soviet achievements in celebrating "fifty years of the atomic fleet" in 2009, with one issue of four stamps including the mothballed *Lenin*. The *Lenin* was launched in 1957 and decommissioned in 1989 when its hull became too worn to endure another season of ice. Two serious accidents damaged its reactors in 1965 and again in 1967. Source: Russian Postal Service.

Soviet and Russian Arctic Explorers.

Soviet and Russian leaders have long supported Arctic exploration and assimilation, from a series of heroic expeditions in the 1930s that led to the loss of human life and ships, but were intended under Stalin to demonstrate that the Soviets *first* transited the Arctic Ocean in one shipping season, to a constant presence—for fifty years!—of drifting research stations north of the Arctic Circle into the 1990s, to the transformation of polar ice, snow, water, and land into a site of gas, oil, platinum, and other operations of service to the state. The explorers were a central aspect of the effort to demonstrate Russian ownership of the Arctic, indeed through such feats as the first flights over the North Pole (1930s) and the first surface ship to the North Pole (the nuclear icebreaker *Arktika*, 1977).

Image 25 In August 2007, the Russian parliamentarian and explorer Artur Chilingarov engaged a deep-sea dive in a bathyscaphe to plant a Russian flag on the bottom of the Arctic Ocean at the North Pole as if to claim the entire polar region for Russia. The expensive expedition included all of the components of Russia's claim to superpower status: a nuclear-powered icebreaker, *Rossiia*, a modern research ship, the *Akademik Fedorov*, the bathyscaphe itself, and Putin's blessings. In a regal ceremony on November 21, 2019, President Putin welcomed Chilingarov's flag-planting expedition and other activities as confirmation of Russia's claim on vast new Arctic territories. He awarded Chilingarov the "The Order for Services to the Fatherland II Degree." Source: Office of the President of the Russian Federation.

From the Glories of the Communist Party to the Glories of State Corporations!

Image 26 A sign of how powerful state corporations in contemporary Russia have replaced Soviet ministries in power, authority, and cultural significance is the honor given to them even in postage stamps, not only in the fact that their owner-oligarchs are essential actors in Kremlin power relationships. This 2016 issue highlights Lukoil, the second largest company in Russia after Gazprom, in the 2020 the ninety-ninth largest public company in the world, and one of the largest global producers of crude oil. We suppose the symbolism here is that a Lukoil worker is at the helm of Russia's (oil) future. Source: Russian Postal Service.

Image 27 Rosatom, a corporation of hundreds of thousands of workers engaged in military nuclear enterprises, also earned a stamp in 2020 on the seventy-fifth anniversary of the start of the atomic bomb project. The theme of the stamp stresses its largely peaceful activities (isotopes, construction, knowledge production), but a bomb and an icebreaker hovering in the background remind us that Russia is always prepared to defend the motherland with its nuclear might. The direct heritage of the Soviet atomic bomb project to Russia today—and the way that nuclear weapons protect the empire—is another crucial message. Source: Russian Postal Service.

Re-writing the History of Hero Projects.

Image 28 Soviet, and now Russian, historians have had a difficult time writing the history of hero projects. *Zeks* died. Projects failed. A number of the heroes later perished as "enemies of the people." Archives were closed. The Russian state has again ruled that several topics are off limits. For example, it is a crime in Russia to denigrate the memory of the "defenders of the USSR" in World War II—or to speak about Putin's war on Ukraine in negative voices. The government has shut down archival access and closed such NGOs as "Memorial" that preserve the memory of the victims of repression. The Russian government built on a clear tradition of rewriting history. Before it, the Soviet state made the final determination who was a hero and who was an enemy, even writing people out of history. In this photograph (right to left), Marshal Kliment Voroshilov, Viacheslav Molotov, Stalin, and Nikolai Yezhov, head of the secret police, visit the Moscow-Volga Canal at its dedication (1937). Yezhov was arrested late in 1938, executed in 1940, and it was ordered that his image be edited out of all copies of this photo, including those already published. Libraries used razor blades to cut this photo out of books. Source: Public Domain via Russian Federation Civil Code of 2006.

Putin Releases Siberian Cranes into the Wild.

Image 29 President Putin has orchestrated a series of photographic sessions to show that he not only instructs nature, especially its resources, to follow state interests, but that he is a man of nature, and that he speaks the language of dolphins, tigers, and polar bears, with all of whom he has posed. He shows concern for "nature" through such government acts as ordering the cleanup of dangerous Arctic detritus left by decades of Russian and Soviet colonists, explorers, factories, and military enterprises, and in his declaration of 2017 as Year of the Environment, even as oil, gas, mining, and transport megaprojects in the Arctic are destroying fragile ecosystems and displacing—again—such indigenes as Nenets reindeer herders. In September 2012, just short of his sixtieth birthday, Putin captained a motorized hang glider to lead Siberian cranes back into the wild. The effort failed. Source: Office of the President of the Russian Federation.

The Crimean Bridge: A Military Object That Also Symbolizes State Power.

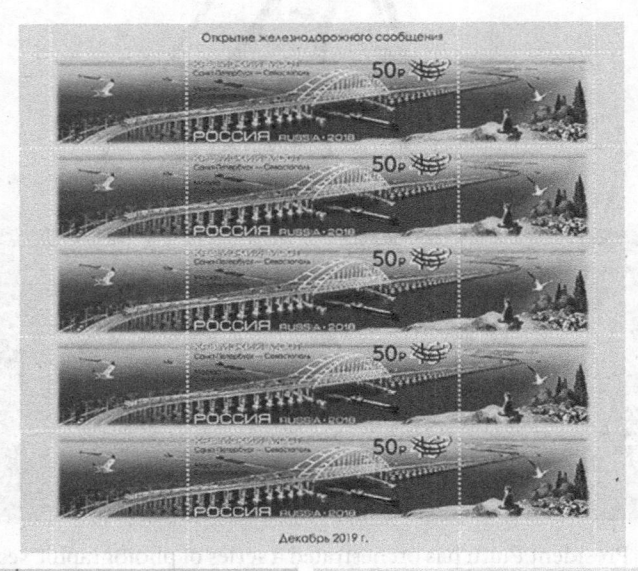

Images 30, 31, and 32 Russian militarists had plans to build a bridge connecting Russia from Krasnodar with Crimea over the Kerch Strait even before Russia's military annexation of Ukraine's Crimea in 2014. Hitler and Stalin both attempted to build such a bridge. Putin's Crimean Bridge, with parallel automobile and railroad components at a cost of $3.7 billion, was dedicated on May 15, 2018. A major hero project of contemporary Russia, along with its space and nuclear programs, the bridge symbolizes Putin's imperial dream to recreate the Soviet empire and has been a supply link for the Russia's war on Ukraine beginning in 2022. Like Stalin's hero projects, the Crimean Bridge is commemorated in postage stamps, here from 2018. It should be noted that the Crimean Bridge has faced several attacks during the ongoing war with Ukraine—and that cracks have appeared in concrete supports. Source: Russian Postal Service.

Vladimir Putin Drives a KamAz Truck.

Images 33 and 34 In early May 2018, during the week of the annual celebration of the Soviet Union's victory over Nazi Germany in World War II, still the crucible event in the nation's geopolitical mindset that insists on vigilance against all enemies, President Putin navigated a dump truck across the Crimean Bridge to link Russia with Crimea in an official memorialization of the structure. The scripted event demonstrated that Putin had completed the military seizure of the Crimean Peninsula from Ukraine to protect Russian citizens against Nazis in Ukraine—who do not exist—and the ever-present danger of American imperialism. The Russian press celebrated the fact that the bridge went up in record time. Putin's use of a KamAz truck (here commemorated in the year the KamAz factory opened in 1974)—that has served as a military transport, construction vehicle, and garbage truck—seemed incongruous with the intended meaning of the courageous leader resurrecting Russian control of Crimea on a modern bridge, as opposed to a truck driver in a vehicle that has changed little in fifty years, making a delivery of Russian imperialism. Source: Office of the President of the Russian Federation; Russian Postal Service.

The Saiano-Shushenskaia Hydropower Station Accident (2009).

Image 35 and 36 But hero projects always run the risk of massive technological failure, for example, at Chernobyl in 1986. In August 2009 the machine hall of a massive power station, the Saiano-Shushenskaia, the sixth largest in the world on the Yenisei River in Siberia, was destroyed when a 1,700-ton turbine burst through its cover, destroying the rest of the station and killing seventy-seven workers. Like BAM, it was late coming on line, well over cost, and operated poorly. Much of its Soviet-era machinery, including the turbine in question, had neared the end of safe operating life (this postage stamp commemorates the station's operation from 1981). In response to the accident, the Putin administration insisted the guilty parties would be identified, the debris cleared away, and the station repaired as quickly as possible. Putin publicly lamented losses at the station, but praised its resurrection as its "second life." Source: Russian Postal Service; Wikimedia Commons.

5

Bridges of Empire

Putin's Failed Crimean Bridge

Between the two shores and two seas,
Far from our birth mothers,
Our fate is not so simple,
We are building the Kerch bridge for the people.
So as not to lose touch with the huge country,
So that he who wants can return home,
There will be something to tell, those who visit,
Everyone is working here, and I drive the pile.

I'm hammering the pile,
I'm hammering the pile,
To the mark, to the point of refusal,
Let it not be easy, let it not happen immediately.
I'm hammering the pile,
I'm hammering the pile,
To the point, to the point of denial.[1]

In early May 2018, during the week of the annual celebration of the Soviet Union's victory over Nazi Germany in World War II, President Vladimir Putin navigated a dump truck across the Crimean Bridge to link Russia with Crimea. Putin looked in control, determined and confident at the wheel of the truck, an ubiquitous Kamaz that has served as a garbage truck, construction vehicle, and military transport since the opening of the truck factory in 1976 in Naberezhnye Chelny on the Kama River, at a typical, Soviet mass construction site built by 100,000 laborers armed with Western technology. Putin's choreographed drive reflected the symbolic end to a long journey that the president commenced in 2000: the restoration of the Russian empire with control of Crimea, a strategic outpost for Russia for dominion over the Black Sea, an unrealized fantasy since the 1830s and the signing of the Treat of Unkiar Skelessi between the Russian and Ottoman Empire that seemed to offer the Russian navy control from a base at Sevastopol to the Dardanelles,

Hero Projects. Paul R. Josephson, Oxford University Press. © Oxford University Press 2024.
DOI: 10.1093/oso/9780197698396.003.0006

and of a second fantasy since the 1930s that Crimea existed for well-off Russian tourists. The bridge, opened officially to automobile traffic at the end of 2018, and with its parallel railroad bridge carrying freight and passengers by the end of 2020, was built at record speed by Russian standards and at astronomical cost, and with tens of thousands of laborers, all also in keeping with Russian traditions of overemployment in state-sponsored projects. The Crimean Bridge, built illegally according to international law because Crimea is a part of Ukraine, grew out of a global tradition of wartime engineering. The third attempt to connect the Crimean Peninsula over the Kerch Strait to Krasnodar, a distance of five treacherous kilometers over roiling waters running between the Black and Azov seas, the first two by Adolf Hitler and Joseph Stalin, this bridge for many Russian citizens symbolized the resurrection of the glorious Russian empire.

If you live by the bridge, you die by the bridge. The dangers of attaching unbounded enthusiasm to the Crimean Bridge with the intent to use it to pursue military ends—and make Muscovites happy over automobile access to their summer playgrounds at Massadra, Golden Sand, and Fox Bay beaches—became apparent on October 8, 2022. A huge and well-timed explosion on the bridge apparently from a transiting tractor trailer collapsed part of the roadway into the Kerch Strait below and set fire to fuel tankers on a train crossing the railroad span of the bridge. Perhaps it was an anonymous, but belated present to Vladimir Putin, the day after his seventieth birthday, to add to those of recent advances of a Ukrainian offense on the eastern and southern fronts against Russia's poorly performing army, which was retreating in disarray over pontoon bridges and rubble as Putin's war of aggression against Ukraine began to collapse. The attack on the bridge came after Putin illegally annexed territory in four Ukrainian provinces. Russian forces had attempted to protect Putin's bridge, deploying decoy barges with radar reflectors, and carrying out smokescreen tests. Yet anticipating such an attack sooner or later, Russian nationals, no doubt courageous patriots, have been fleeing Crimea over the bridge by bus and automobile since March 2022. The Crimean Bridge continues to face attacks into autumn 2023.

Bridges serve commerce. They enable troop movements. They are symbols of cultural achievement. They span spaces, time, and empire: the spectacular Brooklyn Bridge, the Golden Gate Bridge, the Millau Viaduct in Southern France, the Akashi-Kaikyo Bridge connecting Kobe and Awayi Island; arch, trust, suspension, or cable-stayed; and Putin's Crimean Bridge. The Crimean Bridge is intended to permit thousands of automobiles and dozens of trains to connect Russia with its annexed prize, Crimea, which Catherine the Great first annexed for Russia in the eighteenth century. For Putin, the bridge is confirmation of his ability almost single-handedly to restore Russia's economic strength, military power, and national pride less than thirty years after the breakup of the USSR, and a link to the history of the Soviet Union whose collapse he has called the greatest disaster of the twentieth century.

Bridges establish landmarks that are at once majestic, elegant, bold or simple, functional, yet extensive. They require armies of engineers and workers, tons of aggregate, concrete, and steel, and they fit into a network of critical economic, and often military, systems. They reflect cultural capital, engineering knowledge, and economic demand. They span geographies and link cultures and places; they reflect engineering training and paradigms, and social achievements and aspirations.[2] Bridges inspire and awe: the Brooklyn Bridge, at its completion the world's longest suspension bridge; Venice's Bridge of Sighs; the 700-year-old Charles Bridge in Prague; the Tower Bridge of London; the Golden Gate Bridge from San Francisco to Marin County; and among the newer constructions, the ten-lane cable-stayed Zakim Bunker Hill Bridge in Boston (opened in 2003) and the Russkii Bridge in Vladivostok, the longest such bridge at 3,100 m, completed in 2012; and the just-completed $20 billion Hong Kong-Zhuhai-Macau bridge. Bridges reveal the limits of artistic expression under the practical constraints of engineering.[3] How do function, materials, and aesthetics—and raw political adventurism and military power—come together?

In the Russian traditions of building with intense purpose, yet falling behind schedule, placing resources into priority projects to overcome shortfalls, yet lags in supply of material and equipment, and great cost overruns, the Crimean Bridge was built according to an ambitious, yet makable schedule. To achieve the ends of establishment of communications and freighting military and civilian supplies as rapidly as possible between Russia and annexed Crimea over the Kerch Strait, engineers pursued traditional span and support construction rather than seek something more modern and aesthetically pleasing. But the ends of political control and economic security required modest aesthetics rather than those of awe and wonder. There is no wonder about this bridge; it serves state power and reflects accumulated engineering and construction knowledge, and it is raw military ambition.

The Crimean Bridge would be an achievement by any builder, but it is significant for Russia whose bridges go up slowly, lag years behind in meeting pent-up demand, and are cash cows for corrupt builders and officials. The Tsars rarely ordered bridges and forced local people and authorities to build them themselves; peasants and merchants usually struggled across rivers in small launches and ferries. The Soviets showed more interest and more success in conquering spaces, although their bridges were intended to enhance state power and move troops and freight, more than to ease the burdens on the nation's civilian passengers, and they largely left the citizens in major cities without major railway, automobile, and passenger spans until late in the twentieth centuries. The Soviet engineer had such love for concrete and poured so much of it that it is difficult to understand the lags in filling foundations for supports of river crossings. Yet such cities as Arkhangelsk and Novosibirsk got crucial automobile and railway bridges only decades after the need was clear—in the 1950s, 1960s, and later. Ulyanovsk opened a second bridge over the Volga only in 2009, some fifty years after the town officials began to lobby for it.

Big objects—big bridges—have been reborn in contemporary Russia to signify the legitimacy of the regime at home and its presence as a world power abroad, and even bridges fit into this narrative. Dreams of big bridges date to the nineteenth century, but the Russians have not been big bridge builders or skyscraper builders. A list of the world's longest bridges or tallest buildings does not include many Russian efforts. Yet when pressed to show affinity for vertical or horizontal objects, they rise to the occasion: Stalin's seven mixed-style Baroque and Gothic high-rise "wedding cake" skyscrapers built at a time of housing crises and material shortages in the postwar years that dot the Moscow skyline; paeans to industrial extraction that blot the sun and create wind tunnels for urban residents, as the Moscow Vostok Federation Tower, at 372 m the fifty-third tallest building in the world; or the Gazprom "Lakhta" skyscraper in St. Petersburg, the so-called Gazoscreb (Gas Scraper) at 462 m tall that was forced out of city center to the north shore after protests of Petersburgers that were sternly repeated by UNESCO officials about the damage to the city's cultural heritage; and now Putin's Crimean Bridge with its roots in the Tsarist and Stalinist eras.

Engineering Envy

Everywhere in the world military engineers have given great impetus to civil engineering projects in their defense efforts: building breakwaters, deepening harbors, straightening rivers and dredging shoals, laying roads and railroads, and raising bridges. Military engineers, likely the first formally trained engineers in any country, have been central to the improvement of infrastructure for defense and for war. The engineers studied river flows, topography, weather patterns, tides, and so on as they moved up and down the landscape, to the interior, and along the coasts. They surveyed. They built canals. They promoted irrigation systems. Their structures expanded means of communication and facilitated commercial development.

Brief mention of the construction efforts of the US Army Corps of Engineers will provide background to discussion of the development of the Russian engineering effort in this area. The US Army Corps was formally organized in 1802 and served in combat and military construction, in improving transport, in responding to natural disasters, in reworking nature, and in research and development.[4] The Corps built forts, harbors, and levees. It rebuilt the Mississippi River and was crucial to the Panama Canal project.[5] Army engineers directly and indirectly helped in building roadways in national parks, for example, Yellowstone, working in the twentieth century with the Bureau of the Roads and with architectural engineers of the National Park Survey.[6] The involvement of Soviet military engineers and troops in vital national defense construction projects is hardly surprising considering the central role of the US Army Corps of Engineers in the Manhattan Project to build the atomic bomb—and its massive uranium enrichment and plutonium production facilities located in sites from Tennessee to Washington and New Mexico.

Clearly not focused only on reworking the landscape at home—in particular, rivers prone to flood and those that might be transformed as sources for irrigation, or harbors to be deepened and protected by breakwaters—engineers have been active in theaters of war abroad, and also as ambassadors of engineering expertise. US engineers served during the Cold War in Brazil, Italy, Israel, and other countries in the search to strengthen allies and secure new ones through the provision and sale of dams, irrigation systems, and transportation improvements, with the underlying justification being that projects brought prosperity and ensured US hegemony, not menacing Soviet Marxist influence.[7] These technological systems supplemented those of agricultural techniques, fertilizers, pesticides, and seeds tied to the "Green Revolution" foreign policy. And, of course, the Soviets were selling dams, reactors, tractors, and so on for their ideologicaly, foreign policy and hard currency goals.

During World War II, US Army engineers placed floating (pontoon) and fixed bridges across rivers in Italy, France, and Germany. Engineering troops prepared and developed beaches for assault landings in Europe and the Pacific, including of course Normandy, immortalized in memoirs, interviews, and films (*Saving Private Ryan*, 1998), in clearing fields of mines and obstructions, bulldozing battleways along the beaches, fields, and forests, and in the Battle of the Bulge to secure forward motion against hostile troops, obstacles of nature and artificial obstructions emplaced by German engineers. Engineers built in Canada and Alaska, in Assam Province in India, in Yunnan Province in China. The US Army engineers rebuilt bridges, built fortifications, laid lateral roads, and so on in the Korean War. In Vietnam the engineers continued these civil and mechanical engineering projects in support of the US war effort. They introduced the Rome plow, a modified tractor and bulldozer equipped with a special tree-cutting blade to remove vegetation with the thinking that it would enable the fight against the Vietcong who were forced out of guerrilla warfare into denuded plains.[8] (In one of the most immoral acts of the war, the US forces sprayed the carcinogenic defoliant "Agent Orange" from the air in Vietnam's forests to do the Rome plow's work indiscriminately.)

Russian military engineers, similarly, have long served state and society as builders and earth movers, and many of their construction organizations have been reformed into new institutional forms into the twenty-first century. Yet early Russian empire bridge-building efforts lagged. At the turn of the twentieth century, Russian engineers frequently were ordered to their first posts in the countryside from which they learned firsthand how to take advantage of local resources and conditions, while working for local governments called zemstvos, to improve trade and transport. Zemstvos were created after the emancipation of the serfs in 1861 to help bring medicine, education, and public service to rural Russia.[9] Transport was often limited to horse and cart; boats, barges, and ships; and then sleighs along frozen waterways in the winter. In general, backward transport interfered with commerce; agricultural goods might not get to market because of muddy roads and the absence of bridges. An engineer might finish his schooling in Moscow or St. Petersburg and be sent to a provincial town to erect a bridge, perhaps as a diploma project, on the basis of textbook knowledge alone, and be on his own in determining whether a nearby quarry might supply stone for the structure, or a local mill in a wooded region could provide the weight-bearing timbers to proceed with a new bridge. Getting peasant-laborers to hew to the schedule and to the vagaries of modern structures was another major challenge.

For his postgraduate work, Ukrainian specialist Stephen Timoshenko, later known for his *Strength of Materials* (1908), found himself designing a bridge for a local zemstvo. The son of a surveyor who was a former serf, Timoshenko was educated as a railway engineer. Timoshenko recollected being fascinated with building even as a child: "From the sand I built fortresses, castles, and, especially, railroads." He followed his dream to become railway structural engineer, and joined the newly founded St. Petersburg Polytechnic Institute in 1903. Later he pioneered work on buckling—and strength of I-beams—before returning to his native Ukraine and the Kyiv Polytechnic Institute to take a new chair in strength of materials. He helped found the Ukrainian Academy of Sciences in 1918. He fled the USSR in the early 1920s for the United States, fearful that the secret police would arrest him as a nationalist. His work on strength of materials paradoxically has helped build the Crimean Bridge.[10]

If Tsarist officials recognized the importance of roads and railroads belatedly, then the Bolsheviks were determined to modernize transportation and power generation infrastructure from the start. They gazed at American roads, automobiles, subways, factories, and skyscrapers with unbounded technological enthusiasm. They believed their capitalist rivals had something to offer the socialist construction project, namely its technological verve. If only they might "lift" these objects of engineering envy up from the capitalist world, place them down within Bolshevik economic relations, and put the nation to work operating them, then a smoothly operating technological utopia would magically arise to serve the masses. They set out to build hydroelectric power stations as part of Lenin's GOELRO, new roadways to meet what they anticipated to be a Fordist revolution in automobility, and subways (the "metro") to whisk workers seamlessly from home to factory without the din and disruption of public transport that debilitated the proletariat in the capitalist cities.[11] Toward that end, they created a series of new construction organizations focused on roads, bridges, and tunnels, for example, Mostotrest and Metrostroitrest, each of which had gulag and military significance and roots. Virtually all contemporary engineering and construction firms were born from Bolshevik organizations, and they have maintained their buildings, offices, drafting tables, funding, and vision into the twenty-first century. In the Soviet era they could rely on constant and growing state support since an organization, once constituted, would seek out or be assigned new projects to maintain the construct of political legitimacy that there was no unemployment in the USSR; there were no redundant workers, only new projects.

As with virtually every major Russian state corporation, especially those connected with construction and engineering, Mostotrest (the Bridge Building Company) dates to the Stalin era. Established in January 1930 as part of People's Commissariat of Transportation (NKPS), but with a much longer name, Mostotrest was the only specialized bridge-building organization in the country until 1941.[12] Before the war it oversaw the design and building of more than 200 large bridges with a total length of 35,000 m (roughly 175 m in length on average) including the Dnepropetrovsk railway bridge over the Dnipro River, the longest concrete bridge in Europe at the time (1,600 m), and bridges on the Ishim River in Kazakhstan, the Kura in Georgia, and the Yenisei, Zeia, Don, and Neva Rivers. Mostotrest bosses secured their own production, fabrication, and design facilities, and established a large inventory of metalworks. Mostotrest served the industrial heartland and Moscow, while the provinces waited years for long-required bridges to appear at bottlenecks over rivers or highways. During the war, as was usual for Stalinist organizations, Mostotrest's workers heroically overcame every obstacle of Nazi evil, and of capital and labor shortfalls, erecting 516 temporary bridges (at 42 km in total length) and rebuilding 142 more of them with a total length of 16 km. Seven hundred of its employees received orders and medals and other recognition.

At the end of the war in 1945 the Commissariat of Transport formed the Main Administration for the Repair and Construction of Bridges (Glavmostroi) that took in Mostotrest and served as the basis to create territorial bridge-building firms, eventually consisting of twelve provincial facilities. In 1954 this agglomeration was transferred into the newly created Ministry of Transportation Construction. As part of the post-Stalin era of reforms in the economy, the Khrushchev government created a series of construction ministries representing all sectors of the economy (agriculture, transport, heavy industry, and so on) that were intended in theory to overcome bureaucratic barriers of supplies of labor, machinery, and materials that handicapped construction and reconstruction, especially in the provinces. Many of the new ministries took in pieces of the gulag—in essence also construction organizations—as the camps emptied with amnesties, and Mostostroi was one of them.

While Mostostroi has a glorious organizational history, its bridges have not fared as well. When I first went to the USSR as a graduate student in

1984–1985, the Soviet authorities sent my then wife, a professional historian, and me to Moscow—since we had requested to work in Leningrad. We lived in Moscow's Lenin Hills on the main campus of Moscow State University. Nearly daily I took the red line of metro into the city center along a double-decker metro and highway bridge over the Moscow River, apparently the first bridge in the world over a river with a metro station, built by Mostostroi in 1958 from prefabricated stressed reinforced concrete. Only twenty-five years later the bridge station, then called "Lenin Hills" and now called "Vorobevye Hills," was closed for repairs, and it remained closed until 2002; metro engineers were required to reduce train speeds between the university and downtown to a crawl. Only twenty-five years in operation before repairs that take nineteen years to complete is not a good record.

Mostostroi simultaneously worked on the ZIL ("Avtozavodskii") Bridge built between 1958 and 1961 in Moscow. The automobile plant ZIL (Zavod im. Likhachov), originally opened in 1916, was rebuilt with the assistance of the American A. J. Brandt Company in 1932, and reopened as the Stalin Factory (ZiS), then was renamed after the factory director in the 1950s during the Khrushchev era's de-Stalinization campaign. It closed in 2012, but will perhaps someday reopen with its 3.6 million m² of industrial land repurposed into new offices, homes, schools, infrastructure, and cultural facilities. Whatever happens to the former automobile factory, the facility will still rely on the ZiL Bridge, which is infamous as a Moscow traffic bottleneck from the southeast to the center. Mostostroi engineers claim that it was the first such bridge to use the technology of large blocks mounted on pre-stressed reinforced concrete spans of frame-console and continuous systems, that came to be known as the "Russian method." Approved in 1953, finished almost a decade later, the Avtozavodskii Bridge suffered from a significant failing: gradual deformation of the pre-stressed concrete spans. The authorities closed the bridge for the first time only thirty years later in 1992 for work that continued until 1996, but the bridge's failings persisted. A second round of repairs, less than ten years later in 2000–2001, involved major renovations.

Mostostroi continued its glorious efforts to bridge Russia's many rivers until the collapse of the USSR. In the 1990s in new economic circumstances, it somehow managed to preserve its productive potential, integrated new methods and processes, and explored new projects of road and railroad construction. But at the beginning of the 2000s, as a sign of general economic recovery, Mostotrest (renamed again) entered the modern era of Russian bridge building with three new beautiful cable-stayed bridges, in Moscow, St. Petersburg, and Vladimir.[13]

The story of the need to repair, replace, rebuild or raise new bridges played out across the country with similar stories of success, failure, and delay, indicating that only the Crimean Bridge was able to carry, in addition to trucks, buses, automobiles, and trains, the entire authority of the Kremlin. Elsewhere, citizens waited for buses and trams that never came. The Trans-Siberian Railroad had as its western Siberian capital the third largest city in the USSR, Novosibirsk. The Ob (Novosibirsk) hydroelectric power station began full operation after nine years of construction in 1959, modestly whirring at 475 MW, and included a system of locks and a two-lane road across the dam. But the road could hardly serve Novosibirsk itself, some 35 km to the north. A new bridge was required. Every new Soviet bridge, especially modern, massive structures that connected two regions across a river, for example the west bank of the Ob and the center of the burgeoning industrial city, was be celebrated as a true accomplishment of the progressive nation, the coming together of engineers, workers, citizens, and Party officials. Such was the Ob October Bridge that handled pedestrians, trams, and automobiles, and that opened in 1955 at 900 m length to a citywide celebration, with thousands of people coming out to stroll along the bridge at its official proletarian christening. To that time, there had been only a pontoon bridge in the summer, and an ice bridge in the winter. As with many Siberian projects, the bridge, whose blueprints appeared in 1938, was postponed because of the war.[14]

Other cities were not as lucky. Transport from Arkhangelsk proper to the train station on the other side of the Northern Dvina River was by ferry only.[15] On top of this, the station's platforms were too low and too short, and the station was filled with garbage.[16] Obkom (regional party committee) secretary I. S. Latunov wrote Stalin directly concerning construction of a steel bridge across the Northern Dvina River to replace the ferry. Engineers of branch No. 15 of Zheldoproekt, a gulag construction organization, testified that the ferry operated no more than 225 days each year, on 40 days of which the delta ice was so thick that two powerful icebreaking tugs were required to accompany the ferry.[17] During World War II, the authorities ordered a temporary bridge to be built, apparently to transport wounded soldiers arriving at the Arkhangelsk Pier Station by boat or rail to hospitals on the other side.[18] But until 1964, Arkhangelsk residents had to take a ferry—or walk across ice—to get to the Arkhangelsk train station. Further improvements in daily life—and a new bridge—awaited the full flowering of the Khrushchev era, after the general secretary visited the city and saw this bottleneck with his own eyes. He had visited in July 1962 in part to examine the nearby Plesetsk cosmodrome, to witness the testing of an ICBM and cruise missile, to visit nearby Severodvinsk with its nuclear shipbuilding yards, and to tour other nearby military facilities. On his visit to Arkhangelsk, he was disturbed by the ubiquitous rotting, damp, and drafty wooden structures in which people lived. A bridge—and some urban renewal—followed.[19]

Putin is only the second of Russian leaders in the last hundred years to visit Arkhangelsk, a city given impetus by Tsar Peter the Great in the early 1700s in the effort to build a naval yard in the Northern Dvina delta on the White Sea; a statue to Peter, standing on grey granite quarried on the Solovki islands, commemorates his visits to the city in 1693, 1694, and 1702. Like Peter's, Putin's concerns have been entirely military in the Arctic and sub-Arctic; his trips to Arkhangelsk involved dedication of nuclear submarines in nearby Severodvinsk and calls for Arctic assimilation, not for urban improvements in the still wooden, damp city, but now with multitudinous functional Khrushchev- and Brezhnev-era concrete structures. Simply, military demands were the primary impetus to bridge building in the USSR, not municipal concerns, let alone worries about inconvenience to citizens.

Many of the first military engineering detachments formed during World War II were small, flexible operations consisting of platoons of soldiers armed with rudimentary construction equipment who were moved around, far and wide, depending on troop movements, changing fronts, and other considerations, by rail. After World War II, Red Army officers directed mobile bridge operation detachments at a variety of work sites that were slowly consolidated into larger and larger sedentary regional organizations. To take one example, in the darkest days of 1942 when victory was only a dream of propagandists, the Commissariat of Transport in Novosibirsk formed a mobile military-repair road and bridge contingent ("VVMP-14") with a train several wagons in length, each with eighteen to twenty soldiers bunked together, with rudimentary kitchen, bakery, repair shop, smithy, and even steam baths that was relocated to Barnaul in March 1943, and to Siniachikh in July for work on a railroad in the Sverdlovsk region to support regional forestry operations at the site of two prison camps, one for tubercular inmates, and now of a bankrupt lumber and pulp firm. When the Nazis were forced to retreat, VVMP-14 was relocated to reconquered areas, first to the Northern Caucasus, then to Kyiv in 1944 to rebuild the large railroad bridge over the

Dnipro where soldiers lived in *zemlianki* (underground hovels of rock, stone, pieces of lumber and canvas), to Odessa, Zaporozhe, Vitebsk, and to Ufa. In the postwar years as urban construction accelerated, the solders, now organized as Mostootriad-30 (Bridge Building Detachment 30), turned prefabricated concrete forms that became a symbol of Khrushchevean modernity. In the early 1970s, Mostootriad-30 finished a five-year project for a bridge in Ufa over the 1,400 km long Belaia River, a tributary of the Kama River, in the 1980s and 1990s the site of a long-simmering environmental dispute over the determination of the government of Bashkortostan and Russian federal authorities to dam the Belaia to fill a massive reservoir.[20]

Military construction units were assigned work in the postwar reconstruction frenzy at a number of crucial crossings. Mostootriad-72, another wartime creation, played a direct role in the allies' Big Three negotiations among Churchill, Roosevelt, and Stalin in Crimea over the geopolitical order of the postwar world. Stalin hated to travel by airplane. In February 1945 in preparation for his meetings with Roosevelt and Churchill in Yalta, Mostootriad-72 built a bridge, "2-K," at the Kerch Straits. It was not intended for long life, and in fact it failed because of ice floes, but served its temporary purpose of delivering Stalin to the summit. Mostootriad-72 was transferred to the Ural Mountains in the 1950s, and ultimately to Sverdlovsk where its workers lived in forty wagons, only later having trailers, then two-story portable blocks for housing, and still later dormitories on Kachkanarskaia Street. A series of other bridge divisions were deployed and moved about the nation without seeming rationale, order, or geography: no. 82 (near Donetsk, then the Kustanai-Ural railway line, then to the Pacific Ocean and Petropavlovsk, then Kurgan); no. 123 (Dimitrov to Kuntsevo of Moscow region, to Miass in the Ural Mountains, then to build rails for the Uchaly Copper Mine in 1960, and dozens of bridges in Perm, Kungur, Lys'va, Berezniki, and railway lines throughout the Ural Mountains).

In an effort to coordinate the feverish rail construction activities during the war, the authorities established the General Directorate for Military Railroad Restoration (GUVVR). It grew rapidly in the war years, and in the immediate postwar period was central to rebuilding infrastructure. Typical of a Soviet hero organization, it gained tens of thousands of men: in 1941 it commanded thirteen brigades and a total of around 100,000 men, and by July 1941 already 170,000 men. These men and their equipment mostly served near the front where they erected obstacles and built or repaired spans as needed. But dual subordination to GKO (the State Committee for Defense) and NKPS (the

Commissariat of the Means of Communication) hindered GUVVR's work, which was the reason the government had created GUVVR in the first place. One of the most important activities concerned the effort to break through the Leningrad blockade (September 8, 1941–January 27, 1944), the Nazi encirclement of the city on direct orders from Hitler to starve it into submission. Perhaps one million citizens, almost a third of the city, perished from unbearable cold and starvation. GUVVR troops erected 28 km of defenses on the approaches to the city from the Gulf of Finland, and built a special bridge, the "Road of Life," in January 1943 from Shlisselburg to Polyan with a total length of 33 km. The Road of Life was the only way into the city, over frozen lakes. Shipments frequently faced bombing raids from Nazi Junkers. They built the road of life with what was on hand: instead of ballast, snow and ice. The frozen earth, temperatures dropping to −30°, and heavy snows and strong winds handicapped the effort. The soldiers, too, were wasted by hunger, cold, and lack of appropriate clothing and boots.[21] Later, GUVVR served Stalingrad with over 1,000 trainloads of ammunition, weapons, fuel, food, medicines, and other supplies; built and rebuilt roughly 3,000 km of rail and 300 bridges at the Stalingrad, Southwest, and Voronezh fronts; and installed a 1,059 m bridge in Kyiv over the Dniepr in thirteen days.[22]

After the war these many military detachments made huge contributions to re-establishing railroad transport and rebuilding bridges. In all in the European USSR the Nazis had destroyed 65,000 km of rail, or roughly one-half of the entire system, 13,000 bridges, 4,100 stations, 1,600 water towers, 317 depots, 129 nearby factories, 500,000 km of telegraph and telephone lines, 16,000 locomotives, and 428,000 wagons. In the first postwar five-year plan GUVVR troops laid 6,320 km of rail, and rebuilt 2,632 bridges, many in record time, 227 locomotive depots, 57 train stations, and 437,000 m² of housing. They worked coal basins, they re-established trunk lines from the capital in all directions, and completed work in the Caucasus, Western Ukraine, and Belarus. At the beginning of 1950, GUVVR was reorganized as a special division of the army subordinate to MPS (the former NKPS) and from 1954 the Ministry of Transport Construction, and laid rail as far as the Virgin Lands of Kazakhstan to serve Khrushchev's fantastical and failed effort to turn steppe into grain; the Caucasus; the right bank of the Volga River; and West Siberia during another large-scale agricultural campaign to plant grain.[23] In all these incarnations GUVVR was essentially the "Red Army Corps of Engineers."

The construction of new roads, railroads, and bridges did not necessarily mean comfort or convenience in the real practice of moving people and things. Trains in the USSR ran frequently at 30 km per hour, if that. To this day it takes twenty-four hours to travel from Moscow to Arkhangelsk, a distance of only 1,200 km, and sixteen hours by automobile. In the early years of the undercapitalized, hastily built, and poorly assembled railroads—owing to reliance on convict laborers, no doubt—the railroads and their bridges failed almost as quickly as they were built. Facing incessant pressure from the authorities to meet unrealistic production, delivery, and other targets, the locomotives and ties could not keep up. Already by the late 1940s and early 1950s, the recently completed railways heading north from Moscow were falling apart. Tens of thousands of rails had failed. Crashes and accidents were endemic. Engineers had to slow their trains to 15 km/hour. On top of this, 1,148 railway bridges built during World War II in Arkhangelsk province alone of low-grade, untreated pine had rotted, and only a few hundred of them had been replaced.[24] The problem with worn and defective rails persisted into the 1950s, as repairs were hasty and patchwork.[25]

One contemporary bridge building trust, Uralmostroi, dates to the immediate postwar years. Originally the Mostostroi Trust No. 4, Uralmostroi was organized in August 1945 in Rostov-on-the-Don to rebuild hundreds of bridges in South Russia and the North Caucasus destroyed or damaged during the war over the Don, Kuban, Terek, and other rivers. In 1955 it was moved to Cheliabinsk for construction of roads and railway lines including bridges in the Urals, Kazakhstan, and Central Asia. During the Brezhnev-era effort to tap West Siberian oil and gas, it built and modernized bridges in the "Nechernozeme" program, especially for city roads and highways along and over such rivers as the Kama, Irtysh, Ural, Tobol, Miass, Tavda, Viatka, Chusovaia, and even the Ishi and Syrdarya, in all some 7,000 bridges with a total length of 515 km, on average to be sure a modest 70 or 75 m in length. Uralmostostroi claims that its volume of work, and the quality, and quality and number of employees, did not fall during the economic decay of the 1990s. And why? Because of its glorious workers: the 106 employees won a variety of awards and medals, forty of whom became "Honorary Transportation Builders," ten "Meritorious Builders of Russia," and two anointed "Heroes of Socialist Labor."[26]

Lenin's Dire Straits

If you don't sit on gas, oil, or bauxite ore, or if you live in the provinces, then it's hard to get any construction trust to build a bridge, even if you reside in

Lenin's birthplace, the city of Ulyanovsk. It has become Russian tradition that provincial towns suffer the slings of inefficiencies and inconveniences of distance from Moscow with poorly functioning public transport that operates on older equipment, often discarded from the center, miserly repair budgets, and reliance on one or two main transit routes that serve as a catchbasin for daily traffic jams and congeal pedestrians, trams, buses, and private cars in a kissel of smog. Moscow has long been a kind of black hole of money and projects, while the provinces occupy a different century from which they beg for handouts.

Ulyanovsk had its hat in hand for twenty-five years to open a second bridge across the Volga River to connect the two parts of the city, on the left bank with some 350,000 residents, and on the right bank with another 250,000 residents. The old Ulyanvosk bridge for decades had served as the only crossing for 400 km along the Volga. Already in the 1950s the one bridge, part railway, part automobile road and built in the 1910s, was overloaded and needed frequent repairs. It had to be "lifted" in the early 1950s by 10 m to accommodate the rising Volga waters. Stalin had made the crossing harder. As part of his last major gulag project, the Kuibyshev hydroelectric power station, in 1949, he ordered 200,000 prisoners sent to the site on the Volga. When the dam 200 km downstream from Ulyanovsk was closed, it created a reservoir that flooded land both north and south of the city, and increased the width of the Volga by up to 30 km. To protect parts of Ulyanovsk that are now significantly lower than the reservoir, including the Ulyanovsk Ammunition Factory, crucial to the front during World War II and to Cold War demands, the planners installed levees on the right bank. I've walked on the top of the massive levees; they seem substantial, and yet, according to some estimates, "a catastrophic failure would submerge parts of the city comprising around 5% of its total population with as much as 10 m (33 ft) of water."[27] The Kuibyshev reservoir essentially isolated the right from the left bank. By 1982 the roadway on the railway bridge was nearly impassible; potholes revealed a view of the river below.

Ulyanovsk residents asked for a new bridge to honor Lenin and make their commuting manageable. They asked and waited—ten years, through the Yeltsin era economic collapse, and another ten years. In 1995, in a letter to Ulyanovsk region governor Iurii F. Goriachev, the head of Glavgosekspertiza of Russia, Iurii B. Zhukovskii, wrote:

> In 1954–57 when the bridge was raised by 10 m and the supports were raised to this height, due to the filling of the reservoir, channel supports

3, 4, and 5 gave a drawdown and a roll, which threatened to collapse the bridge. When professor of the Moscow Institute of Transport Engineers A. A. Petropavlovsky examined it, it was, according to his words, "criminal negligence" committed during the construction of the bridge in 1913–1916. The channel support . . . shafts and caisson chambers were not filled with concrete masonry, but simply covered with rubble, empty barrels and all sorts of rubbish.[28]

During the 1957 reconstruction, the builders apparently plugged rebar in and around the supports, but this hardly provided the necessary bearing capacity. They exacerbated safety problems by using as roadbed what had become under Nikita Khrushchev the de rigueur material—reinforced concrete slabs that weathered poorly. Over 400 slabs were judged unsafe in three different inspections in the 1980s.

Ultimately, it helped that Lenin's ghost hovered over the Volga waters; how could the authorities leave Lenin's birthplace in such dire straits? To meet symbolic and physical needs of the growing city, the Kremlin had approved modernization of the city in the Eighth Five-Year Plan (1966–1970), with a Lenin memorial, a twenty-three-story hotel, "Venice," where I have had the honor to stay, a new train station, a newly decorated Palace of Pioneers, a children's library, and several schools. New defense industries planned for the left and right bank would increase demand for modern transport even more with a forecast increase in population from roughly 450,000 to 1 million inhabitants. In the town fathers' eyes and hearts, only a new double-decker bridge with a metro line on the lower level could meet the growing travel demands. The metro has never materialized, although a subway has been the dream of all Russian cities of more than half a million people as the citizens across the nation were forced into overpacked and outdated trams, buses, and electric buses on their long commutes. Nor, in Ulyanovsk, did an aviation complex or microelectronics firm materialize. Yet Ulyanovsk's population exceeded 500,000 by 1973, and the old bridge was groaning, if not listing.[29] Some residents had begun to refer to Ulyanovsk as a "nature preserve (zapovednik) of communism and a bastion of stagnation" for its monuments to Lenin.

Like the oligarchy of the 2000s, the Soviet Union was a state of connections between clients and their masters. The first secretary of the Ulyanovsk regional party committee, G. V. Kolbin, knew this well, pushing a plan in October 1984 that gained support of the Council of Ministers for municipal and regional development including a new bridge, a metro, and other major improvements by 1995. Kolbin arrived in Ulyanovsk from Nizhnii Tagil. (He had also previously been second secretary of the Communist Party of Georgia under Eduard Shevardnadze from 1975 to 1983, where, although a typical conservative bureaucrat, he in fact supported a decision to keep Georgian as the state language at a time of a national policy to emphasize Russian language and nationality as the big brother of all little peoples. He himself learned Georgian and seems to have earned the respect of locals for fighting privilege, lines, and shortages, and publicly dressing down bosses of corrupt or incompetent businesses.) From December 1983 to January 1987, as first secretary of the Ulyanovsk, he fought to improve city services, including a new bridge, then in 1986 moved to Kazakhstan when Gorbachev appointed him first secretary of the Kazakh Communist Party in an effort to root out corruption under longtime official Dinmukhamed Kunaev, triggering violent December protests (the "Jeltoqsan") since he was not a Kazakh. Kolbin retired in the 1990s to become a businessman and died in 1998 in the Moscow—not Ulyanovsk—metro of a heart attack.

Kolbin and other local party officials advanced an idea that, by the time of Lenin's 125th birthday in 1995, several things must be built: a circus, a theater, a planetarium, several other projects, and a bridge across the Volga. Why the circus for Lenin's birthday remains unclear. The main state administration for technology assessment (Glavgosekspertiza) of the state construction committee (Gosstroi) picked a northern variant of a bridge across the Volga to push the flow of transportation away from the center of the city. Yet in building the massive structure, the designers faced a series of problems: over thirty times a year 3 m waves buffeted the Volga that prevailed for days on end, and they had already eroded 40 to 90 m of the shore, while the depth of the reservoir in some places exceeded 35 m, and the riverbed consisted of layers of clay. Worst of all, they determined to build a 700 m stretch in an area that on the right bank was prone to landslides. The newly created Ulyanovskmostostroi chose a project submitted by Giprotransmost in Moscow, a design for a two-deck bridge, with cable spans 407 m in length and other spans of 220 m in length that were less expensive and required less labor; yet there was little experience with the proposed project.[30] Indeed, according to a Russian writer, building a bridge on supports 3 to 5 m in diameter, at a depth of 60 m to support a span 50 to 60 m high with spans of 220 m, each weighing 4,200 tons, had never been attempted in world experience. Excavation work alone reached 12 million m^3. To deal with landslides and erosion, they built a 600 m wall of 7.8-ton ferroconcrete tetrapods with riprap backfill. The Presidential Bridge, at nearly 6 km, and at 13 km including the highway approaches, is in fact a truss bridge with one deck—but it is finished.

Yet with these grand designs and technical blueprints, and with Lenin himself no doubt crying out from repose in his Red Square mausoleum, and even recognizing the topographical, hydrological, and geophysical obstacles, what took them so long to build the bridge? Construction commenced in 1989, and things went well to 1992. Unfortunately, federal financing simply disappeared in the Yeltsin decade. Already within five days of the end of the USSR, the Russian Federation Cabinet of Ministers had eliminated central planning of materials and so on, and this of course had an immediate impact on all national projects including major construction efforts. Any future construction went ahead with uncertainties, even after a June 1992 resolution of the government that included the Ulyanovsk bridge as a priority project of the state. As rubles from the center dried up, Governor I. F. Goriachev implored the Kremlin to provide emergency funding so as not to see the bridge work stop. In 1996, construction ceased. Only in 2001 did the span work commence again, although at funding levels about one-quarter of what was needed. A former dyed-in-the-wool Communist Party official and indefatigable bureaucrat who had served the region devotedly for years and who apparently seriously cared for petitioners and especially children, Goriachev turned to the Yeltsin administration for help.[31] To Prime Minister Nikolai Ryzhkov he said, "In Ulyanovsk, they began this big deal, on the left bank is a huge aircraft factory, and [yet] you cannot get across the Volga to it. On the old bridge, it's the real end of the world, there are interminable traffic jams, in addition it is an emergency route, we have to do everything possible to finish the construction of the new bridge." But as always, nothing happened.[32] Goriachev learned that only one-sixth of the financing needed might be provided. He blamed the developing market system and ongoing economic reforms for the delays, and for his tireless and imperious efforts on behalf of the local economy and the bridge came to be known as the "Ulyanovsk Kim Il-sung." Funding dropped to one-twelfth of the promised funds and by 1997 to nothing. Only under President Putin did the country find the economic stability and the will to complete the span, apparently with his personal intervention, from 2005.[33] The importance of the bridge has become clear several times in inclement weather including ice storms when they have had to close the old, Imperial Bridge. Putin did not permit the Crimean Bridge to suffer the same fate of uncertainties and delays.

Stalin's Pylons

War—Nazis invading the Soviet Union, Russia invading Ukraine—seems to be the one path toward building bridges quickly in the Russian orbit. The Germans strove to surmount the Kerch Strait during their occupation of Crimea. Hitler ordered the project, apparently hoping not only to control the Black Sea and the Caucasus, but to establish automobile, truck, and railroad transport to India, where the Nazis believed the Aryan race originated. German soldiers and engineers blitz-moved girders, cement, and other equipment to the spot to begin construction of a railroad and bridge 3.5 km in length across the strait in spring 1943; only 150 days later by late summer, German engineers had built a 4.5 km railroad, and started to move 500 to 800 tons daily of supplies and materiel across their rudimentary bridge. It was not a railroad, but sooner cable cars gliding along wires held up by the supports.[34] But when the Germans retreated in the autumn of 1943, they dynamited the structure, as they lay waste to anything that remained standing when their armies fled westward; in their haste, however, they did not destroy Kerch structure supports entirely and the Red Army attempted to rebuild the shell that was left.[35]

Soviet military planners saw the possibility of using the Nazi bridge for their own purpose; Stalin ordered them not to bomb any intact structure over the strait. He assumed that the USSR soon would turn the tide and finish Hitler's bridge, in part with German supplies and machinery left behind. At the end of November 1944 when the Red Army repulsed the Nazis from Crimea, a bridge of sorts about 4.5 km long was in place, but it was damaged in heavy storms, in particular ice, and Soviet efforts to repair the structure also fell into the turbulence.[36]

Efforts to build the Kerch Strait bridge date to nineteenth century, even in the dreams of British imperialists who hoped somehow to shorten the trip to the jewel of the empire, India. In the early 1930s, as part of the general building frenzy of factories, dams, and power stations, and the "socialist reconstruction" of Moscow, it seemed no imperial project was too far-fetched. Could there also be a Kerch Bridge? At a Kremlin meeting in 1934, Stalin learned that the British government had considered seriously in 1901 a project for a land-based road from Europe to Asia with one variant across Crimea to the Kerch Peninsula and to the Caucasus. The project reached the desk of Tsar Nicholas II but went no further because of the world war. Having heard the report, Stalin observed that, in the process of rapid industrialization, and with engineers and enterprises in place, the USSR could build such a bridge, especially since no one else had succeeded—neither the Brits nor the Tsar.[37] Stalin had in mind not only to build a bridge, but a grand reconstruction project for a railroad in southern Russia: from Kherson through Crimea to Taman on the Russian side of the strait, and then along the Black Sea coast through Sukhumi to Poti. Engineers answered the call with designs and blueprints that included the usual declaration it would be built in record time. But the entire country embraced projects that required steel, iron, and concrete, laborers and bosses, determination and victory, and that also included the declaration to build in record time, and bottlenecks and shortfalls of supplies resulted everywhere. The Kerch Strait project thus forced the Soviets to order girders, supports, piles, and other metal works from the Germans with whom they had had secret military and trade connections since the mid-1920s, the Germans to avoid Versailles Treaty sanctions, the Soviets to build industry and military with Germany assistance. But when Hitler came to power, he sensed that such a bridge and railroad were the way to move tanks toward Asia, and he kept the strategic metalworks in Germany to be used by his engineers during the war.[38]

Apparently, Stalin loved time in Crimea for rest and introspection, perhaps to ponder the next arrests and purges, and he went there when he could by train. He approved a number of construction projects on the peninsula. His right-hand man, and secret police chief, Lavrenty Beria, had gulag camps for labor and priority access to construction materials. They determined to build a Kerch bridge in the late 1930s, and on the eve of the Nazi invasion had already finished the Fedosia-Kerch approach road designed by military engineers. In the final blueprints, typical of the era and of hero projects, massive statues would greet the citizen at each side of the strait, intended to fill people with feelings of patriotism and the glory of the state, one of the omniscient Stalin on the Crimean side to welcome travelers to the peninsula, but not the Tatars who would be forced into murderous exile in 1944, most of them to Uzbekistan, and a huge hammer and sickle, indicating the union of the worker and the peasant, to greet travelers on the Krasnodar, Russia, side.[39] As so many other projects, this one, too, rested on unfinished supports until the Germans were on retreat.

Stalin, Beria, and military leaders returned to the decision to build a railroad bridge over the strait at the end of January 1944 (and weeks before the liberation of Kerch on April 11). Construction actually began on the eastern approach before the Germans had been pushed out of Kerch. Taking as a starting point the German ruins and technology, Soviet engineers developed a design to use 115 spans each at 27 m in length, leading to a section to be built above the navigable section of the strait that was a two-span, 110 m swiveling bridge that turned 90 degrees to allow vessels of any size to pass simultaneously in both directions. The bridge itself was 4.5 km in total length. They considered carefully geological data and data concerning ice floes. They decided first to focus on the bridge and then its approaches, which would enable them to determine the best design for icebreaking and diverting devices on the bridge supports to handle even the most extreme winter conditions. The labor force grew to 10,000. The first wooden piles were driven by the end of April, the first iron piles in May, and the first span was installed by May 10. Pushing onward with 150 days of "shock work," they completed the bridge on target, as usual before a major celebration, in this case on the eve of the twenty-seventh anniversary of the Revolution in November. The first train crossed the bridge on November 3, 1944. The shock workers had driven 2,000 wooden and 2,341 metal piles, installed 15,000 tons of metal works for the span structures and supports, poured more than 5,000 m^3 of concrete, 35,000 tons of stone, 400,000 m^3 of road bed, and laid 69 km of rail.[40]

The second stage of work, involving the replacement of all wooden structures and supports with metal ones, and also the installation of icebreaking devices, was to be completed by January 1, 1945. But this was an impossible order, no matter Stalin's insistence; weather conditions deteriorated rapidly; heavy waves, gale force winds, and ice buffeted the site. In addition, the overloading of existing rail lines with materiel and soldiers to the front prevented freight from getting to the construction site. On December 26, 1944, the site directors sent a telegram to GUVVR to inform officials that a fifteen-day storm had enveloped the strait, and that the workers had managed to install only five ice diverters. A disaster followed in late February 1945, when, in the absence of diverters, thirty-two supports collapsed; bombing the ice by airplanes and artillery failed to break the flows. By February 20, forty-two supports had failed and several sections collapsed. This was lucky since on February 11, a week before the failure, a Soviet delegation leaving the Yalta conference had passed over the bridge. There was talk of rebuilding the structure, or starting anew, and another project was brought forward, but after construction of a caisson near the eastern shore of the strait, the project was considered too risky and expensive and so forgotten. Stalin's pylons interfered with shipping for years.[41]

A government commission recommended a temporary bridge to be installed while preparing a new bridge project in 1945 and 1946; Transmostproekt (now Giprotransmost) offered two variants, with a high span and lower span option, and even built an experimental caisson to explore soil, sand, and bedrock conditions. The high span option came in at about 2 billion rubles. The Stalin Plan to Transform Nature included another Kerch Bridge project. Engineers had in mind in this version a one-deck bridge and only for railroad. Although the blueprints included a massive monument of Stalin gazing off into the waters, Stalin refused to endorse it, referring to the new project dismissively as the "Tsar Bridge." Stalin said, "We deposed the Tsar in 1917." The authorities settled instead a ferry crossing that opened in 1953 and carried two trains daily across the Kerch Strait. After the fall of the USSR, only passenger ferries crossed,[42] and the idea of a Kerch Bridge was left unfulfilled until 2018.[43]

The Bridge of the One-Thousand-Year Presidency

The impetus for a Crimean bridge lacked urgency until ten years after the breakup of the USSR when Vladimir Putin became president. Intending, it seems, from the first to restore the Russian empire, he attacked Georgia, Moldova, and then Ukraine using armed insurrectionists, mercenary proxies, and threats from a once great power. Once he annexed Crimea in 2014, the bridge project was quickly approved, giving credence to the contention that the bridge was planned all along with the annexation of Crimea since shipments of energy, water, food, and so on obviously could not be expected to find their way through Ukrainian territory. Ukraine closed the highways across the Isthmus of Perekop to Krasnoperekopsk or Dzhnkoi to Russian traffic because of the annexation and its proxy war in support of separationists in Ukraine's eastern provinces.

Regarding water, the Ukrainian authorities significantly cut its flow volume into Crimea via the Northern Crimean Irrigation Canal, built in the 1960s to supply Crimea with water from the Kakhovka reservoir in Kherson region that became the site of battles between Ukraine and Russian troops who were routed in November 2022, over control of the Zaporizhzhia NPP and the Kakhovsk reservoir; the cut-off of the canal that runs from Tavriisk to Kerch, small and shallow to begin with, led to failure in the peninsula's harvest in 2014. As result, the Taigan reservoir in central Crimea shrank from 200 hectares to a third of its former size.[44] Even with a bridge linking Kerch and Krasnodar, the question remained whether, as agriculture shrank and water dried up, Russia would have to import food to Crimea at great cost by truck and train on the military bridge. This was another reason for Russia's attack of Ukraine in February 2022: to conquer territory from Kherson to Mariupol to secure Crimea from land as well as by bridge. Russia blew up the Kakhovska dam in June 2023, emptying the reservoir, and putting water supply to Crimea—and to the Zaporizhzhia NPP at further risk.

The cost of the Crimean Bridge, its international ramifications, and other problems associated with its construction were never addressed with the Russian public. Rather, with Crimea in Russian military hands, radio and TV stations filled the airwaves with reporting about the technological achievement of the new span, and how it served Russian residents who waited, at great risk to themselves in the face of Ukrainian fascist aggression, for the critical bridge to the motherland. And if some Russians were skeptical of the project, one never heard voices against it since Putin's media permits only false narratives.

As with the Siberian River diversion project, the idea of a new bridge seems to have found additional support from the former mayor of Moscow, Yuri Luzhkov, who longed for the return of Crimea to Russia. In 2001, arriving in Krasnodar, just across the strait, he symbolically laid the first stone for a bridge, and he promised that Moscow would invest $100 million in the project. A year later, at a meeting of Putin with the Ukrainian president Leonid Kuchma, Luzhkov unveiled a project with a bridge and tunnel and explained its economic significance. Sometime later, engineers determined that projects without tunnels were less expensive than those with tunnels. Growing estimates over the years have indicated the complex project would cost at least $3 billion.[45]

In the patriotic glow of winning the medal count at the 2014 Sochi Olympics, an achievement secured by using state-sponsored doped Russian athletes whose tainted blood and urine samples were switched with the assistance of the secret police (the "FSB"), President Putin personally took the lead in carrying out the annexation of Crimea from Ukraine. His propagandists orchestrated a national frenzy of lies about Ukrainian attacks on Russian nationals that justified the invasion under the slogan "Crimea is ours!"[46] Working with a local people's militias, he ordered uniformed men without insignia, known as "little green men," to seize infrastructure as weapons of war. The army—the little green men—secured airports, ports, radio stations, and TV transmitters, and they intimidated and beat opponents. A plebiscite held just two weeks later, in which, according to Human Rights Watch, perhaps only 15–30 percent of Crimean residents actually voted to "join" Russia, cemented the military takeover. (This was a dress rehearsal for Putin's plebiscite in 2022 in Luhansk and Kherson regions, and in occupied areas of the Donetsk and Zaporizhzhia regions, with Russian soldiers going door to door to order Ukrainians at gunpoint to vote.[47]) The authorities immediately imposed Russian citizenship on residents of the peninsula. Russian forces then attacked human rights, especially, according to the United Nations, of "those who refused to automatically adopt Russian . . . citizenship." Russian laws were substituted, including arbitrary imposition of Russian criminal law that was used to fight "terrorism, extremism and separatism," by which the Russian annexers meant to limit the liberty and security of anyone who opposed annexation and the plebiscite. NGOs, media, and religious communities were required to re-register with an illegal government, and many were denied the right to do so, especially journalists, bloggers, supporters of the Mejlis (the executive representative body of the Tatar people), pro-Ukrainians, and others. Arbitrary arrests, detentions, disappearances, torture, and even execution resulted. Tatars suffered extreme restrictions, while the Russian Federation refused to investigate abuses by their own security forces and armed vigilantes. Some detainees were shipped to penal colonies in Russia. Russian police and soldiers restricted movement, refused to recognize personal documents, deported protestors, and denied travel of children. Health care and other social programs were ceased or interrupted. Ukrainian cultural and educational programs were eliminated. Private and public property was extralegally confiscated.[48]

In an Orwellian address to the nation just after Crimean annexation, Putin justified the Russian seizure of Crimea in Cold War terms and concepts, defining Russia's position as being alone in the world, isolated by the United States, a country that did not respect Russia as it should. He declared he would defend the nation against heavy-handed international war-like behavior directed against Russia, apparently such as that he has employed in Chechnya, Georgia, Luhansk, Donetsk, and Crimea. Refusing to recognize Russia's violation of international law and abrogation of the 1994 Budapest Treaty to guarantee Ukraine's sovereignty over Crimea, Putin appealed to the nationalism of citizens through a series of lies including claims that Russia faced real threats, especially from the United States. Putin justified the military takeover of Crimea by exaggerating the plebiscite's miserly results, and claiming that 82 percent of all voters took part and 96 percent voted in support of reunification with Russia. He referred to the fact that Crimea had long been Russian, it was the spot where Prince Vladimir chose orthodoxy in the tenth century, and made other such ahistorical claims. He noted that 1.5 million of the 2.2 million inhabitants were Russian, he downplayed the exile and murder of Tatars, claiming that Russians suffered first of all. In his speech he criticized the "putsch" of Maidan, Ukraine's autumn 2013 popular uprising that rejected a kleptocratic, pro-Russian regime that had occupied Kyiv. And he repeated the falsehood that Crimean inhabitants asked for help against persistent anti-Russian discrimination; he simply could not ignore their requests for aid, he said. He criticized NATO for massing troops on Russia's borders in pursuit of military ends—which in fact it had not. In all, Putin and his legions saw dangerous, dark forces directed against Russia as they had been in the eighteenth, nineteenth, and twentieth centuries.[49]

The bridge came next to secure the Kremlin's lies. Putin quickly awarded a construction contract for the Crimean Bridge to billionaire Arkady Rotenberg's SGM (Stroigazmontazh) Group.[50] Rotenberg is a personal friend of Vladimir Putin. The SGM Group also handled construction for the Sochi Olympics, which suffered billions of dollars in cost overruns, so that Putin knew what to expect. It came down to a choice between the Mostotrest of the Rotenberg SGM group and SK "Most," a company created by the union of specialists of the Mostootriad-55 and Mostotrest-10 enterprises that had been involved in the construction of BAM. Mostotrest had in recent years had finished big bridges in Irkutsk and St. Petersburg, while SK "Most" built the stayed-cable bridges from Vladivostok to Russian Island, the biggest island of the Eugenie Archipelago. With all this experience, Russian builders still could not handle every detail. They needed to buy machines, steels, and other elements from Swedish, Canadian, and German companies to which they lost access because of sanctions imposed after the annexation of Crimea, and turned to Chinese suppliers. By March 19, 2014, the president had yet to sign laws about the Russian annexation of Crimea, but he had ordered the Ministry of Transport to build a railroad and automobile bridge over the Kerch Strait. In secret, bureaucrats and engineers made plans, keeping everything from journalists. In May 2014 more than fifty engineers, scientists, and managers of SGM, Mostotrest, and Stroitransgaz arrived in Kerch to consider the possible projects.[51]

The huge contract for the bridge logically came to Rotenburg, who had proven himself in the Sochi Olympics. The Rotenberg brothers had moved up from gas stations and security firms, to a vodka factory, to a bank and to the energy supply business, a pattern that reveals the rocky Russia's recovery from the economic decline of the 1990s: if you cannot drive it, drink it, or burn it, then perhaps it has no value. Rotenberg and his brother have known Putin since the 1960s when they shared judo lessons, a friendship that continues to this day with Rotenberg head of a special judo club, the honorary president of which is Putin. Rotenberg also plays pickup hockey with Putin; in an annual charity game, no one boards the president. It seems that Putin and Rotenberg are also closely related in expensive real estate deals that have benefited the Russian parliament, the Federal Narcotics Service, and the Investigative Committee of the Head Procurator's office, with manyfold increases in funding going to housing for those people in elite Moscow neighborhoods for a total of billions of rubles.[52]

But SGM's greatest achievement was Sochi Olympic preparations, where the Kremlin managed to carry out the Winter Olympics in a sub-tropical region. It was the Putin Plan for the Transformation of Nature, his triumph before the world over nature, his ability to showcase Russian athletic achievements, largely through an FSB program to mask drug use by his athletes in pursuit of gold medals. According to Kremlin critics Boris Nemtsov and Leonid Martinyuk, the costly, resource-intensive, and environmentally unsound project was like Nikita Khrushchev's plans for Arctic corn and Brezhnev's Siberian river diversion. It was the epitome of "abuse, corruption, petty tyranny, cronyism, non-professionalism and irresponsibility." By cost per spectator and all other measures, the Sochi Olympics were obscenely overpriced. Private investment disappeared, and the government and its close partners built the entire thing. But since it was built through government contracts, Russian taxpayers indeed paid for nearly all (96%) of the extravaganza.[53] The projects included some of the costliest four-lane road railway and bridges ever constructed in world history, likely the result of corruption.[54]

As in Sochi, where thousands of workers built a winter Olympics in a sub-tropical clime, so in Crimea thousands of workers operated hundreds of machines to build what they called the "Road of Life" between Russia and Crimea, a name that denigrates the meaning of the "road of life" that saved Leningrad from total annihilation during the Nazi blockade. Rotenberg selflessly announced the Crimea Bridge would be "his last project," which he decided to carry out to "contribute to the development of the country"[55] SGM signed a contract with the subsidiary of the federal highway agency Avtodor "Taman'" in February 2015.

Rotenberg had come a long way to build the Crimean Bridge. After he became president, Putin began to bring the resource sectors of the economy under his control through such companies and state corporations as Rosneft, Gazprom, Rosatom, and many others that, through opaque rules and accounting practices, have become personal wealth generators for the oligarchs. Putin assigned Rotenberg essentially a controlling interest in Rosspirtprom that controls nearly half of the nation's booze. From booze, Rotenberg diversified into a new company to build pipelines and the SMP Bank that controlled Rosspirtprom distilleries. (Kristall may be the most famous of the distilleries; it produces "Putinka"—Little Putin—with massive annual sales that also sponsored the US women's Olympic bobsled team in the runup to Sochi.[56]) That the Rosspirtprom name isn't as well known as, say, Gazprom, is partly thanks to a 2006 alcohol-regulation initiative that backfired spectacularly. Attempting to rein in Russia's enormous consumption of alcohol, the state imposed new retail excise stamps, production-monitoring equipment, and other regulations on the largely unchecked alcohol market. The overextended Rosspirtprom couldn't pay its taxes, but the state-run VenechTorgBank bailed out the company and the Rotenbergs. In many cases, the Russian government uses situations like this—alleged failure to pay taxes—to destroy businesses and seize their assets.[57]

As Russian expenses to secure Crimea increased, Putin felt compelled to remind the nation of the importance of his bridge to secure the peninsula's economic well-being. At a March 2016 Kremlin meeting on the socioeconomic development of Crimea its [illegal] integration into the "legal and economic space of the Russian Federation," Putin referred to the 708 billion rubles ($11 billion) budgeted for Crimea to 2020, its growing industrial production, and state-funded projects in energy, agriculture, and tourism that provided jobs to the peninsula. He announced the opening of two high-tension power lines across the strait and the construction of a new thermal power station at 470 MW that raised total production of 1,920 MW, or 600 NW more than current demand. All this, he noted, would enable the peninsula to overcome an "energy blockade" by Ukraine. And he referred to past Kerch Strait bridge projects, for example, that of Nicolas II of the 1900s, to draw attention to the significance of the Crimean bridge for the Russian empire.[58] (He did not refer to Hitler's bridge.) Everything was in place to push across the strait: a military takeover, a plebiscite, logistical demands, well-orchestrated justifications from the Kremlin about the strategic and geohistorical requirements to cross the strait in record time, and a massive, well-funded construction trust that benefited an oligarch friend. This was Putin's "project of the century."

The Design Group Tormasov and Company had hoped to be selected to design and build the bridge. Iurii Borisovich Tormasov, who worked in a Moscow State University mechanics department, joined SpetsStroiProekt to advance a bridge design. He noted that steamships and ferries to serve Crimea between Kuban in Krasnodar were insufficient, and that the creation of normal economic ties between Crimea and its motherland faced significant meteorological and geological obstacles that his bridge would overcome. His design was for a two-level enclosed structure with automobile, rail, bicycle, and pedestrian ways, and water, oil, and electrical conduits, plus helicopter pads. The design employed reinforced, fiber-concrete that would resist ice, and seismically stable spans and supports. Tormasov forecast total time to completion at no more than 2.5 years at a cost of no more than 150 billion rubles, significantly less that SGM and Avtodor's preference at 228 billion rubles ($2.4 billion versus $3.7 billion).[59] Tormasov's futuristic design had no chance given the connections between the Kremlin and SGM.

The director of the bridge construction of Stroigazmontazh, Leonid Ryzhenkin, confidently predicted on-time completion of the bridge, even ahead of other countries' experiences with bridge works. He noted how the company had analyzed recent examples of bridge building in China, Malaysia, the United States, and Canada that showed no less than three years usually passes in the design of a bridge. Yet by February 19, 2016, construction the Crimean span had already begun. This was a large-scale technology par excellence with steel manufacture, concrete and aggregate operations, special machine tools, pile drivers, excavators, pile drivers, welders, and divers assembled to move forward, as if it was a Soviet construction project with the entire nation contributing to its successful completion. There were 3,800 laborers on the Russian side, and 2,000 more on the Ukrainian (Crimean) side, living in nondescript trailers, although certainly better than sleeping in tents at a gulag camp. They worked according to the shift method, thirty days on, fifteen off, and they were paid 50,000 rubles (about $820) twice a month through a debit card. They came from the Far East, Nizhnii Novgorod, and Moscow environs—everywhere. This was a modern Soviet Komsomol campaign project.[60] Stroigazmontash drove hundreds of piles, erected scores of supports, and placed spans from Crimea to the "motherland" over the island of Tuzla. Closer to the Crimean shore, the engineers designed a 35 m high arch to permit ship passage. Even Soviet hyperbole returned in reporting on the sheer weight of project: the builders announced the bridge used 12 million tons of construction materials—twice the amount needed to build the pyramid at Cheops, the oldest and largest of the Giza pyramids with a volume of 2.6 million m³.[61] And keeping in mind past failed efforts, they designed the bridge to last 100 years, dissipate ice floes, and withstand a massive earthquake. SGM engineers anticipated that by 2035, 40,000 automobiles would be crossing the structure daily.[62]

Putin called his bridge "a historical mission," and on repeated visits to the work site referred to it as "the most important public project" to integrate Crimea into the motherland.[63] This was indeed a hero project. On March 14, 2018, he personally inspected the construction of the automobile section of the bridge where construction had begun some two years earlier, and met workers on Tuzla Island to inspect asphalting, guardrail construction, and light standards.[64]

Technology, even Putin's technology, cannot control the weather. The builders scheduled 100 days per year on which storms, strong winds, heavy fogs, and deep freezes would still or slow them. Yet the workers installed the girders that united the island and corridor for the passage of ships on schedule. Precisely here the Turkish freighter *Lira* collided with supports for the technical bridge being built to facilitate main bridge construction. No one was injured, but one of the bridge's pillars was completely destroyed and several others were badly damaged. There was no pilot on the *Lira*, but ships of its class and size are permitted to sail the Kerch without one.

Preliminary studies in the 1970s indicated not to build the Crimean Bridge where they built it precisely because of the absence of sufficient ocean floor foundation. Rather than drive piles into the depths, they should have excavated, poured concrete and aggregate under pressure, and then driven in the piles. The promotional literature indicates, however, a pristine and quite bay, a calm blue sea, and no waves whatsoever, let alone ice floes.[65] Perhaps it was difficult to meet each technical point because the project blueprints and designs fill a total of 450 volumes; from the time from adoption to approval of the project, the engineers produced more than one volume per day on average! Engineers ultimately chose a traditional Russian beam bridge on piles, although with piles 70 m long—four times the length of those employed in the 1944 version of the bridge, and twice as thick. For the ship passage section of the bridge—the largest span—there are 95 piles, each 1,420 cm in width driven to a depth of 80 m into the ocean floor, with a total span width of 227 m and ship passage of 85 m and height of 35 m. Is the bridge expensive? The Chinese Jiaozhou Bay Bridge at 36 km was $1.5 billion, or $41 million per km. The Crimean Bridge was $173 million per kilometer, four times as expensive. The builders think this is a fair price given the technical challenges of geology, seismology, and currents. All went according to plan: the rail bridge was dedicated in December 2019 and opened to rail traffic in June 2020, and over one million vehicles including 800,000 buses crossed the roadway in the eighteen months after its opening in 2018.[66]

Several Soviet institutions were reincarnated to ensure the bridge spanned the water without public worry. To speed the project, the builders and engineers failed to carry out environmental studies required by law, but instead went with Soviet Gidroproekt research from the 1970s. Archeologists and other social scientists were given a short few weeks to undertake digs and surveys before heavy machinery destroyed their efforts. Similarly, they moved people out of work zones with promises of new comfortable housing in the appropriately named neighborhood of "Cement Industrial Settlement"—this after claiming there would be no "oustees." Second, the authorities established a citizens' group with laymen and specialists, a so-called Committee of Social Control, as a way to convince any doubters that this is a project of democracy with all social issues considered. Management instituted voluntary *subbotniki* (Saturdays given over to unpaid labor) for workers joyously to clean up the garbage. And in the tradition of exhorting Communist Youth League (Komsomol) members to join "shock work" projects across the empire to harness their enthusiasm to the faltering wheel of labor shortages and indifference, so too students from six different engineering institutes were involved in construction to contribute cheap labor. Third, in keeping with the cult of war so prevalent in the nation, by 2015 the worksite already had its own memorial to sailors of World War II. Finally, the authorities have established constant environmental monitoring under the authority of Rospriorodnadzor in ten different directions from 300 sampling points, and there is no doubt the samplers will find nothing wrong, while an afforestation program is being carried out to turn beaches into pine barrens.[67]

Many people remained skeptical about the design and prospects for the bridge, and not only Americans and Ukrainians, but Russian engineers. They argue that a 19 km bridge (including all approaches, not only the bridge) over the Tuzla Spit may not endure because of poor designs and geophysical and climatological circumstances. Georgy Rosnovsky called the design "the most complicated and expensive option." There are deep-lying mud volcanoes and a sludgy bottom, as well as high seismic activity. He argued this required the piles to be much deeper, and with spans over 200 m to ensure they aren't damaged during freezes.[68] Russian engineer Yuri Sevenard added his worries about extreme weather. Several anonymous Moscovites have dubbed the project "idiotism"; after all, the Moscow-Kharkiv-Simferopol train handled the tourist traffic, and freight is needed only to feed the peninsula, and even local Crimean leaders think a new ferry or two—at 7 billion rubles or so— would foot the bill better than a 300 billion ruble bridge. To rebuild the ferry terminals would also require Ukrainian agreement by law.[69] Other detractors point out that the construction of the bridge without Ukrainian consent was a violation of international law.[70] But to push the bridge ahead quickly, the authorities ignored environmental impact statements, facilitated in part by the fact that the Duma passed a bill to allow for unmonitored construction, and with permits a mere formality since it was designed and built simultaneously, they ignored the worries of critical engineers, and they ignored the sovereignty of Ukraine.[71]

Crimea and Twenty-First-Century Bolshevism

As part of the effort to indicate that "Crimea is ours!," print media have published a series of historical articles to justify the illegal construction of the Crimean Bridge. *Tekhnika-Molodezhi* (Technology—For Youth!) ran special issues on Crimea in 2015–2016 concerning the Russian Civil War of 1918– 1920 and the eventual expulsion of the remnants of the White armies under Baron Peter Wrangel from the peninsula in November 1920. The media have played up victory by the Bolsheviks over the monarchists as if to justify the current war in Crimea. These journals have not, of course, addressed the history of Crimea in the 1920s when the Bolsheviks ruthlessly suppressed Tatar nationalism, in the 1940s when Stalin exiled hundreds of thousands of Tatars from the peninsula, half of whom died, nor the role of "little green men" in subjugating Russia's desired place for summer sojourns in 2014. Like Soviet publications, the Russian press touts the glory of the Crimean Bridge in its tons, meters, and poured concrete: 5,500 piles with a total length of 300 km and 240,000 tons that are driven into sea floor. Ignoring the unfortunate precedent of the hated Third Reich, one journalist celebrated the fact that the deepest piles and supports must weather 94 m of water, and they are guaranteed corrosion resistant for 1,000 years, like a Reich. The article shouts that "The Crimean Bridge Is Being Built on 1,000 Year Foundations!"[72]

State-controlled media produced a Soviet-style film—a love story—about the Crimean Bridge. With a screenplay by Margarita Simonian, editor in chief of the state-sponsored propaganda network RT, and directed by her husband, Tigran Simonian, *Crimean Bridge* is an unlikely love story that takes place between a young couple during the building of the bridge. They will be united from different sides when the span is complete. The film strangely acknowledges and simultaneously ignores the deportation of the Crimean Tatars. The male lead, Damir, is a Tatar, who says of his countrymen, "They were sent away—that means it had to be," and at other points in the film, he has approving words for Stalin. The film depicts Crimea as a land of sun and beautiful women, not of Russian imperial plans, naval bases, and Ukrainian and Tatar exclusion.[73]

The bridge has been the focus of children's coloring books that explain how the bridge was built, accompanied by poetic technical explanations.[74] There are Soviet-style literary celebrations, for example *Krymskii Most*, an "almanac of the Russian Union of Professional Writers,"[75] that reproduced from Viktor Krotov's "Surozhskie skazki" the following lines from "Bulldozer on the Beach"[76]:

> A bulldozer came to the beach.
> It rakes up stones and smooths the sand.
> It growls, puffs, and tries and tries.
> Many are resting about,
> Fewer than grains of sand, but more than pebbles.
> But almost no one notices the bulldozer.
> And who will notice—just smile.
> The bulldozer is quite a toy.
> And growls-puffs quite a child's voice.

The point may be that the bulldozer is just a brief interlude onto the beautiful sandy beach, or perhaps that bridges and bulldozers are necessary for today's Russian tourists in annexed territories.

Engineering documents proselytize Putin's bridge as a sign of rebirth of the nation and its empire, and the epitome of technological display, while also embracing the Soviet lexicon of hero projects. One brochure celebrates the "Crimean Spring. We are building the future," and describes the "grandiose and unbelievable project of the century with which all Crimea and Russia—and with incredulity surprise the rest of the world—recognize the project with hope and pride." The brochures instruct readers about the majestic roadways (hardly present anywhere else in Russia), the 7,000 piles, the 250,000-ton spans, the thousands of workers, the forecast 14 million passengers and 13 million tons of freight per year. As a tool of the presidential economy, the Crimean Bridge is supposed to enable investment as much as ease of travel between Crimea and the mainland. As always, Russian promoters of big digs claim they are preserving the historical heritage of their site, having properly carried out geoacoustic and geomagnetic surveys in support of archeological digs. Yet the construction site was a beehive of destruction: villages for the shift workers, supply yards, 40 km of approach and service roads, barrels of leaking petrochemicals, oil spills and leaks, and the bridge itself that destroyed hurriedly inspected historic sites.

Perhaps in some way the Crimean Bridge suggests the challenges of any such massive engineering project, for example, the Big Dig in Boston. Already in the 1940s the automobile "overwhelmed downtown [Boston] streets." In response, the city built an elevated highway, the Central Artery, with the Summer Tunnel to Logan Airport. It was "ugly . . . unappealing . . . and confusing." Immediately, 75,000 vehicles hounded the roadway daily, and by the turn of the century 200,000 vehicles joined in creating massive traffic jams. This led to the Central Artery/Tunnel Project, the so-called Big Dig, with construction beginning in 1991 to remove the elevated road and put it underground, building a new harbor tunnel and two bridges over the Charles River, the Zakim Bridge at ten lanes the widest in the world, drilling tunnels underground without disrupting the highway or traffic or subways or utilities by using a slurry wall technique, or creating a lot of noise. Workers built 5 miles of 3-foot thick slurry wall and moved 500,000 truckloads of dirt for the underground roadway. The original estimated cost of $4 billion rose to $15 billion when completed, and the tunnel was criticized as being aesthetically unappealing.[77] And traffic is still a mess. The engineers ignored the major law of highway construction: "If you build it, then they will come." A second, Aristotelian notion also holds here: "Nature abhors a vacuum." In a word, any effort to deal with congestion by enabling more vehicles to enter the streets will invite more vehicles and clog those streets—usually within a matter of weeks. Putin's bridge risks earthquakes, ice flows, and storms. And it was built to wage war on Ukraine.

The bridge over the Kerch Strait is not necessary infrastructure, nor a solution to traffic problems, but a symbol of presidential power in the Kremlin, its command of resources, and of imperial conquest. Europe and the United States imposed sanctions on Russia for conquering Crimea, war in Eastern Ukraine, and for facilitating the shooting down a Malaysian passenger jet, MH17, on July 17, 2014, killing all 298 people on board. The bridge signifies disregard for international law. Ultimately, like many bridges in human history, the Crimean Bridge was a military structure, in this case conceived in the runup to a war with Ukraine. It has roots in engineering expertise developed primarily in Red Army detachments and gulag operations that were transformed by the state into massive corporate construction firms. These firms marshalled steel, lumber, and stone; aggregate and concrete; earthy moving machines and men in armies of technological verve. Like many of the visionary projects explored in this book, the Crimean Bridge had imperial predecessors in the thinking of Tsarist and British officials, and in completed, if temporary, bridges of Adolf Hitler and Joseph Stalin. It may indeed be, according to Russian media, that a red cat, adopted by the construction workers, was the first across the Crimean Bridge, even before Vladimir Putin jumped in a KamAz truck for a photo opportunity. At least, that's what the construction workers say. And they claim the cat was looking for a kitty. But this claim is simply a poor effort at humor, a forced smile to obscure the fact that the bridge remains a weapon of war and expansion that has now come under attack.[78]

6

Nostalgic Engineering

Big Technology and Russia in the Twenty-first Century[*]

—Россия впереди, так было и так будет.[1]
—"Russia builds cutting-edge nuclear icebreakers. We have had the most powerful icebreaker fleet in the world, and this will remain so."[2]

In the 1920s, Soviet leaders, educators, scientists, and engineers attempted to convert a largely illiterate and peasant population into conscious workers in support of an advanced socialist economy.[3] The creation of the New Soviet Man and Woman involved various educational programs to advance newly trained peasants and workers into positions of proletarian responsibility, propaganda efforts at workers' clubs and "red corners" in factories and other facilities, "red teepees" among reindeer herders in the tundra, and vigilant campaigns to eradicate religious belief, in part by supplanting religious icons with new icons of the Bolshevik order. These icons were political posters with current messages about labor and work, devotion to the state, new cultural norms, and the new glorious symbol of socialism—modern technology. Such new artifacts of modernity as tractors, power lines, dams, light bulbs, and spacious, well-illuminated factories were the focus of myriad posters, and their glorious, even heroic construction was a central message of many of the speeches of Bolshevik leaders and planners, as it has been into the contemporary era.

Many of the founders of the Soviet state saw technology as a panacea for the geographical tricks played on the empire—its massive and sparsely populated Arctic and sub-Arctic regions that were rich in lumber, and in mineral and fossil fuel reserves, weather patterns unconducive to modern agriculture in parched Central Asian republics, and so on. They believed technology would magically overcome the natural and economic problems of development that

Hero Projects. Paul R. Josephson, Oxford University Press. © Oxford University Press 2024.
DOI: 10.1093/oso/9780197698396.003.0007

faced the nation, at the same time protecting it militarily—and enabling military gambits to secure more territory. They saw new industrial behemoths arising in the taiga and tundra wherever resources were located that drew peasants and workers like magnets to the forge, and that produced every strategic product that the nation required, with copious amounts of electricity flowing from dams and boilers to factories and fields, with tractors overnight transforming backward agriculture and farmers in the fields into the modern agribusiness of collectivized farms, and in all securing the nation for the inevitable war with the capitalist nations that surrounded it.[4] One need only recall one of the major slogans of early Bolshevism and its state plan for the electrification of the country: "Communism equals Soviet power plus electrification of the entire country." To put it into contemporary terms, the slogan might read: "Our motherland will be secured on the basis of modern technology tied to the strength and vision of our political leaders, along with gas, aluminum, and other commodities."

As this book has indicated, big technology remains a crucial feature for Russian leadership in the twenty-first century. Contemporary big projects—in coal, in oil and gas, in waterworks, dams and canals, in a planned Arctic railroad, in bridges over troubled waters, in myriad nuclear transport and power units—have their roots in the Soviet period. They were dreams and projects of Tsarist engineers and the visions and campaigns of Soviet planners and politicians, and they still issue forth in presidential proclamations and documents of research and design institutes, virtually all of which were founded in the Soviet period but have found new life from petrodollars and new will from within the Kremlin walls. Under Vladimir Putin the Russian state has vigorously pursued a return to the world stage as a rival to the United States and the European Union in economic and military matters; as a scientific superpower; and as an empire, in its own terms, stretching from the European plain to the Pacific Ocean, attacking Moldova and Georgia, and seizing territory from Ukraine in unprovoked war; all to be a powerful state, and since resource assimilation undergirds state power, therefore a powerful resource state.

The thinking behind the effort to recreate a powerful state centers on a series of important factors. The first is the belief among leaders that Russia was all-powerful as the leading nation of the USSR, and that it was wronged by the Western powers, the United States in particular, when the Soviet Union collapsed in the 1990s. Under President Putin, Russia has regained its standing and self-respect as a leader in a reconstituted bipolar world. The

second is that mineral and natural resources make the Russian state powerful. Putin himself argued this point in his master's essay completed at the
Mining Institute in St. Petersburg in 1998.[5] The third is that big technology
is the key instrument to building state power, especially that in line with the
"hero projects" and "projects of the century" of past leaders. We have traced
the institutional momentum of these projects and the institutes pushing
them into the twenty-first century.

Another factor is the way that the political culture of the Soviet past has
been recreated in the style and trappings of the Russian president and in his
embrace of megaprojects. Many of the leading Russian officials are, like Putin,
siloviki, literally men of power, people who entered Russian politics from the
security, armed forces, or police branches of service. They are former KGB
agents, federal inspectors, or highly placed defense operatives. It is not surprising that they would be nostalgic about the power and glory of the former
Soviet Union, that they recall with pride the days of military and scientific
parity with the United States, or that they see large-scale technologies as the
key for securing the nation's security and economic might in the twenty-first
century, in particular since they often benefit personally and financially from
their positions as heads of ministries and oil companies or in the government.

Through various earth-moving, nuclei-splitting, and resource-extracting
organizations and companies, Russian leaders have resumed Soviet-like
projects to demonstrate that the country remains a technological superpower,
and they use state-controlled media to present images of oligarchs, and especially President Putin, engaged with modern technology—Russia's massive aluminum factories and hydropower stations, its nuclear reactors, gas
fields, and pipelines. Like Soviet leaders—and leaders in many countries—
Putin uses photo opportunities to show himself as a friend of nature at the
same time as a master of it. These photos harken to the Soviet practice of connecting leaders to technological enthusiasm—and big projects—factories,
dams, canals, and so on—in posters, slogans, photographs, and mass media
reporting. Soviet posters, themselves born from the transplanting of technological images into religious icons, have been reborn as corporate logos,
for example, the ubiquitous Gazprom flame. Putin embraces this approach
of photo "ops" with the flame on display nearby. By video link or in person
he dedicates the "starts" of pipelines and "openings" of factories of nuclear reactors. He has reintroduced special Soviet "days" that celebrate the
achievements of such employees of big technology as atomic workers and
cosmonauts, he gives awards to successful managers, and he publicly sacks

them when they irritate him. And he carries out war on Ukraine to reconstitute the glorious Soviet heritage with Russia at its head.

Much of the world attention on Russian resources and technological verve centers on the development of gas and oil, exploitation of reserves in Siberian and polar regions, and the phenomenal growth of such state corporations as Gazprom. We have considered oil and gas extraction as a megaproject in the spread of the Yamal Peninsula pipeline, railroad and bridge infrastructure in difficult geographic and geological conditions north of the Arctic Circle. A brief comment on Gazprom reinforces conclusions about the importance of hero projects in contemporary Russia for their economic, political, and geopolitical significance. Gazprom is the thirty-second largest publicly owned company in the world, with assets of $330 billion and 469,000 employees. Gazprom "holds the world's largest natural gas reserves. The Company's share in the global and Russian gas reserves amounts to 16 and 71 per cent respectively." And "the Company owns the world's largest gas transmission system, the total length of which within the boundaries of Russia reaches 175.2 thousand kilometers. Gazprom sells more than half of its gas to Russian consumers and exports gas to over 30 countries within and beyond the former Soviet Union."[6] Further, "hydrocarbons account for 25% of Russia's GDP, 50% of its government revenue, and 70% of its export earnings," with oil having played a central role in Russia's recovery from the 1990s, in helping to show Putin as a great leader, and in making Russia an "energy superpower," even if oil and gas dependency is bad for the country's long term development ("the resource curse").[7] Like other large-scale technological systems, Gazprom as big oil and gas technology is central to the Russian narrative of what I call "nostalgic engineering"—a fascination with Soviet engineering projects of the past as part of the justification for contemporary engineering projects. The thinking is that big projects of the Soviet period succeeded, so they must succeed in the twenty-first century. In this chapter, I examine that narrative for technologies generally and consider President Putin's personal role, and that of the *siloviki*, in furthering it.

Putin and his advisors have embraced technological achievements of the past and drawn clear connections with the big technological projects of the present. They have incorporated the president himself through a kind of personality cult that ties his leadership successes to the rebuilding of a new, powerful, technologically advanced Russia, a country capable of standing up to the United States and NATO, and of providing an alternative to the corrupt and decadent West with its embrace of gay rights and other ostensible immoralities.[8] The constant praise of Putin bears some resemblance to the cults of personality in the Stalin, Khrushchev, and Brezhnev era in which technological achievements played a major role. The Kremlin's response to world conditions is largely driven by the technological momentum of past projects, both because they exist in blueprints and because large-scale centralized approaches to resource development have been the tried and true way of securing military and economic might. Hero projects provide legitimacy to the current leadership as well. Many of these megaprojects were born in the Stalin era in the gulag, and others owe their genesis to later Soviet leaders. Like past leaders, the current leadership tends to ignore their environmental and social costs, the latter including the failure to stimulate the simultaneous development of human capital. Yet the pursuit of big technology, as it was for the Bolsheviks, is a rational choice if the goal is unbridled state power and wealth, if legitimacy devolves from it, and if the symbolism of technological verve remains crucial to society.

Many Russians—from citizens to leaders, from oligarchs to babushkas—lament the breakup of the USSR, they yearn for great power status, and Putin himself called the 1991 dissolution of the Soviet Union the greatest geopolitical catastrophe of the twentieth century. The number of Russians "pining for the Soviet past has been steadily rising under Putin since he returned to the presidency in 2012," and except during a short period around 2012 it has never been below 50 percent.[9] Citizens lament the loss of a stable, if gray existence, with a certain social safety net, and relatively low prices for food, housing, and health that characterized life under the Soviets, although they do not pine for many other aspects of the Soviet system—bans on foreign travel, limits on free speech, close supervision of daily life and thought by political and police operatives, poor-quality goods and country-wide shortages, and international isolation. Yet because of the current government's actions at home and abroad in war they face all of these restrictions again in one way or another. They take solace in recalling the heights of Soviet civilization—Sputnik, Yuri Gagarin, Tokamak fusion devices, the Bratsk hydropower station, and other technological feats. This fascination with the Soviet technological past that enables individuals to overplay the successes, ignore the failures, and remain ignorant of the social and environmental costs of those achievements is all a part of nostalgic engineering.[10]

Twenty-first-century Russian nostalgia for Soviet technology reflects a variety of phenomena. First, trust in current Russian leadership to restore national pride, protect the fatherland, and provide for the masses resembles that of the Soviet past. Similarly, big projects, past and present, demonstrate enlightened and legitimate leadership. These big projects enable the government to claim the ability to manipulate a hitherto capricious nature, at the same time securing borders against geopolitical threats in an uncertain world. Narratives and tropes about power and prestige, control and mastery, pride and sacrifice that characterized Soviet projects in space, in Arctic conquest, in extracting and manipulating resources through nuclear power, in modern roads, bridges, and railroads through the vast stretches of the land, and in canals and hydropower stations, have been reborn in contemporary Russian versions.[11] The nostalgia for the Soviet past is not surprising, in that many aspects of political culture have been restored and because many of these projects have grown out of expensive antecedents that were mothballed in the late 1980s and 1990s. The projects have reappeared as symbols of the technological might of the new Russian state. Similarly, scientists and engineers refer wistfully to Soviet antecedents of their projects, even if those projects collapsed, or were of uncertain reliability—witness the reverence for the *Lenin* icebreaker whose failed reactors were jettisoned unceremoniously into the Arctic Ocean—or the thousands of other objects of high radioactivity that the Soviets dumped in the region.[12]

The Russian government, and Putin in particular, have been active in fostering nostalgia for the Soviet technological sublime. The technological sublime, as David Nye explores in a book on the US experience and the fascination with railroads, bridges, dams, skyscrapers, electrification, and so on, describes the way people respond to technology with awe and wonder, and how it helps to bring a diverse society together, and contributing to a sense of "specialness."[13] So, in Russia, a nation with dozens of distinct geographical regions and scores of ethnic groups, the Russian leadership uses technology to weave a history of common purpose, of unique achievements ("First in the world!" "Furthest north!" "First polar navigation!"), and of national mission, if megaprojects as a rule benefit Moscow and the center first of all, and come at the expense of the provinces. To put it simply, pipelines and railroads on the Yamal Peninsula, coal mines in Siberia, hydroelectric power stations in Siberia, floating reactors in the Arctic, and a bridge across the Kerch Strait are of the same cloth—and concrete and steel—as Soviet achievements.

We Were First into Space! Putin Celebrates Gagarin

The Russian leadership has promised the construction of a lunar base by 2030, and a mission to Mars soon thereafter, in spaceships powered by nuclear reactors. Putin has pursued these space "firsts" by forcing the construction of a new space city on Russian territory to replace that at Baikonur, Kazakhstan, lost with the breakup of the USSR. At the same time, Putin recognizes the importance of Soviet achievements in space as convincing evidence that the conquest of Mars is possible, even if economic life at home may be difficult. To draw connections between technological achievements that enhance state power and the contribution of the people to them, Putin celebrates a series of holidays, many of which were established in the Soviet era in honor of such great figures of Russian and Soviet history as secret police, linguists, and seamstresses: Victory Day (May 9); Day of Knowledge (September 1); Day of People's Unity (November 4, to celebrate freedom from "Polish occupiers" in 1612); Day of Workers of Narcotics Control (March 11); Day of Submariners (March 19); Day of Philologists (March 25); Day of Textile and Light Industry Workers (the second Sunday in July); days of builders, miners, of workers of oil and gas industry, of tankists, of mothers, jurists, heroes of the fatherland, of soldiers in the strategic rocket service; of course, of employees in the secret police; and Day of the Cosmonauts on April 12 to commemorate Russian space leadership and the day Yuri Gagarin rocketed into space in 1961. One day stands out for acknowledging technological failure: Day of Those Killed in Radiation Accidents and Catastrophes (April 26, the anniversary of the Chernobyl disaster, itself the result of a combination of poor reactor design, a foolishly designed and risky experiment, and technological hubris).

Contemporary Russian leaders have been increasingly vocal in celebrating the big science and technology of the Soviet period, and especially its space achievements—the first satellite, Sputnik, and man, Yuri Gagarin, into space, in 1957 and 1961 respectively, the first extravehicular activity, the first woman in space, Valentina Tereshkova, and on and on. Space has been centrally important to Russian self-image and imagination. Gagarin, for example, was a new kind of hero—a hero of the potentialities of Soviet society under Khrushchev, and of reborn faith in the communist future. Under Putin, Gagarin's heroism is a model of service to the Russian Federation.[14] Russian newspaper articles on space themes typical for April any year will refer to the cultural heritage of Gagarin. According to one, "space" like nothing else symbolized and cultivated in the people and the country the desire to be the first and became a kind of national idea. The cosmos was "a celebration." Cosmonaut Valentina Tereshkova said, "The thought that only we could do it (go to space first) was lost in the 1990s and we immediately went in reverse."[15] A catastrophic loss of finances, the absence of plans and projects, brain drain of personnel to the West, and interruptions in leadership of the space program sent the system into crisis, which current leadership intends to repair.

In the view of Russian leaders, the United States was responsible for the Russian space program "going into reverse." According to Deputy Prime Minister Dmitrii Rogozin, responsible for the space and defense industries, in the 1990s the West unfairly took advantage of a weakened Russia to steal its engineering and scientific achievements on the cheap. After the collapse of the USSR, a series of public failures, as opposed to the secret ones of the Soviet era—for example, the loss of the highly touted Phobus-2 satellite that disappeared on its last approach to Mars's moons, and several other space freight vehicles and satellites—rocked the industry. Other countries began to forget Russia, treating it, Rogozin believed, as a junior partner, not a power in space research.[16] In an article on the importance of space in Russian culture, Viktor Marakhovskii, a cultural journalist, concluded that "However, we remain ourselves—and that is why we read with such avidity, for example, the news about the joint announcement by Rosatom and Roskosmos about the nuclear rocket engine that will allow astronauts to reach Mars in a month and a half and return. . . . We really need space."[17]

No less than Chinese, European, or US space agencies, Roskosmos has determined to revitalize its programs in recent years. Putin has shown particular interest in this effort. This required overcoming the sense in Russian consciousness that the nation had declined, restoring pride, instituting radical reforms, and paying for space with oil revenues. In January 2016, Putin thus signed an order to create Roskosmos, a government corporation in the form of Rosatom to mimic nuclear successes, to resurrect Russia leadership in the cosmos on the basis of its extensive experience, rocket engines, and other performance criteria. His deputy, Rogozin, concurred that space research would take on the role of an "effective instrument of raising national pride." Rogozin claimed that by the early 2010s, Russian space research was ready again to provide practical benefits to citizens, foster innovation in industry, telecommunications, medicine, transport, and of course defense. Beyond these promised contributions to the quality of daily life, Roskosmos planners have also begun, as in Soviet times, to advance fantastic visions for space exploration, as noted, to the moon and Mars.[18]

Putin has been cultivating a "cult of space" since early in his presidency, and equated Soviet firsts with Russian destiny in the cosmos. In 2001, on the fortieth anniversary of Yuri Gagarin's liftoff for three earth orbits as the very first man in space, Putin declared that "We have the right to take pride in the fact that this huge, scientific-technical breakthrough was achieved in our country."[19] On Gagarin Day in 2004, Putin stated that "Russians will always be proud that the first man in space was a citizen of our country." He reminded citizens that Gagarin—and by extension Russia—"without exaggeration opened the cosmic era," an era of "human greatness." Putin continued, "Space today remains the horizon, movement toward which is connected with scientific discoveries, progress, and the utilization of untapped earlier possibilities."[20] He underlined the close connections between Soviet and Russian practices by announcing a series of public (and Soviet-like) awards he now bestows annually at the Kremlin on Day of Cosmonauts.[21] For its part, the space industry has joined the Gagarin bacchanalia with the publication of biographies of space heroes and collections of previously secret documents.[22] The cosmonauts have been the subject of, and wrote, children's books, too.

The rocket engines of space culture have generated approval among Russian citizens. Eighty percent of Russians see investment in space in contemporary Russia as worthwhile and necessary. This was a sharp turnaround from just a few years earlier, when people scrambled to make ends meet and groused about expensive projects.[23] One group of happy patriots produced a film to glorify Gagarin and made note of Putin's restoration of respect for the motherland through Gagarin. In it, the narrator intones monotonously in front of a somnolent crowd, droning on about the glories of the great USSR. He admonishes, "We have lost the great power—the USSR. But our great leader V. V. Putin will resurrect that technological might."[24]

On the fifty-second anniversary of Yuri Gagarin's flight into space in 2011, Putin unveiled his $50 billion determination for Russia to preserve its status in space from a new flight center, Vostochny, built on Russian territory in the Amur region of the Far East. Vostochny would also save Russia roughly $150 million annually in rent to Kazakhstan. Delays and corruption in construction have blighted work on the new space city, with billions of dollars in cost overruns. But the impressive facility moves ahead, if not closer to space. Beginning in 2012, 10,000 workers built 115 km of roads, 125 km of railways, an oxygen-nitrogen factory, and a company town, like those of the Soviet period, with housing for 25,000 people in the sparsely populated region.[25]

Like all leaders, Putin makes it a point to show up at construction projects important to the state. Putin visited Vostochny in April 2016 to watch the space park's inaugural launch. Because of a delay in that launch, Putin publicly upbraided Rogozin and Roskosmos head Igor Komarov.[26] As the official opening of the Vostochny Cosmodrome approached in April 2017 on the eve of Cosmonauts Day, Putin invited two great living legends of Soviet space, Aleksei Leonov and Valentina Tereshkova, together with the daughter of the founder of the Soviet space program, Sergei Korolev, and the daughter of Gagarin, Elena, to the Kremlin to watch a new Russian film, *Time of the First* (*Время первых*), about the great achievements of Soviet cosmonauts, and in particular the first space walk in 1965 by Leonov himself. Putin opened the showing before a crowd of notable personalities and officials by congratulating everyone on the holiday and reminding them that Russian space achievements of Russia were indeed something about which to be proud.[27] He announced that Russia would send manned flights from Vostochny by 2018,[28] but that date has been pushed back to 2025, and no doubt in keeping with contemporary hero projects under the stress of international isolation will be pushed back again and again by several years.

Russian officials insist that the goal of the current space program is to conquer the moon, with a trip to Mars also in the offing. Indeed, on Gagarin day in 2014, Putin announced a Gagarinesque plan to colonize and mine the moon as befitting a highly developed high-tech nation.[29] Russia's current mission to establish a lunar base thus is not an historical mission alone, but a national one. "It has become the subject of national pride," Putin declared.[30] The satellite "Luna-Globe" (Луна-Глоб, also called Luna-25 to indicate its inheritance from the Soviet program and Luna-24 launched in 1976) is the first step to the base. Its launch was postponed several times, and on August 19, 2023, the thirty-second anniversary of the failed communist coup again Mikhail Gorbachev, it crashed into the moon leaving only a crater. One of the leading figures of space research, Vitalii Melnikov, died a few weeks later, apparently from eating poison mushrooms. He joined a number of other oligarchs and bureaucrats who have died recently—mysteriously jumping out of windows or committing suicide rather than face being called out by Putin for their failures. The launches of Luna-26 through Luna-30 are scheduled for later in the 2020s, but frankly who can anticipate any firm schedule now.[31] Sometimes nostalgia is more important than reality.

Arctic Pasts, Presents, and Futures

Russian museums and press centers play an important role in nostalgic representations of Soviet engineering including such technological achievements as breakers churning through ice floes. Museums of local lore, history, nature, and cultural development (*kraeved* museums, of which there are at least 800 in Russia), and those at such technological "installations" as nuclear power stations, physics research institutes, and so on, proudly chronicle Soviet and Russian achievements. Many expositions stress the continuity between the Soviet empire and the technological and geopolitical feats of contemporary Russia.[32] To take one example: the *Lenin* museum—the moored icebreaker of the heroic past that operated from 1959 until 1989, when it was retired because of a thinning hull—has been called the "pride of Murmansk" and an object of "cultural and citizen significance" as the first ship to cover the entire polar circumference. (I myself managed to get aboard the ship in the 1990s, but Atomflot determined to turn it into a museum to be open to the public, a step completed in 2010.[33]) The *Lenin* has become one of Rosatom's six special press information centers across the country, each with interactive expositions, film theater, and other modern museum devices. Given the large number of reactors concentrated within the city limits, the *Lenin* museum staff claim that the residents of Murmansk are without a doubt thrilled by the possibility to receive reliable information on the work of the various nuclear enterprises—including the *Lenin*.[34]

Russian shipbuilders, administrators, and officials have understandably great nostalgia for the Soviet Union, which created the world's greatest icebreaker fleet. They often refer to the *Lenin* as the epitome of Soviet know-how with its elegant interior of polished wood handrails, door frames, cabinets, library, saunas, swimming pool, formal dining room, and cafeteria, all as a symbol of Russia's inevitable mission to secure the Arctic Circle.[35] Many Russian leaders and citizens remember the *Lenin* as a civilian and peaceful technology as distinct from those of the militaristic Western nations. The *Lenin* was "the honorable work taken on by the entire Soviet people and proved conclusively that the 'socialist atom' was peaceful and creative."[36] It was the "pride and joy of the great game of the Soviet Union in the Arctic" that has now "dropped anchor at eternal guard in local icy waters" as a relic of the Cold War. And thirty years later, Russia has again begun to push into the Arctic with new icebreakers. This will reconfirm Russia's rightly and destined position as leader of conquest and assimilation in the Far North as she proudly engages Canada, the United States, Norway, and even China for influence—and military and economic expansion—in the region.[37]

Like Soviet leaders who celebrated the achievements of explorers, the finding of mineral wealth, the human conquest of tundra, and the building of strategic mono-industrial cities, so Russia's leaders today imagine Arctic development as key to Russia's future, and a source of significant economic and military might. Russian leaders have recreated the imagery and artifacts of the Soviet era to demonstrate the continuity between eras and the fate of the fateful outcome. In August 2007, Russian parliamentarian and explorer Artur Chilingarov engaged a deep-sea dive to plant a Russian flag on the bottom of the Arctic Ocean at the North Pole, as if to claim the entire polar region.[38] The expensive expedition included the components of Russia's renewed claim of superpower symbolism. A nuclear-powered icebreaker, *Rossiia*, led a research ship, *Akademik Fedorov*, to get into position for Chilingarov's descent in a bathysphere. In a regal ceremony, President Putin welcomed Chilingarov's flag-planting expedition as confirmation of Russia's claim on vast new Arctic territories.

Chilingarov and his colleagues produced a popular scientific coffee-table volume in the style of Stalin-era books on the Arctic. The book celebrated the return to the Arctic of floating research stations that had filled the Arctic in the Soviet era from the 1950s without interruption until the 1990s when the funding crises of the Yeltsin years ended the glorious scientific presence in the Arctic. The book referred explicitly to a Soviet classic, N. N. Zubov's *V tsentre Arktiki* (1948), as a model, and to the pathbreaking efforts of Soviet explorers and the heroic North Sea Route administration, Glavsevmorput. And, of course, the book's authors supported Russia's claims to increased share of the Arctic, and they asserted that foreign governments sought to displace Russia from her rightful control over the Northern Sea Route because of their desire to control petroleum resources on the Arctic shelf.[39]

For military-strategic, economic, and socio-cultural reasons, the Putin presidency has embraced the Soviet Arctic legacy and converted it into a contemporary narrative about preparedness, defense of the motherland, and glorious assimilation of hydrocarbons.[40] Putin has built upon the Stalinist program of Arctic conquest in a variety of government documents that are similar in goals and tone.[41] A 2008 government decision on the basic directions of Russian Arctic policy through 2020 included a called for the creation of special units of Arctic troops to be vigilant against potential threats; in 2011 the first such units appeared. A special motorized brigade prepared for Arctic conditions would be stationed at the Kola Peninsula 200th motorized regiment base. In September 2012, President Putin called for a great leap forward à la Stalin's industrialization campaign of the 1930s to rejuvenate Russian military industry to be prepared for Arctic security.[42]

It is precisely Arctic projects that have garnered the attention of the government which consume up to 10 percent of all investment in the country. At an Arctic Forum in April 2019, Putin outlined the extensive hydrocarbon works sponsored by the state and its corporations, for example, the Yamal Liquid Natural Gas project, and the Bovanenkovskoe and Kharasaveyskoe gas fields. Toward the ends of these projects, Putin again referred to Arctic infrastructure, including the Northern Latitudinal Railway (NLR) with its Stalinist roots. The NLR was added to the investment queue to open "the natural riches of the Polar Urals and Yamal, and in the long term, the north of Krasnoyarsk Territory of the Russian Federation." This project, which Putin endorsed without any sense of irony in 2012, is based on Stalin's "Road of Death," a gulag railroad project, it will be recalled, that pushed across the Arctic Circle eastward toward Igarka with the loss of tens of thousands of men.[43] The NLR will supplement the Northern Sea Route that will be opened "without fail year-round." Displaying not a small amount of pride, Putin pointed out, in 2019, that it would quadruple freight traffic to 80 million tons by 2025, up from 20 million tons in 2018, and three times the Soviet record of 6.5 million tons sent in the 1980s. Icebreakers were the key, nuclear-powered icebreakers, with "at least 13 heavy-duty linear icebreakers, including nine nuclear icebreakers" by 2035.[44]

One of Putin's close associates, Igor Sechin, a member of the *siloviki*, a former deputy prime minister, but now CEO of Rosneft, the state oil company, also is enamored of ships, yachts, and shipbuilding like other oligarchs, including nuclear shipbuilding and repairs. He employed Rosneft, together with Rosneftegaz and Gazprombank, to underwrite and expand the Far Eastern "Zvezda" shipbuilding company in its company town of Bolshoi Kamen, an operation established in 1954, but in conjunction with the repair of smaller commercial fishing vessels. In the twenty-first century, "Zvezda" works mainly on naval ships, having repaired some 600 warships and auxiliary vessels, and fifty-three nuclear and thirteen diesel submarines, and it employs 4,000 people. A series of government decrees led to the upgrading of facilities to undertake repairs and construction on all vital military and civilian marine facilities.[45] The civilian operations include oilrigs. The head of "Zvezda," Sergei Tseluiko, called the complex "the latest page in the history of Russian shipbuilding. Before our eyes it is becoming the largest shipyard in Russia, designed for the construction of all types of ships and production platforms for work on the Russian shelf." These activities were "on behalf of the president and the government of the Russian Federation." President Putin described the facility as "of great importance for the entire national shipbuilding industry." And, of course, in these days of nostalgia, Putin showed up at the dedication of the expanded Zvezda Shipbuilding Complex on September 1, 2016.[46]

While the sublime endeavor to build, launch, and operate icebreakers remains heroic, it comes with many dangers. *Icebreaker* (2016), a Russian disaster film directed by Nikolai Khomeriki, is based in part on the real events that occurred in 1985 with the icebreaker *Mikhail Somov* that was trapped by Antarctic ice and spent 133 days in forced drift.[47] This film recalls the Stalin-era spectacles of the *Sedov*, *Cheliuskin*, and other icebreakers forced by nature to winter in deep Arctic ice pack that were played out on the national stage as the coming conquest of the Arctic. Sailors and explorers perished, but those spectacles indicated instead Bolshevik resolve, certitude of victory over the elements, and they made heroes out of frozen men. The disasters occurred not because of the failings of captains and sailors, but because Stalin and the Party leadership pushed them, unprepared and with inadequate ships, to be heroes before the nation. For example, the *Cheliuskin*, in fact, was not an icebreaker, but a Danish-built steamship, refitted with extra steel plates on the hull in the attempt at the first Arctic crossing from Murmansk to Vladivostok in 1933. The political requirement to demonstrate a Stalinist victory over the elements forced the ship deeper into the autumn ice almost to the Bering Straits. This was a symbol of the heady times of Stalinist superhuman plans. But once icebound, the ship's hull failed and sank, and the members of the expedition were forced to set up an ice camp in the Chukotka Sea to winter in a constant battle against changing conditions. Eventually, under the watchful gaze of Stalin and the nation, the *Cheliuskintsy* built a runway out of snow and ice and were evacuated by airplane. The fact that one-third of the expedition members were Communist Party members or members of the Komsomol, we are told, secured victory of the Arctic. As Soviet propagandists duly noted, "This of course was a huge advantage that not one of the past bourgeois expeditions [to the Arctic] knew about."[48] Also, in keeping with Stalinist practices, a number of the shipmates including officers were later arrested for the fiasco as "wreckers," even as others were immortalized in books, posters, and stamps. Indeed, Soviet postage stamps of the era often celebrated the heroes of nature—as Russian stamps do to this day, leaving no doubt about the importance of a continuing narrative of technological conquest. The stamps immortalize Otto Smidt, head of Glavsevmorput in the 1930s; the *Arktika*, the first surface ship to the North Pole; and 2015 issues of Russian Arctic oil platforms and tankers.[49]

The Role of the President in Creating the Technological Sublime

After becoming president in 2000, Putin embraced a series of images and realities of Russian technological prowess to push the nation's economic recovery and bolster its self-image. It is not surprising that a man of Soviet origins, a KGB official, an old-style patriot, would find programs and policies of the past to rebuild state power and to augment his own stature in the present. Working with his advisors and with powerful oligarchs, he sought not only personal wealth, but a return of Russia to its preeminent geopolitical position, in large part by recreating the resource empire that had stretched from the North Pole to Central Asia and from Europe to the Pacific.[50] He has praised the Soviet development model that arose under Stalin as instructive for Russia's rapid economic growth, taking credit for that growth even if recovery had much to do with sales of oil and gas abroad at higher and higher prices. In his master's thesis about natural resources and the state, defended at the Mining Institute, a state organization dating to Catherine the Great, Putin declared that "the stable development of Russia in the next years should be based on the orderly growth of its parts, and first of all on its mineral-resource potential." On the one hand, he wrote that the mining, extraction, and enrichment complexes should be "regulated by the government purely by market mechanisms," by which he meant legal, financial-credit, and infrastructural and informational support, as well as efforts to ensure safety and prevent accidents. Yet he called for "strengthening the economic foundations of federalism in relation to ownership of natural resources," by which we now know he meant state control.[51]

At the same time, Putin began carefully to cultivate an image of a modern-day leader who understood the complexities of the domestic and geopolitical worlds, but was deeply concerned, as an omniscient Tsar, about the challenges facing the ordinary citizen in daily life. He has relied heavily both on real technological achievements and on the messages and imagery associated with them. He subtly takes credit for factory modernization, pipeline openings, ship, submarine and spacecraft launchings, powering up of nuclear reactors, and building bridges into conquered territories.[52] The Kremlin uses its own website, kremlin.ru, and media outlets, 90 percent which are now state-controlled, to disseminate images of Putin as tamer of wild animals, Arctic explorer, Lake Baikal archeologist, and truck driver across the nearly complete Crimean Bridge.[53] This is not only political banality. Putin truly has assembled great authority in Russia among the public, and he clearly embraces the effort in speeches, public appearances, and technological feats to orchestrate his image as protector of Russian values and its borders against such threats as America, NATO, immorality, homosexuality, and so on.

Indeed, the country's achievements in science and technology have been tied to a growing cult of personality around Putin that resembles those of Stalin, Khrushchev, and Brezhnev. The cult involves a style of political leadership in which the Tsar or Party secretary—or president—is surrounded by boyars, other party members, or oligarchs—whose power depends on the central figure and their allegiance to him.[54] Toward this end, in his terms as president, Putin has chipped away significantly at democratic reforms and the fragile rights of nascent civil society, in part to secure an agenda of breakneck resource development. He established control over the regional governors by making it almost impossible for opposition politicians to run for office. Putin weakened significantly the federal environmental protection agency and gave the provincial governments responsibility for enforcement of laws but without adequate staff or personnel. Putin's FSB at first interfered with the activities of NGOs and required those with international funding to register as "foreign agent," and now is shutting down many of them, including Memorial, an organization dedicated to preserving the memory of the millions of people repressed under Stalinism.[55] If Russia is not the USSR, then why does it fear so much preservation of past memory? Why does it fear the fact that the gulag helped build the Soviet empire?

Putin strongly believes that resource exploitation is crucial to Russia's economic and military strength. His Ministry of Natural Resources manages the nation's great mineral and natural wealth through the fire sale of resources, not any effort at conservation, let alone preservation.[56] Yet Putin simultaneously shows concern for "nature" through government acts and public displays. The acts include ordering the cleanup of dangerous Arctic detritus left by decades of Russian and Soviet colonists, explorers, factories, and military enterprises, and Putin's declaration of 2017 as Year of the Environment.[57] The public displays include a series of well-known and well-orchestrated photographs in which Putin has appeared in natural surroundings in poses that are intended to reveal his power over nature itself: leading wild cranes back to the wild, revealing a virile chest while holding a rifle, tranquilizing tigers, mastering the Arctic, cavorting with dolphins—and speaking their language.

In resurrecting some of the trappings of Soviet rule, the Russian president always addresses the people on New Year's Eve with his greetings and wishes for a prosperous future for citizens and the nation. In this nationwide TV oration, Putin normally raises high notes of nation (working together as "a united team"), health and happiness for family, and the guidance of the church, but he also notes "pressing tasks in the economy, research, technology, healthcare, education and culture."[58] And he has taken the opportunity to urge a special kind of circumspection about the state of the world. In 2016 he called on his countrymen and women to "believe in ourselves, in our strengths and in our country. We are working, and working successfully, and we are achieving much. I would like to thank you for the victories and achievements, for your understanding and trust, and for your true, sincere care for Russia." But he reminded listeners that "not everyone is at the holiday table today. Many of our citizens are away from home, ensuring Russia's security, working at enterprises, on duty in hospitals, and operating trains and aircraft," and conveyed best wishes "to all those who are now fulfilling their labour and military duties."[59]

The president receives high officials in his Kremlin office to hear them report on their posts and ministries. He praises their technological achievements and criticizes their lags. The choreographed meetings take place in Putin's office where Putin faces the supplicant across a table. He listens carefully to the report and then responds with a few questions—or usually a terse, "Thank you for your work on behalf of the nation." Three days before Atomic Workers' Day, on September 25, 2015, for example, Putin entertained Sergei Kirienko, the head of Rosatom, who listed the burgeoning business of the nuclear corporation: dozens of reactors under construction or on order, thirty-three in operation, advances in floating nuclear power stations, and so on. Putin responded, "Lately a lot has been done, over the last ten years, perhaps, a particularly noticeable jump, a leap, it can be said. I want to congratulate you, and everyone who works in the industry, on the upcoming [Nuclear Workers'] holiday."[60]

Many of the president's meetings involve celebration of technology or its workers. Soviet leaders and officials developed a whole series of awards, prizes, and honors for workers, with special titles, ruble prizes, and other incentives: honorary worker, hero of socialist labor, state prizes, and orders of the red banner of labor, in the Stalin period "Stakhanovite" for those who established new norms. Russia has reinstalled prizes, awards, and titles that are the same as Soviet-era ones or highly reminiscent of them. Putin is a master at awarding favored workers and officials with these titles. On September 25, 2007, Putin announced awards to "workers and veterans of the atomic industry" on the occasion of their professional atom workers day. These almost 200,000 sector employees were "patriotic scholars, engineers, designers and other specialists of several generations" who had built in "our country" the first nuclear power station, the first nuclear submarine, and the first icebreaker. Putin referred to the dynamic growth of this sector of the economy and was confident they would maintain their tradition of great contributions to national strength.[61] The holiday dated to 2005 and a Putin declaration. He and his advisors chose the date September 28, 1942, to draw explicit connections with Soviet achievement: on that day the State Committee for Defense had organized the atomic bomb project.

Putin's behavior harkens to the Soviet period not only in the formal trappings of the office. In a series of speeches over the last decade, President Putin has pointed directly and indirectly to the importance of strengthening the Russian empire through modern technology in a way often reminiscent of the language of Joseph Stalin, and with similar references to the dangers and problems that face the nation.[62] In a speech in 2018 Putin touted the achievements of the Russian nation in establishing "sustainability and stability in almost all areas of life." Yet he also referred to domestic and international challenges that the country has "had to face over the course of its history."[63] He repeated the warnings of previous Russian and Soviet leaders concerning the mission of the empire: the troubling international situation, especially of the efforts of the United States to establish hegemony over world forces; and uncertainty at home, including of enemies of Russian values and beliefs that have penetrated the nation, for example, those of decadence—and gay life, anti-Orthodox religious proselytization, and the dangerous presence of immigrants and other foreigners within Russia's borders.

Stalin's views of empire, technology, planning, and expertise have been instructive for Putin. For Stalin, the most important doctrine related to empire and frontier was the notion of "socialism in one country." Stalin rejected

Lev Trotsky's belief—and that of many other Marxists—in world revolution. World revolution meant that the Soviet revolution could not ultimately succeed without proletarian revolution in other leading industrial nations, although the USSR would lead the way toward that stage. Stalin pushed world revolution off to some distant time. He contended that internal enemies—Trotskyites, wreckers, counter-revolutionaries—had been defeated—liquidated—but that the nation faced hostile capitalist encirclement. The nation had to redouble industrialization efforts and militarization efforts in face of that threat until such time as the USSR was an unassailable fortress. He declared, "Our Red Army, Red Navy, Red Air Fleet, and the Chemical and Air Defense Society must be increased and strengthened to the utmost."[64]

Technological modernization was central to state power under Stalin. In a famous speech at the first All-Union Conference of Workers of Socialist Industry on February 4, 1931, Stalin called for "Bolshevik tempos" of work, and for making up in ten years the distance that separated the socialist fortress from capitalist countries by mastering technology and becoming experts in industrial modernization.[65] Stalin believed that only state-sponsored centralized knowledge production secured the revolution. The notion that the New Soviet Man and New Soviet Woman would master science and technology and control nature also was important in thinking about the empire. Mastery of nature through planning and brute force, overcoming of backwardness through education, proselytizing progress and patriotism, and creating industry where once was emptiness all were essential elements to Stalinist programs.[66]

Drawing perhaps on Stalin's admonishment that the USSR must embrace modern technology or risk falling further behind the West, Putin warned, "The speed of technological progress is accelerating sharply. It is rising dramatically. Those who manage to ride this technological wave will surge far ahead. Those who fail to do this will be submerged and drown in this wave." He claimed, "Technological lag and dependence translate into reduced security and economic opportunities," and he noted the main threat of "falling behind. If we are unable to reverse this trend, we will fall even further behind." Toward this end, Putin called for the creation of modern infrastructure. He said, "Russia is a country with a vast territory, and its active, dynamic life cannot be concentrated in several metropolitan cities. Big cities must distribute their energy, and serve as a support for the balanced, harmonious spatial development of the whole of Russia. . . . Particular attention will be paid to the social and infrastructural development of rural areas."[67] Unfortunately, the government has had little success in promoting the growth of infrastructure for the benefit of broader swaths of society. It has ignored rural regions. Rather, as Putin himself acknowledges, the government supports large-scale projects, and defend them as he might, they are in regions with low population densities and serve state power and state corporations, if at the same meeting time Russia's military strategic interests.

Although not addressing technology directly, Putin has used Victory Day celebrations to remind the nation of the dangers facing the empire, with the implication that state policies including those for hero projects will protect citizens. Claiming the presence of fascists in Ukraine and Crimea, he justified annexation of Crimea and Russia's proxy war in Eastern Ukraine. On Victory Day on May 9, 2019, the president offered his "congratulations to you on the 75th anniversary of the liberation of Sevastopol and Crimea from the Nazi invaders." Ignoring Russia's violent conquest of Crimea by Catherine the Great in the eighteenth century, and Soviet ethnic cleansing of Crimean Tatars in the first half of the twentieth, he claimed that "Sevastopol has always played a special role in our country's history, strengthening its statehood, establishing traditions of civic consciousness and patriotism. Russia's reliable [naval] outpost on the Black Sea, it staunchly endured enemy's assaults and entered unforgettable pages to the military chronicles of our Fatherland."[68] And in 2022, repeating the same far-fetched accusations of fascists in control of Kyiv, he unleashed the Russian army in an attack on independent Ukraine, all in the effort to push Russian borders toward Europe, secure land-based routes to Crimea through Ukrainian territory, and re-establish some semblance of past Russian empires. Thus, for Putin, the empire—extending from the Arctic to Central Asia, and from the Black Sea to Siberia—must be secured through modern technology, including military technology.

The Kremlin as a Modern Resource State

Does the Russian citizen in the 2020s embrace the State's magnificent projects to tame the Arctic, open the flow of oil and gas from the tundra, raise power stations in frigid Siberia, weld pipelines across the Yamal Peninsula, sail icebreakers from Arkhangelsk to Dikson and build bridges across the Kerch Strait? From the time of Stalin to Brezhnev, the Soviet citizen had little reason to question the importance of hero projects. Indeed, the new Soviet Man and Soviet Woman were proudly patriotic to participate in them—and to see new skyscrapers, canals, hydropower stations, the Metro, and so on appear through the labor of their own hands. They saw successes in nuclear power and space as confirmation of the fact that the socialist motherland was moving ever closer to communism and challenging outmoded capitalism for supremacy. Only in the late Gorbachev period did large numbers of citizens question the Soviet development model, its large-scale approaches to construction, extraction, and transportation, and the environmental and other costs of these projects.

It would seem that Russian citizens in the 2020s approve of state infrastructural, construction, and other big technology projects. Anecdotal evidence reveals that many people are impressed with these structures as signs of modernity and state power, and they relish the restored military prestige of the nation. Public opinion surveys show strong support for Russian space and other projects, even if they are less happy about changes in pension, insurance, and other laws and rules that have put a greater financial burden on the average citizen. For example, in a 2021 survey of the All-Russian Center for the Study of Public Opinion (VCIOM), the vast majority of participants (91%) agreed that Russia needs to participate in space exploration to develop science and high technology, and to maintain defense capability of the country. The percent agreeing was somewhat lower among the youngest Russians aged eighteen to twenty-four (84%), but still quite high. Respondents saw space R&D as providing the possibility to compete with the United States, European Union, and China on equal terms.[69]

Regarding the Arctic region, on the eve of the expedition to put a Russian flag on the polar floor in 2007, also according to VTsIOM, not quite half of Russians (44%) believed that Russia should pursue "a firm course in the struggle for 'its sector' of the Arctic" because of its economic development; a smaller number of respondents (16%) believed that the assimilation of the Arctic was better postponed to the distant future to avoid conflict.[70] And six years later, Russians seemed to be more bellicose about the Arctic and their rights to the region. Two-thirds of Russians believe that it is necessary to suppress attempts by foreign environmental organizations to hinder the development of the Russian Arctic. Only 20 percent of respondents took the opposite position.[71] The government's attack on NGOs had produced bitter frozen fruit for the Arctic environment, with few voices to protect it from rapacious research development.

While Western politicians would relish the Russian president's approval ratings, polling data reveal, however, a noticeable decline in Putin's popularity since 2012, and especially since he announced plans to tighten welfare programs, raise the retirement age, and cut other social programs while increasing military expenditures to balance the budget. If Russians approve the annexation of Crimea, then they find less to celebrate in terms of the nation's wealth and achievements—since little of it comes their way. But Russian leaders are convinced that the large-scale projects have been crucial to the political, economic, and military might of the nation.

Yet there is some evidence to indicate that the government's efforts to create an image of a technologically superior nation have not fully succeeded fully in communicating the desired messages of modernity, security, and omniscient leadership. Other than full support for Russia's decision to annex Crimea and carry out a proxy war in Ukraine, support for government policies and Putin has been falling. Nearly 90 percent of Russians in 2016 believed Crimea should be part of Russia, and in 2019, 86 percent still supported or mostly supported its annexation.[72] Otherwise, citizens more and more recognize that Russia lacks any effective economic strategy to turn the economy around other than hope for oil and gas to go up in price. In a recent survey, less than half (only 45%) of Russians said they would vote for Putin, down from 67 percent at the beginning of 2018. For a man who has ruled Russia longer than anyone else than Stalin, this is a comedown. (Seventy percent of Russians think that Stalin's rule was good for the country, and over 51% have a favorable view of the tyrant-murderer.) If "a majority of Russians (62%) continue to support Russia's annexation of Crimea . . . [then] but only three in ten (29%) would like the same for Donetsk and Luhansk." Paradoxically, "majorities of Russians say Moscow's recent international actions have worsened the economy (58%), standards of living (64%), and relations with the United States (78%)."[73]

But most citizens remain satisfied, even enthralled, with Putin's leadership. Popular fascination with Putin and the yearning for a strong leader as in the glory days of the USSR have led to kitsch in art and society. One can now buy Putin rugs, Putin bikinis, Putin *shkatulki* (hand-carved, ornamented wooden boxes), some with the boss attired as a Tsarist general, and Palekh boxes (black-lacquered art works with intricate paintings from history, culture, and now Putin). Teenage and twenty-some-year-old girls fantasize about an audience with the virile former KGB agent, tattooing their bodies, wearing "Putin" swimwear, and decorating their nails in honor of the president. They hold bikini car washes in support of his campaigns. One Tomsk artist knit sweaters of Putin, Gagarin, and Father Frost.[74] One can buy the presidential fragrance for men, "Leaders," inspired by Vladimir Putin; an erotic calendar in honor of the president, posed by Moscow State University female students; and the "*Little Brown Book of Putin*, a three-volume collected speeches of the president, at only 29,000 rubles ($450).[75]

A number of contemporary public practices to promote public involvement in hero projects resemble Soviet tactics of encouraging citizens to the embrace of technology without full accounting of risks. One involves engaging local schoolchildren in art competitions to celebrate nuclear power stations or dams. In Kaliningrad region, children in 2013 drew pictures that celebrated the joys of a future filled with cheap electrical energy. The weekly newspaper *Vestnik RusGidro* has published paintings and drawings of schoolchildren about the glories of river engineering. The winning painting revealed a "machine in the garden"—a beautiful pastoral scene that in no way indicated the significant environment changes and impact on flora and fauna of massive new hydroelectric power stations (no. 4, April 2014).

Perhaps because showcasing the technological sublime is not enough in the face of growing concerns among many Russians about unemployment, low wages and huge income differentials, and rampant corruption, the Kremlin has begun to address these issues as well. While government officials continue to tout plans for moon shots or a base on Mars to rebuild Gagarinesque enthusiasm, or celebrate the launch of a fourth-generation icebreaker and the achievement, at long last, of the promised Great Northern Sea Route, and even maintain plans for an Inland Siberian Sea, they also recognize that the average Russian wants more in terms of simple daily comforts. Putin himself indicated this need. In February 2019 in a speech to the parliament, Putin set forth an ambitious social program like Brezhnev's "Food Program" of the early 1980s, which promised to refill stores and demonstrate the Communist Party truly had citizens' needs in mind. Putin had ignored social concerns for several years, indeed while squeezing the public to balance the budget (in the face of declining oil revenues), by reducing education funding and pensions by stipulating later retirements. The latter move, effectively cutting pensions, was widely unpopular. The volatile and lower prices of oil and sanctions had already weakened an economy that is reliant on oil and gas for revenues, even before a raft of sanctions imposed on Russia for the war on Ukraine, which has caused significant hardships for citizens. In keeping with a pro-natalist policy in the struggle against Russia's dangerously low birth rate—that in the last thirty years has been exceeded by the natural death rate—Putin promised massive subsidies to families with children, including one-time birth payouts and mortgage subsidies; and more spending on anti-poverty programs. The Soviet "hero mother" award for women with ten or more children has been reborn. Yet there is no doubt that the nation has fallen into a deep demographic crisis with the population actually shrinking. Why don't younger Russians want to start families when they can share in the glories of megaprojects?

Elsewhere, in the face of growing public anger over pollution and waste, Putin asked the parliament to support efforts to modernize waste-management systems and pollution control, including a 20 percent reduction in industrial emissions over six years.[76] But these efforts, too, have lagged, as should be expected given Russian environment laxness, and it may be that Russian citizens have begun to recognize the costs associated with emphasis on big projects that leave them behind financially and carry environmental risks: polluted rivers, altered floodplains, migrating petrochemicals, decaying dams and other technogenic leaks, disasters, and accidents. One such environmental problem provoked demonstrations beginning in 2019: Moscow's plans to export its garbage to the provinces. This has been called the "most noticeable wave of protest in Northern Russia since 1990s."[77]

What remains is the determination of the Russian state to employ large-scale technologies to develop resources and renew a semblance of great power status after the political and economic crises of the 1990s. In the 1990s many citizens and leaders believed—and many of them still believe—that Western nations, in particular the United States, did not respect Russian sovereignty, and took advantage of its temporary weakness to steal or acquire its resources, science, and technology on the cheap. The technology of space, nuclear power, Arctic conquest, and so on underpinned the new and continuing efforts to recreate the empire and generate feelings of belonging and accomplishment among the people. As Russians look north toward the Arctic, east to the polar Ural Mountains and Siberia, south to Central Asia, and to the Crimean Peninsula in the Black Sea, one can sense the nostalgia they and their political and economic leaders of Russia feel for resource development programs that are similar to those of the Soviet era.

Large-scale projects seem to have inspired public support. Yet who truly benefits from the projects, the nation as a whole, or the oligarchs who own and run the state corporations and resource extraction operations, and with them the Kremlin? The nostalgia for the Soviet era offers great hopes and visions for Russia, but also suggests significant dangers of contemplating the imperial past while seeking the future through hero projects.

Epilogue

Hero Projects as Nostalgia for the Future

From the Tsars to the commissars, from the Bolsheviks to the oligarchs, and from Lenin to Putin, the Russia development model has been centered on hero projects to bring the vast landscapes of tundra, taiga, steppe, and desert, from the European plain to the Pacific Ocean, and from the Arctic Ocean to the mountainous regions of Central Asia, within the orbit and control of the Moscow. Each project had the goal both of resource exploitation in support of state power and incorporation of local peoples—whether Slavs or Muslims, Nenets or Evenk, Lithuanians, Estonians, and Latvians, and Georgians, Azeris, and Armenians—into such transformationist projects as railroads, waterworks, and mines. The benefits were intended for all citizens, but we have seen that the Kremlin used hero projects essentially to enrich its own leaders by building an economically powerful and militarily secure empire. Hero projects were tautologically big technologies in which Russia often lagged behind Europe and America—roads, dams, and the like—but also were such high-tech projects as nuclear power plants and spaceships that revealed to the world—and to citizens—that Russia was a scientific superpower. The extensive costs of hero projects, their environmental and social consequences, and their military purposes have rarely been questioned by leaders or citizens alike, but were essential to the political narrative of the need for an all-powerful, imperial state to withstand the dangers of hostile nations that would otherwise seek to weaken Mother Russia. Hero projects served cultural purposes as well. They brought together engineers and planners, workers and managers, Slavs, Kazakhs, and Uzbeks, leaders and citizens in the common effort to celebrate construction of a better world.

Hero projects have been pursued around the globe, if not always for imperial purposes. In many places, at many times, the interests of political leaders, economic planners, engineering specialists, and publics have coincided to engage massive waterworks projects to improve on the natural world; raise such new infrastructure as bridges, tunnels, and highways; undertake great voyages across the oceans, into the seas, over the North Pole, and into space; and tap the earth's natural and mineral resources in pursuit of political, economic, and military power—and the betterment of the lives of citizens.

Some of the projects, if expensive, hubristic, and questionable in terms of social utility, are glorious—for example, landing a man on the moon or building the world's largest skyscraper in Dubai—while many others are violent and destructive: strip mines; nuclear bombs and missiles; pipelines and oil derricks; highways, dams, and other infrastructure with large rights-of-way that require the ousting of people from their homes, often poor people, local people, indigenous people whose land and other resources suddenly "stand in the way of progress," and who must give way, move out, and start anew elsewhere, sometimes with assistance, often not. Such infrastructural projects as railroads and highways may enable commerce and accelerate economic growth. They are also often boondoggles—witness Boston's "Big Dig." Geopolitics often make or break hero projects, at times generating unquestioned support for them, for example, the space race or nuclear power during the Cold War. The dams of China, India, Brazil, and Russia in the twenty-first century; the copper mines of the United States, Chile, Indonesia, Peru, and Russia, and coal operations, albeit many in decline; and other resource-oriented projects seem to move ahead without pause because of the need for strategic minerals or fossil fuels, and they often do so with inadequate attention to local concerns, and with irreversible impacts on the environment, largely because public concerns about them have not be aired or have been stifled.

Domestic affairs crucially play a big role here, especially in authoritarian regimes. Strongmen—and they are usually men, and they are usually men who like to be seen as all-powerful—have a particular affinity for symbolic large-scale projects of this sort. In the absence of sufficient public scrutiny, often because the state restricts protests and denies rights to such basic institutions of civic culture as the rights to free speech and to gather—and to protest—the men and their projects move forward without pause, stumbling perhaps because of accidents or other technological failures—a nuclear reactor disaster, a hydropower station catastrophe, a mine collapse with significant loss of life—but rarely because their promoters worry about the displaced, the unemployed, or the environment, and even more rarely because they recognize any fault in hero projects. In authoritarian regimes, leaders may speak about "the public," the rights of the citizen, the benefit of jobs and compensation versus some perturbance in ecosystems social disruptions.

But the projects benefit state power and those in powerful positions in the orbit of government and business. Think of the multibillion dollar projects of Philippine president Rodrigo Duterte that comprised some seventy-five flagship projects: six airports, nine railways, thirty-two highways and bridges, and four seaports intended to lower production costs, raise income, facilitate commerce, and create jobs, at nearly $200 billion.[1] The megaprojects of Turkish president Recep Tayyip Erdoğan include a "28-mile canal linking the Black Sea to the Sea of Marmara—estimated to cost $15 billion, though critics say the figure is closer to $65 billion, and it will displace some 800,000 people."[2] And then there are Putin's projects.

Putin's projects—and Russian hero projects over the last century—share many of these features of technological verve and hubris; "irreversibility"; cultural symbolism; and benefit to the state and those close to the state. Russian projects stand out because of their heavy reliance on extractive industries, their nostalgic importance, indeed their ties to a kind of political and technological culture of a bygone era. Many of the projects in fact were first hatched in the Soviet period; many of them date to the Stalin years and were engaged using gulag slave labor. Even today, many leaders and citizens see little fault in, or chose to overlook, the human costs of Stalinist industrial development if the result has been the creation of a scientific superpower. In Russia, big projects muddle along—because of state power, because of their Soviet legacy, because of their cultural meaning, but not because they necessarily produce value for the average citizen, for example, higher living standard, better public health, meaningful and well-paying jobs, or an end to the disparities between life in the provinces and that in glittering Moscow and St. Petersburg.[3]

A major factor in this state of affairs is precisely the allegiance of the Russian Federation to extractive industries—oil and gas, coal, nickel, copper, and platinum, now even water as an international commodity. The president himself has long argued that the nation can be strong and the people secure only if the state manages Russia's vast resources carefully and firmly. Thus, extractive industries pursue state-sponsored and -funded hero projects. The Yamal Peninsula has become the gas well of the tundra, and no more, operated by shift workers. The nascent plans to restart Stalin's great polar railroad across taiga and tundra, through desolate, thinly settled regions, over the Ural Mountains and to the Yenisei River, makes sense in this kind of economy. And since Russia and Russians feel isolated and mistreated in the international sphere—especially since their annexation of Crimea and their invasion of Ukraine—geopolitical and military considerations provide another crucial impetus to Putin's projects. Extractive industries provide support to the revitalization of the Russian military, with new bases and new transportation technologies that enable the government to demonstrate that the motherland is secure.

Many people know that gulag prisoners were behind—or under—the infrastructural projects of the 1930s, 1940s, and 1950s, and that many mills, smelters, dams, and railroads still operating in the twenty-first century were built largely by *zeks*—these prisoners. Surely, the massive loss of life in Ukraine during collectivization, in the northern railway camps, along the rails of BAMlag, and at dozens of other frenzied building campaigns to create a socialist fortress, involved unconscionable personal, family, social, and environmental costs. It is obvious that today's inheritors of gulag institutions and projects had nothing to do with the practices or approaches of the Stalin era. Putin's projects rely on the shift system and migrant labor, and not on prison labor. Yet fully 38 percent of Russian citizens consider Stalin to be the "greatest leader of all times and all peoples," with President Putin in second place at 24 percent, and Russian leaders argue that there is much to be learned and appreciated in the Stalinist economic development model.[4] Many Russian officials speak reverentially for Stalin—even if not pronouncing his name—for having created a powerful economy against all odds.[5] The worker and his union were emasculated, and they remain emasculated under current leaders. Civic culture, in the form of NGOs and public access to the technology assessment process, remains weak and is getting decidedly weaker under the thumb of state intervention. One wonders whether some of the hugely expensive projects being advanced—the Evenkiiskaia GES in Siberia, open-cast mines in Kemerovo, nuclear-powered oil drilling platforms and tankers—would move ahead so easily if their costs and risks were more openly aired. And one wonders if the war on Ukraine would be possible without the insistence of an authoritarian leader who can rely on hero projects to fuel the war machine.

On top of this, contemporary Russian political culture, and the culture of technology, in many ways resembles the power arrangements between the Kremlin, the ministries, the provinces, and the citizens of the Soviet period. Through authoritarian laws and practices, Putin, his advisors, and central economic actors have chipped away at democratic institutions at all levels: the relations between the president and governors, the state and NGOs, citizens and the police all reflect more much-closed avenues of disputation, disagreement, and protest. The resulting oligarchy pushes a resource state to its perfection of extraction and production to benefit the center. State industries from the hydroelectric company Rusgidro to the nuclear corporation Rosatom play to the public from glossy public relations offices with equally glossy publications in the effort to demonstrate unquestioned economic and social benefits of their projects and to defuse opposition over safety, environmental, and other concerns. Gazprom officials issue a variety of monthly publications that reveal how wells and drills can share space with herders and reindeer. A variety of quasi-public bodies and expert commissions enable some airing of safety and environmental concerns. But big power and mining projects are so important to the state that its representatives will not tolerate public dissent that goes beyond some arbitrary limit. Companies and ministries see their responsibilities to get the ore, gas, and oil out of the ground. NGOs have been shut down, their offices raided, and they have been likened to spies by the FSB, being called officially "foreign agents." The environment is suffering the consequences of pollution, inadequate investigatory powers into accidents and waste disposal practices, and fines that are cheaper to pay than for businesses to change polluting practices. From the Yamal Peninsula to the Kuzbass, environmental quality is declining. Many Russian citizens, if not most, live in environments where water and air are significantly below official pollution standards.

Yet a kind of technological verve has been reborn in Russia in the twenty-first century. The Soviet ministries reincarnated as state corporations have picked up literally and figuratively where the ministries left off when the USSR collapsed and projects were mothballed in the Russian 1990s. Research and engineering firms, branch industrial laboratories, and the projects they supported were all closed down in the absence of financing. Bridges, canals, space and Arctic research, nuclear power plants, roads and railways—all were slowed, and at many worksites construction simply stopped as the facilities became hulking, empty concrete monuments to a failed system. President Yeltsin and the Duma (parliament) were unable to find financing or determine which projects merited support. Now these hero projects, many of which date to the Stalin period, others to the Brezhnev era, and in some cases that even have Tsarist roots, have been restarted: massive hydropower stations; nuclear icebreakers; diversion canals; floating nuclear power stations; and again Stalin's polar railroad, among many other projects with suspect environmental and social consequences. When engineers look to the past to consider some of these projects, they rarely refer to the failures of the *Lenin* icebreaker, the Chernobyl explosion, the desiccation of the Aral Sea, or the

Virgin Lands campaign as a way to learn how to avoid dangers. They instead talk about the great Soviet legacy of cosmonaut Yuri Gagarin, the pride of Soviet citizens in state-sponsored megaprojects and their importance to the motherland, and the boldness of their leaders. Salaries are low for most citizens, pensions are inadequate, but Russian citizens seem not to blink at the claim that the motherland must re-establish Russian greatness through lunar bases, a nuclear-powered Arctic, vast networks of gas wells, pipelines, and railroads, and transfer canals of great cost, but suspect utility.

Putin's projects may accomplish little to improve public health.[6] Dangerous pollutants that often with hero products, according to the Russian Federal Center of Public Health and Epidemiology of the State Consumer Protection Agency, fill the air, drinking water, and places of work; they result from industrial activities, farming, and transportation activities; they exist in schools; and they lead to a variety of infections, diseases, and parasites. At least 50 million people—more than a third of the Russian population—live in regions where at least some of these harmful substances exceeded by five times maximum norms in 2015.[7] Similarly, while water quality improved from 2008 to 2009 by 9.3 percent in terms of chemical content and by 1.2 percent in terms of microbiological indices, still in the northwest region of the country and Ural regions nearly 40 percent of drinking water does not meet norms. And so on for chemical and microbiological indices, pesticides, and nuclear waste.[8]

Sadly, and murderously, Vladimir Putin, a loyal admirer of Stalin, has proudly embraced scorched policies in his war on Ukraine as victory slips from his hands. He has targeted cities, power stations, and power lines, hit hospital and kindergartens, attacked nuclear facilities to convert them into dirty bombs, and ordered the demolition of such hero projects as the Kakhova Hydroelectric Power Station to transform Soviet-era structures into massive-scale weapons against land and people.[9] The construction of the Kakhovka hydroelectric power station (357 MW), dam, and reservoir on the Dnipro River, while completed under Khrushchev in 1956, commenced in 1950, and was one of a series of such waterworks pursued in Stalin's grandiose Plan for the Transformation of Nature (1948). The "hero" waterworks on the Dnipro, Don, Volga, and other major European rivers served the Kremlin's effort to subdue Eastern Europe by creating a unified electrification, irrigation, and transport network that harnessed resources to the Kremlin's military and economic plans to be prepared for the next, inevitable war.

Putin pursued his own "hero projects" to build state power—but is ready to sacrifice them for his war on Ukraine. Beyond oil and gas operations, and a megalomaniacal effort to complete Stalin's fantastical and disastrous construction of a trans-Arctic railway, the most obvious Putin hero project, the Crimean Bridge, was intended ultimately to funnel Russian citizens and supplies into Crimea in support of the war. As noted, the bridge was completed at a cost of almost $4 billion after four years as a state priority. Putin, in self-indulgent choreography, drove the very first vehicle, a supply truck, across the Crimean Bridge in 2018. The Russian postal service quickly issued commemorative stamps. How ironic that tens of thousands of Russians are now fleeing Crimea over the bridge, to return to uncertain sanctuary in Russia. The bridge itself has been hit by artillery and truck bombs several times, and its columns are already cracking, not because of the war, but because of the earlier effort to finish the project in Stalinist fashion—well before target dates as a symbol of enlightened leadership.

But the Crimean Bridge did not help Putin prepare for his full-scale attack of Ukraine, and so he turned to the demolition of the Kakhovka Reservoir. With a capacity of 18.2 km^3, it served regional agriculture needs and was the source of the North Crimean Canal, built in the 1960s, that eventually supplied 85 percent of Crimea's water, mostly for agriculture, but also for municipal and industrial purposes. Destroying the dam will cut water supply to Crimea, require rationing in towns and cities, and substantially cut Crimean grain, fruit, and vegetable harvests. The blowing up of Kakhovka will interrupt water supply to the irrigation systems in Kherson and Zaporizhzhia regions, mostly in the occupied lands from which Russia is retreating, will require closing of factories in Marganets, Nikopol, and Pokrov, and will destroy any remaining fisheries. Once the war has ended, it will take Ukraine years to rebuild the dam; without water, lands in the south of Ukraine will dry out. But this is Russia's goal: to force the population to leave the region en masse.

Another demonstration of Putin's megalomaniacal tactics that involve hero projects center on nuclear power plants (NPPs) in Ukraine. Ukraine operates fifteen reactors at four stations that produced over half of the country's electrical energy. In March 2022, Russian troops occupied the Zaporizhzhia NPP, with six reactors the largest station in Europe, on the Dnipro River and just 200 km from Crimea. The terrorist detonation of the Khakhovka dam threatens the ZNPP because the station relies on water from the Kakhovka Reservoir to cool the shutdown reactors and the spent fuel stored on site. Thus, Russian troops, retreating in anticipation of a Ukrainian offensive, destroyed a dam and threatened nuclear safety in one cynical move before running off to Russia. For a time, Russian soldiers in 2022 even took over the Chernobyl disaster exclusion zone, perhaps not understanding the danger to themselves, and it is unlikely that their commanders let them know of the risk of acute radiation sickness and later cancers. But for several weeks, during their occupation, they raised radioactive dust and interfered with safe storage of vast quantities of hazardous waste, and, having risked nuclear safety across Europe, hurriedly withdrew.

The Russian use of hero projects—as tools of economic development and as tools of war—should remind us of their great costs however they are employed and their transient irreversibility. Around the globe, institutes and projects acquire great momentum and power. Leaders, bankers, and engineers can always make the arguments that to stop a bridge mid-river is a sign of failure, a waste of money, and simply an irrational choice given the intended purposes of the object. Putin's projects are distinguished not by their momentum alone, but also their service to enrichment of the Kremlin in symbolic, financial, political, and military ways: RUSAL smelters fed by the Saiano-Shushensk hydroelectric power station, the $27 billion Gazprom and Novatek Arctic Gates offshore natural gas terminal in the Ob River Delta, and the Crimean Bridge to link Russia with conquered Crimea. The media have been filled with photographs of President Putin—dedicating a pipeline or ship, riding a lorry across an imperial span—that reveal a vision of a powerful state, strategic military acumen, and engineering excellence. The photographs of the lorry-driver president reveal that Putin's projects serve precisely a resource empire whose leader seeks to exploit mineral and natural resources in service of the state, not the leader who once whispered with dolphins,. It must be kept in mind, ultimately, that an ever-present aspect of ravenous hero projects is that heroes eventually die.

Acknowledgments

This book has involved two journeys. One journey was that from my original conceptualization and research to an in-depth exploration of hero projects and their strategic, military, economic, and cultural significance for the Russian empire. Nicholas Breyfogle, Thane Gustafson, Tim LeCain, and Pey-Yi Chu offered critical comments both on the details and on the overall meaning of the book. Several anonymous reviewers showed great patience with my effort, they encouraged greater attention to the important lessons in this work, and this forced me to write a much better book. My colleague and friend, Lauren Kerr, created the index. Crucially, Tatiana Kasperski shared her rich and vital insights into Russian history and culture, and the history of technology, and has tolerated my workaholic approach to writing. Dave McBride at Oxford University Press found promise in *Hero Projects* and helped me to complete it when I had doubts.

The research on this book was supported by the National Science Foundation through NSF Project 1534860, "A History of Large-Scale Environmental-Engineering Projects in Russia," and in part by the HoNEST (History of Nuclear Energy and Society) project funded by Euratom grant 662268, and by grants from Colby College. I am deeply grateful to my program officer at NSF, Dr. Frederick Kronz, for his advice, guidance, and support. Two articles in *Global Environment* also resulted from this work.

Unfortunately, *Hero Projects* involved a second journey. I have charted the use of hero projects to serve the state goals of economic power and military preparedness. Citizens in the Russian empire—Slavs, Central Asians, indigenes, and many others in this multinational state—have rarely benefited directly from these projects. Even such basic necessities as clean water do not exist for most inhabitants in 2022, according to Russian federal standards. Instead, the nation has engaged hero projects with an emphasis on military and resource intensive projects, and this approach leaves the vast majority of citizens behind in standard of living and other quality-of-life measures. Russian leaders and citizens themselves to this day justify this emphasis by referring to the great losses of life in World War II—four generations ago—and the need to thwart all sorts of dangers that continue to threaten them. Since the Cold War they have conceived the major dangers as American and

European aggression, and also Western decadence that might weaken Russia from within. Leaders have for decades promised the nation that they will never again permit attack by securing the borders and filling the empty spaces of the empire with strategic industries. But they have used hero projects not solely to protect, but to carry out wars on others: Hungary, Czechoslovakia, Afghanistan, Chechnya, Georgia, and Ukraine.

Thus, this book about empire, resources, and technology turned out also to be about preparing the USSR and Russia for war: using gulag prisoners to extract Pechora basin coal that was shipped along rails built by gulag prisoners to engage Hitler; pushing the frontier beyond the Ural Mountains into Siberia to develop strategic minerals and nuclear weapons during the Cold War; harnessing oil and gas to use it as a cudgel against European energy independence; and remilitarizing the post–Cold War Arctic at great risk to geopolitical stability and the global environment. Yet hero projects have left Russia paradoxically unprepared for war, as military failures in World War II, Afghanistan, and now Ukraine demonstrate. Before World War II, for example, hero projects were directed to prepare the USSR for an inevitable war against "hostile capitalist encirclement." Yet in marshaling resources and manpower for the life-and-death struggle against Nazi Germany in World War II, Stalin and military leaders threw men and machines into battle with little distinction, commanded soldiers that to retreat one step was treason, and ordered the Soviets to destroy their own farmland and industry which they could not protect from the enemy. Hero projects could produce coal, pig iron, and cement but not prevent, let alone slow, Blitzkreig, and 25 million Soviets died.

Since 2014, Russia has set out to conquer independent Ukraine to incorporate it into the remnants of the Russian empire, first by annexing Crimea in violation of the Budapest Memorandum of 1994, and now through the full-scale invasion of sovereign Ukraine. There was no threat to Russia that justified its murderous missile assault on Ukrainian civilians, their homes and hospitals, schools and research centers, let alone their assault on nuclear power stations and the Chernobyl exclusion zone. It is a war based on lies and fabrications about a nonexistent enemy, and denial of the Ukrainian nation, and even of its language and culture, as real. Hero projects—bridges, pipelines, nuclear facilities—have been laid over the landscape in the effort to reassemble a tottering and irreparable empire, the Soviet Union, into "Russia," by a treacherous leadership.

The second journey in this book thus involved the effort to write a history of the economic, military, and cultural significance of large-scale projects in Russia, and their importance to the Kremlin to wage war. In the last twenty-five years, Russia has transformed into an international outlaw whose soldiers have carried out human rights abuses in war in Chechnya, Georgia, and now Ukraine. Russia may be wealthy in oil, gas, forests, and platinum, and Russia may have nuclear weapons, but Russia's war has isolated it from the modern world not only economically, but culturally. Some nations will buy its commodities, but no one will respect its policies or follow its lead.

I dedicate this book to my family. Thank you, Tatiana, for still insisting I go for long training runs when I put down the laptop, and to my younger children, Nina and Emile, who are indispensable in reminding me of the joys of finding a new park, or of cycling, sunbathing, and jumping in the ocean. And special love to Isaac because he still jumps into the ocean.

Barcelona, Spain
Vinalhaven, Maine
November 2022

Note on Sources

I use a slightly simplified US Library of Congress system of transliteration for Russian-language names and words, except for those words and names commonly "Anglicized," and in some cases for ease of reading have dropped the soft sign (') and hard sign ("): Trotsky instead of Trotskii, Yenisei and Yamal instead of Enisei and Iamal, Ob instead of Ob', and so on.

Notes

Introduction

1. Alexander Etkind, *Internal Colonization: Russia's Imperial Experience* (London: Wiley, 2011).
2. Paul Josephson, *Industrialized Nature* (Washington, DC: Island Press, 2002).
3. In *Seeing like a State* (New Haven, CT: Yale University Press, 1998), James Scott advances several arguments important to this book about state power, citizens, and nature. Michael Adas, *Machines as the Measure of Men: Science, Technology, and Ideologies of Western Dominance* (Ithaca, NY: Cornell University Press, 1989); Etkind, *Internal Colonization*; and Alfred Crosby, *Ecological Imperialism* (Cambridge: Cambridge University Press, 1986), consider the interrelationship between science, technology, and the environment. See also R. Macleod, "Passages in Imperial Science: From Empire to Commonwealth," *Journal of World History* 4 (1993): 117–150; A. Alam, "Imperialism and Science," *Race and Class* 19 (1978): 239–251; G. Basalla, "The Spread of Western Science," *Science* 156 (1967): 611–622; P. Palladino and M. Worboys, "Science and Imperialism," *ISIS* 84 (1993): 91–102; and L. Pyenson, "Cultural Imperialism and Exact Sciences Revisited," *ISIS* 84 (1993): 103–108. Of interest are also Nicholas Thomas, *Entangled Objects: Exchange, Material Culture and Colonialism in the Pacific* (Cambridge: Cambridge University Press, 1991); and David Arnold, *The Problem of Nature: Environment, Culture and European Expansion* (Hoboken, NJ: Wiley, 1996).
4. Cathy Frierson, trans. and ed., *Aleksandr Nikolaevich Engelgardt's Letters from the Country, 1872–1887* (New York: Oxford University Press, 1993).
5. Richard Pipes, "The Russian Military Colonies, 1810–1831," *Journal of Modern History* 22, no. 3 (1950): 205–219. Arakcheev apparently ordered the hanging of cats because of his fondness for nightingales.
6. Iakov Demchenko, *O navodnenii Aralo-Kaspiiskoi nizmennosti dlia uluchsheniia klimata prilezhashchikh stran* (Kyiv: S. P. Iakovlev, 1900).
7. On the discourse over the worrying state of health of Russian forests, see Jane Costlow, *Heart-Pine Russia: Walking and Writing the Nineteenth-Century Forest* (Ithaca, NY: Cornell University Press, 2013).
8. Loren Graham, *The Soviet Academy of Sciences and the Communist Party, 1927–1932* (Princeton, NJ: Princeton University Press, 1967); and Kendall Bailes, *Technology and Society under Lenin and Stalin: Origins of the Soviet Technical Intelligentsia, 1917–1941* (Princeton, NJ: Princeton University Press, 1978).
9. On the Sharashki (engineering gulag camps), see Asif Saddiqi, "Atomized Urbanism: Secrecy and Security from the Gulag to the Soviet Closed Cities," *Urban*

History 49, no. 1 (2022): 1–21. See also G. Ozerov, *Tupolevskaia Sharaga* (Frankfurt am Main: Posev, 1973). For a thorough overview of the gulag in Soviet history, see Anne Applebaum, *Gulag: A History* (New York: Anchor Books, 2004); Paul R. Gregory and Valery Lazarev, eds., *The Economics of Forced Labor: The Soviet Gulag* (Stanford, CA: Hoover Institution Press, 2003).

10. According to one historian, "the concepts of empire and imperialism" had been in steady decline from 1980s with that of colonialism with its globalization and transnationalism on the rise. Precisely because of the effort to understand "internal colonization," empire has again become an important focus again. See Stephen Howe, "Imperial and Colonial History," in *Making History*, at https://www.history.ac.uk/makinghistory/resources/articles/imperial_post_colonial_history.html.

11. Etkind, *Internal Colonization*.

12. Josephson, *Conquest of the Russian Arctic* (Cambridge, MA: Harvard University Press, 2015), chapter 4. See also GAAO (State Archive of Arkhangelsk Region), F. 1735, op. 1, ed. khr. 480, 13–15, 17–18; and GAMO (State Archive of Murmansk Region), F.194, op. 1, d. 1, ll. 25, 27, 62, 74; and d. 50, ll. 4–5.

13. Among other studies of the Soviet empire, in particular nationality policy, see Robert Conquest, *Stalin: Breaker of Nations* (New York: Penguin, 1991); Jeremy Smith, *The Bolsheviks and the National Question, 1917–1923* (London: Palgrave, 1999); Terry Martin, *The Affirmative Action Empire: Nation and Nationalism in the Soviet Union, 1923–1939* (Ithaca, NY: Cornell University Press, 2001); and Francine Hirsch, *Empire of Nations: Ethnographic Knowledge and the Making of the Soviet Union* (Ithaca, NY: Cornell University Press, 2005).

14. On the transformation of the Kola Peninsula into an industrial region, see Andy Bruno, *The Nature of Soviet Power: An Arctic Environmental History* (Cambridge: Cambridge University Press, 2016).

15. Alan Barenberg, *Gulag Town, Company Town: Forced Labor and Its Legacy in Vorkuta* (New Haven, CT: Yale University Press, 2014).

16. David Moon, *The Plough That Broke the Steppes: Agriculture and Environment on Russia's Grasslands, 1700–1914* (Oxford: Oxford University Press, 2013).

17. Stephen Brain, "The Great Stalin Plan for the Transformation of Nature," *Environmental History* 15, no. 4 (October 2010): 670–700.

18. Julia Obertreis, *Imperial Desert Dreams. Cotton Growing and Irrigation in Central Asia, 1860–1991* (Gottingen: Vandenhoeck & Ruprecht, 2017).

19. Paul Dukes, *A History of the Urals: Russia's Crucible from Early Empire to the Post-Soviet Era* (New York: Bloomsbury, 2015).

20. Loren Graham, *Lonely Ideas: Can Russia Compete?* (Cambridge, MA: MIT Press, 2013).

21. Thomas Hughes, "Technological Momentum in History: Hydrogenation in Germany, 1893–1933," *Past and Present*, no. 441 (1969): 106–132. See also Hughes, "The Evolution of Large Technological Systems," in *The Social Construction of Technological Systems: New Directions in the Sociology and History of Technology*, ed. W. E. Bijker, T. P. Hughes, and T. J. Pinch (Cambridge, MA: MIT Press, 1987), 51–82.

22. Loren Graham, "The Formation of Soviet Research Institutes: A Combination of Revolutionary Innovation and International Borrowing," *Social Studies of Science* 5, no. 3 (August 1975): 303–329.

23. Paul Josephson, "Science Policy in the Soviet Union, 1917–1927," *Minerva* 26, no. 3 (Autumn 1988): 342–369.

24. Barenberg, *Gulag Town, Company Town*.

25. D. V. Ushakov, A. M. Ablazhei, and Iu. M. Pliusnin, "Sotsial'no-ekologicheskie problemy korennogo naseleniia Evenkin v svete vozmozhnogo stroitel'stva gidroelektrostantsii na Nizhnei Tunguske," *Vestnik Novosibirskogo Gosudarstvennogo Universiteta. Seriia Filosofiia* 10, no. 1 (2012): 65–72. In a recent article, using terminology of the Brezhnev era, a journalist asked whether RusGidro would succeed in building the Evenki GES, the next "project of the century." See Mikhail Karpov, "Stroika veka: Udastsia li postroit' samuiu moshchnuiu v strane GES," *Lenta*, September 11, 2016, at https://lenta.ru/articles/2016/09/11/evenkiyskaya_ges/.

26. Paul Josephson, "'Projects of the Century' in Soviet History: Large Scale Technologies from Lenin to Gorbachev," *Technology and Culture* 36, no. 3 (July 1995): 519–559.

27. Josephson, *Industrialized Nature*.

28. See Douglas Puffert, "Path Dependence," *Economic History H-Net* at https://eh.net/encyclopedia/path-dependence/. See also Paul David, "Path Dependence, Its Critics and the Quest for 'Historical Economics'," in *Evolution and Path Dependence in Economic Ideas: Past and Present*, ed. P. Garrouste and S. Ioannides (Edward Cheltenham, England: Elgar Publishing, 2000), chapter 7; and James Mahoney, "Path Dependence in Historical Sociology," *Theory and Society* 29, no. 4 (August 2000): 507–508.

29. Paul Josephson, *Fish Sticks, Sports Bras, and Aluminum Cans: The Politics of Everyday Technologies* (Baltimore: Johns Hopkins University Press, 2015), chapter 6.

30. David Lilienthal, *TVA: Democracy on the March* (New York: Harper and Brothers, 1944).

31. Kate Brown, *Manual for Survival* (New York: W. W. Norton, 2019).

32. "Vladimir Putin: Posle avarii Saiano-Shushenskaia GES poluchila vtoruiu zhizn," *Ruskline*, August 27, 2013, at http://ruskline.ru/news_rl/2013/08/27/vladimir_putin_posle_avarii_sayanoshushenskaya_ges_poluchila_vtoruyu_zhizn/.

33. Tatiana Kasperski, "From Legacy to Heritage: The Changing Political and Symbolic Status of Military Nuclear Waste in Russia," *Cahiers du monde russe* 60, no. 2–3 (2019): 517–538 Among the dozens of excellent compilations and reports that indicate the extent of the Soviet Cold War legacy, see the Bellona Foundation reports: Nils Bøhmer et al., *The Arctic Nuclear Challenge* (Oslo: Bellona Foundation, 2001); and Igor Kudrik et al., *The Russian Nuclear Industry—The Need for Reform* (Oslo: Bellona Foundation, 2004).

34. Ulrich Beck, "The Anthropological Shock: Chernobyl and the Contours of the Risk Society," *Berkeley Journal of Sociology* 32 (1992): 153–165; and Beck, *Risk Society: Towards a New Modernity* (London: Sage, 1992).

35. Graham, *Ghost of the Executed Engineer* (Cambridge, MA: Harvard University Press, 1993); Paul Josephson et al., *An Environmental History of Russia* (New York: Cambridge

University Press, 2013); and Nicholas Breyfogle, "At the Watershed: 1958 and the Beginnings of Lake Baikal Environmentalism," *Slavonic and East European Review* 93, no. 1 (January 2015): 147–180.

36. Novatek, "NOVATEK and Gazprom Neft Sign Agreement of Joint Arctic Development," January 6, 2019, at http://www.novatek.ru/en/press/releases/index. php?id_4=3241.

37. P. L. Paskova, ed., *Poliarnaia magistral'* (Moscow: "Veche," 2007).

38. Josephson, "Горное дело и металлургия в Арктике: советские моногорода," *Уральский исторический вестник*, no. 2 (43) (2014): 125–135. (In Russian.)

39. Barenberg, *Gulag Town, Company Town*.

40. John McCannon, *Red Arctic* (New York: Oxford University Press, 1998).

Chapter 1

* My thanks to Dr. Ekaterina Emeliantseva at the University of Zurich for organizing, and the other participants of a conference on "Cultures of Secrecy in Soviet Life," January 2017, in which I presented an early and much shorter version of several of the ideas in this chapter.

1. E.g., John Armstrong and David M. Williams, "London's Steamships: Their Functions and Their Owners in the Mid-Nineteenth Century," *London Journal* 42, no. 3 (2017): 238–256.

2. See the essays in Bruce Mazlish, ed., *The Railroad and the Space Program: An Exploration in Historical Analogy* (Cambridge, MA: MIT Press, 1965).

3. On serfdom, see Terence Emmons, *Emancipation of the Russian Serfs* (New York: Holt, Rinehart & Winston, 1970); David Moon, *The Abolition of Serfdom in Russia* (Abingdon: Routledge, 2002).

4. On BAM, Christopher Ward, *Brezhnev's Folly: The Building of BAM and Late Soviet Socialism* (Pittsburgh: University of Pittsburgh Press, 2009). For an early variant of technological display, see Matthew Payne, *Stalin's Railroad: Turksib and the Building of Socialism* (Pittsburgh: University of Pittsburgh Press, 2011).

5. E. V. Agbalian, V. Iu. Khroshavin, and E. V. Shinkaruk, "Otsenka ustoichivosti ozernykh ekosistem Iamalo-Nenetskogo avtonomnogo okruga," *Vestnik TGU* 1, no. 1 (2015): 45–54; UNIAN, "Ekologi b'iut trevogu: 'Gazprom' prodolzhaet aktivnoe zagriaznenie Arktiki—SMI," October 24, 2014, at http://www.unian.net/world/1000 464-ekologi-byut-trevogu-gazprom-prodoljaet-aktivnoe-zagryaznenie-arktiki-smi. html; and Bellona, "Dismal Spill Findings on Russian State Oil Giant Should Give Norwegian Partner Statoil Pause," *Bellona*, August 20, 2012, at http://bellona.org/ news/fossil-fuels/oil/2012-08-dismal-spill-findings-on-russian-state-oil-giant-sho uld-give-norwegian-partner-statoil-pause.

6. D. I. Mendeleev, *O neftianom promysle v Amerike i ob otnoshenii k russkomu neftianomu promyslu na Kavkaze*, in Mendeleev, *Sochineniia*, vol. 25 (Leningrad-Moscow: Izdatel'stvo AN SSSR, 1952), originally published 1877.

7. "How Did the Baku Oil Industry Grew [*sic*] under Tsarist Russia?" January 26, 2016, at   https://exploringhist.blogspot.com/2016/01/how-did-baku-oil-industry-grew-under.html; and Mir-Yusif Mir-Babayev, "Baku-Batumi—The World's Longest Pipeline," January–February 2015, at http://www.visions.az/en/news/618/3b2f9122/.

8. G. F. Chirkin, *Kolonizatsionno-ekonomicheskie zadachi zheleznykh dorog* (Leningrad: Tipografiia Murman Zh. D., 1926).

9. Steven Marks, *Road to Power* (Ithaca, NY: Cornell University Press, 1991).

10. Among the many fine studies of nineteenth-century Russian industrialization, see William Blackwell, *The Beginnings of Russian Industrialization, 1800–1860* (Princeton, NJ: Princeton University Press, 1968); Alexander Gerschenkron, *Economic Backwardness in Historical Perspective* (Cambridge, MA: Belknap Press of Harvard University Press, 1962); Joseph Bradley, *Guns for the Tsar. American Technology and the Small Arms Industry in Nineteenth-Century Russia* (DeKalb: Northern Illinois University Press, 1990); Theodore H. Von Laue, *Sergei Witte and the Industrialization of Russia* (New York: Columbia University Press, 1963).

11. N. V. Protas'ev, *Proekt soedineniia Ekaterininskoi gavani na Murmane s set'iu russkikh zheleznykh dorog* (Petrozavodsk: Olonetskaia Gubernskaia Tipografiia, 1910) and A. M. Арнольдов, *Zheleznodorozhnaia kolonizatsiia v Karel'sko-Murmanskom Krae: Po materialam, razrabotannym kolonizatsionnym otdelom pravleniia dorogi* (Leningrad: Leningradskii Gublit, 1925).

12. "Barracks for Prisoners of War along the Murmansk Railway," at https://www.wdl.org/en/item/5138/, as accessed December 16, 2016.

13. Malcolm R. Hill, "Russian Iron Production from the Repeal of Serfdom to the First World War," *Icon* 22 (2016): 115–138; Peter Gatrell, *Industrial Expansion in Tsarist Russia, 1908–14* (1982); Barry Goodwin and Thomas Grennes, "Tsarist Russia and the World Wheat Market," *Explorations in Economic History* 35, no. 4 (October 1998): 405–430; Peter Gatrell, *Russia's First World War. A Social and Economic History* (Harlow: Pearson, 2005); and Anthony Heyward, "Russia's Railways in War and Revolution, 1914–25: What Really Happened?" Russia's Great War and Revolution at http://russiasgreatwar.org/media/military/railways.shtml.

14. Payne, *Stalin's Railroad.*

15. N. A. Voloshinov, "Zhelezno-dorozhnaia razvedka mezhdu Angaroi i severnoiu okonechnost'iu Baikala," *Izvestiia VSORGO* 20, no. 5 (1889): 1–14. See also G. M. Budagov, *K proektu pereustroistva Sibirskoi zheleznoi dorogi* (St. Petersburg: Izdat. Sobr. Inzh. Put. Soobshch., 1905); G. N. Vil'rat, *Zheleznye dorogi Sredne-Sibirskogo kraia i ikh gruzovye potoki* (Irkutsk: Pervaia Gos. Tipografiia, 1925).

16. "O stroitel'stve Baikalo-Amurskoi Magistrali" established the path from Taishet—North Baikal—Tyndinskii—Urgal—Komsomolsk-na-Amure—to Sovetskaia Gavan'. See RZhD, "Istoriia Stroitel'stva BAMa," at http://www.rzd-expo.ru/history/Istor iya%20stroitelstva%20BAMa/.

17. M. V. Mishechkina et al., eds., *Stroika No. 503 (1947–1953 gg.): Dokumenty. Materialy. Issledovaniia*, vyp. 1 (Krasnoiarsk: Grotesk, 2000), at http://www.memorial.krsk.ru/Articles/503/00.htm

18. Dmitrii Mishchenko, "Baikalo-Amurskaia Magistral'—Nachalo istorii goroda Tynda (1929–1950 gg.)," *Uroki istorii XX vek*, June 6, 2009, at http://urokiistorii.ru/node/253.

19. Mishchenko, "Baikalo-Amurskaia Magistral'."

20. Mishchenko, "Baikalo-Amurskaia Magistral'."

21. Vasilii Grossman, *Zhizn' i sud'ba* (Moscow: Knizhnaya Palata, 1988), 790–791.

22. Irina Shcherbakova, "Dnevnik okhrannika GULAGa," *Uroki istorii XX vek*, February 2, 2011, at http://urokiistorii.ru/history/people/1364.

23. Shcherbakova, "Dnevnik."

24. "Severnyi Zheleznodorozhnyi ITL (Sevzheldorlag, Sevzheldorstroi)," at http://www. memo.ru/history/NKVD/GULAG/r3/r3-306.htm.

25. Asif Siddiqi, "Scientists and Specialists in the Gulag: Life and Death in Stalin's Sharashka," *Kritika* 16, no. 3 (2015): 557–588, and L. L. Kerber, *Stalin's Aviation Gulag: A Memoir of Andrei Tupolev and the Purge Era*, ed. Von Hardesty (Washington, DC: Smithsonian Institution Press, 1996).

26. Karta Pamiati, "Kladbishche Zakliuchenykh Sevzheldorlag," at http://www.mapo fmemory.org/11-94.

27. TASS, "Glava IaNAO: most cherez Ob' v Salekharde sdelaet Pripoliarnyi Ural dostupnee dlia turistov," February 15, 2019, at https://tass.ru/ural-news/6121802.

28. Doocuments in TsKhIDK (ЦХИДК, the Central Repository of Historical Documentary Collections—Центра хранения историко-документальных коллекций, including its RGVA (Russian State Military Archive, Российский государственный военный архив, РГВА)—reveal the nature of the murder of the Polish officers at Katyn. See Bibliotekha "Katyn'," " 'Razgruzka' lagerei Narkomchermeta Sevzheldorlag," at http://www.katyn-books.ru/library/katyn-prestuplenie-protiv-chelovechestva10.html.

29. N. S. Lebedeva, "Katyn'. Plenniki neob"iavlennoi voini," *Katyn Files*, June 3, 2011, at http://katynfiles.com/content/book-katyn-1.html#doc71

30. See "Katynskie materialy," July 11, 2020, at http://katynfiles.com/content_docs.html for all of the documents, photos, and other materials.

31. Lebedeva, "Katyn'. Plenniki neob"iavlennoi voini." See APRF (Archive of the President of the Russian Federation), F. 3, Zakrytyi paket 1, Podlinnik. Katyn, Dokumenty ludobojstwa, Warszawa, 1992, pp. 34–40, at http://katynfiles.com/content/book-katyn-1.html#doc217.

32. See TsKhIDK, F. 1/P, op. 13, d. 3, l. 183, and RGVA, F. 40, op. 1, d. 44, l. 9, and d. 71, l. 10 at "Katynskie materialy," July 11, 2020.

33. V. S. Parsadanova, *K istorii Katynskogo dela—Katynskaia drama*, p. 117; RGVA, F. 40600, op. 1, d. 44, ll. 9–10, and TsKhIDk, F. 1/p. op. 1e, d. 3, l. 188, all at http://kat ynfiles.com/content_docs.html.

34. "Katynskie materialy."

35. Viktor Murzin, "Proklataia doroga," July 1997, *Vokrug sveta*, at http://www.vokrugsv eta.ru/vs/article/991/

36. E. S. Sergeevich Seleznev, *Proizvodstvennaia deiatel'nost' ITL GULZhDS NKVD/MBV na Zapadnom Uchastke BAMa, 1937–1953 gg.*, Candidate of History Thesis, Irkutsk State Pedagogical University, 2009. In the middle of 1935, there were 170,000 people

in BAMlag and 200,000 in May 1938—of a total of perhaps 1.8 million in the entire gulag.

37. Murzin, "Proklataia doroga."

38. Antik Forum, "Rel's uzkokoleinyi s markirovkoi A. O. B. Z. 1878 g. Lot 1," February 8, 2011, at http://www.antik-forum.ru/forum/archive/index.php/t-8821.html.

39. For discussion of the re-educational aspects of the gulag, see "Death and Redemption," Russian History Blog, May 2012, at http://russianhistoryblog.org/category/blog-conversations/death-and-redemption/. Historians still debate the gulag's function in redemption of prisoners from their political and ideological failings. But for me, its rapid transformation into a construction organization reveals that its primary function was to produce grist for the mills of Stalinist industry.

40. For example, the lumber city of Kotlas, as an embarkation point, had its own GULZhDS division, founded in 1940 on the basis of Sevzheldorlag, Sevdvinlag, and Kotlaslag. Its prison population ranged from 19,000 to 35,000 prisoners; on the outskirts of Kotlas are several gulag cemeteries. See "Kotlasskii otdel GULZhDS NKVD," *Virtula'nyi Muzei Gulaga*, at http://www.gulagmuseum.org/showObject.do?object=7102566&language=1.as, as accessed January 5, 2017.

41. N. Nemchenko, "Shtrikhi k portretu V. A. Barabanov" (1999), in *Stroika No. 503 (1947-1953 gg.): Dokumenty. Materialy. Issledovaniia*, at http://www.memorial.krsk.ru/Articles/503/04.htm.

42. See *Mertvaia doroga* (2013), directed by Denis D'iakonov, a documentary film on this last Stalin hero project, at https://www.prlib.ru/item/343388.

43. Mishechkina, *Stroika No. 503*.

44. V. Lamin, "Sekretnyi Ob"ekt 503," *Nauka v Sibirii*, no. 3, p. 4; no. 5, p. 6; and no. 10, p. 6, all 1990, and Nash Ural, "Mertvaia doroga (Transpoliarnaia magistral')," May 24, 2013, at http://nashural.ru/Mesta/mertvaya-doroga.htm.

45. Blake McKelvey, "A Half Century of Southern Penal Exploitation," *Social Forces* 13, no. 1 (October 1934–May 1935): 114.

46. McKelvey, "A Half Century." See also J. A. Holmes, "Road Building with Convict Labor in the Southern States," in United States Department of Agriculture, *Yearbook of Agriculture* (Washington, DC: USDA, 1901), 321–326; and Jane Zimmerman, "The Penal Reform Movement in the South during the Progressive Era, 1890–1917," *Journal of Southern History* 17, no. 4 (November 1951): 462–492.

47. See, e.g., Gazprom, http://www.gazprom.ru/nature/, and http://www.gazprom.ru/social/; http://www.gazprom.ru/press/journal/; Novatek, "Fotogaleriia," at http://www.novatek.ru/ru/press/photo/. In autumn 2022, Gazprom's website ceased to work.

48. Paskova, ed., Poliarnaia magistral' (Moscow: "Veche," 2007).

49. Gorky's support for the Stalinist regime after his criticism of Bolshevik authoritarianism and self-imposed exile in protest, his return to the USSR in 1928, his support for the Belomor Canal, his celebration of socialist realism, and his joyfulness over such other Stalinist projects as Igarka are hard to explain. See Andrew Barratt and Edith W. Clowes, "Gor'ky, Glasnost' and Perestroika: The Death of a Cultural Superhero?" *Soviet Studies* 43, no. 6 (1991): 1123–1142; and Lidiia Spiridonova, "Gorky and Stalin

(According to New Materials from A. M. Gorky's Archive)," *Russian Review* 54, no. 3 (1995): 415–417.

50. Konstantin Gnetnev, *Belomor Kanal: Vremena i sud'by* (Petrozavodsk: Ostrova, 2008). See also Cynthia Ruder, *Making History for Stalin: The Story of the Belomor Canal* (Gainesville: University of Florida Press, 1998).

51. S. Marshak, "Uvazhaemye deti," in *Sobranie sochinenii v 8 tomakh*, v. 6 (Moscow: Khudozhestvennaia Literatura, 1971), 304–312, at http://s-marshak.ru/works/prose/prose17.htm.

52. Yuri Slezkine, *Arctic Mirrors: Russia and the Small Peoples of the North* (Ithaca, NY: Cornell University Press, 1994).

53. N. Kapitanova, "Anatolii Matveevich Klimov," *Cheliabinskaia Oblastnaia Detskaia Biblioteka im. V. Maikovskogo*, October 27, 2015, at http://www.chodb.ru/news/1001/, as accessed January 2, 2016.

54. Mariia Mishechkina and Aleksandr Toshchev, *"My iz Igarki": Nedetskaia sud' ba detskoi knigi* (Moscow: Bozvrashchenie, 2000), 26.

55. Kur'er.Sreda.Berdsk, "Epokha Brezhneva ili Luchshie Gody SSR," December 19, 2013, http://www.kurer-sreda.ru/2013/12/19/125754-epoxa-brezhneva-ili-luchshie-gody-sssr.

56. See the 1978 film on Brezhnev's Siberian travels by the same name, *Vsegda s narodom*, at https://www.youtube.com/watch?v=kX_ywjsCkRY.

57. Svetlana Fedotova, "Poezdka General'nogo Sekretaria TsK KPSS Leonida Brezhneva v Sibir' i na Dal'nii Vostok cherez Perm," *Realnaia Perm'*, September 14, 2016, at https://www.newsko.ru/articles/nk-3372260.html.

58. G. I. Marchuk, "Strategiia nauchnogo poiska," in *Gorizonty sibirskoi nauki*, ed. N. A. Pritvits (Novosibirsk: Zap-Sib Knizhnoe Izdatel'stvo, 1979), 7–19.

59. Brezhnev, "Otchetnyi Doklad Tsentral'nogo Komiteta KPSS XXIII S"ezdu Kommunisticheskoi Partii SSSR," March 29, 1966, in Brezhnev, *Leninskim Kursom*, vol. 1 (Moscow: Izdatpolit, 1976), 315.

60. On BAM, see Ward, *Brezhnev's Folly*. For another perspective of BAM during its formative, camp years, see Alun Thomas, "On Guard at BAMlag: Representations of Guards in the 1930s Gulag Press," *Soviet and Post Soviet Review* 41, no. 1 (2014): 3–32.

61. Video, "Pesnia o BAMe. O. Fel'tsman, R. Rozhdestvenkii. Slyshish' vremia gudit BAM," July 11, 2012, at http://avatarija.blogspot.com/2012/07/video_7289.html.

62. V. Shainskii and R. Rozhdestvenskii, "Idut po BAMu POEZDA," http://izmerov.narod.ru/rsong/rrs0204.html. The Russian is: "Сквозь расстоянья и года, Размеренно и строго, Идут по БАМу поезда, Работает дорога."

63. Rustem Faliakhov, "Tynda: Ulitsa Diogenov," *Gazeta.ru*, September 21, 2016, at https://www.gazeta.ru/social/bam/2016/09/21/10205897.shtml.

64. Andrei Sidorchik, "'Zoloto BAMa. Kak zavershali posledniuiu velikuiu stroiku SSSR," *Argumenty i fakty*, October 1, 2014, at http://www.aif.ru/society/history/zoloto_bama_kak_zavershali_poslednyuyu_velikuyu_stroyku_sssr; and TASS, "Vospominaem BAM," at http://tass.ru/bam-40, as accessed November 3, 2022.

65. Fiona Hill and Clifford Gaddy, *The Siberian Curse: How Communist Planners Left Russia out in the Cold* (Washington, DC: Brookings Institution, 2003).

66. McCannon, *Red Arctic*.

67. Hill and Gaddy, *The Siberian Curse*.

68. "Vorota Arktiki," *Pikabu*, at https://pikabu.ru/story/vorota_arktiki_5666414, as accessed November 5, 2022

69. Gazprom, "Obskaya-Bovanenkovo Railroad," at http://www.gazprom.com/about/production/projects/mega-yamal/obskaya-bovanenkovo/.

70. Oil and Gas World, "Yamal LNG," September 26, 2020, at https://oilandgas.world/viewtopic.php?f=64&t=334.

71. Gazprom, "Obskaya-Bovanenkovo Railroad."

72. Railway-Technology.com, "Obskaya-Bovanenkovo Railroad, Russia," October 29, 2009, at http://www.railway-technology.com/projects/obskaya-bovanenkovo/.

73. Gazprom, "Obskaya-Bovanenkovo Railroad."

74. Sofiia Zorina, "Chistaia territoriia," *Sibirskaia neft'*, no. 128 (February 2016): 30–34.

75. N. N. Zaporotskaia, "Karta 'Goriachikh Tochek' i potential'nykh konfliktov mezhdu promyshlennymi kompaniiami i korennymi molochiclennymi narodami Kamchatki," Materials from the Project of the Center for Assistance to Minority Peoples of the North (RITTs), supported in part with funds from the United Nations, at https://arctic consult.org/2017/07/16/2013-запороцкая-н-н-карта-горячих-точек-и/.

76. See *Gigiena i sanitaria*, no. 1 (2012): 14–16.

77. E. V. Agbalian, "Sostoianie okruzhaiushchei sredy v Arktike," *Uspekhi sovremennogo estestvoznaniia*, no. 4 (2011): 74–76.

78. A. A. Dudarev and J. O. Odland, "Forty-Year Biomonitoring of Environmental Contaminants in Russian Arctic: Progress, Gaps and Perspectives," *International Journal of Environmental Research Public Health* 19 (2022).

79. Bryan Sage, "Ruptures in the Trans-Alaska Oil Pipeline: Causes and Effects," *Ambio* 9, no. 5 (1980): 262–263; Erich H. Follmann and John L. Hechtel, "Bears and Pipeline Construction in Alaska," *Arctic* 43, no. 2 (June 1990): 103–109; Susan Cargill Bishop and F. Stuart Chapin III, "Patterns of Natural Revegetation on Abandoned Gravel Pads in Arctic Alaska," *Journal of Applied Ecology* 26, no. 3 (December 1989): 1073–1081. See also R. B. Weeden and D. R. Klein, "Wildlife and Oil: A Survey of Critical Issues in Alaska," *Polar Record* 15 (1971): 479–494.

80. Agbalian, "Otsenka ustoichivosti ozernykh ekosistem."

81. UNIAN, 'Ekologi b'iut trevogu."

82. A. V. Golovnev and I. V. Abramov, "Oleni i gaz: Strategii razvitiia Iamal," *Vestnik arkheologii, antropologii i etnografii*, no. 4 (27) (2014): 122–131.

83. Irina Fedosseva, "'Gazprom' zakryvaet na Iamale 200 kilometrov zheleznoi dorogi," *Znak*, June 4, 2015, at https://www.znak.com/2015-06-04/proekt_na_kotoryy_byli_potracheny_milliardy_koncernu_ne_nuzhen_foto.

84. V. A. Isakov, "Main Types and Causes of Deformations on Railways and Roads in the Norilsk Industrial District," in *Proceedings of the Tenth International Conference on Permafrost, "Resources and Risks of Permafrost Areas in a Changing World,"* ed. V. P. Melnikov, D. D. Drozdov, and E. Romanovsky, Salekhard, Yamal-Nenets Autonomous District, Russia, 25–29 June 2012, vol. 2 (2012): 133–136, at ttp://ipa. arcticportal.org/publications/conference-proceedings; and Ivan Sokolov, Nikolai

Volkov, and Vladislav Isaev, "Cone Penetration Testing for Railways on Permafrost," in *Exploring Permafrost in a Future Earth, Book of Abstracts*, ed. Frank Günther and Anne Morgenstern, XI International Conference on Permafrost, 20–24 June 2016, Potsdam, Germany, 1135–1136.

85. Aleksandr Zhelenin, "Slyshish', vremia gudit—BAM," *Rosbalt*, July 9, 2014, at http://www.rosbalt.ru/blogs/2014/07/09/1290119.html. See also Sergei Dolya, "Severomuiskii Tonnel'—Smertonosnyi uchastok BAMa," November 15, 2016, at https://sergeydolya.livejournal.com/1122496.html.

86. Nina Serebrennikova, "Putin v den' 40-letiia BAMa pozhelal tyndintsam uspekhov i Zdorov'ia," *2x2*, July 9, 2014, at https://2x2.su/society/news/putin-v-den-40-letiya-bama-pozhelal-tyndincam-uspe-56342.html.

87. Kira Latukhina, "Putin poobeshchal peshit' problemy stroitelei BAMa," *Rossiiskaia gazeta*, July 8, 2014, at https://rg.ru/2014/07/08/bam-site.html.

88. TASS, "Putin zaiavil ob uvelichenii propusknoi sposobnosti BAMa i Transsiba k 2025 gody," February 20, 2019, at https://tass.ru/ekonomika/6138160.

89. Vesti, "Putin: O razvitii BAMa, Transsiba, konkurentsii i vyxode na novye rynki," August 27, 2018, at https://www.vestifinance.ru/articles/105976.

90. Ekaterina Skobitskaia, "Putin prizval uvelichit' propusknuiu sposobnost' BAMa i Transsiba," *DP*, November 30, 2012, at https://www.dp.ru/a/2012/11/30/Putin_priz val_uvelichit_p.

91. Interfax, "Iakunin poprosil Putina prosledit' za vydeleniem deneg na BAM," July 8, 2014, at https://www.interfax.ru/business/384720.

92. AFP, "Russian Prisoners to Build Siberian Railway Line," *Moscow Times*, June 11, 2021, at https://www.themoscowtimes.com/2021/06/10/russian-prisoners-to-build-siberian-railway-line-a74186.

93. Granted, railroad rights of way are far less disruptive than automobile roads. See *Rail Transport and Environment. Fact and Figures* (CER, June 2008). But historically, rails have been greatly disruptive of ecosystems directly and indirectly. They bring other economic development and settlers interested in making a new life, making a fortune, and taking what may be there before others do. The result has been scarred landscape and indigenes and others whose lives are fully disrupted. On Honduras, e.g., see John Soluri, *Banana Cultures* (Austin: University of Texas Press, 2005); on Tanzania, C. A. Conte, "The Forest Becomes Desert," *Land Degradation and Development* 10, no. 4 (1999): 291–304; on India, Madhav Gadgil and Ramachandra Guha, *The Use and Abuse of Nature* (New Delhi: Oxford University Press, 2000); and Alex Ruuska, "Ghost Dancing and the Iron Horse," *Technology and Culture* 52 (July 2011): 574–597.

94. Valeriia Komarova, "'Gazprom' podkliuchilsia k proektu stroitel'stva Severnogo shirotnogo khoda," *RBK*, March 30, 2017, at https://www.rbc.ru/business/30/03/2017/58dcd4c29a79470d2519d01a; Paskova, *Poliarnaia magistral'*; "'Ural Promyshlennyi–Ural Poliarnyi,'" *Rossiiskaia gazeta. Prilozhenie "Regiony RG" (Ural'skii Federal'nyi Okrug)*, October 23, 2007; V. P. Timoshenko, "Megaproekt 'Ural Promyshlennyi–Ural Poliarnyi': Inertsiia sovetskoi epokhi v sravnitelnoi perspektive," *Ekho*, no. 2 (2013): 48–60; and Irina Zhuravleva and Mikhail V'iugin,

"Eto zaval. Za mnogie gody ne sdelano nichego, poetomu nachnutsia poiski krainikh," *URA*, February 20, 2014, at http://ura.ru/articles/1036261388.

95. Rambler, "Severnyi shirotnyi khod podelili na piaterykh," November 19, 2018, at https://news.rambler.ru/other/41289986; Znak, "Proekt Severnogo shirotnogo khoda-2 ot Bovanenkovo do Sabetty—Podeshevel na 40 mlrd," March 20, 2019, at https://www.znak.com/2019-03-21/proekt_severnogo_shirotnogo_hoda__2_ot_bovanenkovo_do_sabetty_podeshevel_na_40_mlrd; and Regnum, "Severnyi shirotnyi khod prodolzhit Transpoliarnaia magistral," February 21, 2019, at https://regnum.ru/news/economy/2577527.html.

96. Komarova, " 'Gazprom' podkliuchilsia k proektu stroitel'stva Severnogo shirotnogo khoda."

97. President of the Russian Federation, "Start of Oil Shipping Operations at Vorota Arktiki (Arctic Gate) Terminal," May 25, 2016, http://en.kremlin.ru/events/president/news/51994.

98. Gazprom, "Gazprom Neft Confirms First Ever Maritime Shipments of Yamal Oil Via New Arctic Gates Sea Terminal," May 25, 2016, at http://www.gazprom-neft.com/press-center/news/1113245/.

99. Russian Trains, "Luxury Overnight Trains," https://www.russiantrains.com/en/page/overnight-luxury-trains?gclid=CjwKCAjwieuGBhAsEiwA1Ly_nWs2fHPnanw_dvuhMYfLon99yjzPxQZyxenXQ-NsX60CLNqxR-ExmhoCoRsQAvD_BwE.

100. The Trans-Siberian Travel Company, "LUXURY & PRIVATE TRANS-SIBERIAN RAILWAY EXPRESS TRAINS & TOURS," https://www.thetranssiberiantravelcompany.com/tours/luxury-private-train-tours/.

Chapter 2

* My thanks to Tim LeCain for helpful critical comments on this chapter.

1. See Lewis Siegelbaum, *Stakhanovism and the Politics of Productivity in the USSR, 1935–1941* (Cambridge: Cambridge University Press, 1988).

2. An open pit is typically a relatively small footprint with deep penetration, but coal is typically deposited and stripped in relatively shallow but extensive layers.

3. Andrew Roy, *The Practical Miner's Companion; or, Papers on Geology and Mining in the Ohio Coal Field* (Columbus, OH: Westbote, 1885), 97.

4. Timothy Mitchell, *Carbon Democracy* (New York: Verso, 2011)

5. T. N. Gvozdkova, V. I. Golik, and Iu. I. Razorenov, "Kuzbass v istorii gornoi promyshlennosti Rossii," *Vestnik Kuzbass TekhUniversiteta*, no. 6 (2014): 155–160.

6. Alfred Rieber, "The Rise of Engineers in Russia," *Cahiers du monde russe et soviétique* 31, no. 4 (1990): 539–568.

7. Susan McCaffray, "The Association of Southern Coal and Steel Producers and the Problems of Industrial Progress in Tsarist Russia," *Slavic Review* 47, no. 3 (1988): 464–482; Aleksandr Fenin, *Coal and Politics in Late Imperial Russia*, trans. Alexandre Fediaevsky, ed. Susan P. McCaffray (Dekalb: Northern Illinois University Press, 1990); Ian Blanchard, "Russian Railway Construction and the Urals Charcoal

Iron and Steel Industry, 1851–1914," *Economic History Review* 53, no. 1 (2000): 107–126; Raymond Goldsmith, "The Economic Growth of Tsarist Russia 1860–1913," *Economic Development and Cultural Change* 9, no. 3 (1961): 441–475; Thomas Owen, "The Russian Industrial Society and Tsarist Economic Policy, 1867–1905," *Journal of Economic History* 45, no. 3 (1985): 587–606.

8. V. I. Lenin, "To A. I. Rykov and I. I. Radchenko," trans. R. Cymbala, in *Collected Works*, vol. 44 (Moscow: Progress, 1975), 456–458, at https://www.marxists.org/archive/lenin/works/1920/oct/28b.htm.

9. Bertrand Russell, "Bertrand Russell on Lenin," excerpted from *Lenin, Trotsky and Gorky* at http://skepticva.org/excerpt-Lenin.html. Lenin also apparently thought that it was better to make spirits from peat than from potatoes, and in this way avoid paying peasants in alcohol for their spuds.

10. Edward Charles Jeffrey, *The Origin and Organization of Coal* (Lancaster, PA: Intelligencer, 1924), 5–6.

11. Gvozdkova, "Kuzbass v istorii gornoi promyshlennosti Rossii."

12. R. S. Bikmetov, "Spetskontingent v ekonomike Kuzbassa (1930–1940 gg.)," *Polit.ru*, March 19, 2009, at http://polit.ru/article/2009/03/19/spetskontingent/.

13. J. R. Hughes argues that regional interests and local party officials had a significant role in shaping the attack on Siberian peasants for the grain, and he presents evidence to show that the outcome and the policies for dealing with the grain crisis were not only the result of high party politics of Stalin and his closest associates. See Hughes, "The Irkutsk Affair: Stalin, Siberian Politics and the End," *Soviet Studies* 41, no. 2 (April 1989): 228–253. See also Derek Lambie, "Stalin's Secret Train Trip to Siberia," *Siberian Times*, October 16, 2014, at http://siberiantimes.com/other/others/features/stalins-epic-secret-train-trip-to-siberia/.

14. "Siblag," *Istoricheskaia entsiklopediia Sibiri*, 2009, at http://irkipedia.ru/content/siblag_istoricheskaya_enciklopediya_sibiri_2009.

15. "Siblag," *Istoricheskaia entsiklopediia Sibiri*.

16. "Siblag," *Istoricheskaia entsiklopediia Sibiri*.

17. "Siblag," *Istoricheskaia entsiklopediia Sibiri*.

18. Bikmetova, "Spetskontingent v ekonomike Kuzbassa," and Liubov' Gvozdova, "Stalinskie lageria na territorii Kuzbassa," at http://www.memorial.krsk.ru/Articles/1997Gvozdkova.htm.

19. Bikmetova, "Trudoposelentsy na Shakhtakh Kuzbassa (1930–seredina 1950 gg.)," *Vestnik kuzbasskogo GosTekhUni*, no. 1 (2004): 113–120.

20. Bikmetova, "Trudoposelentsy."

21. Bikmetova, "Trudoposelentsy," "Siblag," *Istoricheskaia entsiklopediia Sibiri*, and "Spetskontingent"; and S. L., "Soviet Coal Production since the War," *The World Today* 7, no. 12 (December 1951): 518–528.

22. On the Shakhty Affair as explored in these paragraphs, see Sergei Alumov, "Shakhtinskoe delo," July 29, 2017, at https://diletant.media/articles/36331375/; and S. A. Kislitsyn, *Shakhtinskoe delo* (Rostov-na-Donu: Izd-vo NMTS "Logos," 1993). On the context for Shakhty and other assaults on scientific autonomy, see Graham, *Ghost of the Executed Engineer*.

23. B. N. Lokhanov, "Open-cut Mines in the Kuzbass: Progress and Prospects," *Soviet Mining* 3, no. 5 (1967): 523–527.

24. History, Irkutskgorelektrotrans, at http://www.irkget.ru/history/tramway-22-02-49.htm.

25. V. A. Krotov, ed., *Materialy konferentsii po izucheniiu proizvoditel'nykh sil Vostochnoi Sibiri* (Irkutsk: Izdat. AN SSSR, 1948).

26. A. V. Vinter and V. I. Veitz, "Energeticheskie resursy vostochnoi Sibiri i razvitie energetiki Baikalo-Cheremkhovskogo Kompleksa." As a sign of the significance of this work for 1947 and Russia in the 2010s, it was reprinted in *Vostochno-Sibirskaia Pravda,* September 25, 2012, at http://www.vsp.ru/2012/09/25/energeticheskie-resursy-vostochnoj-sibiri-i-razvitie-energetiki-bajkalo-cheremhovskogo-kompleksa-2/.

27. Vinter and Veitz, "Energeticheskie resursy."

28. V. V. Zvonkov, *Velikie stroiki kommunizma i transport* (Moscow: Izdat. AN SSSR, 1952). A Stalinist, he contributed to the series of scientific-popular books that appeared in the early 1950s to celebrate the Stalin Plan for the Transformation of Nature.

29. "Syr'evye resursy legkikh metallov vostochnoi Sibiri i ikh ispol'zovanie," in *Trudy vostochno-sibirskogo filiala AN SSSR*, vyp. 13, vol. 2 (1958).

30. I. P. Bardin, ed., *Razvitie proizvoditel'nykh sil vostochnoi Sibiri: Energetika* (Moscow: Izdat. AN SSSR, 1960).

31. Boris Rumer, "Current Problems in the Industrialization of Siberia," *Final Report to the National Council for Soviet and East European Research*, December 1982, 1–2. See also Fiona Hill and Clifford Gaddy, *The Siberian Curse: How Communist Planners Left Russia out in the Cold* (Washington, DC: Brookings Institution, 2003).

32. Nataliya Kibita, *Soviet Economic Management under Khrushchev: The Sovnarkhoz Reform* (London: Routledge, 2013)

33. A. M. Moshkin, "What Is a Territorial-Production Complex?" *Soviet Geography* 3, no. 9 (1962): 49–55.

34. Richard E. Lonsdale, "The Soviet Concept of the Territorial-Production Complex," *Slavic Review* 24, no. 3 (1965): 466–478.

35. Lonsdale, "The Soviet Concept of the Territorial-Production Complex."

36. Stephen Rutt, "The Soviet Concept of the Territorial-Production Complex and Regional Development," *Town Planning Review* 57, no. 4 (1986): 425–439.

37. Philip Pryde, *Environmental Management in the Soviet Union* (Cambridge: Cambridge University Press, 1991), 239–240.

38. Rutt, "The Soviet Concept of the Territorial-Production."

39. Ivan Peschinskii, "Remont Berezovskoi GRES mozhet zatianut'sia," *Vedomosti*, May 27, 2017, https://www.vedomosti.ru/business/articles/2017/05/26/691596-remont-berezovskoi-gres; and Finmarket, "Tretii energoblok Beezovskoi GRES vosstanovim, ego zhdut v energosisteme," March 22, 2017, at http://www.finmarket.ru/interview/?id=4492214.

40. See "Excavator rotary ERSHRD-5250" at http://hekmat.at/Pages/UploadedData/Contents/1391714112_634850317759090039.pdf and http://nkmz.com/?id=514.

See also photos of the monster at http://hekmat.at/Pages/UploadedData/Contents/1391714112_634850317759090039.pdf.

41. David Remnick, *Lenin's Tomb* (New York: Random House, 1993), chapters 14 and 27.

42. Stephen Crowley, *Hot Coal, Cold Steel: Russian and Ukrainian Workers from the End of the Soviet Union to the Post-Communist Transformations* (Ann Arbor: University of Michigan Press, 1997).

43. Lewis Siegelbaum, "Labor Pains in the Soviet Union; Miners' Hopes Deferred," *The Nation*, May 27, 1991, 693–694.

44. A. A. Vasil'chenko, *Ptitsy Khamar-Davana* (Novosibirsk: Nauka, 1987).

45. "Gagina, Tatyana Nikolaevna," at http://irkipedia.ru/content/gagina_tatyana_nikolae vna. Born into the family of a forest rangers in 1925, in 1944 Gagina entered the biology program at Irkutsk University, graduating in 1949, and continued study throughout Siberia for the rest of her life including extensive fieldwork. She coauthored the *Red Book* of Kemerovo province on fauna and was a leading member of a number provincial societies of sports hunters and fishers, birders, and other organizations.

46. Olg'a Shcheglova, "'*Kuznetskii Alatau*': *Mesta zapovednye* (Kuznetskii Alatau, 2012). See also A. A. Vail'chenko, E. A. Maksimenko, and S. G. Babina, "Regional'nye problemy zapovednogo dela," in *15-letiiu gosudarstvennogo prirodnogo zapovednika "Kakasskii,"* ed. V. A. Stakheev (Abakan: Izdat. Khakasskogo Gos. Universiteta, 2006), 25–30.

47. Vadim Borisov and Simon Clarke, "The Russian Miners' Strike of February 1996," *Capital and Class* 20, no. 2 (1996): 23–30.

48. Alessandra Stanley, "Russian Miners Strike, Defying Yeltsin," *New York Times*, February 2, 1996, at https://www.nytimes.com/1996/02/02/world/russian-miners-strike-defying-yeltsin.html; and Reuters, "Russian Coal Miners' Union Votes to End Strike," *New York Times*, December 12, 1996, at https://www.nytimes.com/1996/12/12/world/russian-coal-miners-union-votes-to-end-strike.html.

49. Igor Artemiev and Michael Haney, "The Privatization of the Russian Coal Industry: Policies and Processes in the Transformation of a Major Industry," (World Bank [?], April 2002).

50. Thane Gustafson, *Wheel of Fortune* (Cambridge, MA: Harvard University Press, 2012); Marshall Goldman, *Petrostate: Putin, Power and the New Russia* (New York: Oxford University Press, 2008).

51. On Magnitogorsk, see John Scott, *Behind the Urals* (Bloomington: Indiana University Press, 1989), originally published in 1942.

52. Jamestown Foundation, "Tuleev Wins Landslide in Kemerovo," *Monitor* 3, no. 195 (October 20, 1997), at https://jamestown.org/program/tuleev-wins-landslide-in-kemerovo/; Elizaveta Pestova, "Russia's Kuzbass Coal Region Is on the Verge of an Ecological Catastrophe," *Open Democracy*, November 23, 2017, at https://www.opendemocracy.net/od-russia/elizaveta-pestova/russias-kuzbass-coal-region.

53. Pestova, "Russia's Kuzbass Coal Region."

54. Much of the following section comes from a gleaning of Sharon LaFreniere, "A Hotbed of Crime in Cold Siberia," *Washington Post*, January 7, 1999, at https://www.washingtonpost.com/archive/politics/1999/01/07/a-hotbed-of-crime-in-cold-siberia/65c32 2d5-a8d7-48b6-9306-1750bbeafa87/?utm_term=.fe5f0f369750; Kompromat, "Zamy

Tuleeva vymogali razrez," November 15, 2016, at http://www.compromat.ru/page_37483.htm; Kompromat, "U Amana opiat' vzorvalos' . . .," January 12, 2003, at http://www.compromat.ru/page_14273.htm; Igor Lavrenkov and Tat'iana Kosacheva, "Aman Tuleev prizval splotit'sia vokrug Vladimira Putina," November 23, 2017, *Kommersant*, at https://www.kommersant.ru/doc/3475821.

55. Pestova, "Russia's Kuzbass Coal Region."

56. SUEK Press Service, "Nazarovskie ugol'shiki v chisle luchshikh v Rossii," July 2017 (?), http://www.nazarovograd.ru/news/4691.html.

57. Aljazeera, "Kemerovo Governor Resigns over Deadly Shopping Centre Fire," *Aljazeera*, April 1, 2018, at https://www.aljazeera.com/news/2018/4/1/kemerovo-governor-resigns-over-deadly-shopping-centre-fire.

58. LaFreniere, "A Hotbed of Crime in Cold Siberia."

59. Kuzbassrazrezugol', "O Nas," at http://www.kru.ru/ru/about/us/, and Kuzbassraz-rezugol', "Istoriia," at http://www.kru.ru/ru/about/history. See also SUEK, "Leader in Powering the World," at http://www.suek.com/about-us/.

60. Aljazeera, "Kemerovo Governor Resigns."

61. MFD, "Ugol'nye kompanii Erunakovskogo mestorozhdeniia vveli v ekspluatatsiiu zheleznodorozhnuiu liniiu," July 30, 2003, at http://mfd.ru/news/view/?id=87050.

62. A. M. Tuleev and S. V. Shatirov, *Ugol' Rossii v XXI veke: Problemy i resheniia* (Moscow: Sovershenno Sekretno, 2003).

63. Vladimir Slivyak, "Russia: The Land without Doubt or Debate," Heinrich Boll Stiftung, November 18, 2015, at https://www.boell.de/en/2015/11/10/russia-land-without-doubt-or-debate.

64. D. A. Dodin, *Minerageniia Arktiki* (St. Petersburg: Nauka, 2008), 271–272, and Interview with David Abramovich Dodin, December 22, 2009, St. Petersburg.

65. Dodin, *Mineral'no-syr'evye resursy rossiiskoi Arktiki*, 723–725.

66. EPA, "Coke Ovens: Pushing, Quenching and Battery Stacks: National Emission Standards for Hazardous Air Pollutants," at https://www.epa.gov/stationary-sources-air-pollution/coke-ovens-pushing-quenching-and-battery-stacks-national-emission.

67. "Coke-Oven Emissions," at https://ntp.niehs.nih.gov/ntp/roc/content/profiles/coke ovenemissions.pdf.

68. Edward Wong, "Coal Burning Causes the Most Air Pollution Deaths in China, Study Finds," *New York Times*, August 17, 2016, at https://www.nytimes.com/2016/08/18/world/asia/china-coal-health-smog-pollution.html.

69. Allan Rodgers, "Coking Coal Supply: Its Role in the Expansion of the Soviet Steel Industry," *Economic Geography* 40, no. 2 (2016): 113–150.

70. "V zone ekologicheskogo bedstviia skoro okazhutsia vse," *Grad' Achinsk*, April 24, 2014, at https://achgrad.ru/stati/ekologiya/item/345-v-zone-ekologicheskogo-bedstv iya-skoro-okazhutsya-vse.html.

71. For example, "Na khimkobinate 'Enisei' v rezultate vzryva obrushilos' zdanie," *Pravda*, June 20, 2014, at http://www.pravdapfo.ru/news_pravda_jizni/na-himko mbinate-enisey-v-rezultate-vzryva-obrushilos-zdanie.

72. See Timothy LeCain, *Mass Destruction* (New Brunswick, NJ: Rutgers University Press, 2009).

73. Andrew Isenberg, *Mining California* (New York: Hill & Wang, 2005).

74. See Laura Henry, "Russia's Environment and Environmental Movement," in *Understanding Contemporary Russia*, 2nd ed., ed. Michael L. Bressler (Boulder, CO: Lynne Rienner, 2018), 275–301; and Laura Henry (with Joshua P. Newell), "The State of Environmental Protection in the Russian Federation: A Review of the Post-Soviet Era," *Eurasian Geography and Economics* 57, no. 6 (2016): 779–801; "Civil Society under the Law 'On Foreign Agents'"; and "Oil Extraction and Benefit Sharing in an Illiberal Context: The Nenets and Komi-Izhemtsi Indigenous Peoples in the Russian Arctic" (with Maria Tysiachniouk, Machiel Lamers, and Jan P. M. van Tatenhove), *Society and Natural Resources* 31, no. 5 (2018): 556–579.

75. "'Nachni s doma svoego' detskaia ekologicheskaia ekspeditsiia 2010 goda po Sibiri," *Priroda Sibiri*, no. 7 and 8 (2010): 28–34, at http://prirodasibiri.ru/?id_page=24&id_r azd=113.

76. "UK 'Kuzbassrazrezugol' napravit 31 mln rublei na letnii detskii otdykh," May 31, 2018, at http://www.kru.ru/ru/press/news/uk-kuzbassrazrezugol-napravit-31-mln-rubley/.

77. Ellen Barry, "Rescuers Are Counted among Dead as Toll Rises in Russian Mine Blasts," *New York Times*, May 10, 2010.

78. Golos Kuzbassa, "Shtab Soiuza zhitelei Kuzbassa. Novokuznetsk," May 23, 2010, at http://goloskuzbassa.livejournal.com/.

79. Voices from Russia, "Chapel in Memory of Dead Miners in the 2010 Raspadskaya Mine Disaster Opened in the Kuzbass," August 17, 2012, at https://02varvara.wordpr ess.com/tag/2010-raspadskaya-mine-explosion/.

80. Michael Specter, "Far North in Russia, the Mines' Fatal Blight," *New York Times*, March 28, 1994, 1; T. W. Kienlen, "The Future of Coal," *Analysts Journal* 10, no. 4 (August 1954): 77–80; E. Willard Miller, "Strip Mining and Land Utilization in Western Pennsylvania," *Scientific Monthly* 69, no. 2 (August1949): 94–103; Paul H. Rakes, "Technology in Transition: The Dilemmas of Early Twentieth-Century Coal Mining," *Journal of Appalachian Studies* 5, no. 1 (Spring 1999): 27–60; Judith Shapiro, *Mao's War against Nature: Politics and the Environment in Revolutionary China* (New York: Cambridge University Press, 2001); LeCain, *Mass Destruction*; Joyce Barry, "Mountaineers Are Always Free?: An Examination of the Effects of Mountaintop Removal in West Virginia," *Women's Studies Quarterly* 29, no. 1/2, Earthwork: Women and Environments (Spring–Summer, 2001): 116–130; Silas House, "A Conscious Heart," *Journal of Appalachian Studies* 14, no. 1/2 (Spring/Fall 2008): 7–19; Michael Wallace, "Dying for Coal: The Struggle for Health," *Social Forces* 66, no. 2 (December 1987): 336–364.

81. N. E. Bufina, "Vozdeistvie ugol'noi promyshlennosti na ekologicheskuiu situatsiiu v Kuzbasse v XX–XXI vekakh," *Vestnik KemGU*, no. 2 (54) (2013): 33–34.

82. Bufina, "Vozdeistvie."

83. Valentina Ivakina, "V plenu u razrezov: Gde i pochemu v Rossii bastuiut protiv dobychi uglia," *Saltzone*, June 2, 2017, at https://salt.zone/radio/7699.

84. Ivakina, "V plenu u razrezov."

85. "Belovskoe vodokhranilishche: Otdykh i rybalka," May 7, 2015, at http://webmandry. com/belovskoe-vodohranilishhe-otdyh-i-rybalka-foto-i-video-karta-belovskogo-morya/.

86. "Kuzbassovtsy mogut lishit'sia otdykha na Belovskom More," *City-N*, May 22, 2017, at https://www.city-n.ru/view/396628.html.

87. "Zapretit' otkrytie razreza na granitse Belovskogo vodokhranilishchina, 3 naselennykh punktov, GRES!!" (2017 [?]), at https://www.change.org/p/президент-рф-запретить-открытие-разреза-на-границе-беловского-водохранилища-3-населенных-пунктов-грэс.

88. RUSAL, a massive company of 61,000 employees, the sixth largest aluminum producer in the world at 4.2 million tons annually and 7 percent of world production, runs under Oleg Deripaska, one of the richest men in Russia, who is a close friend of Vladimir Putin, and has worked with Paul Manafort, Donald Trump's campaign manager, on a variety of Russian election efforts.

89. "Zhiteli Achinska obrashchaiutsia k prezidentu iz-za ekologii," *Zapad24*, September 29, 2015, at http://zapad24.ru/news/achinsk/37098-zhiteli-achinska-sostavlyayut-peticiyu-prezidentu-po-deyatelnosti-agk.html.

90. Pestova, "Russia's Kuzbass Coal Region."

91. Lesser reserves consist of the Moscow basin; in the Urals the Kizelovskii, Cheliabinsk, and South Ural deposits; in Siberia the Minusinsk, Cheremkhovskii, Ulugkhemiskii, and Tungusk reserves; and in the Far East the South Iakutsk basin of high-quality coal on the basis of which a territorial industrial complex (TPK) was created, and also the Bureinskii, Cuchanskii, and Lenskii basins and Kamchatka sites.

92. G. I. Gritsko, "Emissions of Pollutants into the Atmosphere and Hydrosphere of the Kuznetsk Coal Basin," in Committee on Improving the Effectiveness of Environmental Nongovernmental Organizations in Russia et al., *The Role of Environmental NGOs: Russian Challenges, American Lessons. Proceedings of a Workshop* (Washington, DC: National Academy of Sciences Press, 2001), 109–110.

93. Pestova, "Russia's Kuzbass Coal Region."

94. Gritsko, "Emissions of Pollutants," 113–114.

95. Gritsko, "Emissions of Pollutants," 113–114.

96. Slivyak, "Russia: The Land without Doubt or Debate."

97. Unian, "US State Dept: Russian Proxies' Plans to Flood Coal Mine in Donbas, Site of Nuclear Test, Could Threaten Drinking Water," April 14, 2018, at https://www.unian.info/war/10080866-u-s-state-dept-russian-proxies-plans-to-flood-coal-mine-in-donbas-site-of-nuclear-test-could-threaten-drinking-water.html.

Chapter 3

* My deep thanks to Professor Nicholas Breyfogle and other participants in the Water, Culture, and Society in Global Historical Perspective Conference at Ohio State University where I "presented" an early version of this paper in May 2016 by internet; I could not attend the conference because of the death of my dear, close friend Erik Seastead.

1. A contemporary variation on the Russian proverb "Chem dal'she v les, tem bol'she drov (The farther into the forest, the more the firewood)."

2. On Lenin's technological utopianism and his support for GOELRO, see Josephson, *Would Trotsky Wear a Bluetooth?* (Baltimore: Johns Hopkins, 2009), chapter 1. For the final program of GOELRO written "at the request of Lenin" and adopted in December 1920, see G. M. Krzhizhanovskii, "Plan elektrifikatsii RSFSR," in *Izbrannoe* (Moscow: Gosizdatpolit, 1957), 65–189.

3. G. A. Beresnev and Iu. Gromov, *Ogni sedogo Volkhova* (Leningrad: Lenizdat, 1967), 12–13, 22.

4. D. Saslavsky, *Dnieprostroi: The Biggest Dam in the World* (Moscow: Cooperative Publishing Society of Foreign Workers in the USSR, 1932), 3–4, 8–10.

5. Obertreis, *Imperial Desert Dreams*.

6. A. Malyavin, "Razgrom Irtura—'gromkoe' delo Samarskoi GybChK," December 30, 2106, at http://a-malyavin.livejournal.com/86661.html.

7. "Voistinu, 'net proroka v svoem otechestve' . . .," at http://korenev.org/index.php/ru/2011-04-07-13-55-37/2011-04-07-14-16-28/114-2012-02-13-20-30-39. On the murderous effort to transform the steppe into a powerful agricultural region and the human costs for the Kazakh people of Russian nature transformation projects, see Sarah Cameron, *The Hungry Steppe: Famine, Violence, and the Making of Soviet Kazakhstan* (Ithaca, NY: Cornell University Press, 2018).

8. See Rizenkampf, *Trans-Kaspiiskii Kanal* (Moscow: VSNKh, 1922), published at http://www.cawater-info.net/library/rus/hist/rizenkampf3/index.htm.

9. "Voistinu, 'net proroka v svoem otechestve.'"

10. On the American West, see Mark Reisner, *Cadillac Desert* (New York: Penguin, 1986); on Brazil, Josephson, *Industrialized Nature*. On Indian dams, see Government of India, Ministry of Power, "Policy on Hydro Power Development," October 26, 2022, at https://powermin.gov.in/en/content/policy-hydro-power-development; and Mayank Aggarwal, "The Return of the Mega Hydropower Projects across India," *Mongabay*, June 17, 2020, at https://india.mongabay.com/2020/06/the-return-of-the-mega-hydropower-projects-across-india/. See also Donald Worster, *Rivers of Empire* (New York: Pantheon, 1985).

11. Obertreis, *Imperial Desert Dreams*; Ruder, *Making History for Stalin*; Klaus Gestwa, *Die "Stalinschen Großbauten des Kommunismus". Sowjetische Technik- und Umweltgeschichte 1948–1967* (München: Oldenbourg Wissenschaftsverlag, 2010).

12. *Rezoliutsii XVII S"ezda VKP (b)* (Moscow: Partizdat, 1934), 15–16.

13. Lilienthal, *TVA*.

14. Richard White, *The Organic Machine* (New York: Hill & Wang, 1985); and Kate Brown, *Plutopia* (New York: Oxford University Press, 2013).

15. Shiu-Hung Luk and Joseph Whitney, eds., *Megaproject: A Case Study of China's Three Gorges Project* (Armonk: M. E. Sharpe, 1993), 3–39; Xibao Xu, Yan Tan, and Guishan Yang, "Environmental Impact Assessments of the Three Gorges Project in China: Issues and Interventions," *Earth-Science Reviews* 124 (2013): 115–125; and Cheng Lin et al., "Managing the Three Gorges Dam to Implement Environmental Flows in the Yangtze River," *Frontiers in Environmental Science* 6 (2018), at https://www.frontiersin.org/articles/10.3389/fenvs.2018.00064. On Australia's audacious

project, see Snowy Hydro, "The Snowy Scheme," 2020, at https://www.snowyhydro.com.au/generation/the-snowy-scheme/; and C. M. Gray, "The Snowy Mountains Scheme," *Journal of the Royal Society of Arts* 104, no. 4988 (1956): 887–910.

16. Dmitrii Vorob'ev, "Kogda gosudarstvo sporit s soboi: Debaty o proekte 'povorota rek'," *Neprikosnovennyi zapas*, no. 2 (46) (2006), at http://magazines.russ.ru/nz/2006/2/vo8.html. On the Lower Lena GES, see "Kiusiur. Chekurovskie shcheki. 'Lenskaia truba'," September 30, 2012, at https://uritsk.livejournal.com/70486.html.

17. NKVD SSSR, *Kanal Moskva-Volga. Spravochnye dannye* (Dmitriv: NKVD, 1936), 6–7, 13, 27–28.

18. R. Ia. Khiger, *Arkhitektura rechnykh vokzalov* (Moscow: GosArkhIzdat, 1940), 3. For more details on construction of the canal, see the biweekly journal, *Stroitel'*, nos. 14–15 (September 1937), entire, with articles on excavation, concrete works, armatures, mechanical works; *Pionerskaia pravda*, April 28, 1935; and *Moskva-Volga*, a documentary film (1937), at http://moskva-volga.ru/videoteka/. See also *Kanal Moscow-Volga. Materialy dlia agitatorov i propagandistov. Dlia vnutrennego pol'zovaniia* (Dmitrov: Izdat. Stroitel'stva Kanala Moskva-Volga, 1935); and A. Rasstanov, *Moskva-Port. Ocherki* (Dmitrov: KBO Dmitlaga, 1937).

19. Aleksandr Rozanov, *Moi kanal. Pesni storiki. Biblioteka perekovki* (Dmitrov: Dmitlaga NKVD SSSR, 1936).

20. I. L. Averbakh, *Ot prestupleniia k trudy* (Moscow: OGIZ, 1936).

21. A. Zholdasov, "Na ruinakh velikoi stroiki," *Tsentraziia*, February 2, 2003, at https://centrasia.org/newsA.php?st=1044278400.

22. M. I. Kuz'min, "Bol'shoi Ferganskii Kanal," *Gidrotekhnika i melioratsiia*, no. 3 (1965); H. E. Adler, "Turkistan in Transition," *Geographical Journal* 107, no. 5/6 (1946): 230–235; and A. A. Grigoryev, "Soviet Plans for Irrigation and Power: A Geographical Assessment," *Geographical Journal* 118, no. 2 (1952): 168–179.

23. V. A. Berg, *Zashchita gidrostantsii ot vozdushnogo napadeniia* (Moscow: Stroizdat Narkomstroiia, 1940).

24. Mark Harrison, *Accounting for War* (New York: Cambridge University Press, 1996); Denis Brand, *L'expérience soviétique et sa remise en cause* (Paris: Sirey, 1993).

25. Walter Sanning, "Soviet Scorched-Earth Warfare: Facts and Consequences," at http://www.ihr.org/jhr/v06/v06p-91_Sanning.html.

26. Brain, "The Great Stalin Plan."

27. On the plan, its significance and background, see Stephen Brain, *Song of the Forest: Russian Forestry and Stalinist Environmentalism, 1905–1953* (Pittsburgh: University of Pittsburgh Press, 2011); W. deJong-Lambert, *The Cold War Politics of Genetic Research: An Introduction to the Lysenko Affair* (Dordrecht: Springer, 2012), 92–94; Douglas Weiner, *A Little Corner of Freedom: Russian Nature Protection from Stalin to Gorbachëv* (Berkeley: University of California Press, 2002), 89–90.

28. Some of the material in this section was published earlier in Josephson, "The Stalin Plan for the Transformation of Nature and the East European Experience," in Doubravka Osakova, ed., *Stalin's Plans for the Transformation of Nature and Their Impact in Eastern Europe* (Oxford: Berghahn Books, 2016), 1–41.

29. The most important works on the Volga River history are: Evgenii Burdin, *Pokorenie Volgi: Stalinskaia model' gidrostroitel'stva v Rossii* (Chisinau, Moldava: Lambert Academic Publishing, 2011); *Volzhskaia Atlantida: Tragediia velikoi reki* (Ul'ianovsk: "Pechanyi Dvor," 2005); *Volzhskii Kaskad GES: Triumf i tragediia* (Moscow: ROSSPEN, 2011); and *Vklad zakliuchennykh GULAGa v stroitel'stvo volzhskikh gidrouzlov (1932–1958 gg.)* (Ul'ianovsk: UlGPU, 2013). See also Dorothy Zeisler-Vralsted, *Rivers, Memory, and Nation-Building: A History of the Volga and Mississippi Rivers.* (New York, Oxford: Berghahn Books, 2014); and Janet M. Hartley, *The Volga: A History of Russia's Greatest River* (New Haven, CT: Yale University Press, 2021). My deep thanks to Professor Burdin for inviting me to Ulyanovsk to meet him and his students, and to become familiar with his rich and deeply impressive work.

30. On the role of innocent men and women—prisoners of Stalinism—in the construction of the mighty symbols of the Stalin Plan, see O. V. Lavinskaia and Iu. G. Orlova, eds., *Zakliuchennye na stroikakh kommunizma. Gulag i ob'ekty energetiki v SSSR. Sobranie dokumentov i fotografii* (Moscow: ROSSPEN, 2008).

31. Burdin, *Pokorenie Volgi*; Gestwa, *Die „Stalinschen Großbauten des Kommunismus"*; and Josephson, *Industrialized Nature*.

32. F. P. Gromyko, *Energiia rek—na sluzhbu kolkhozam* (Ivanovo: Ivanovskoe Oblastnoe Gosudarstvennoe Izdatel'stvo, 1949), 3. See also M. Davydov and M. Tsunts, *Rasskaz o velikikh rekakh* (Moscow: Gosizdat kul'turno-prosvetitel'noi literatury, 1955); and F. G. Basov, *Ispol'zovanie vodnoi energii rek na kolkhoznykh gidrostantsiiakh* (Voronezh: Voronezhskoe Oblastnoe Knigoizdatel'stvo, 1940).

33. Burdin, *Pokorenie Volgi*.

34. For thorough analysis of the genesis of these large irrigation projects and the engineering proclivity to impose concrete, canals, drainage, and pumps on the landscape, with health doses of chemicals, see Obertreis, *Imperial Desert Dreams*. The Central Asian projects reflected a view of nature also as an enemy of the people, and the Soviets were determined to subjugate "her" with big technology and water.

35. See the brilliant book of the late Maya Peterson, *Pipe Dreams: Water and Empire in Central Asia's Aral Sea Basin* (Cambridge: Cambridge University Press, 2019), on this subject.

36. On the precursors of the Urundar'inskaia Expedition, see N. A. Severtsov, *Puteshestviia po Turkestanskomu Kraiu*, at http://www.vostlit.info/Texts/Dokumenty/M.Asien/XIX/1840-1860/Severcov_2/framepred12.htm.

37. *Niva*, no. 18 (1874): 287.

38. "Sel'skokozhiaistvennye predpriatiia," April 23, 2012, at http://tsikly.ru/hozyaystvo/selskoe/63-selskoxozyajstvennye-predpriyatiya.html.

39. Vitalii Shentalinskii, "Vsled za zhivoi vodoi," *Vokrug sveta*, October 1982 (no. 10), at http://www.vokrugsveta.ru/vs/article/2541/.

40. F. I. Bylin et al., *Tekhnologicheskie karty na meliorativno-stroitel'nye raboty* (Leningrad: Lenizdat, 1966).

41. Zholdasov, "Na ruinakh velikoi stroiki"; V. Shishikin, "Proekty perebroski stoka severnykh rek v respubliki Srednei Azii," at http://www.science-techno.ru/nt/article/proekty-perebroski-stoka-severnykh-rek-v-respubliki-srednei-azii/page/2, as accessed December 14, 2014.

42. "Sel'skokozhiaistvennye predpriatiia," April 23, 2012, at http://tsikly.ru/hozyaystvo/selskoe/63-selskoxozyajstvennye-predpriyatiya.html.

43. Zholdasov, "Na ruinakh velikoi stroiki"; Roman Poberezhniuk, "Oazis v pustyne ili mirazh?" *Ezhenedelnik*, June 27, 2008, at http://2000.net.ua/2000/aspekty/istorija/42544; and L. Konstantinov, *Karakumskie vstrechi* (Barnaul: Altaiskoe Knizhnoe Izdatel'stvo, 1953); "Dolina Murgaba," May 20, 2012, at http://tsikly.ru/rayoni/hlopok/122-dolina-murgaba.html.

44. Il'ga Mekhti, "Elegiia o zhazhde," *Khronika Turkmenistana*, May 1, 2014, at http://www.chrono-tm.org/2014/05/elegiya-o-zhazhde/.

45. Mekhti, "Elegiia o zhazhde"; Shentalinskii, "Vsled za zhivoi vodoi."

46. *XX S'ezd Kommunisticheskoi Partii Sovetskogo Soiuza, 14–25 Fevralia 1956 goda. Stenograficheskii otchet*, Vol. 1 (Moscow: Gosizdatpolit, 1956), 252–253.

47. Evgeniia Liping, "Kaskad GES ub'et Angaru," April 30, 2010, *BaikalInfoRU*, at http://baikal-info.ru/friday/2010/16/008001.html

48. S. I. Kuznetsov, *Lagaria GULAGa i GUPVI na territorii irkutskoi oblasti* (Irkutsk: Ottisk, 2007).

49. Rosneft, "Angarsk Refinery," at https://www.rosneft.com/business/Downstream/Neftepererabotka/OilRefineries/AngarskRefinery/.

50. O. V. Afanosov, "V zvedenie zapadnogo uchastka BAMa," at http://taishettoday.ru/15, http://penpolit.ru/papers/detail2.php?ELEMENT_ID=937; "Vostochnyi poligon—Transsib i BAM," at http://cargo.rzd.ru/static/public/ru?STRUCTURE_ID=5128&layer_id=3290&id=2088; "Zakonchen pervyi uchstok BAM, 1975," at https://histrf.ru/lenta-vremeni/event/view/zakonchien-piervyi-uchastok-bama; O. V. Afanasov, "Uchastniki lagernykh vosstanii 1953–54 gg. v Ozerlag," *Memorial*, http://www.memorial.krsk.ru/Articles/2000Afanasov.htm. See also A. M. Kriukov, *BAM—Trassa muzhestva. Puti i trevogi. Zapiski voennnogo zheleznodorozhnika* (Petrozavodsk: "Karelia," 1979). Unfortunately, none of these websites was working as of November 2022.

51. One of the first books on the development of Baikal, Marshall Goldman, *The Spoils of Progress: Environmental Pollution in the USSR* (Cambridge, MA: MIT Press, 1972), remains the classic policy history. See also Nicolas Breyfogle, "At the Watershed: 1958 and the Beginnings of Lake Baikal Environmentalism," *Slavonic and East European Review* 93 (2015): 147–180.

52. Gosudarstvennyi Arkhiv Novosibirskoi Oblasti (GANO), F. D-97, op. 1, d. 35a and d. 48; F. R-1020, op. 2, d. 32, op. 7, d. 1, op. 7, dd. 3 op. 7; f. P-4, op. 35, d. 400 and d. 11 and d. 431; and F. P-11796, op. 1.2, d. 36, 11, 53, 53a and 367, as discussed at "Unikal'nye dokumenty Gosudarstvennogo Arkhiva Novosibirskoi Oblasti o proektirovanii i stroitel'stve novosibirskoi GES," at http://bsk.nios.ru/content/unikalnye-dokumenty-gosudarstvennogo-arhiva-novosibirskoy-oblasti-o-proektirovanii-i.

53. Masha Sorokina, "Novosibirskaia GES: Kak vse nachinalos," August 12, 2011, at http://sib.fm/articles/2011/08/12/novosibirkaya-ges-kak-vsyo-nachinalos (website not working November 2022). See also L. Pashchenko, "Ne zabudem vovek, kak moguchuiu Ob' pokoril chelovek!" *Sovetskaia Sibir'*, July 10, 2006, at http://www.sovsibir.ru/news/67023.

54. Sorokina, "Novosibirskaia GES," and Pashchenko, "Ne zabudem vovek, kak moguchuiu Ob' pokoril chelovek!"
55. "Kanalu Volga-Don 60 let," *Gidrotekhnika XXI vek* 9, no. 2 (2012): 14–18.
56. Petr Godlevskii, "'Volgo-Don 2,'—Shag v budushchee," *Delovaia pressa*, January 23, 2008, at http://www.businesspress.ru/newspaper/article_mId_21962_aId_440703. html; and "Medvedev ne iskliuchaet vozmozhnosti realizatsii proekta Volgodon-2," *StroiSMI*, February 5, 2008, at https://www.stroysmi.ru/novosti/medvedev-ne-iskl yuchaet-vozmozhnosti-realizatsii-proekta-volgodon-2/.
57. Anatolii Chalykh, "Varianty soedinenniia Volgi i Dona," at http://sarkel.ru/istoriya/ istoriya_kazachestva/varianty_soedineniya_volgi_i_dona/.
58. "Vpered v shestidesiatye?!," at http://n-discovery.spb.ru/news_full.php?id=3914.
59. Ibid.; and Tat'iana Khmel'nik, "O malykh GES zamolvite slovo. Etim elektrostantsiiam mozhet pomoch' tol'ko energeticheskii krizis," August 1, 2009, at http://zagorod.spb. ru/articles/2733.
60. Khmel'nik, "O malykh GES."
61. Aleksei Mironov, "Nicheinye GES," *Ekspert Severo-Zapad*, no. 17 (September 10, 2001), at http://expert.ru/northwest/2001/17/17no-cover2_53096/.
62. "Iz-za proryva nefteprovoda proizoshlo zagriaznenie reki," *Tomskaia nedelia*, September 13, 2011, at http://www.tomsk.ru/news/view/47299/.
63. "V Novosibirske odin iz pritokov Obi otpravliaut nefteprodukty," *Altaiskaia pravda*, October 1, 2013, at http://altapress.ru/story/116993.
64. "Chem opasno obmelenie tomskikh rek?" *Tomskaia nedelia*, May 20, 2012, at http:// www.tomsk.ru/news/view/56618/.
65. L. M. Kipriianova and E. Iu. Zarubina "Reke Berd' grozit mnogo bed," *Nauka v Sibiri*, June 28, 2012, http://www.sbras.ru/HBC/hbc.phtml?20+641+1.
66. Iakov Demchenko, *O navodnenii Aralo-Kaspiiskoi nizmennosti dlia uluchsheniia klimata prilezhashchikh stran* (Kyiv: S. P. Iakovlev, 1900), at https://www.prlib.ru/ item/686131.
67. On Siberian River diversion, see Philip Micklin, "The Status of the Soviet Union's North-South Water Transfer Projects before Their Abandonment in 1985–86," *Soviet Geography*, 5 (1988): 287–329; Micklin, "The Siberian Water Transfer Schemes," in *The Aral Sea*, ed. P. Micklin et al. (Berlin-Heidelberg: Springer-Verlag, 2014), 381–403; and Robert Darst, "Environmentalism in the USSR: The Opposition to the River Diversion Projects," *Soviet Economy* 4, no. 3 (1988): 223–253. See also A. S. Berezner, *Territorial'noe pereraspredelenie rechnogo stoka evropeiskoi chasti RSFSR* (Leningrad: Gidrometeoizdat, 1985).
68. V. A. Vasilenko, "Ostrozhno, snova 'Povorot'!" *Eko*, no. 8 (2003): 3–20. See in partic- ular Sergei Zalygin, *Povorot* (Moscow: Mysl, 1987). Zalygin contributed mightily to the killing of the project.
69. One of the best discussion of the history of fantasies of Siberia river diversion is Dmitrii Vorob'ev, "Kogda gosudarstvo sporit s soboi: Debaty o proekte 'Povorota Rek," *Zhurnal'nyi zal*, no. 2 (46) (2006).
70. Davydov and Tsunts, *Rasskaz o velikikh rekakh*.
71. Ibid.

72. Shishikin, "Proekty perebroski stoka severnykh rek v respubliki Srednei Azii."

73. Ibid.

74. "Astana rassmatrivaet vozmozhnost' stroitel'stva kanala iz Irtysha v Ishim Stoimost'iu $3.3 mlrd," October 7, 2013, *Novosti-Kazakhstana*, at http://www.newskaz.ru/econ omy/20131007/5632823.html.

75. United Nations, "The Aral Sea Basin Programs," at https://kazaral.org/en/ifas/asbp/, and "UN Aral Sea Programme," at http://undp.akvoapp.org/en/project/525/. See also Iu. S. Kamalov, "Aral'skoe more, problemy, legendy, reshenie," *Soiuz zashchity Arala i Amudar'i*, at http://ecodelo.org/3676-aralskoe_more_problemy_legendy_resheniya-basseinovyi_podkhod.

76. Government of the Russian Federation, *General'naia skhema razmeshcheniia ob"ektov elektroenergetiki do 2020 goda*, Pasporiazhenie no. 215-r, February 22, 2008 (Moscow: Government of the Russian Federation, 2008), 5.

77. Ibid., 11.

78. Ibid., 15, 24, 136.

79. See http://www.boges.ru/press-tsentr/fotomaterialy/ for a photogallery of the Boguchanskaia GES. Construction photos have disappeared from RusGidro's web-site. See also Plotina.Net! "Gidrogigantomaniia: Novye gigantskie GES na Angare i Pritokakh Amura," February 27, 2014, at http://www.plotina.net/gidrogigan tomania/.

80. Plotina.Net! "Znakom'tes': Nizhneboguchanskaia GES," at http://www.plotina.net/nizhneboguchanskaya-ges/.

81. Andrei Zakhvatov, "Stanet li Rossiia 'vodnym donorom'?" August 1, 2008, at http://www.rosbalt.ru/main/2008/08/01/509404.html.

82. Letter of Iu. Luzhkov, "Prezidentu Rossiiskoi Federatsii V. V. Putinu," January 25, 2002, at *Zelenyi mir. Spetsial'nyi vypusk*, no. 11 (December 2002), at http://razumru.ru/pseudo/rivers/dreams.htm. See also Andrei Moiseekno, "Kanal imeni Moskvy," *Komsomol'skaia pravda*, December 22, 2002; "Proekt perebroski chasti stoka severnykh i sibirskikh rek. Spravka," at http://eco.rian.ru/documents/20081030/154087032.html; and Tatiana Chernova, "'Za' i 'protiv' techeniia . . .," *Novaia gazeta*, December 23, 2014, at http://www.ng.ru/scenario/2014-12-23/13_sibreka.html.

83. Yuri Luzhkov, *Voda i mir* (Moscow: Moskovskie Uchebniki i Kartolitografiia, 2008).

84. "Budet voda—budet mir," *Izvestiia*, May 22, 2009.

85. Fred Pearce, "Russia Reviving Massive River Diversion Plan," *New Scientist*, February 9, 2004, at http://www.newscientist.com/article/dn4637-russia-reviving-massive-river-diversion-plan.html#.VRBpNGR4odk.

86. V. I. Danilov-Danil'ian, "I meru nado znat' meru, ili korabl' pustyni s rogami," at http://www.iwp.ru/monograf/luzkov/mer.html.

87. Chernova, " 'Za' i 'protiv' techeniia."

88. Letter of Luzhkov.

89. Danilov-Danil'ian, "I meru nado znat' meru."

90. Danilov-Danil'ian, "I meru nado znat' meru." On Sochi's grotesque costs, see Boris Nemtsov and Leonid Martyniuk, *Zimniaia Olimpiada v subtropikakh* (2013) at http://www.nemtsov.ru/old.phtml?id=718789, as accessed March 29, 2015.

91. Viktor Maltsev, "Chto nam stoit reku perestroit!" *Leninskaia smena*, June 1, 2014, at http://www.lensmena.ru/2014/06/3484367/.

92. V. Sokolikova, "Almaz v korone Enisei," *Sovetskaia Khakasiia*, February 16, 1962.

93. Ia. Zhukovskii, "Saianskaia zvezda," *Sovetskaia Rossiia*, April 25, 1963; "Izyskateli prishli v Saiany," *Krasnoiarskii rabochii,* December 27, 1961; Iu. Zakharov, "Saiano-Shushenskaia GES . . . na vyborskoi storone," *Pravda*, October 14, 1965; V. Leont'ev, "Sainskie budni," *Krasnoiarskii komsomolets*, August 29, 1974. On the concrete pourers: S. E. Kolenkov, *My—Gidrostroiteli* (Kransoiarsk: Krasnoiarskoe Knizhnoe Izdatel'stvo, 1983); V. M. Vlasov, "K otsenke kachestva betona polotiny Saiano-Shushenskoi GES," *Gidrotekhnicheskoe stroitel'stvo*, no. 10 (1988): 41–43, and Vlasov, "Otsenka rezerva prochnosti betona plotiny Saiano-Sushenskoi GES," *Gidrotekhnicheskoe stroitel'stvo*, no. 5 (1989): 11–16.

94. N. Kuleshov, "Na Brebne plotiny," *Sovetskaia Khakasiia*, November 3, 1982, 1.

95. "Dlia giganta energetiki," *Ogni Saian*, May 10, 1980.

96. *Ogni Saian*, April 26, 1975, 1–2, entire.

97. S. Ezhov, "Plotina v chelovecheskom aspekte," *Sovetskaia Khakasiia*, May 23, 1991, 2.

98. "V avarii na GES nashli vinovnykh," *Izvestiia*, December 11, 2009.

99. Diana Krivtsova, "Zhelezo vosstanovim, liudei—ne vernut'," *Trud*, August 24, 2009, at http://www.trud.ru/article/24-08-2009/227583_zhelezo_vosstanovim_ljudej_ne _vernut.html.

100. "Vladimir Putin: Posle avarii Saiano-Shushenskaia GES poluchila vtoruiu zhizn'," August 27, 2013, at http://ruskline.ru/news_rl/2013/08/27/vladimir_putin_posle_ avarii_sayanoshushenskaya_ges_poluchila_vtoruyu_zhizn/.

101. Bellona, "Prekrasheno ugolovnoe delo v otnoshenii zhurnalista, osveshavshego avariiu na SShGES," *Bellona*, September 7, 2009, at http://bellona.ru/2009/09/07/ prekrashheno-ugolovnoe-delo-v-otnosheni/. Afanasyev's report is "Srochno! Na SSh GES pogibaiut liudi. Pros'ba perepostit' vsem," August 19, 2009, at https://ruk hakasia.livejournal.com/8476.html.

102. RIA Novosti, "Avariia na Saiano-Shushenskoi GES v avguste 2009 goda," August 17, 2013, at http://ria.ru/spravka/20130817/956779489.html#ixzz34kLlbS49; and RIA Novosti, "Avariia na Saiano-Shushenskoi GES v avguste 2009 goda," August 17, 2013, at http://ria.ru/spravka/20130817/956779489.html.

103. Vladimir Tarasov, "Mekhanizmy Saiano-Shushenskoi avarii. Fakty i gipotezy," *Taiga. info*, May 9, 2011, 17.

104. Tagir Irbek and A. Prokopchuk, "SSh GES: Vozmozhnost' katastrofy perspektivy S-ShGES v vesenie-letnee polov," April 15, 2010, *Plotina.Net!*, at forums.drom.ru/ Vladivostok/t1151373422.html.

105. V. I. Goldanskii, "Vozrodrim energeticheskoe chudo Saian 'Imeni 75'," *Prirodno- resursnye vedomosti*, no. 11–12 (November–December 2009), 250–351, at http:// www.priroda.ru/reviews/detail.php?ID=9800.

106. Plotina.Net!, "Otvergnutaia versiia katastrofy na Saiano-Shushenskoi GES," *Plotina. Net!*, August 23, 2016. See also Vladimir Babkin, *O regulirovanii rechnogo stoka v XXI veke* (Moscow: Triumf, 2018), written because of the SShGES disaster—precisely because of safety issues. Babkin worked at the station thirty-nine years until he was fired in 2001.

107. "Putin i Kuznetsov nabliudali iz Kremlia za tseremoniei zapuska boguchanskoi GES," *Krasnoiarskii rabochii*, October 16, 2012, at http://www.krasrab.net/news/Putin_i_Kuznetsov_nablyudali_iz_Kremlya_za_tseremoniey_zapuska_Boguchans koy_GES/?sphrase_id=11184.

108. "Saiano-Shushenskaia GES v Khakasii v 2016 godu ustanovila rekord po vyrabotke elektroenergii," *TASS*, February 1, 2017, at http://tass.ru/ekonomika/3987106.

109. Andrew Kramer, "Decaying Soviet Infrastructure Shows Its Era," *New York Times*, August 20, 2009, at https://www.nytimes.com/2009/08/21/business/global/21ru ble.html.

110. Alexander Shurshev, "Avariia na Saiano-Shushenskoi GES: Problemy eshche vpreredi?" *Bellona*, February 22, 2010, at http://bellona.ru/2010/02/22/avariya-na-sayano-shushenskoj-ges-problem/.

111. Ushakov et al., "Sotsial'no-ekologicheskie problemy."

112. Ushakov et al., "Sotsial'no-ekologicheskie problemy."

113. Amnesty International, "Russia: A Year On, Putin's 'Foreign Agents Law' Choking Freedom," November 20, 2013, at http://www.amnesty.org/en/news/russia-year-putin-s-foreign-agents-law-choking-freedom-2013-11-20.

114. Sergei Baimukhametov, "Kuda smotrit FSB?" *Russkii bazar*, no. 32 (694), http://russ ian-bazaar.com/ru/content/15434.htm. See also "Prokuratura na saite Poltina.Net! ekstremizma net," July 3, 2009, http://uhhan.ru/news/2009-08-19-1182.

115. See Federal'nyi Zakon Rossiiskoi Federatsii ot 18 dekiabria 2006 g., N 232-F3, at http://www.rg.ru/2006/12/23/kodeks-izmeneniya.html. For discussion of public involvement in the environmental policy process, see Henry, "Social Mobilization and the Strong State," and Henry, "Complaint-Making as Political Participation in Contemporary Russia," *Communist and Post-Communist Studies* 45, 3–4 (September–December 2012): 243–54.

116. Dale E. Peterson, " 'Samovar Life': Russian Nurture and Russian Nature in the Rural Prose of Valentin Rasputin," *Russian Review* 53, no. 1 (January 1994): 81–96.

117. Evgeniia Liping, "Kaskad GES ub'et Angaru," *BaikalInfoRU*, April 30, 2010, at http://baikal-info.ru/friday/2010/16/008001.html.

118. Natalia Ozhogina, "Proshchai, Angara!," *Vremia*, April 20, 2007, at http://angvre mya.ru/sobesednik/4819-.html.

119. Margarita Baranova, "Siberia: Sold Down the River," *Ecologist*, November 9, 2013.

120. "O sanitarno-epidemiologicheskoi obstanovke v Altaiskom krae v sviazi s pavodkovoi situatsiei na 11.06.2014," at http://www.rospotrebnadzor.ru/about/info/news_region/news_details_region.php?ELEMENT_ID=1933.

121. "Korrespondent Altapress.ru osmotrel zonu navodneniia," *Altaiskaia pravda*, June 6, 2014, at http://altapress.ru/story/135546.

122. RFE/RL, "At Least 1,000 Evacuated amid Floods in Siberia's Altai Krai," June 9. 2014, at http://www.rferl.org/content/at-least-1000-evacuated-amid-floods-in-siberias-altai-krai/25415156.html.

123. "O sanitarno-epidemiologicheskoi obstanovke v altaiskom krae."

124. FEMA, *2017 Hurricane Season: FEMA After-Action Report* (Washington: FEMA, July 12, 2018).

125. President of Russia, "Meeting on Relief Efforts Following Floods in Altai, Khakassia and Tyva," http://eng.kremlin.ru/transcripts/22469; and Vladimir Putin, "Effektivno rabotaiut vse vedomstva i rukovoditeli regionov, postradavshikh ot pavodka na Altae," June 10, 2014, http://altapress.ru/story/135358.

126. A. Nadtochii, "'Zolotye' berega Novosibirskogo Vodokhranilishcha," *Nauka v Sibiri*, no. 30–31 (August 9, 2012), at http://www.sbras.ru/HBC/hbc.phtml?16+644+1.

127. A. Nadtochii, "Zametki s nauchnoi konferentsii po problemam bezopastnosti Novosibirskogo Vodokhranilishcha," *Nauka v Sibiri*, no. 13 (2948), March 29, 2012, at http://www.sbras.ru/HBC/hbc.phtml?8+629+1.

128. Ibid.

129. *Organizatsiia i provedenie radiatsionnogo monitoringa Ob'-Irytshkogo rechnogo vasseina v granitsakh Khanty-Mansiikogo Avtonomnogo Okrug-Igry v 2010 gody* (Khanty-Mansiisk: Sluzhba po kontroliu i nadzoru v sfere okhrany koruzhaiushchei sredy, 2010). On heavy metals and radioactive isotopies (^{137}Cs, ^{90}Sr, and Pu) in water bodies, see also the journals *Radiobiologiia, Vodnye resursy, Raditsionnaia bezopasnost' i zashchita AES*, and *Radiatsionnaia gigiena*.

130. "Beloiarskaia AES. Spravka," at http://www.anti-atom.ru/ab/node/1932.

131. RT, "Almost All Water in Russia is Undrinkable," February 12, 2009, at http://rt.com/news/almost-all-water-in-russia-is-undrinkable/.

132. "Rossiia zaiavila o togovnosti podkliuchit'sia k stroitel'stvu Nikaraguanskogo Kanala," *Vzgliad*, October 26, 2015, at http://vz.ru/news/2015/10/26/774381.html.

133. President of Russian Federation, "V Bishkeke sostoialis' Peregovory Vladimira Putina s Prezidentom Krigizii Almabekom Atambaevym," September 20, 2012, at http://www.kremlin.ru/news/16509; and N. A., "Prezident Uzbekistana rezko vyskazalsia protiv stroitel'stva Kambaratinskoi i Rogunskoi GES," *Fergana News*, September 7, 2012, at http://www.fergananews.com/news/19412.

134. Dmitrii Usol'tsev, "Za schet Sibiri: Minsel'khoz nameren podelit'sia vodoi s kitaitsami," *Kolokol Rossii*, May 12, 2015, at http://kolokolrussia.ru/ekonomika/za-schet-sibiri-minselhoz-nameren-podelitsya-vodoy-s-kitaycami#hcq=2Zd1tSp.

135. Ibid.

136. Aleksandr Shirokorad, "Rossii i Belarusi—Istoriia i perspektivy," part 1, *Soiuznoe gosudarstvo*, March 19, 2013, at https://www.postkomsg.com/history/196530/.

137. Valerii Erofeev, "Zakliuchennye kanaloarmeitsy. Po materialam gazety *Za reshetkoi*," February 15, 2014, at http://tyurma.com/zaklyuchennye-kanalo/kanalrmeitsy.

138. Rosmorrechflot, "Ot Volgi do Eniseia," *Vestnik rosmorrechflota*, no. 1 (2014): entire.

Chapter 4

1. Emails from Julian Cooper to the author, March 29 and 30, 2016. See also Julian Cooper, "Minatom: The Last Soviet Industrial Ministry," in *Shaping the Economic Space in Russia*, ed. S. Harter and G. Easter (Aldershot: Ashgate, 2000), 147–161. See also Rosatom, "About Us," at https://www.rosatom.ru/en/about-us/.

2. For a history of the Soviet nuclear enterprise and Chernobyl's meaning, see Zhores Medvedev, *The Legacy of Chernobyl* (New York: W. W. Norton, 1999).

3. Government of Russian Federation, "O gosudarstvennoi korporatsii po atomnoi energii 'Rosatom,'" Federal Law no. N317-F3, December 1, 2007, at: http://www.rg.ru/2007/12/05/rosatom-doc.html; and Aleksandr Emel'ianenkov, "Krylatyi 'Rosatom' pod sen'iu novoi korporatsii distsiplinu povenchaiut s rynkom," November 14, 2007, at http://www.rg.ru/2007/11/14/kirienko-rosatom.html. See also Emel'ianenkov, *Ostrova Sredmasha* (Moscow: Parad, 2005).

4. Emel'ianenkov, "Krylatyi 'Rosatom.'" For a more detailed analysis of the reforms aiming at consolidation of the Russian nuclear industry, see Igor Kudrik, Charles Digges, Alexander Nikitin, Nils Bøhmer, Vladimir Kuznetsov, and Vladislav Larin, *Russian Nuclear Industry: The Need for Reform*. Bellona Report Vol. 4 (November 2004), at http://bellona.org/publication/russian-nuclear-industry-the-need-for-reform. See also Gaukhar Mukhatzhanova, "Russian Nuclear Industry Reforms: Consolidation and Expansion," *James Martin Center for Nonproliferation Studies Research Story*, May 22, 2007, at http://cns.miis.edu/stories/070522.htm.

5. Paul Josephson, *Red Atom* (Pittsburgh: University of Pittsburgh Press, 2005); Medvedev, *Legacy of Chernobyl*; David Holloway, *Stalin and the Bomb; the Soviet Union and Atomic Energy, 1939–1956* (New Haven, CT: Yale University Press, 1994); Sonja Schmid, *Producing Power* (Cambridge, MA: MIT Press, 2015); Kate Brown, *Plutopia* (New York: Oxford University Press, 2013); and Tatiana Kasperski, *Les politiques de la radioactivité: Tchernobyl et la mémoire nationale en Biélorussie contemporaine* (Paris: Pétra, 2020).

6. General'naia skhema razmeshcheniia ob"ektov elektroenergetiki do 2020 goda, Pasporiazhenie no. 215-r, February 22, 2008 (Moscow: Government of the Russian Federation, 2008); and Kurchatov Institute, *O strategii iadernoi energetiki Rossii do 2050 goda* (Moscow: KIAE, 2012).

7. L. V. Gureyeva, V. V. Egorov, and V. L. Podberezniy, "Coupling of AST-500 Heating Reactors with Desalination Facilities," International Atomic Energy Agency (IAEA), 1997, accessed May 10, 2015, at http://www.iaea.org/inis/collection/NCLCollectionStore/_Public/28/076/28076304.pdf.

8. Government of the Russian Federation, "Ob utverzhdenii gosudarstvennoi programmy Rossiiskoi Federatsii 'Razvitie Atomnogo Energopromyshlennogo Kompleksa,'" Postanovlenie no. 506-12, June 2, 2014, at http://government.ru/media/files/41d4e579a4d19542262a.pdf.

9. Government of Russian Federation, "Ob utverzhdenii programmy razvitiia atomnoi energetiki Rossiiskoi Federatsii na 1998–2005 gody i na period do 2010 goda," Postanovlenie no. 605, October 6, 2006, at http://pravo.gov.ru/proxy/ips/?docbody=&prevDoc=102124526&backlink=1&&nd=102109273.

10. Government of the Russian Federation, "O general'noi skheme razmeshcheniia ob"ektov elektroenergetiki do 2020 goda," Rasporiazhenie no. 215-r, February 22, 2008, at http://pravo.levonevsky.org/bazaru09/raspor/sbor05/text05919/index21.htm, and "O programme deiatel'nosti gosudarstvennoi korporatsii po atomnoi energii 'Rosatom' na dolgosrochnyi period (2009–2015 gody)," Postanovlenie no. 705,

September 20, 2008, at http://pravo.gov.ru/proxy/ips/?docview&page=1&print=1&nd=102124526&rdk=2&&empire.

11. Government of Russian Federation, "O reorganizatsii kontserna 'Rosatom' putem prisoedineniia k nemu federal'nykh gosudarstvennykh unitarnykh prepriatii atomnoi energetiki," Rasporiazhenie No. 1207-R, September 8, 2001, at http://russia.bestpravo.ru/fed2001/data03/tex14729.htm; Government of Russian Federation, "Ob utverzhdenii pravil otchisleniia predpriiatiami i organizatsiiami, ekspluatiruiushchimi osobo radiatsonno pasnye proizvodstva i ob"ekty (atomnye stantsii), sredstv dlia formirovaniia rezervov, prednaznachennykh dlia obespecheniia bezopasnosti atomnykh stantsii na vsekh stadiiakh zhiznennogo tsikla i razvitiia," Postanovlenie no. 68, January 30, 2002 at http://www.consultant.ru/document/cons_doc_LAW_138047/; Rosbalt, "Deviat' grazhdanskikh FGUPov atomnoi otrasli preobrazovany v OAO," December 26, 2007, at http://www.rosbalt.ru/business/2007/12/26/443818.html; RIA Novosti, "Zachem Rossii 'Atomenergoprom'?" May 10, 2007, at http://ria.ru/analytics/20070510/65207809.html; Vadim Ponomarev, "Iadernyi Renessans," *Ekspert*, October 10, 2017, at http://expert.ru/siberia/2012/48/yadern yij-renessans/; Rossiiskoe Atomnoe Soobshchestvo, " 'Iadernyi Renessans' i Russiia," November 16, 2011, at http://www.atomic-energy.ru/news/2011/11/16/28737.

12. "VVER Reactor," at http://www.rosatom.ru/en/rosatom-group/engineering-and-construction/modern-reactors-of-russian-design/.

13. World breeder reactor experience has shown the LMFBR to be a costly, risky endeavor. France's first breeder reactor went through a series of sodium fires and breakdowns, while the Superphenix, the world's first "commercial" LMFBR at 1,200 MW operated for roughly fourteen years but was shut down in 1998 and produced very little electricity. See Mycle Schneider, "Fast Breeder Reactors in France," *Science and Global Security* 17 (2009): 36–53. Japan's effort failed for similar technical and safety reasons. The United States abandoned the breeder because of proliferation concerns.

14. On Shevchenko, see Stefan Guth, "Wachtürme unter Kränen. Zwangsarbeit in der post-stalinistischen UdSSR am Beispiel der Atomstadt Ševčenko/Aktau, 1970," *Traverse. Zeitschrift für Geschichte* 24, no. 1 (2017): 153–159, and "Stadt der Wissenschaftlich-Technischen Revolution. Ševčenko, Kasachstan," in *Goldenes Zeitalter der Stagnation? Perspektiven auf die sowjetische Ordnung der Brežnev-Ära*, ed. Boris Belge and Martin Deuerlein (Tübingen: Mohr Siebeck, 2014), 97–130. On the Soviet breeder reactor program, see Josephson, *Red Atom*, 47–80.

15. Zhores Medvedev, *Nuclear Disaster in the Urals* (London: Angus & Robertson, 1979).

16. For a lyrical and revealing personal account of the history of Zarechnyi, see Sergei Goncharov, *Zarechnyi: Polnaia istoriia Atomgrada* (Ekaterinburg: Sokrat, 2014).

17. http://www.anti-atom.ru/ab/node/1932 and MChS, "Intsident na Beloiarskoi AES (SSSR), sviazannyi s Bol'shoi Tech'iu v Parogeneratore no 5 Energobloka BN-600," at http://rb.mchs.gov.ru/mchs/radiation_accidents/m_other_accidents/1982_god/Incident_na_Belojarskoj_AJES_SSSR_svjaza. Neither of these webpages is working. See also Andrei Ozharovskii, "Beloiarskaia AES: ChP ko Dniu Atomshchik," *Bellona*, September 28, 2013, at http://bellona.ru/2013/09/28/beloyarskaya-aes-chp-ko-dnyu-atomshhika/.

18. In the absence of http://www.anti-atom.ru/ab/node/1932, see A. V. Trapeznikov et al., *Migratsiia radionuklidov v presnovodnykh ekosistemakh*, 2 vols. (Ekaterinburg: Izdatel'stvo Ural'skogo Universiteta, 2007).

19. Atominfo.ru, 2006, "Iurii Kazanskii: Reaktor BN-800—Eto vopros liderstva Rossii," at http://www.atominfo.ru/news/air288.htm.

20. Rosatom, "Modern Reactors of Russian Design," at http://www.rosatom.ru/en/rosa tom-group/engineering-and-construction/modern-reactors-of-russian-design/.

21. Kirill Bortnikov, "Edinstvennyi v mire: Na Beloiarskoi AES rabotaet reaktor na bystrykh neitronakh," *Vesti*, December 22, 2015, https://www.vesti.ru/doc.html?id= 2700947.

22. Ibid.

23. Atominfo.ru, 2006, "Iurii Kazanskii: Reaktor BN-800."

24. TASS, "Stoimost' stroitelstva reaktora na bystrykh neitronakh BN-800 otsenivaetsia v 145.m Mlrd rublei," January 20, 2016, at http://www.atominfo.ru/newsm/t0547.htm.

25. Rosatom, "Modern Reactors of Russian Design," at http://www.rosatom.ru/en/rosa tom-group/engineering-and-construction/modern-reactors-of-russian-design/.

26. RIA Novosti, "Russia Planning 3 Advanced Fast-Breeder Reactors at Beloyarsk Nuclear Power Plant by 2030," July 23, 2014, at http://atominfo.ru/en/news3/ c0959.htm.

27. Nuclear Engineering International, "Russia Defers BN-1200 Until after 2035," *NEIMagazine*, January 20, 2020, at https://www.neimagazine.com/news/newsrus sia-defers-bn-1200-until-after-2035-7581968; RIA Novosti, "Konstruktor: Novyi Rossiiskii Blok AES BN-1200 mozhno vozvesti za 10 let," June 26, 2017, at https:// ria.ru/atomtec/20170626/1497313701.html; Kurchatov Institute, *O strategii iadernoi energetiki Rossii*, 38–39; RIA Novosti, "NIKIET Institute Completes Design of BREST-300 Fast Reactor," September 5, 2014, at http://atominfo.ru/en/news4/d0078. htm; Yu. G. Dragunov, V. V. Lemekhov, A. V. Moiseev, and V. S. Smirnov, *Lead-Cooled Fast-Neutron Reactor* (BREST) (Moscow: NIKIET, May 2015), at https://www.iaea. org/NuclearPower/Downloadable/Meetings/2015/2015-05-25-05-29-NPTDS/Russi an_Projects/28_Smirnov_Brest_on_IAEA_eng.pdf.

28. Dmitrii Mamontov, "Ballada o bystrykh neitronakh," *Populiarnaia mekhanika*, no. 1 (January 2010), at https://www.popmech.ru/science/9816-ballada-o-bystrykh-ney tronakh-unikalnyy-reaktor-beloyarskoy-aes/.

29. Ana Uzelac, "IAEA Backs Controversial Neutron Reactor Plan," *Moscow Times*, November 11, 2000.

30. Aleksandr Nikitin, "Rosatom State Corporation," *Bellona*, November 26, 2007, at http:// bellona.org/news/nuclear-issues/nuclear-russia/2007-11-rosatom-state-corporat ion; Nikitin, "Atomnaia otrasl' i ekologicheskoe dvizhenie: Tochki sotrudnichestva," X International Forum-Dialog "70 Years of the Russian Nuclear Industry. Dialog of Generations," Moscow, Russia, November 12–13, 2015, at https://bellona.ru/2015/11/ 17/fd-nikitin/. See also Galina Raguzina, "'Ozhivshii' BN-800: Reaktor budushchego ili perezhitok proshlog," *Bellona.ru*, July 29, 2014, at http://bellona.ru/2014/07/29/ ozhivshij-bn-800-reaktor-budushhego-ili-pe/. According to Bellona, "During a con-versation about the future of nuclear power with students of the Moscow Engineering

Physics Institute, Russian President Vladimir Putin voiced a number of theses that suggest that the president is poorly informed about the state and prospects of nuclear energy in the world and is in captivity from myths diligently cultivated by the nuclear scientists themselves." See Andrei Ozharovskii Bellona, "Mnenie: Vladimir Putin v MIFI rasprostranial mify o iadernoi energetike," *Bellona*, February 3, 2015, at http://bellona.ru/2014/02/03/mnenie-vladimir-putin-v-mifi-rasprost/.

31. James M. Acton, "The Myth of Proliferation-Resistant Technology," *Bulletin of the Atomic Scientists* 65, no. 6 (2009): 49–59; and Thomas B. Cochran et al., "It's Time to Give Up on Breeder Reactors," *Bulletin of the Atomic Scientists* 66, no. 3 (2010): 50–56.

32. The barge was decommissioned in 1977 after the US Army spent over $3 million on trying to install an emergency core cooling system at a cost three times than originally estimated, and because of fears of terrorist attacks in the Panama Canal Zone. In all, the US Army seems to have acquired seven of the floating reactors that operated from the late 1950s until the 1960s and in one case to 1976, and ranged in power from 200 kw (an experimental apparatus) to 10 MW, that it abandoned as too expensive to operate. See Letter, Fred Schafer, Director, US General Accounting Office, October 19, 1977, to Senator William Proxmire.

33. B. D. Fishbein and G. M. Gorelov, "Sovremennyi proekt atomnogo gazoturbinnogo lokomotiva," Patent 2284932 S1 (2006) and MIRAES, "Atomovoz. Poezd na atomnoi tiage v SSSR i Rossii," April 28, 2019, at https://miraes.ru/atomovoz-poezd-na-atomnoy-tyage-sssr-rossia/.

34. Vasiliii Semashko, "Pervuiu belorusskuiu AES razreazali avtogenom," November 21, 2007, at http://news.tut.by/society/98447.html; and A. V. Smirnov et al;, "Belarus': Vyvoz unikal'nogo topliva," *Bezopasnost' iadernykh tekhnologii i okruzhaiushchei sredy*, no. 1 (2011): 96–97.

35. A. V. Karpenko, "Floating NPP FAPP 'Breakwater-3'," October 18, 2018, at http://nevskii-bastion.ru/volnolom-3/.

36. Claire Bigg, "Amid Nuclear Scare, Russia Pushes Ahead with Controversial Floating Reactors," RFE/RL, April 22, 2011, at http://www.rferl.org/content/russia_pushes_ahead_with_controversial_floating_nuclear_reactors/9502474.html; Interview with Professor Jacopo Buongiorno, Zoom, December 28, 2020, 11:00 to 11:40 EST.

37. On the history of floating reactors, see V. M. Vorob'ev (director of the PATES department), "Razrabotka proektov plavuchikh Atomnykh Stantsii," in V. A. Siderenko, *Istoriia atomnoi energetiki Sovetskogo Soiuza i Rossii* (Moscow: Isdat AT, 2004), 154–168; and Bigg, "Amid Nuclear Scare."

38. A. Nikitin and L. Andreev, *Plavuchie atomnye stantsii* (Oslo: Bellona, 2011), 44.

39. Iurii Baranaev, "Budushchee vse-taki est'," *Atominfo*, April 15, 2008, at http://www.atominfo.ru/news/air3807.htm.

40. See the nearly 400-page A. A. Sarkisov, *Atomnye stantsii maloi soshchnosti*, 2 vols. (Moscow: Akadem-Print, 2015).

41. Kurchatov Institute, *O strategii iadernoi energetiki Rossii*, 36–38.

42. Rosatomenergo, "Rosenergoatom: Port g. Peveka prinial pervye v etom godu suda s gruzom dlia stroitel'stva PAES," October 29, 2017, at http://www.atominfo.ru/newsq/x0811.htm.

43. Atominfo, "Glavgosekspertiza odobrila stroitel'stvo pervoi v mire plavuchei AES na Chukotke," January 1, 2018, at http://www.atominfo.ru/newsr/y0398.htm.

44. Yevgenia Borisova, "Floating Nuke Plant Drawing Opposition," *St. Petersburg Times*, March 16, 2001; and Greig Ebeling, "Russians Float Their Nuclear Ideas," *Proposition One Committee*, September 30, 1997, at http://prop1.org/2000/safety/970930ru.htm.

45. TASS, "Obshchaia stoimost' pervoi v mire plavuchei AES sostavit 30 mlrd rublei," April 10, 2016, at http://www.atominfo.ru/newso/v0295.htm.

46. RIA Novosti, "Baltiiskii zavod 18 maia zalozhit pervuiu v mire olavuchuiu AES," May 5, 2009, at http://www.atomic-energy.ru/news/2009/05/05/3834; and Russian Atomic Society, "V Peterburge dosrochno izgotovili parogeneratory dlia pervoi v mire plavuchei AES," February 11, 2009, at http://www.atomic-energy.ru/news/2009/02/11/2200.

47. Alla Cherednichenko, "Kto razogreet merzlotu," *Sankt-Peterburgskie vedomosti*, August 3, 2017, at https://spbvedomosti.ru/news/obshchestvo/kto_razogreet_merzl otu/

48. Bailes, "Technology and Legitimacy"; Scott Palmer, *Dictatorship of the Air* (Cambridge: Cambridge University Press, 2006).

49. President of the Russian Federation, "Na bortu ledokola '50 let Pobedy' Vladimir Putin provel zasedanie . . .," May 2, 2007, at http://kremlin.ru/events/president/news/39116.

50. Oleg Bukharin, "Russia's Nuclear Icebreaker Fleet," *Science and Global Security* 14 (2006): 25–31.

51. Evgenii Beliakov, "Arkticheskie vezdekhody," *Komsomol'skaia pravda*, October 7, 2011, at http://kp.ru/daily/25767/2751896/.

52. Andrey Ozharovsky, "Lozh' na pervom: Po mneniiu zhurnalistov na ledokole Lenin avarii ne bylo," May 6, 2009, at http://www.bellona.ru/weblog/andrey-ozharovsky/1241708613.5.

53. "Rossiia prazdnuet 35-letie pokoreniia Severnogo poliusa ledokolom 'Arktika'," *Komsomol'skaia prava*, August 16, 2012, at http://www.kp.ru/online/news/1224536/.

54. "Ledokol 'Arktika' otpravili na pensiiu," *Komsomol'skaia Pravda*, October 3, 2012, at http://kp.ru/online/news/148296/.

55. Andrei Mikhailov, "Korabli-legendy: 'Arktike' pokorilas' Arktika," *Pravda*, August 17, 2012, at https://www.pravda.ru/society/fashion/models/17-08-2012/1125045-arctica-0/

56. "'Est' podozreniia, chto proekt bol'she sviazan s osvoeniem deneg, chem s polucheniem rezul'tata,'" *Kommersant*, August 24, 2012, at http://kommersant.ru/doc/2007338.

57. Kirill Iablochkin and Mikhail Rychagov, "Atomnaia 'Arktika': Rossiia sputstila na vodu samyi bol'shoi v mire ledokol," *Zvezda TV*, June 16, 2016, at http://tvzvezda.ru/news/opk/content/201606151824-qznv.htm.

58. Sergei Romashenko, "V Rossii sorvan roszakaz na stroitel'stvo ledokola 'Arktika'," July 12, 2017, at http://www.dw.com/ru/в-россии-сорван-госзаказ-на-строительство-ледокола-арктика/a-39651649.

59. OKBM im. I. I. Afrikantova, *Publichnyi otchet "OKBM Afrikantov"* (Nizhnii Novgorod: OKBM im Afrikantova, 2017).

60. "Istoriia TsKB," *TsKB "Aisberg,"* at https://iceberg.org.ru/about-us/.
61. Vladimir Dzaguto, "'Atomflot' v 2016 godu pomog perevezti po sevmorputi 7 mln tonn gruzov," *Kommersant,* September 29, 2017, at www.kommersant.ru/doc/34238811.
62. Ibid.; World Nuclear News, "Nuclear Icebreaker 'Ural' Completes Sea Trials," *World Nuclear News,* November 3, 2022, at https://www.world-nuclear-news.org/Articles/Nuclear-icebreaker-Ural-completes-sea-trials.
63. Olga Samofalova, "Moshchneishii v mire ledokol obespechit Rossii liderstvo v Arktike," *Vzgliad,* June 16, 2016, at https://vz.ru/economy/2016/6/16/815324.html.
64. Meduza, "Atomnye ledokoly byli i budut national'noi gordost'iu strany," *Meduza,* February 14, 2016, at https://meduza.mirtesen.ru/blog/43632835582/atomnyie-ledokolyi-byili-i-budut-natsionalnoy-gordostyu-stranyi.
65. Ibid.
66. Ibid.
67. Regnum, "Atomflot: Ledokolov mnogo ne byvaet," December 8, 2017, at https://regnum.ru/news/2355252.html; and Rambler, "'Atomflot' planiruet zakazat' eshche dva ledokola LK-60," *Rambler,* December 6, 2017, at https://news.rambler.ru/army/38601883.
68. Anna Liesowska, "More Details Announced for the Arctic Northern Sea Route Expansion," *Siberia Times,* December 16, 2014, at http://siberiantimes.com/business/siberianexport/news/n0062-more-details-announced-for-the-arctic-northern-sea-route-expansion/.
69. MPO Chernomorsko-Azovskaia Territorial'naia Organizatsiia RPSM, "Ledokoly Atomflota proveli po sevmorputi 87 sudov v khode navigatsii 2017 goda," http://www.novosur.ru/news/1338-ledokoly-atomflota-proveli-po-sevmorputi-87-sudov-v-khode-navigatsii-2017-goda.html.
70. BMPD, "'Atomflot' rassmatrivaet vozmozhnost' stroitelstva ledokolov na szhizhennom gaze vmesto atomnykh," September 24, 2017, at https://bmpd.livejournal.com/2865185.html.
71. Fontanka, "Rogozin: Upravliat' sevmorputem budet Rosatom," December 5, 2017, at https://www.fontanka.ru/2017/12/05/070/.
72. NOAA, *Oil Spill Case Histories 1967–1991,* Hazardous Materials Response and Assessment Division, Report No. HMRAD 92-11 (Seattle: National Oceanic and Atmospheric Administration, September 1992).
73. Ibid.
74. V. P. Kuznetsov, V. V. Kushtan, and A. A. Mirzoev, "Arkticheskii vyzov mirnogo atoma," *Stroim flot sil'noi strany* 3, no. 20 (2014): 43.
75. Andrey Allakhverdov and Vladimir Pokrovsky, "Russian Academy President Narrowly Wins Reelection," *Science* 320 (June 6, 2008): 1270–1271.
76. http://www.anticompromat.ru/putin/ozero.html and http://www.anticompromat.ru/kovalch1/kovalch1bio.html.
77. Vladimir Pokrovsky, "Putin Tightens Control over Russian Academy of Sciences," *Science,* June 27, 2017, at https://www.science.org/content/article/putin-tightens-control-over-russian-academy-sciences.
78. Kuznetsov et al., "Arkticheskii vyzov," 43–49.

79. Ibid., 45.

80. Among dozens of articles and reports available, see TASS, "Rossiiskaia Akademiia Kosmonavtiki: lunnaia baza budet poluchat' energiiŭ ot AES," *TASS*, May 24, 2016, at http://www.atominfo.ru/newsn/u0334.htm.

81. Kelsey Atherton, "Russia Wants to Test a Nuclear Space Engine in 2018," *Popular Science*, March 11, 2016, at https://www.popsci.com/russia-wants-to-test-nuclear-space-engine-in-2018.

82. TNEnergy, "Iadernyi dvigatel' Rosatoma i Mars," *TNEnergy*, March 3, 2016, at https://tnenergy.livejournal.com/44817.html.

Chapter 5

1. Konstantin Khomenko, "I Drive the Piles," at RIA Novosti, "Stroiteliam Krymskogo mosta posviatili pesniu," August 12, 2016. https://crimea.ria.ru/20160812/1106739599.html. Translated by the author.

2. Eda Kranakis, *An Exploration of Engineering Culture, Design, and Research in Nineteenth-Century France and America* (Cambridge, MA: MIT Press 1996).

3. On the Brooklyn Bridge, see David McCullough, *The Great Bridge* (New York: Simon & Schuster, 2012). On the poetry, art, and engineering of bridges and towers, see David Billington, *The Tower and the Bridge: The New Art of Structural Engineering* (Princeton, NJ: Princeton University Press, 1985). See also V. Chandra et al., "Landmark Cable-Stayed Bridge over the Charles River, Boston, Massachusetts," *Transportation Research Record* 1845, no. 1 (2003): 19–27.

4. US Army Corps of Engineers, "The Beginnings to 1815," at http://www.usace.army.mil/About/History/Brief-History-of-the-Corps/Beginnings/.

5. US Army Corps of Engineers, "Improving Transportation," at http://www.usace.army.mil/About/History/Brief-History-of-the-Corps/Improving-Transportation/; and US Army Corps of Engineers, "US Army Engineers and the Building of the Panama Canal, 1907–1914," at http://www.armyengineer.com/history/panama/engineers/Army_Engineers/army_engineers.html.

6. National Park Service, "The History of the Construction of the Road System in Yellowstone National Park, 1872–1966," at https://www.nps.gov/parkhistory/online_books/yell_roads/hrs2-2.htm;

7. US Army Corps of Engineers, "US Army Corps of Engineers: A Brief History."

8. Ibid.

9. Terrence Emmons and Wayne Vucinich, eds., *The Zemstvo in Russia: An Experiment in Local Self-Government* (Cambridge: Cambridge University Press, 1982). See also Sergei Vitte, *Konfidentsial'naia zapiska ministra finansov stats-sekretaria S. Iu. Vitte (1899 g.)* (Stuttgart: J. H. W. Dietz, 1903).

10. Damjan Čakmak, "The Life and Work of Stephen P. Timoshenko," *Doktorski Studij na FSB: Uvod u Znanstveno Istraživački Rad*, 2016/2017, at https://www.fsb.unizg.hr/brodogradnja/UZIR-Essay-2017-Cakmak.pdf.

11. Karl Schlögel, *Moscow 1937* (Cambridge: Polity Press, 2012).

12. On the history of Mostotrest used in these paragraphs, see "Sozdanie Mostotrest," *Mostotrest,* at http://mostotrest.ru/about/history/; "OAO Mostotrest," *Vikipedia,* https://dic.academic.ru/dic.nsf/ruwiki/228321#.D0.98.D1.81.D1.82.D0.BE.D1.80. D0.B8.D1.8F.

13. Mostotrest, "Istoriia," at http://www.mostro.ru/about/history/.

14. D. V. Dretser, "Istoriia stroitel'stvo i otkrytiia Oktaibr'skogo mosta goroda Novosibirska . . .," *Biblioteka Siberskogo Kraevedeniia,* at http://bsk.nios.ru/content/istoriya-stroitelstva-i-otkrytiya-oktyabrskogo-mosta-goroda-novosibirska-po-dok umentam. See also Dmitrii Bukevich, "56 let nazad berega Obi v Novosibirske sviazal kommunal'nyi most," *Komsomolskaia pravda,* October 23, 2011, at https://www. kp.by/daily/25775/2759120/?geo=3

15. This history of the Arkhangelsk bridge is taken from my *Conquest of the Russian Arctic* (Cambridge, MA: Harvard University Press, 2014).

16. Gosudarstvennyi Arkhiva Arkhangel'skoi Oblasti (GAAO), Otdel DSPI, F. 296, op. 2, d. 191, l. 33.

17. GAAO Otdel DSPI, F. 296, op. 2, d. 1389, l. 57, 68.

18. GAAO Otdel DSPI, F. 296, op. 1, d. 1332, ll. 30, 49.

19. "54 goda nazad Arkhangel'sk posetil Nikita Khrushchev," *Pravda severa,* July 22, 2016, at http://pravdasevera.ru/society/-cw38cyr2.

20. Greenpeace and other environmental organizations and others succeeded in stopping the project that would have flooded the "Shulgan-Tash" nature preserve.

21. "Vosstanovlenie zheleznodorozhnogo transporta vo vremiia i posle Velikoi Otechestvennoi Voiny," *Zheleznodorozhnik,* March 6, 2020, at http://xn--d1abacdejqd wcjba3a.xn--p1ai/istoricheskaja_spravka/vosstanovlenie.html

22. "Zheleznodorozhnye Voiska RF," February 28, 2012, at ttp://xn--b1amah.xn--d1ad.xn--p1ai/wiki/Железнодорожные_войска_РФ; and Zheleznodorozhnik, "Vosstanovle."

23. "Zheleznodorozhnye Voiska RF"; Zheleznodorozhnik, "Vosstanovle."

24. GAAO Otdel DSPI, F. 296, op. 2, d. 908, ll. 31–36, and d. 1389, ll. 47–51.

25. GAAO Otdel DSPI, F. 296, op. 2, d. 1882, l. 99.

26. Uralmostostroi, "Istorii," http://uralmostostroy.ru/about/istoria/.

27. Gennadii Andreevich El'tsov, "Chto nam stoit most postroit'," *Monomakh,* September 2009, no. 3, at http://monomax.sisadminov.net/main/view/article/864.

28. Ibid.

29. Ibid.

30. Ibid.

31. "Goriachev Iurii Frolovich," *Izvestnye liudi Ul'ianovskoi oblasti,* at http://people.uonb. ru/?p=55.

32. El'tsov, "Chto nam stoit."

33. Ibid.; Margarita Nazarenko, "Istoriia grandioznoi stroiki . . . 8 Let so dnia otkrytiia novogo mosta cherez Volgu," November 24, 2017, at https://ulpressa.ru/2017/11/24/istoriya-grandioznoy-stroyki-brandergofer-8-let-so-dnya-otkryitiya-novogo-mosta-cherez-volgu/.

34. For a film clip of the Nazi Kerch Strait "bridge," see https://crimea.vgorode.ua/news/sobytyia/253873-ystoryia-kryma-kerchenskyi-most-obraztsa-1944-hoda-vydeo.

35. Rambler, "Pochemu ni Stalin, ni Gitler ne smogli stroit' Kerchenskii most," *Rambler*, January 5, 2018 at https://news.rambler.ru/other/38824267. See also M. S. Rudenko, "Istoriia stroitel'stvo i razrusheniia mosta cherez Kerchenskii proliv," *Transportnoe stroitel'stvo*, no. 6 (1991).

36. Iu. Ia. Ivanichenko and V. I. Demchenko, *Obrechennyi most* (Moscow: Veche, 2016), 1, at https://www.litmir.me/br/?b=255174.

37. Ibid.

38. Rambler, "Pochemu ni Stalin, ni Gitler."

39. AMD, "Stalinskii proekt Kerchenskogo mosta 1949 g.," March 5, 2016, *PVO*, at http://pvo-info.ru/?p=1442.

40. "Istoriia stroitel'stvo mosta i strategicheskoe znachenie," *Zhil'e v feodosii*, http://www.kvartiri-feodosii.ru/info/FotoobzorNovostey/137/.

41. Oleg Totskii, "Kerchenskii most 1944 goda," March 12, 2014, *TOV*, at https://tov-tob.livejournal.com/127847.html; Rudenko, "Istoriia stroitel'stvo."

42. Aleksandr Levinskii and Elizaveta Maetnaia, "Most nash: Kak Arkadii Rotenberg poluchil podriad na storiky veka," *Forbes*, March 15, 2016, at http://www.forbes.ru/kompanii/infrastruktura/282637-most-nash-kak-arkadii-rottenberg-poluchil-podr yad-na-stroiku-veka.

43. Rudenko, "Istoriia stroitel'stvo," and "Kerchenskii most: Pochemu Stalin zabrakoval stroiku veka," May 29, 2016, at https://inforeactor.ru/29917-kerchenskii-most-poch emu-stalin-zabrakoval-stroiku-veka.

44. Mansur Mirovalev, "Dam Leaves Crimea Population in Chronic Water Shortage," *Al Jazeera*, January 4, 2017, at https://www.aljazeera.com/indepth/features/2016/12/dam-leaves-crimea-population-chronic-water-shortage-161229092648659.html.

45. Levinskii and Maetnaia, "Most nash."

46. World Anti-Doping Agency (Richard McClaren), "The Independent Person 2nd Report," December 9, 2016, at https://www.wada-ama.org/sites/default/files/resour ces/files/mclaren_report_part_ii_2.pdf.

47. Ivanna Bilych, *Human Rights on Occupied Territory: Case of Crimea* (New York: Razom, 2015). See also Voice of America, "Voting Ending in 'Sham' Annexation Polls in Four Ukrainian Regions," *VOA News*, September 27, 2022, at https://www.voanews.com/a/voting-ending-in-sham-annexation-polls-in-four-ukrainian-regions-/6764 836.html.

48. Office of the United Nations High Commissioner for Human Rights, *Situation of Human Rights in the Temporarily Occupied Autonomous Republic of Crimea and the City of Sevastopol (Ukraine)* (Geneva: UN, 2017). According to another study, "The illegitimate Crimean and Russian *de facto* authorities target those ethnic, religious, and national groups that oppose the annexation. Indigenous Crimean Tatars are fre-quently suspected of this sort of broadly defined 'anti-Russian activity'." See Bilych, *Human Rights on Occupied Territory*.

49. President of the Russian Federation, "Obrashchenie prezidenta Rossiiskoi Federatsii," March 18, 2014, at http://kremlin.ru/events/president/news/20603.

50. The SGM group generally supplies offers engineering, logistics, construction, and re-pair works, for gas and oil pipelines and for railways. Stroigazmontazh receives reg-ular contracts from the Russian government. It has over 16,000 employees. Rotenberg

made his career selling vodka to the masses and then selling pipe to Gazprom through two companies worth 28.9 billion rubles with a profit of 4.4 billion rubles in 2008. Stroigazmontazh is also critical to the Nord Stream pipeline and several other pipelines in the south.

51. Levinskii and Maetnaia, "Most nash."
52. http://putinism.net/?p=1375; Offshore Leaks, "Arkady and Boris Rotenberg," data from the Panama Papers, at https://offshoreleaks.icij.org/stories/arkady-and-boris-rotenberg?n=0.
53. Boris Nemtsov and Leonid Martynyuk, *Winter Olympics in the Sub-Tropics: Corruption and Abuse in Sochi. An Independent Expert Report* (2015), 5–13.
54. Ibid., 20–27.
55. Levinskii and Maetnaia, "Most nash."
56. Nick Zaccardi, "US Women's Bobsledders Sponsored by Russian Vodka," *NBC Sports*, November 8, 2013, at https://olympics.nbcsports.com/2013/11/08/us-bobsled-russian-putinka-vodka/.
57. Mark Lawrence Schrad, "Vodka Politics: Alcohol, Autocracy, and the Secret History of the Russian State," *New Yorker*, February 20, 2014, at https://www.newyorker.com/business/currency/in-sochi-the-mark-of-a-russian-vodka-oligarch.
58. President of the Russian Federation, "Soveshanie po voprosam stroitel'stva Krymskogo mosta i sotsial'no-ekonomicheskogo razvitiia Kryma i Sevastopolia," March 18, 2016, at http://kremlin.ru/events/president/news/51534.
59. Design Group Tormasov and Co. and SpetsStroiProekt, *Proekt-Kontseptsiia: Universal'nyi transportnyi perekhod cherez Kerchenskii proliv* (Moscow: 2014).
60. Andrei Koshak, "Na 2 km blizhe k Krymu," *Gazeta.ru*, April 22, 2016, at https://www.gazeta.ru/auto/2016/04/21_a_8189045.shtml.
61. *Krymskii most*, 10, 12, 14, 15, 24–25, 30, 66.
62. Andrei Koshak, "Na 2 km blizhe k Krymu."
63. *Krymskii most*, 9, 45.
64. President of the Russian Federation, "Osmostr gotovogo uchastka Krymskogo mosta," March 14, 2018, at http://kremlin.ru/events/president/news/57057.
65. "Rossiiskii uchenyi zaiavil, chto dostraivat' Krymskii most budet ogramnoi oshibkoi," *IStatus*, March 16, 2018, at http://statuspress.com.ua/ukrainian-news/rossijskij-uchenyj-zayavil-chto-dostraivat-krymskij-most-budet-ogromnoj-oshibkoj.html, www.youtube.com/watch?v=f8oOoeAF3Xc.
66. Levinskii and Maetnaia, "Most nash"; Aleksandr Valiyev, "'Like Being a Slave . . .,'" *RFE/RL*, August 7, 2016, at www.rferl.org/a/russia-crimea-kerch-bridge-workers-abuse-unpaid/27906011.html; and Aleksandr Iankovskii, "Doroga v Krym: Pochemu rossiiskie kompanii ne khotiat stroit' Kerchenskii most," *Krym.Realii*, December 28, 2016, at www.ru.krymr.com/a/28200474.html.
67. *Krymskii most*, 10, 12, 14, 15, 24–25, 30, 66.
68. Georgii Rosnovskii, "Rossiiskii most cherez Kerchenskii proliv dolgo ne prostroit," *Fokus*, April 18, 2016, at focus.ua/world/348338/.
69. Levinskii and Maetnaia, "Most nash."
70. Forum TVS, "Dlia stroitel'stva mosta v Krym nuzhno soglasie Ukrainy," March 24, 2016, at www.forum-tvs.ru/index.php?showtopic=121888.

71. Halya Coynash, "Russia's Crimea Bridge Could Collapse Anytime," *Atlantic Council*, January 10, 2017, at http://www.atlanticcouncil.org/blogs/ukrainealert/russia-s-crimea-bridge-could-collapse-anytime; Otkrytaia Rossiia, "Kerchenskii most na Britanskie Virginskie Ostrova," April 26, 2016, at openrussia.org/post/view/14614/.

72. Andrei Vaganov, "Krymskii most stroitsia na Tysiacheletnikh Osnovaniiakh," June 22, 2016, *Nezavisimaia gazeta*.

73. Robert Coalson, "Love Conquers Truth: New Romantic Comedy by RT Chief Simonyan Spins Crimea Drama," *RFE/RL*, November 2, 2018, at https://www.rferl.org/a/love-conquers-truth-new-romantic-comedy-by-rt-head-simonyan-spins-crimea-drama/29579470.html.

74. Andrei Usachev et al., *Raskraska "Krymskii most"* (KrymMost, 2017?).

75. Tat'iana Mikhailovskaia, *Krymskii most* (Moscow: Izdatel'skie Resheniia, 1917?).

76. The beautiful Russian original reads:

> На пляж приехал бульдозер.
> Камни сгребает, песок выглаживает.
> Рычит, пыхтит, старается.
> Отдыхающих вокруг много.
> Меньше, чем песчинок, но больше, чем камушков.
> Но никто почти не замечает бульдозер.
> А кто заметит—только улыбнётся.
> Бульдозер-то совсем игрушечный.
> И рычит-пыхтит совсем детским голоском.

77. Henry Petroski, "Big Dig, Big Bridge," *American Scientist* 92 (July–August 2004): 316–320; Thomas Hughes, *Rescuing Prometheus* (New York: Vintage Books, 2000); National Academy of Engineering et al., *Completing the "Big Dig": Managing the Final Stages of Boston's Central Artery/Tunnel Project* (Washington, DC: National Academies Press, 2003).

78. *Krymskii most* (2017?), 13.

Chapter 6

* My thanks to Otto Boele, whose call to write about nostalgia led to a very early version of what became this chapter, and to Otto, Ksenia Robbe, and Boris Noordenbos for their comments.

1. "Russia is ahead, as it was and as it will be!" "Atomnye ledokoly byli i budut national'noi gordost'iu strany," *Meduza*, February 14, 2016, at https://meduza.mirtesen.ru/blog/43632835582/atomnyie-ledokolyi-byili-i-budut-natsionalnoy-gordostyu-stranyi.

2. President of Russia, "Presidential Address to the Federal Assembly," March 1, 2018.

3. James T. Andrews, *Science for the Masses: The Bolshevik State, Public Science, and the Popular Imagination in Soviet Russia, 1917–1934* (College Station: Texas A&M University Press, 2003).

4. Josephson, *Would Trotsky Wear a Bluetooth?*

5. V. V. Putin, "Mineral'no syr'evye resursy v strategii razvitiia rossiiskoi ekonomiki," in *Rossiia v okruzhaiushchem mire: 2000*, ed. N. N. Marfenin (Moscow: Izdatel'stvo MNEPU, 2000), 1–3, 10. Originally published in *Zapiski Gornogo Instituta* 144, no. 1 (1999). See Harley Balzer, "The Putin Thesis and Russian Energy Policy," *Post-Soviet Affairs* 21, no. 3 (2005): 210–225.

6. Gazprom, "About Gazprom," at https://www.gazprom.com/about/.

7. Peter Rutland, "Petronation? Oil, Gas and National Identity in Russia," *Post-Soviet Affairs* 31, no. 1 (January 2015): 67.

8. Ibid., 70.

9. Tom Balmforth, "Russian Nostalgia for Soviet Union Reaches 13-year High," *Reuters*, December 19, 2018, at https://www.reuters.com/article/us-russia-politics-sovietun ion-idUSKBN1OI20Q.

10. In many ways, nostalgic engineering is a perfect case for nostalgia generally. According to Svetlana Boym, nostalgia "appears to be a longing for a place but is actually a yearning for a different time." She writes that "the nostalgic desires to obliterate history and turn it into private or collective mythology, to revisit time as space, refusing to surrender to the irreversibility of time that plagues the human condition." In addition, as Boym notes, nostalgia can be future-oriented in that "the fantasies of the past determined by the needs of the present have a direct impact on the realities of the future." See Svetlana Boym, *The Future of Nostalgia* (New York: Basic Books, 2001).

11. One measure of the importance of big technology in the Russian media is mentions of these artifacts in leading newspapers. For example, in *Novaia gazeta* there have been 556 articles that consider icebreakers in one way or another going back to 1999, while Yuri Gagarin has been mentioned 557 times and the northern sea route over 1,000 times. In *Kommersant*, from May 2016 to May 2017, there were 173 mentions of "icebreaker," 64 of Gagarin, and so on.

12. Aleksei Iablokov et al., *Fakty i problemy sviazannye so sbrosom radioaktivnykh otkhodov v moria, primykaiushchie k territorii Rossiiskoi Federatsii* (Moscow: Priemnaia Prezidenta Rossiiskoi Federatsii, 1993); United States Congress Office of Technology Assessment, *Nuclear Wastes in the Arctic: An Analysis of Arctic and Other Regional Impacts from Soviet Nuclear Contamination* (Washington, DC: OTA, 1995); and Olav Stokke, "Nuclear Dumping in Arctic Seas: Russian Implementation of the London Convention," in *The Implementation and Effectiveness of International Environmental Commitments*, ed. David Victor, Kal Raustiala and Eugene Skonikoff (Cambridge, MA: MIT Press, 2001), 475–517.

13. David Nye, *American Technological Sublime* (Cambridge, MA: MIT Press, 1994).

14. Andrew L. Jenks, *The Cosmonaut Who Couldn't Stop Smiling: The Life and Legend of Yuri Gagarin* (DeKalb: Northern Illinois University Press, 2012).

15. "55 let nazad Gagarin triumfal'no otkryl eru pilotiruemoi kosmonavtiki," *TASS*, April 12, 2016, http://tass.ru/kosmos/3194610.

16. "55 let nazad Gagarin."

17. Viktor Marakhovskii, "Gagarin—Eto my," *Russkaia Sila*, April 12, 2016, at http://rus ila.su/2016/04/12/gagarin-eto-my/.

18. "55 let nazad Gagarin."

19. "Putin Praises Space Hero," *BBC*, April 12, 2001, at http://news.bbc.co.uk/2/hi/eur ope/1273224.stm.

20. "Putin: Gagarin—rossiianin, i eto zvuchit gordo," *RIA nauka*, April 12, 2004, https:// ria.ru/science/20040412/566915.html.

21. Putin, "Spisok letchikov-kosmonavtov i rabotnikov raketno-kosmicheskoi promyshlennosti, nagrazhdennykh gosudarstvennymi nagradami," *President of the Russian Federation*, April 12, 2004, at http://kremlin.ru/supplement/1904.

22. E.g., Viacheslav Vil'iamskii, *Yuri Gagarin v zapoliar'e* (Rostov-on-Don: Neformat, 2016).

23. V. Putin, 'Vstupitel'noe slovo na torzhestvennom sobranii, posviashchennom dniu kosmonavtiki', *President of the Russian Federation*, April 12, 2004, at http://kremlin. ru/events/president/transcripts/22419.

24. "Gagarin—doroga v kosmos! Putin—doroga k suverenitetu!" April 12, 2016, at https://m.ok.ru/video/11070276897.

25. AFP/Reuters, "Russia Launches Rocket from New Vostochny Cosmodrome after Delay," April 28, 2016, at http://www.abc.net.au/news/2016-04-28/russia-launches-first-rocket-from-vostochny-after-delay/73674. For discussion of the political, so-cial, and cultural importance of the space race to Soviet Russia, see Asif Siddiqi, *The Red Rockets' Glare: Spaceflight and the Soviet Imagination, 1857–1957* (Cambridge: Cambridge University Press, 2010).

26. AFP/Reuters, "Russia Launches."

27. "Putin vmeste s kosmonavtami otsenil novyi fil'm o pokorenii kosmos 'Vremia pervyk'," *TASS*, April 12, 2017, at http://tass.ru/kosmos/4175425.

28. "Putin otmetit Den' kosmonovtiki na kosmodrome Vostochnyi," *NTV*, April 12 2013, http://www.ntv.ru/novosti/556296/; and Shaun Walker, "Putin Aims for the Stars with a £ 33bn Space Programme," *Independent*, April 12, 2013, http://www.independ ent.co.uk/news/world/europe/putin-aims-for-the-stars-with-33bn-space-progra mme-8570462.html.

29. "Is Vlad Keen on a Trip?," *Daily Mail*, April 12, 2014, at http://www.dailymail.co.uk/ news/article-2602291/We-coming-Moon-FOREVER-Russia-sets-plans-conquer-colonise-space-including-permanent-manned-moon-base.html.

30. V. Putin, "Vstupitel'noe slovo na torzhestvennom sobranii." See also "Putin: Rossiiskaia kosmicheskaia programma dolzhna vesti strany vpered," *NTV*, April 12, 2017, http:// www.ntv.ru/novosti/1795087/.

31. "Putin otmetit Den' kosmonovtiki na kosmodrome Vostochnyi"; "Zapusk issledovatel'skoi stantsii 'Luna-Glob' perenesen na 2020 god," *Kosmicheskaia lenta*, January 25, 2018, at https://kosmolenta.com/index.php/1176-2018-01-25-luna-2025.

32. On museums and science, see Sharon Macdonald, ed., *The Politics of Display: Museums, Science, and Culture* (London: Routledge, 1998); Sonja Schmid, "Celebrating Tomorrow Today: The Peaceful Atom on Display in the Soviet Union," *Social Studies of Science* 36, no. 3 (2006): 331–365; and Egle Rindzeviciute, "Nuclear Energy in Russia: From the Future Technology to Cultural Heritage," *Tiltas*, November (2016), x–xx.

33. "Ledokol Lenin mozhet stat' ob"ektom," *The Arctic*, September 3, 2015, at https://ru.arctic.ru/tourism/20150903/155907.html.

34. A. M. Kamakhina, *Arkticheskii vystavochnyi tsentr "Atomnyi Ledokol Lenin," istoriia sozdaniia, osnovnye napravleniia deiatel'nosti i perspektivy razvitiia*, unpublished paper (Murmansk: "Lenin," 2015?).

35. The aesthetics and craftsmanship of the peaceful atom did not extend from the interiors to the reactors that on two occasions experienced serious accidents and were dumped unceremoniously off the coast of Novaia Zemlia. The first three-reactor power source was replaced at Zvezdochka in Severodvinsk with a two-unit power source, a "unique" operation that took four years.

36. "Tomnyi ledokol 'Lenin'. Atomnye ledokoly Rossii," *Howtoshka*, http://howtoshka.ru/obrazovanie/68253-atomnyj-ledokol-lenin-atomnye-ledokoly-rossii.html.

37. http://www.tv21.ru/news/2017/02/04/rossiya-v-arktike-samyy-znachitelnyy-voennyy-proryv-posle-raspada-sssr-pochemu-zamgubernatora-grigoriy-stratiy-ulybnulsya-otvechaya-britanskomu-zhurnalistu. Webpage no longer functions.

38. I discuss Chilingarov's adventures in "Putin, the Arctic and the Environment," *Global Environment* 9 (2016): 376–413.

39. A. Chilingarov, V. M. Gruzinov, and Iu. F. Sychev, *Ocherki po geografii Arktiki* (Obninsk: Artifeks: 2009), 48. See also Alexander Oreshenkov, "Arctic Diplomacy," *Russia in Global Affairs*, no. 4 (December 2009), at http://eng.globalaffairs.ru/number/n_14250.

40. Lassi Heininen (with Heather Nicol), "The Importance of Northern Dimension Foreign Policies in the Geopolitics of the Circumpolar North," *Geopolitics* 12, no. 1 (February 2007): 133–165.

41. *The Foundations of State Policy of the Russian Federation in the Arctic Region*, adopted by the President of the Russian Federation D. Medvedev, September 18, 2008, pdf, at http://img9.custompublish.com/getfile.php/1042958.1529.avuqcurreq/Russian+Strategy.pdf?return=www.arcticgovernance.org.

42. "Putin Sees Stalin's Industrialization as Model," *Moscow Times*, September 3, 2012, at http://www.themoscowtimes.com/business/article/putin-sees-stalins-industrialization-as-model/467476.html.

43. "Stroitel'stvo i osvoenie pechorskoi zheleznoi dorogi. Istoricheskii ocherk," http://www.sakharov-center.ru/asfcd/auth/?t=page&num=12784.

44. President of Russia, "The Arctic: Territory of Dialogue," Plenary session of the International Arctic Forum," April 9, 2019, at http://en.kremlin.ru/events/president/news/60250; E. V. Agbalian, V. Iu. Khoroshavin, and E. V. Shinkaruk, "Otsenka ustoichivosti ozernykh ekosistem Iamalo-Nenetskogo Avtonomnogo Okruga k kislotnym vypadeniiam," *Vestnik Tiumenskogo Gosudarstvennogo Universiteta. Ekologiia i Prirodopol'zovanie* 1, no. 1 (2015): 45–54; UNIAN, "Ekologi b'iut trevogu: 'Gazprom' prodolzhaet aktivnoe zagriaznenie Arktiki – SMI," *UNIAN*, October 24, 2014, http://www.unian.net/world/1000464-ekologi-byut-trevogu-gazprom-prodoljaet-aktivnoe-zagryaznenie-arktiki-smi.html.

45. Dal'nevostochnyi Zavod Zvezda, "Istoriia zavoda," at http://www.fes-zvezda.ru/about/history/.

46. Sudostroitel'nyi Kompleks "Zvezda," at http://www.sskzvezda.ru/index.php/ru/.

47. "Plenniki Antarktiki. Nastoiashchaia istoriia spaseniia ledokola 'Mikhail Somov,'" *AiF*, October 20, 2016, at http://www.aif.ru/society/history/plenniki_antarktiki_nastoyashchaya_istoriya_spaseniya_ledokola_mihail_somov.

48. V. K. Buinitskii, *812 dnei v dreifuiushchikh l'dakh* (Moscow: Glavsevmorput, 1945), 117.

49. For an autobiography of one of Stalin's hero-pilots, see M. Vodop'ianov, *Poliarnyi letchik. Rasskazy* (Leningrad: Leningradskoe Gazetno-zhurnal'noe i Knizhnoe Izdatel'stvo, 1954).

50. Karen Dawisha, *Putin's Kleptocracy* (New York: Simon & Schuster, 2014).

51. Putin, "Mineral'no syr'evye resursy v strategii razvitiia rossiiskoi ekonomiki."

52. It should be noted that Putin, too, wants glorious achievements in civilian aeronautics with a new jet, the Sukhoi-100, to compete with Boeings and Airbuses, to date with little success and great expense.

53. For example, Olga Khvostunova, "A Complete Guide to Who Controls the Russian News Media," *Index on Censorship*, December 9, 2013, at https://www.indexcensorship.org/2013/12/brief-history-russian-media/.

54. Edward Keenan, "Muscovite Political Folkways," *Russian Review* 45, no. 2 (April 1986): 115–81.

55. Amnesty International, "Russia: A Year On, Putin's 'Foreign Agents Law' Choking Freedom," November 20, 2013, at http://www.amnesty.org/en/news/russia-year-putin-s-foreign-agents-law-choking-freedom-2013-11-20.

56. Josephson, "Putin, the Arctic and the Environment," *Global Environment* 9 (2016): 376–413. See the works of Stephen Brain, Nicholas Breyfogle, Douglas Weiner, Maya Peterson, and Andy Bruno.

57. In a series of public lessons on the importance of nation, family, science, and Russian culture, Putin declared 2008 as Year of the Family, 2009 Year of the Younger Generation, 2010 Year of the Teacher, 2011 Year of Russian Cosmonautics, 2012 Year of Russian History, 2013 Year of Environmental Protection, 2014 the Year of Culture, 2015 Year of Literature, and 2016 Year of Cinema.

58. President of the Russian Federation, "New Year Address to the Nation," December 31, 2018, at http://en.kremlin.ru/events/president/news/59629.

59. President of the Russian Federation, "New Year Address to the Nation," December 31, 2016, at http://en.kremlin.ru/events/president/news/53683.

60. V. Putin, "Vstrecha s glavoi goskorporatsii 'Rosatom' Sergeem Kirienko," President of the Russian Federation, September 25, 2015, at http://kremlin.ru/events/presid ent/news/50373. See Jeffrey Brooks, *Thank You, Comrade Stalin!* (Princeton, NJ: Princeton University Press, 2001), for discussion of the rise of public rituals of thanks and humiliation, of awards, and the like that commenced in the Stalin era.

61. V. Putin, "Vladimir Putin pozdravil rabotnikov i veteranov atomnoi promyshlennosti s professional'nym prazdnikom," *Office of the President of the Russian Federation*, September 28, 2007, http://kremlin.ru/events/president/news/42702.

62. Vladimir Filonov, "Putin Sees Stalin's Industrialization as Model," *Moscow Times*, September 3, 2012, at https://themoscowtimes.com/articles/putin-sees-stalins-industrialization-as-model-17445; and Keenan, "Muscovite Political Folkways."

63. President of Russia, "Presidential Address to the Federal Assembly," March 1, 2018, at http://en.kremlin.ru/events/president/news/56957.

64. Joseph Stalin, "On the Final Victory of Socialism in the USSR," January 18, 1938 (published in *Pravda* on February 12, 1938), at https://www.marxists.org/reference/archive/stalin/works/1938/01/18.htm.

65. Joseph Stalin, "Speech at the First All-Union Conference of Leading Personnel of Socialist Industry," February 4, 1931, as published in *Pravda*, no. 35 (February 5, 1931), at https://www.marxists.org/reference/archive/stalin/works/1931/02/04.htm.

66. On the New Soviet Man as hero, see Jay Berman, "Valerii Chkalov: Soviet Pilot as New Soviet Man," *Journal of Contemporary History* 33 (1998): 135–152.

67. President of Russia, "Presidential Address to the Federal Assembly," March 1, 2018.

68. President of Russia, "Victory Day Address, May 9, 2019, at http://en.kremlin.ru/events/president/news/60491.

69. "VTsIOM: Bol'shinstvo rossiian schitaiut, chto strane neobkhodimo prodolzhit' osvoenie kosmosa," *TASS*, April 12, 2021, at https://tass.ru/obschestvo/11121829.

70. "VTsIOM: Rossiiane soglasny borot'sia za Arktiku," *RBC*, August 24, 2007, at https://www.rbc.ru/society/24/08/2007/5703c8b39a79470eaf7669fa.

71. "VTsIOM: 60% rossiian podderzhali presechenie aktsii protiv osvoeniia Arktiki," *RIA novosti*, October 3, 2013, at https://ria.ru/20131003/967501586.html.

72. Levada-Center, "Crimea: Two Years Later," June 10, 2016, at https://www.levada.ru/en/2016/06/10/crimea-two-years-later/, and "Crimea: Five Years," April 11, 2019, at https://www.levada.ru/en/2019/04/11/crimea-five-years/.

73. Stepan Goncharov and Denis Volkov, "Russians Want Crimea; Prefer Luhansk and Donetsk Independent," *Chicago Council/Levada Center*, April 3, 2019, at https://www.thechicagocouncil.org/publication/russians-want-crimea-prefer-luhansk-and-donetsk-independent.

74. Anastasia Gnedinskaia, "Tomskaia khudozhnitsa sviazala v svitere Putina, Gagarina i Deda Moroza," *Moskovskii komsomolets*, April 18, 2016, at http://www.mk.ru/social/2016/04/18/tomskaya-khudozhnica-svyazala-v-svitere-putina-gagarina-i-deda-moroza.html.

75. "'Leaders', inspired by Vladimir Putin," *Liveleak* at https://www.liveleak.com/view?i=abc_1451501120; "Studentki MGU sdelali eroticheskii kalendar' dlia Putina," *LibyMax*, October 7, 2010, at http://libymax.ru/?p=15420; and Putin, *Slova, meniaiushchie mir. Kliuchevye tsitaty Vladimira Putina*, deluxe edition at $180 at https://www.ozon.ru/context/detail/id/137872147/. An alternative Putin calendar is available with students of the law department at the university protesting Putinism by posing with yellow ribbons of silence closing their lips, but with captions asking questions about graft, corruption, loss of freedom of speech and to gather freely, and about the murder of the journalist Anna Politkovskaia. See D. Kachalov, "Vtoroi kalendar' ot studentok MGU," *dkachalov*, October 11, 2010, at http://dkachalov.livejournal.com/117850.html. Kremlin Kitsch has a partner in the US White House: there are, to be sure, Trump Eau de Toilette for $45, Ivanka's own perfume for $70, and Donald's *America: Great Again* (2015), for comparative reading analysis.

76. Henry, "Russia's Environment and Environmental Movement," in *Understanding Contemporary Russia*, 2nd ed., ed. Michael L. Bressler (Boulder, CO: Lynne Rienner, 2018), 275–301; and Leonid Bershidsky, "Putin Is Finally Ready to Look Homeward," *Bloomberg*, February 20, 2019, at https://www.bloomberg.com/opinion/articles/2019-02-20/russia-s-vladimir-putin-turns-to-domestic-policy.

77. Email of Dmitry Kozlov, to the author and others, April 12, 2019. See also "Thousands Rally in Russia's Komi Republic against New Landfill," *RFERL*, June 3, 2019, at https://www.rferl.org/a/thousands-rally-in-russia-s-komi-republic-against-new-landfill/29978612.html.

Epilogue

1. Richard Heydarian, "Duterte's Ambitious 'Build, Build, Build' Project to Transform the Philippines Could Become His Legacy," *Fortune*, February 28, 2018, at https://www.forbes.com/sites/outofasia/2018/02/28/dutertes-ambitious-build-build-build-project-to-transform-the-philippines-could-become-his-legacy/#802e5311a7f4.

2. Carlotta Gall, "A Canal through Turkey? Presidential Vote Is a Test of Erdogan's Building Spree," *New York Times*, June 21, 2018, at https://www.nytimes.com/2018/06/21/world/europe/turkey-election-ergodan-canal-megaprojects.html.

3. Anne Garrels, *Putin Country: A Journey into the Real Russia* (New York: Picador, 2017).

4. Levada Tsentr, "Vydaiushchiesia liudi," June 26, 2017, at http://www.levada.ru/2017/06/26/vydayushhiesya-lyudi/.

5. Filonov, "Putin Sees Stalin's Industrialization as Model."

6. Josephson, "Putin, the Arctic and the Environment."

7. N. Zh. Kozhoka et al., eds., *O sanitarno-epidemiologicheskoi obstanovke v Rossiiskoi Federatsii v 2009: Gosudarstvennyi doklad* (Moscow: Federal'nyi Tsentr Gigiena i Epidemiologii Rospotrebnadzora, 2010), 6–7.

8. Ibid., 30–31, 74, 225, and 395.

9. Paul Josephson, "The Deep Historical Roots of Russia's Scorched Earth Policy," *Engelsberg Ideas*, Jun 14, 2023, at https://engelsbergideas.com/essays/the-deep-historical-roots-of-russias-scorched-earth-policy/.

Index